Ruling by Norms

Leiden Studies on the Frontiers of International Law

VOLUME 14

The titles published in this series are listed at *brill.com/lsfi*

Ruling by Norms

Technical Experts and the Making of International Cybersecurity Law

By

Arun Sukumar

BRILL | NIJHOFF

ISSN 2212-4195
ISBN 978-90-04-73760-0
ISBN 978-90-04-73761-7 (PDF)
DOI https://doi.org/10.1163/9789004737617

Library of Congress Control Number: 2026947511

Brill Nijhoff and Koninklijke Brill BV are part of De Gruyter Brill.
www.degruyterbrill.com

Questions about General Product Safety Regulation: productsafety@degruyterbrill.com

Cover illustration: Image generated by Manus AI.

For Lila

You taught me language; and my profit on't/Is,
I know how to curse.

William Shakespeare (*The Tempest*, I.ii.365–366)

Contents

Acknowledgments

"Your children are not your children", wrote Khalil Gibran, "but the sons and daughters of Life's longing for itself." And so it is with this monograph. Love's labor of six years, it is not the end of a journey, but rather the beginning of what I hope will be a fruitful life engaging with academic scholarship. My family, friends, colleagues, and mentors were a source of strength and inspiration as I took the difficult, initial steps in this journey.

The expansive scope of this book – it studies the development of rules for international cybersecurity by several institutions over two decades – would simply not have been feasible had it not been for the generosity of practitioners and scholars working in this field. Sixty-seven diplomats, lawyers, technical experts, and civil society members – including seventeen UN negotiators – spared an hour of their time to share their ringside views and insights into international cybersecurity governance. Most of them did so in 2020 and 2021, amidst extremely challenging personal and professional circumstances brought on by the onslaught of COVID-19. I cannot thank them adequately for their patience and kindness, and hope the reader will find their insights as illuminating as I did. Due to the sensitivity and ongoing nature of cybersecurity negotiations, some interviewees opted to remain anonymous. While thanking them, I also wish to specifically acknowledge the encouragement and guidance I have received over the years from James Lewis (Center for Strategic and International Studies), Duncan Hollis (Temple University), Adam Segal (Council on Foreign Relations), Kerstin Vignard (Johns Hopkins University), and Samir Saran (Observer Research Foundation). Jim, Duncan, Adam, Kerstin, and Samir have offered me countless professional opportunities to present my research on international cybersecurity. Securing access to high-level diplomats for interviews or to closed-door groups and discussions for participant observation would have been unlikely had it not been for my prior interactions with various practitioners, which they facilitated.

In particular, I am grateful to Dennis Broeders, not only for enriching this book through his own research and insights, but also for taking a chance on me and offering me a post-doctoral fellowship at Leiden University. Dennis has built a first-rate international cybersecurity research program at Leiden, and it is a privilege to be part of his team.

I owe a great intellectual debt to my PhD advisor and committee. I was fortunate to have Ian Johnstone as my advisor at Fletcher throughout my graduate student days. The rigor and quality of Ian's feedback throughout the dissertation process were matched only by his dedication to my professional growth as a scholar who is open to new ideas and arguments. Joel Trachtman joined my committee despite knowing that he would himself have to navigate some unfamiliar theoretical and methodological terrain to evaluate my conclusions about international law-making for cybersecurity. Joel put me through my paces, constantly challenging me to distill complex concepts and ideas into jargon-free language that would be intelligible to anyone interested in the global cybersecurity landscape. Finally, I am grateful to Tomer Broude, who graciously agreed to join my committee, and never compromised on providing thorough feedback on my drafts, despite his increasing academic and administrative commitments at the Hebrew University of Jerusalem's Faculty of Law. That Tomer managed to do a line-by-line review of my final draft while juggling his responsibilities as dean of the law faculty during a testing and turbulent moment in Israel's legal and political history is simply incredible. I am privileged to call these senior scholars and towering figures in their respective fields as mentors.

Without Vedica Kant's unflinching support and solidarity, the PhD itself would have been an arduous journey. She was not only a sounding board for my arguments, but also a loyal companion and empathetic listener during moments of doubt and anxiety that invariably accompany the writing of any book. Vedica's own professional rise during this time and masterful navigation of challenges that confronted her in a heavily male-dominated corporate environment humbled and inspired me.

This book is dedicated to my three-year-old, Lila. The poet Gibran also wrote that we can only give children our love and not our thoughts. Alas, how I wish that were not true. I have undertaken this journey for myself. I hope, however, that it will motivate my daughter to embark on challenging but ultimately rewarding quests in the pursuit of knowledge.

Tables

CHAPTER 1

Ruling by Norms

1 Of Technical Experts and International Lawyers: A Memo from History

"The day of the plain man has passed", declared Harold Laski in 1930.[1] The business of governance in the 20th century, he argued, had been increasingly relegated to "experts" – individuals with "possession of specialized knowledge".[2] Laski's commentary was directed at public affairs in general, but it also coincided with a period of heightened involvement by technical experts in modern global governance. The interwar years saw specialists in varied domains such as finance, trade, labor, health, communications, and science and technology, at the frontlines of modern diplomacy,[3] whether in the form of "economic conferences",[4] "transgovernmental"[5] interactions between technical committees, municipal administrations, line ministries, or bureaucracies, "intercolonial" networks,[6] or expert "commissions".[7] In fact, the thirties –

1 Harold Joseph Laski, "The Limitations of the Expert," Harper's Magazine, December 1, 1930, https://harpers.org/archive/1930/12/the-limitations-of-the-expert/.

2 *Laski, Limitations of the Expert.*

3 "Technical Activities," accessed September 28, 2020, https://www.unog.ch/80256EDD006AC19C/(httpPages)/05BBB89F97399EF4C1256F350049DF51?OpenDocument; *see generally*, Daniel Laqua, ed., *Internationalism Reconfigured: Transnational Ideas and Movements Between the World Wars*, 1st ed. (London: Bloomsbury Academic, 2011).

4 W. Leslie Runciman, "The World Economic Conference at Geneva," *The Economic Journal* 37, no. 147 (September 1, 1927): 465–472, https://doi.org/10.2307/2223577.

5 Martin David Dubin, "Transgovernmental Processes in the League of Nations," *International Organization* 37, no. 3 (1983): 469–493.

6 Tomoko Akami, "Imperial Polities, Intercolonialism, and the Shaping of Global Governing Norms: Public Health Expert Networks in Asia and the League of Nations Health Organization, 1908–1937," *Journal of Global History* 12, no. 1 (March 2017): 4–25, https://doi.org/10.1017/S1740022816000310.

7 Renee Redman, "The League of Nations and the Right to Be Free from Enslavement: The First Human Right to Be Recognized as Customary International Law – Freedom: Beyond the United States," *Chicago-Kent Law Review* 70, no. 2 (December 1, 1994): 759; J. P. Daughton, "ILO Expertise and Colonial Violence in the Interwar Years," in *Globalizing Social Rights: The International Labour Organization and Beyond*, ed. Sandrine Kott and Joëlle Droux (London: Palgrave Macmillan UK, 2013), 85–97, https://doi.org/10.1057/9781137291967_6.

HTTPS://DOI.ORG/10.1163/9789004737617-002

perhaps affirming Laski's argument – has been termed as the "golden age for [the] expert activities" of the League of Nations.[8]

How exactly did technical experts influence the creation of rules for these various specialized domains? The fact is, modern international law as an autonomous legal discipline, *i.e.*, a discipline with clearly defined sources and rules of interpretation, had just begun to emerge during this period. A few months before Laski published his commentary, the League of Nations convened a Codification Conference in The Hague, as a "first attempt on a worldwide basis to codify and develop whole fields of international law".[9] Only in 1920 had an Advisory Committee of Jurists been formed to draw up the statute of the Permanent Court of International Justice (PCIJ). This Committee spent most of its time discussing how to elect PCIJ judges, taking merely three meetings to draw up draft Article 35 of the PCIJ statute – which would later become Article 38 of the Statute of the International Court of Justice – on the sources of international law.[10] Ake Hammarskjöld, secretary to this Committee and the first Registrar of the PCIJ would note later that this discussion on the sources of international law was "purely platonic" and without much "practical value".[11] Yet, between 1920 and 1928, the number of registered international treaties increased remarkably from 70 to 1904.[12] Most of those instruments were concerned with topics such as communications, health, labor, movement of commodities and persons, customs and taxation, treatment of refugees or prisoners of war, exploitation of natural resources,

8 Ludovic Tournès, "American Membership of the League of Nations: US Philanthropy and the Transformation of an Intergovernmental Organisation into a Think Tank," *International Politics; Basingstoke* 55, no. 6 (November 2018): 866, http://dx.doi.org/10.1057/s41311-017-0110-4.

9 "International Law Commission | About the Commission: Origin and Background," accessed October 2, 2020, https://legal.un.org/ilc/league.shtml.

10 League of Nations, ed., *Procès-Verbaux of the Proceedings of the Committee, June 16th-July 24th 1920, with Annexes: Procès-Verbaux Des Séances Du Comité, 16 Juin-24 Juillet 1920, Avec Annexes* (Clark, NJ: Lawbook Exchange, 2005); Malgosia Fitzmaurice, "The History of Article 38 of the Statute of the International Court of Justice," The Oxford Handbook of the Sources of International Law, October 26, 2017, 182 https://doi.org/10.1093/law/9780198745365.003.0009; Alain Pellet and Daniel Müller, "Part Three | Statute of the International Court of Justice, Ch.II Competence of the Court, Article 38," in *The Statute of the International Court of Justice (3rd Edition): A Commentary*, ed. Andreas Zimmermann et al. (Oxford, UK: Oxford University Press, 2019), 736.

11 Ole Spiermann, "'Who Attempts Too Much Does Nothing Well': The 1920 Advisory Committee of Jurists and the Statute of the Permanent Court of International Justice," *The British Year Book of International Law; Oxford 73*, no. 1 (2003): 216.

12 Hatsue Shinohara, "International Law and World War I," *Diplomatic History* 38, no. 4 (2014): 890.

etc.[13] Many of them, as noted earlier, were drafted by the League of Nations' specialized agencies. Rulemaking in these domains was less a doctrinal exercise – in other words, driven by legal reasoning based on the sources of international law – than one shaped by practices of the League's agencies that brought together international lawyers, diplomats, civil servants, and technical experts to address matters that urgently required global cooperation.

For instance, the practice of involving public health experts from the Global South and "trustee states" of the League shaped the 1926 International Sanitary Regulations by turning the instrument's focus to diseases from tropical countries and establishing regional "epidemiological intelligence bureaus" for data gathering on disease outbreaks.[14] The League's creation of an "International Committee of Statisticians" resulted in their setting standards for publishing trade and customs data by states.[15] The League of Nations Health Organization's (precursor to the World Health Organization) close cooperation with the Rockefeller Foundation in New York resulted in practices such as the funding and facilitation of expert exchanges and fellowships that created an "epistemic community" of health experts in the LNHO.[16] This community advised the League to shift its focus from "preventive" to "positive" health indicators of populations, resulting in the LNHO collecting data not only on morbidity and mortality rates but also on broader demographic socioeconomic data that was correlated to health.[17]

These practices were neither adopted in a random manner nor was the participation of technical experts a chance occurrence. They reflected the deeply held belief of actors within the League, especially the League's secre-

13 *See generally*, "Chronological Index of Treaties Index," *League of Nations Treaty Series* Index No. 1 (1920–1926): 448–529.

14 Patricia Anne Sealey, "The League of Nations Health Organisation and the Evolution of Transnational Public Health" (PhD Thesis, The Ohio State University, 2011), 112; Anne Sealey, "Globalizing the 1926 International Sanitary Convention," *Journal of Global History* 6, no. 3 (November 2011): 434–447.

15 Roser Cussó, "Building a Global Representation of Trade through International Quantification: The League of Nations' *Unification of Methods in Economic Statistics*," *The International History Review* 42, no. 4 (July 3, 2020): 714–136, https://doi.org/10.1080/07075332.2019.1619611.

16 Paul Weindling, "Philanthropy and World Health: The Rockefeller Foundation and the League of Nations Health Organisation," *Minerva* 35, no. 3 (1997): 269–281; Ludovic Tournès, "American Membership of the League of Nations: US Philanthropy and the Transformation of an Intergovernmental Organisation into a Think Tank," *International Politics; Basingstoke* 55, no. 6 (November 2018): 852–869; Iris Borowy, *Coming to Terms with World Health: The League of Nations Health Organisation* 1921–1946 (Peter Lang, 2009), 142.

17 *Weindling*, 278.

tariat, that rulemaking had to transcend "national loyalties and political ideologies".[18] Scholars have variously described this animating belief as "*le esprit d'internationalite*", the "internationalist milieu", and "*l'esprit de Genève*".[19] The League's secretariat and specialized agencies developed recruitment and operational practices that involved lawyers, civil servants, and technical experts who demonstrated said internationalist spirit and rose above national fealties.[20] This belief was the product of a specific, historical circumstance: officials recognized that the League had to inculcate an internationalist spirit to forge greater cooperation among states and avoid a repeat of the First World War. For this purpose, there had to be a corpus of dedicated civil servants and technocrats who put national interests aside and worked to advance global governance in specialized domains. A strong, sub-conscious disposition towards global mindedness shaped practices of the League.[21] Those practices in turn guided interactions between international lawyers and technical experts, and as demonstrated above, influenced the scope of the League's specialized rules themselves.

2 Global Governance on the Fly: The Rise of Informal Initiatives

At first blush, the world of 2025 may look far removed from that of the 1920s and the most productive years of the League of Nations. The internationalist spirit is certainly on the wane, as developed and developing countries flex

18 Antoine Vauchez, "Statesmen of Independence: The International Fabric of Europe's Way of Political Legitimacy," *Contemporary European History* 27, no. 2 (2018): 183–201, https://doi.org/10.1017/S0960777318000127.

19 Robert de Traz, "L'Esprit de Genève," *Journal of the Royal Institute of International Affairs* 8, no. 6 (1929): 637, https://doi.org/10.2307/3015688; Jean-Michel Guieu, "La SDN et ses organisations de soutien dans les années 1920. Entre promotion de l'esprit de Genève et volonté d'influence," *Relations Internationales*, no. 151 (2012): 11–24.

20 M. Moraes, "Internationalism as an Organisational Practice: The League of Nations Secretary-General, 1918–1946" (http://purl.org/dc/dcmitype/Text, University of Oxford, 2020), https://ora.ox.ac.uk/objects/uuid:b5c37bd9-fc74-4a18-8e28-5655aa7345cd; Susan Pedersen, "Back to the League of Nations," *The American Historical Review* 112, no. 4 (2007): 1091–1117.

21 Guillaume Sacriste and Antoine Vauchez, "The Force of International Law: Lawyers' Diplomacy on the International Scene in the 1920s," *Law & Social Inquiry* 32, no. 1 (2007): 83–107; Karen Gram-Skjoldager and Haakon A. Ikonomou, "Making Sense of the League of Nations Secretariat – Historiographical and Conceptual Reflections on Early International Public Administration," *European History Quarterly* 49, no. 3 (July 1, 2019): 420–444, https://doi.org/10.1177/0265691419854634.

their sovereign muscle on matters such as trade, migration, and cross-border data flows. More importantly, there is such a "thing" today called public international law (PIL). Or, as Collins and Bohm phrase more elegantly, international law is today an "ontological reality"[22] – it is an autonomous discipline organized around formal sources identified in Article 38(1) of the ICJ statute, and whose application is guided by legal doctrine that has evolved over time through treaties and practice. It is practiced, in Oscar Schachter's famous formulation, by an "invisible college"[23] of international lawyers who represent states in diplomatic delegations, multilateral negotiations, and before international tribunals; teach in universities and dedicated academies from The Hague to Seoul; spend years in the legal and political affairs divisions of intergovernmental organizations as civil servants; and who are ensconced within non-governmental entities, such as businesses, transnational advocacy organizations, think-tanks, and task forces. Certainly, the practicalities and exigencies of global governance continue to drive the creation of multilateral rules as they did in the golden twenties. However, doctrinal rules of interpretation and the acceptability of legal arguments – which in turn shapes the "justificatory discourse" and compliance of states[24] – are more robustly debated than ever in various professional settings.

Even as international lawyers have in this manner helped develop a coherent, professional discipline, international law-making is once again evolving. The business of global governance is increasingly conducted through informal institutions, understood as those institutions that are neither constituted by a treaty nor have a permanent secretariat.[25] The "organizational space" of rule-making and legal interpretation has today become "congested" as multilateral institutions that once were the mainstay of the post-war world compete with "dense complexes" of fluid, informal, and task-specific entities.[26] Non-binding,

---

22 Richard Collins and Alexandra Bohm, "International Law as Professional Practice: Crafting the Autonomy of International Law," in *International Law as a Profession*, ed. Jean d'Aspremont et al. (Cambridge: Cambridge University Press, 2017), 69.

23 Oscar Schachter, "Invisible College of International Lawyers," *Northwestern University Law Review* 72 (1977): 217.

24 *See* Abram Chayes and Antonia Handler Chayes, *The New Sovereignty: Compliance with International Regulatory Agreements. The New Sovereignty* (Harvard University Press, 1998), https://doi.org/10.4159/9780674262638.

25 Felicity Vabulas and Duncan Snidal, "Cooperation under Autonomy: Building and Analyzing the Informal Intergovernmental Organizations 2.0 dataset," *Journal of Peace Research, 58*(4), 2021, 859–869.

26 Kenneth W. Abbott, Jessica F. Green, and Robert O. Keohane, "Organizational Ecology and Institutional Change in Global Governance," *International Organization* 70, no. 2 (2016): 247–277.

political agreements are on the rise, leading scholars of international law[27] and international relations[28] to contemplate whether they portend the "death of the treaty".[29] Especially notable is the emergence of "adhocracies"[30] or "ad hoc coalitions"[31] of specialized governance that have no institutional template to guide their discussions. These bodies develop policies on recruitment, deliberation, and decision-making on the fly. Many informal bodies cease to exist almost as abruptly as they are created.

Two factors make this development evoke comparisons with rulemaking by the League of Nations specialized agencies. Firstly, the rise of informal institutions have brought technical experts from businesses, standards bodies, and academia to the fore of global governance once again. Much like the "golden age" of the League, expert involvement in global governance has deepened in recent years.[32] This is not surprising. Informal governance mechanisms have become popular partly because private actors with deep pockets and significant convening power – for example, technology companies, civil society coalitions, and standards bodies[33] – have actively promoted them. In contrast to treaty mechanisms, where private actors have limited avenues for meaningful participation, informal governance arrangements have tended to be more open and inclusive. The participation of technical experts in informal bodies set up specifically to address complex scientific tasks is understandable. It is also not a phenomenon that escaped criticism. The pervasive involvement of "experts" who profess domain knowledge, but who simply manage (and subvert) the popular aspirations or felt needs of peoples to perpetuate systemic

---

27 Curtis A. Bradley, Jack Goldsmith, and Oona A. Hathaway, "The rise of nonbinding international agreements: An empirical, comparative, and normative analysis," *U. Chi. L. Rev.* 90 (2023): 1281.

28 *See generally* Kenneth W. Abbott and Thomas J. Biersteker, *Informal Governance in World Politics* (Cambridge University Press, 2024).

29 Joel P. Trachtman, "Reports of the Death of Treaty Are Premature, but Customary International Law May Have Outlived Its Usefulness," *AJIL Unbound* (2014), *108*, 36–40. https://doi.org/10.1017/S2398772300001811.

30 Ian Johnstone and Joshua Lincoln, "Global Governance in an Era of Pluralism," *Global Policy* 13, no. 4 (2022): 563–570, https://doi.org/10.1111/1758-5899.13085.

31 Yf Reykers et al., "Ad Hoc Coalitions in Global Governance : Short-Notice, Task – and Time-Specific Cooperation," *International Affairs*, 2023, https://doi.org/10.1093/ia/iiac319.

32 *See* Ole Jacob Sending, *The Politics of Expertise: Competing for Authority in Global Governance* (University of Michigan Press, 2015); Vincent Pouliot and Jean-Philippe Thérien, *Global Policymaking: The Patchwork of Global Governance*, 1st ed. (Cambridge University Press, 2023), 174–203.

33 Tim Büthe and Walter Mattli, *The New Global Rulers: The Privatization of Regulation in the World Economy* (Princeton University Press, 2011).

inequities has prompted a rethinking of global governance altogether.[34] However, as informal institutions begin to address questions around the application of existing international law to specialized domains – how those rules apply becomes an even more pertinent question in the absence of a specific treaty[35] – technical experts arguably emerge as crucial interlocutors in the identification and application of rules.

Secondly, the rise of informal governance initiatives brings into focus the practicalities of legal interpretation in those initiatives.[36] Informal bodies cannot articulate binding agreements. Their contribution to advancing legal discourse around a particular domain is nevertheless significant.[37] As the first report on "non-legally binding international agreements" by the International Law Commission's Special Rapporteur on the topic notes, "the fact that these agreements are not legally binding does not mean that international law is not likely to apply to them in some respects, or that they do not produce any legal effect".[38] Indeed, informal initiatives can contribute to generating intersubjective legal meaning around key concepts or principles for specific domains.[39] Even where interpretive differences exist between states or other stakeholders, these initiatives can help define the contours of what constitutes acceptable legal reasoning or argumentation.[40] Therefore, studying the process by which informal governance initiatives address international law-finding becomes important. Many informal initiatives are set up to address specific

---

34 David Kennedy, *A World of Struggle: How Power, Law, and Expertise Shape Global Political Economy* (Princeton University Press, 2016).

35 Martha Finnemore and Duncan B. Hollis, "Constructing Norms for Global Cybersecurity," *The American Journal of International Law* 110, no. 3 (2016): 425–479.

36 Nikolas M. Rajkovic, Tanja E. Aalberts, and Thomas Gammeltoft-Hansen, "Introduction: Legality, Interdisciplinarity and the Study of Practices," in *The Power of Legality: Practices of International Law and Their Politics*, ed. Nikolas M. Rajkovic, Tanja E. Aalberts, and Thomas Gammeltoft-Hansen (Cambridge: Cambridge University Press, 2016), 1–26, https://doi.org/10.1017/CBO9781316535134.002.

37 Joost Pauwelyn, Ramses A. Wessel, and Jan Wouters, "When Structures Become Shackles: Stagnation and Dynamics in International Lawmaking," *European Journal of International Law* 25, no. 3 (August 1, 2014): 733–763, https://doi.org/10.1093/ejil/chu051.

38 ILC, *First report on non-legally binding international agreements, by Mathias Forteau, Special Rapporteur,* Seventy-fifth session., Supp. No. 10, UN Doc. A/CN.4/772, 3/58 (2024).

39 Mark A Pollack and Gregory C Shaffer, "11 The Interaction of Formal and Informal International Lawmaking," in *Informal International Lawmaking*, ed. Joost Pauwelyn, Ramses Wessel, and Jan Wouters (Oxford University Press, 2012), https://doi.org/10.1093/acprof:oso/9780199658589.003.0012.

40 Steven Ratner, "Persuasion About/Without International LawThe Case of Cybersecurity Norms: Steven Ratner," in *Talking International Law: Legal Argumentation Outside the Courtroom*, ed. Ian Johnstone and Steven Ratner (Oxford University Press, 2021), https://doi.org/10.1093/oso/9780197588437.003.0006.

policy concerns, which in turn guide their discussions on international law. These initiatives often troubleshoot urgent problems, such as the prevention of a looming climate-related disaster, mitigation of a major epidemic or cybersecurity incident, orchestrating collective military action against terrorist groups, etc. The ascertainment and application of existing international law by these forums is guided as much by technical, economic, or military concerns, as it is by doctrinal methods. This is why the Special Rapporteur also noted that the ILC should "proceed with [...] caution" on how non-binding or informal agreements interact with the sources of international law.[41] The focus should be on the "*practical* aspects" [emphasis original] of law finding, noted the report, and not necessarily doctrinal or theoretical concerns.[42]

3 Informal Cybersecurity Governance, Technical Experts, and International Law-Ascertainment

Both the above considerations are relevant in the context of cybersecurity governance, which is the focus of this book. This book studies how technical experts have shaped the application of international law to state behavior in cyberspace. The international cybersecurity regime typifies the increasingly informal and *ad hoc* character of global governance. At the time of writing, there is treaty or no authoritative entity to articulate legally binding rules for international cybersecurity. In its stead, informal initiatives – intergovernmental, multistakeholder, and private – have proliferated, many of them seeking to develop a "framework of responsible state behavior" in cyberspace. By developing such a "framework", this book demonstrates, such initiatives and specifically the technical experts involved in them have also advanced "international cybersecurity law".[43] In other words, informal initiatives have played an important role in determining what existing rules apply and how those rules apply to state activities in cyberspace. These initiatives make up rules of procedure as they go; often have a rotating cast of members, advisers or consultants to assist with their goals; frequently identify new cybersecurity topics that are relevant to their work or address serious incidents and develop-

41 *First report on non-legally binding international agreements, by Mathias Forteau, Special Rapporteur*, n.38.

42 *Ibid.*

43 "International cybersecurity law" refers in this context to the corpus of rules or legal principles widely (but not universally) accepted by the states and non-state interlocutors (businesses, civil society, legal scholars, etc.) involved in international cybersecurity governance.

ments that have captured states' attention; and determine as they go along how best to report their findings or outcomes. Unsurprisingly, there are significant differences in the makeup and approaches of intergovernmental and multistakeholder bodies involved in cybersecurity governance.

The fluid character of these initiatives notwithstanding, informal governance in cybersecurity as a whole has proven remarkably persistent.[44] Take for instance, the UN Group of Governmental Experts (UN GGE), which is arguably the preeminent, intergovernmental group involved in international cybersecurity governance.[45] A small informal group whose membership has historically ranged from 10 to 25 "Experts" nominated by respective states and whose duration is ordinarily never more than a year, the UN GGE has been reconstituted six times over two decades. The UN GGE on cybersecurity is the longest running *ad hoc* body of its kind since the UN first established expert groups on security-related issues in 1968.[46] Over the years, discussions in cyber GGEs have become geopolitically charged, but it is worth highlighting that technical experts have historically played an important role in these negotiations. The "Experts" – with a capital "E" – nominated by many states to lead their delegations in the GGE tended in the past to be technical experts, although they have more recently been replaced by professional diplomats.[47] UN GGE Experts lead delegations that often include national security advisors, international lawyers, and technical experts. UN GGEs are created by the UN Secretary General upon request from the UN General Assembly, and their consensus reports are usually adopted as UNGA resolutions. The UNGA has offered little or no guidance to the cyber GGEs on what issues they should discuss, or how they should discuss them. The framework of cybersecurity governance that UN GGEs have developed, as this book demonstrates, is a

44 Arun Sukumar, Dennis Broeders, and Monica Kello, "The Pervasive Informality of the International Cybersecurity Regime: Geopolitics, Non-State Actors and Diplomacy," *Contemporary Security Policy* 45, no. 1 (January 2, 2024): 7–44, https://doi.org/10.1080/13523260.2023.2296739.

45 "Developments in the Field of Information and Telecommunications in the Context of International Security – UNODA," accessed March 1, 2023, https://www.un.org/disarmament/ict-security/.

46 "Means to Reinforce Research on Nuclear Disarmament Verification: Report on a Series of Regional Conversations," Matters No. 13 (VERTIC, November 2017), http://www.vertic.org/media/assets/Publications/VM13.pdf.

47 *Interview with Guilherme Patriota*, July 29, 2021; Heli Tiirmaa-Klaar, "The Evolution of the UN Group of Governmental Experts on Cyber Issues," Cyberstability Paper Series New Conditions and Constellations in Cyber, 5 (The Hague Centre for Strategic Studies, December 2021), https://hcss.nl/wp-content/uploads/2021/12/Klaar.pdf.

suo motu outcome of procedures and deliberates that the group has evolved over time.

Multistakeholder and private groups involved in international cybersecurity governance are even more loosely organized. Prominent multistakeholder initiatives like the Global Commission on the Stability of Cyberspace (GCSC)[48] and the Paris Call for Trust and Security in Cyberspace[49] were backed by major players in cyberspace like the Netherlands, France, and Microsoft, but functioned in an autonomous manner with little guidance from their sponsors. These initiatives articulated guidelines of responsible state behavior in cyberspace, drawing on a mix of closed-door working group meetings, public consultations, and inputs from research advisory meetings.

Multistakeholder initiatives are short-lived and do not tend to last as long as the UN processes. However, with the rise in scale and sophistication of malicious cyber operations globally, there has been a proliferation of bespoke initiatives to address them. Examples of such multistakeholder initiatives include "Let's Talk Cyber",[50] "Community Talks on Cyber Diplomacy",[51] and the "European Cyber Agora",[52] all of which are organized as interactive discussions or workshops on specific cybersecurity incidents or governance topics. While "Community Talks", organized by the cybersecurity company Kaspersky, was spread over two years, "Let's Talk Cyber" and "European Cyber Agora", sponsored by the Canadian government and Microsoft respectively, were held over two days. Additional examples of such discussions include those organized jointly in 2016 and 2017 by the UN Institute for Disarmament Research (UNIDIR) and the US think tank Centre for Strategic and International Studies (CSIS) in Geneva and Singapore, as well as the annual cyber norms conference hosted by the Computer Science and Artificial Intelligence Laboratory at

---

48 "Report – Global Commission on the Stability of Cyberspace," accessed June 22, 2024, https://cyberstability.org/report/.

49 Ministère de l'Europe et des Affaires étrangères, "Cybersecurity: Paris Call of 12 November 2018 for Trust and Security in Cyberspace," France Diplomacy – Ministry for Europe and Foreign Affairs, accessed June 17, 2024, https://www.diplomatie.gouv.fr/en/french-foreign-policy/digital-diplomacy/france-and-cyber-security/article/cybersecurity-paris-call-of-12-november-2018-for-trust-and-security-in.

50 "Informal Multi-Stakeholder Cyber Dialogue," accessed June 21, 2024, https://letstalkcyber.org/.

51 "Community Talks on Cyber Diplomacy: Summary of a Short Series of Multi-Stakeholder Conversations," accessed June 21, 2024, https://media.kaspersky.com/en/community-talks-on-cyber-diplomacy.pdf.

52 "European Cyber Agora, June 2–3, 2021 – Microsoft," accessed June 21, 2024, https://www.microsoft.com/en-eu/cyber-agora/.

MIT.[53] These workshops and conferences have all seen robust participation from technical experts.

In recent years, technical standards bodies have themselves evinced interest in informal governance initiatives. Since 2018, the Institute of Electrical and Electronics Engineers (IEEE) has been the principal technical sponsor and publishing host for the papers selected by CyCon, an "international conference on cyber conflict".[54] CyCon is organized by the Cooperative Cyber Defence Centre of Excellence (CCDCOE), a NATO think tank, and features high-level participation from Western states. The 2019 edition of CyCon featured the release of an "Interactive Cyber Law Toolkit", a "web-based resource for legal professionals who work with matters at the intersection of international law and cyber operations".[55] Similarly, the Asia-Pacific Network Information Centre (APNIC), the Regional internet Registry that manages and distributes IP addresses across Asia, has brought together technical experts and international lawyers in a series of "interdisciplinary dialogues" produced as podcasts.[56] The internet Engineering Task Force has in the past invited members of the GCSC to brief the technical standards community about norms of responsible state behavior in cyberspace.[57]

Apparent from even this cursory overview of the institutional landscape of cybersecurity governance is that it is dominated by informal initiatives, in which technical experts play *some* role. The aforementioned initiatives have been important to developing what has come to be known among various stakeholders as the "framework of responsible state behavior in cyberspace".[58] This framework comprises four pillars.[59] Voluntary and aspirational guidelines for the conduct of states, called "cyber norms", are central to the

53 "Report of the International Security Cyber Issues Workshop Series" (UNIDIR/ Center for Strategic and International Studies, 2016), https://www.unidir.org/files/publications/pdfs/report-of-the-international-security-cyber-issues-workshop-series-en-656.pdf.

54 "International Conference on Cyber Conflict – CyCon," accessed July 18, 2024, https://ccdcoe.org/cycon/.

55 "International Cyber Law: Interactive Toolkit," accessed June 21, 2024, https://cyberlaw.ccdcoe.org/wiki/Main_Page.

56 *Electronic correspondence with Pablo Hinojosa*, February 13, 2021.

57 "Rough Guide to IETF 102," *IETF Journal* (blog), accessed June 23, 2024, https://www.ietfjournal.org/rough-guide-to-ietf-102/.

58 "Unpacking the GGE's Framework on Responsible State Behavior: Cyber Norms" (Global Partners Digital, December 2019), https://www.gp-digital.org/wp-content/uploads/2019/12/unpacking_gge_cyber-norms.pdf.

59 "Background to UN Discussions on Responsible State Behavior – Unidir," *Cyber Policy Portal of the United Nations Institute for Disarmament Research* (blog), January 27, 2022, https://nationalcybersurvey.cyberpolicyportal.org/background-to-un-discussions-on-responsible-state-behaviour/.

framework. Equally relevant are capacity-building initiatives and confidence-building measures (CBMs) between states to secure digital networks and prevent them from being used for malicious cyber attacks. Finally, responsible behavior in cyberspace is also about complying with existing international law. The applicability of international law to state behavior in this domain has been a highly contentious matter. States spent years at the UN discussing whether existing rules apply at all to cyberspace, before agreeing to identify and apply some of those rules. While debates on international law unfolded at the UN, multistakeholder and private initiatives have frequently relied on legal principles to clarify what constitutes responsible conduct in cyberspace.

Studying how technical experts influence law-finding by these informal initiatives – and therefore the overall development of "international cybersecurity law" – is challenging because of the sheer institutional diversity and regime complexity[60] in this domain. Yet, this is an important research endeavor given the rising role of private actors in modern global governance and the concurrent rise of informal governance initiatives in which they are prominent participants. Acknowledging that law-finding in these informal initiatives to be driven by practical and policy-oriented considerations rather than strictly doctrinal methods, this book foregrounds the operating practices of those initiatives to study the role of technical experts. In fluid and ad hoc settings such as the UN GGE or the Global Commission on the Stability of Cyberspace, law-finding or ascertainment is governed by the "logic of practicality",[61] the book demonstrates. Put differently, the ascertainment of international law applicable to cyberspace is guided by the practices developed by these institutions, which in turn reflect their core beliefs about how cyberspace should be governed. Institutional practices determine not only when participants turn to legal reasoning and argumentation to address cyberspace governance, but also how technical experts participate in and influence international cybersecurity law discourse.

3.1 Making Sense of International Law-Finding by Informal Initiatives

What does it mean to say that legal interpretation and argumentation in informal governance initiatives is a practical affair? Do the short durations and

60 Karen J. Alter and Kal Raustiala, "The Rise of International Regime Complexity," *Annual Review of Law and Social Science* 14, no. Volume 14, 2018 (2018): 329–349.

61 Vincent Pouliot, "The Logic of Practicality: A Theory of Practice of Security Communities," International Organization 62, no. 2 (2008): 259.

pursuits of limited objectives by informal initiatives – responding to a major cybersecurity incident or protecting specific sectors of critical infrastructure – mean they simply stumble through their discussions to arrive at governance outcomes? Not quite. Despite the diversity of the abovementioned initiatives, the fact remains that there is today a remarkable degree of acceptance among states on which existing rules apply to cyberspace, and how they apply to state behavior in various scenarios.[62] Stakeholders in informal initiatives have developed a shared vocabulary around responsible state behavior in cyberspace, which includes legal principles and interpretations of those principles. To be sure, states, including "like-minded" partners such as the United States and European Union states, disagree frequently on the application of specific legal principles to this domain. While there is disagreement, there is also a common understanding among most actors, including among states such as China and Russia,[63] as to what constitutes acceptable legal discourse on international cybersecurity. In other words, states know what other states are talking about when they talk about the international law of cyberspace.

As noted earlier, this book demonstrates that the emergence of such shared understandings in international cybersecurity law is owed to the practices of various informal governance institutions. Far from being randomly established, practices are "socially meaningful and organized patterns of activities" within an institution or society.[64] They form the "infrastructure of social and political interaction"[65] through which actors in that social setting engage and understand each other. As scholars of international relations and international law have demonstrated, practices of global governance institutions

---

62 *See generally*, Chris Carpenter and Duncan B. Hollis, "A Victim's Perspective on International Law in Cyberspace," *Lawfare* (blog), August 28, 2023, https://www.lawfaremedia.org/article/a-victim-s-perspective-on-international-law-in-cyberspace.

63 Zhixiong Huang and Kubo Mačák, "Towards the International Rule of Law in Cyberspace: Contrasting Chinese and Western Approaches," *Chinese Journal of International Law* 16, no. 2 (June 1): 271–310; "The 2nd 'Frontier Forum on International Rules in Cyberspace' Successfully Held," *Wuhan University School of Law*, accessed February 21, 2024, https://law.whu.edu.cn/info/1699/13932.htm; A Anatoly A. Streltsov, "Application of International Humanitarian Law to Armed Conflicts in Cyberspace," 2012, https://digital.report/wp-content/uploads/2016/04/169747-Streltsov-ENG.pdf.

64 Vincent Pouliot and Jean-Philippe Thérien, "Global Governance in Practice," *Global Policy* 9, no. 2 (2018): 163–172.

65 Vincent Pouliot, "Global Governance in the Age of Epistemic Authority," *International Theory* 13, no. 1 (March 2021): 152.

reflect and reinforce certain core dispositions that drive interactions among its participants, whether states or non-state actors.[66]

Framed differently, these participants come to share a "deeply internalized" belief or set of beliefs about how a domain should be governed.[67] Practices of institutions in which states and non-state actors are interlocutors appear commonsensical – reflecting the "right way" to go about the business of governance – because they draw on those ingrained beliefs. The notion of background beliefs or subconscious dispositions that drive a community's actions is a complex one, and has been interpreted variously by social theorists from John Searle to Pierre Bourdieu.[68] In IR theory and especially international legal scholarship, Bourdieu's concept of "*habitus*" has been influential and widely applied to study how institutions develop background beliefs about global governance.[69] It is easier to describe what the *habitus* is characterized by, and what it does, than what it is. A community's *habitus* generates "expectations unconsciously acquired by individuals [in that community] through experience and socialization".[70] Each community or institution, whether social, cultural, political, or economic in nature, has its own *habitus*. To the individual participating in the *habitus*, its practices seem "sensible and reasonable".[71]

International relations and legal scholars drawing on Bourdieu's *habitus* note that core beliefs about communities of global governance may be owed

66 Jérémie Cornut, "The Practice Turn in International Relations Theory," in *The International Studies Encyclopedia* (Wiley-Blackwell, 2017), https://www.oxfordreference.com/display/10.1093/acref/9780191842665.001.0001/acref-9780191842665-e-0456.

67 Anne van Aaken and Moshe Hirsch, "Introduction: International Legal Theory and the Cognitive Turn," in *International Legal Theory and the Cognitive Turn*, ed. Anne van Aaken and Moshe Hirsch (Oxford University Press, 2025), https://doi.org/10.1093/9780198909293.003.0001.

68 *See generally*, Ian Johnstone and Arun Mohan Sukumar, "Constructivism, Interpretation, and Cognitive Studies," in *International Legal Theory and the Cognitive Turn*, ed. Anne van Aaken and Moshe Hirsch (Oxford University Press, 2025), https://doi.org/10.1093/9780198909293.003.0004.

69 *See*, Rebecca Adler-Nissen, *Bourdieu in International Relations: Rethinking Key Concepts in IR* (Routledge, 2012); Mikael Rask Madsen and Salvatore Caserta, "International Judicial Habitus: Pierre Bourdieu and the Cognitive Turn" in Mosche Hirsch and Anne van Aaken (eds), *International Legal Theory and the Cognitive Turn*, (Oxford University Press, 2025); Deepak Nair, "Using Bourdieu's Habitus in International Relations," *International Studies Quarterly* 68, no. 2 (2024): sqae007, https://doi.org/10.1093/isq/sqae007.

70 Pierre Bourdieu, *Outline of a Theory of Practice*, trans. Richard Nice, Cambridge Studies in Social and Cultural Anthropology (Cambridge: Cambridge University Press, 1977), 72.

71 Bourdieu (1977), 79.

to "material conditions of existence".[72] These conditions could be geopolitical, economic, military or drawn from other, objectively discernible, historical factors.[73] Beliefs about governing a specific domain, say cyberspace, or the ozone layer, or artificial intelligence, generate unique practices that allow states and private actors to anticipate, understand or respond to others' governance proposals. Practices become mutually intelligible and socially significant because they draw on these beliefs, and consequently, they also become the main vehicle for learning by participants in governance institutions. In other words, if core beliefs provide participants with a "feel for the game", practices shape how they play that game, and navigate its various scenarios.[74]

It is important to distinguish between background beliefs and knowledge from "representative knowledge", i.e., knowledge gained through vocational means.[75] To be sure, "representative knowledge" matters: a technical expert, international lawyer, arms control diplomat or human rights activist may approach global governance from the prism of their training and professional experience. However, such knowledge submits itself to, and its application is shaped by, the core beliefs and dispositions of the community to which the practitioner belongs. State and non-state actors may indeed have closely held prior interests as they enter the regime complex of cybersecurity or environmental governance, but which of those interests are advanced and how they are advanced are both shaped by the practices of the institutions in which they participate. In Pouliot's elegant formulation, "it is not only who we are

---

72 Pierre Bourdieu, *In Other Words: Essays Towards a Reflexive Sociology* (Stanford University Press, 1990) *c.f.* Vincent Pouliot and Frédéric Mérand, "Bourdieu's Concepts: Political Sociology in International Relations," in *Bourdieu in International Relations: Rethinking Key Concepts in IR*, ed. Rebecca Adler-Nissen (Routledge, 2012).

73 To say that the "practice turn" in international relations and international law has been truly faithful to Bourdieu would be an overstatement. Many notable theorizations, including those identified in this chapter, modify Bourdieu's framework to meet the realities of global governance, where membership, fealty, and/or sustained participation in institutions can be less readily ascertained than in national, societal, or ethnic communities to which his sociological analysis is more tailored. *See Nair* (*2024*), *n.69*, whose review of the state of the art emphasizes that IR theorizations often sidestep the causes and origins of "primary socialization" of diplomats and other actors along vectors such as race, gender, and family backgrounds. This book does not go into a deeper review of Bourdieu's work but rather highlights the analytical utility of certain *Bourdieusian* concepts like *habitus* and *doxa*.

74 Pierre Bourdieu, *Practical Reason: On the Theory of Action*, 25 (Stanford University Press, 1998).

75 Sebastian Schmidt, "Foreign Military Presence and the Changing Practice of Sovereignty: A Pragmatist Explanation of Norm Change," *American Political Science Review* 108, no. 4 (2014): 817–29, https://doi.org/10.1017/S0003055414000434.

that determines what we do; it is also what we do that determines who we are".[76]

3.2 The Role of Communities of Practice

Having laid the conceptual ground for understanding the significance of practices in international relations, it is also important to frame the social setting in which practices acquire salience. If the global governance of a domain is indeed a practical affair, then practical know-how about governance seldom circulates within a single institution. Such beliefs and attendant practices often transcend "institutional affiliations and boundaries", and are shared among states and private actors involved in domain governance.[77] This is hardly surprising. After all, regime complexes of actors and overlapping institutions are ubiquitous in contemporary international relations. Common membership or participation results in "practical know-how" about advancing governance circulating across multiple institutions – as Bueger et al note, this know-how is the common background knowledge that shapes intentional practices, notwithstanding their diversity across said institutions.[78] Further, regime complexes may have focal institutions that play a critical role in developing rules or guidelines.[79] While focal institutions can contribute to path dependency[80] within the regime, it is rarely the case that an institution singlehandedly advances the governance agenda. As Hoffmann and Yeo demonstrate, "low sovereignty costs associated with informal focal organizations" generate a process of "breakout layering" around said organizations, resulting in even more informal institutions to address specific governance themes.[81]

76 Vincent Pouliot, *International Security in Practice: The Politics of NATO-Russia Diplomacy* (Cambridge: Cambridge University Press, 2010), 5.

77 Emanuel Adler et al., "Communities of Practice in World Politics: Advancing a Research Agenda," *Global Studies Quarterly* 4, no. 1 (2024): https://doi.org/10.1093/isagsq/ksad070.

78 Christian Bueger et al., "Global Ordering and the Interaction of Communities of Practice: A Framework for Analysis," *Global Studies Quarterly* 4, no. 1 (2024): https://doi.org/10.1093/isagsq/ksad079.

79 *See generally*, Daniel W. Drezner, "The Power and Peril of International Regime Complexity," *Perspectives on Politics* 7, no. 1 (2009): 65–70, https://doi.org/10.1017/S1537592709090100.

80 C. Randall Henning and Tyler Pratt, "Hierarchy and Differentiation in International Regime Complexes: A Theoretical Framework for Comparative Research," *Review of International Political Economy* 30, no. 6 (2023): 2178–2205, https://doi.org/10.1080/09692290.2023.2259424.

81 Stephanie C. Hofmann and Andrew Yeo, "Historical Institutionalism and Institutional Design: Divergent Pathways to Regime Complexes in Asia and Europe," *European Jour-*

Such layering contributes to a considerable degree of overlap in membership, ideas, and mandates in the regime complex. Even where the format and composition of institutions vary, therefore, participants in the broader regime complex may come to share common beliefs about the goals of governance and even methods to advance it.

Take, as an illustration, the case of global non-proliferation regimes. Most modern non-proliferation treaties and institutions seek to regulate the export of "dual use" technologies, i.e., technologies that have both civilian and military uses. This is an article of faith, internalized by diplomats, technical experts and other practitioners involved in non-proliferation regimes, whether those regimes pertain to conventional, chemical, biological, or radiological weapons and material. Invoking a technology's "duality of purpose" is tacitly associated with certain state responsibilities, mechanisms or triggers of multilateral cooperation to regulate it, and even moral or ethical obligations to limit its deployment.[82] Core beliefs about duality also generate diplomatic and expert practices that are instantly recognizable and whose meaning is understood by all actors, regardless of their institutional affiliation. For example, an international NGO's publishing an annual index of states with good or poor nuclear security[83] (reputational and material consequences), or an expert body's moving of a "doomsday clock" closer to midnight (cultural and socio-cognitive impact). One does not need to belong to the *Bulletin of the Atomic Scientists* or the IAEA to understand what is signaled through these practices.

Because negotiators, NGOs, and experts participate in this manner through multiple institutions with overlapping mandates, it is more appropriate to frame practices as being intrinsic to a "community". A "community of practice" (CoP) refers to a "constellation of agents"[84] characterized by "mutual engagement, [the pursuit of] a joint enterprise, and a shared repertoire of words, gestures, tools, stories, symbols and ways of doing things".[85] CoPs

---

nal of International Relations 30, no. 2 (2024): 306–332, https://doi.org/10.1177/13540661231170717.

82 Lena Riecke, "Unmasking the Term 'Dual Use' in EU Spyware Export Control," *European Journal of International Law* 34, no. 3 (2023): 697–720, https://doi.org/10.1093/ejil/chad039; Seumas Miller and Michael J. Selgelid, "Ethical and Philosophical Consideration of the Dual-Use Dilemma in the Biological Sciences," *Science and Engineering Ethics* 13, no. 4 (2007): 523–580, https://doi.org/10.1007/s11948-007-9043-4.

83 "NTI Nuclear Security Index," *The Nuclear Threat Initiative*, April 16, 2024, https://www.nti.org/about/programs-projects/project/nti-index/.

84 Vincent Pouliot, "The Logic of Practicality: A Theory of Practice of Security Communities," International Organization 62, no. 2 (2008): 259.

85 Etienne Wenger, *Communities of Practice: Learning, Meaning, and Identity*, 73 (Cambridge University Press, 1999).

build the "normative and epistemic ground for action" in the real world.[86] Practitioners within the community hold "complementary dispositions and expectations" but they need not bear the same interests and may frequently disagree with each other through commonly recognized practices.[87] Wenger-Trayner describes the creation of a CoP as the "social process of negotiating competence" over time:[88] participants in a CoP understand and evaluate their actions and those of others through a common structure of beliefs, and even if they may not agree with each other, their actions are mutually intelligible.

Indeed, Lave and Wenger-Trayner noted that the term community did not "imply necessarily co-presence, a well-defined, identifiable group, or socially visible boundaries".[89] Membership in a CoP simply means "participation in an activity system about which participants share understandings concerning what they are doing and what that means in their lives and for their communities".[90] Adapting this loosely held concept in international relations, Emanuel Adler and Michael Barnett argue that a CoP has three distinct features.[91] *First*, its members have "shared identities, values, and meanings". *Second*, practitioners in the CoP have "many-sided and direct relations", and interact routinely through "some form of face-to-face encounter and relations in numerous settings". *Third*, they "exhibit a reciprocity" that reflects a degree of "long-term interest, and perhaps even altruism". Long-term interest, in particular, "derives from knowledge of those with whom one is interacting". Scholarship on practices and communities of practice in international relations has encompassed a wide range of actors and institutions, including ministries of foreign affairs,[92] organs and specialized agencies of the United

86 Emanuel Adler and Vincent Pouliot, "International Practices: Introduction and Framework," in *International Practices*, ed. Emanuel Adler and Vincent Pouliot, 1st ed. (Cambridge University Press, 2011), 17, https://doi.org/10.1017/CBO9780511862373.003.

87 Emanuel Adler, *World Ordering: A Social Theory of Cognitive Evolution*, 1st ed. (Cambridge University Press, 2019), 202, https://doi.org/10.1017/9781108325615.

88 Valerie Farnsworth, Irene Kleanthous, and Etienne Wenger-Trayner, "Communities of Practice as a Social Theory of Learning: A Conversation with Etienne Wenger," *British Journal of Educational Studies* 64, no. 2 (April 2, 2016): 139–160, https://doi.org/10.1080/00071005.2015.1133799.

89 *Lave and Wenger* (1991), 98.

90 *Lave and Wenger* (1991), 98.

91 Emanuel Adler and Michael Barnett, "A Framework for the Study of Security Communities," in *Security Communities*, ed. Emanuel Adler and Michael Barnett, Cambridge Studies in International Relations (Cambridge: Cambridge University Press, 1998), 29–66, https://doi.org/10.1017/CBO9780511598661.002.

92 Iver B. Neumann, "Returning Practice to the Linguistic Turn: The Case of Diplomacy," *Millennium* 31, no. 3 (July 1, 2002): 639–649; Gëzim Visoka, "Metis Diplomacy: The Everyday Politics of Becoming a Sovereign State," *Cooperation and Conflict* 54, no. 2 (June 1,

Nations such as the UN Security Council[93] and the World Bank,[94] regional organizations,[95] and domains of global governance such as peacekeeping and anti-piracy.[96]

3.3 Communities of Practice and International Law-Ascertainment

If at least some CoPs in global governance apply and interpret international law to various domains, how does one identify practices that specifically shape law-ascertainment? The practices of international lawyers, within and outside institutional settings where they interpret existing rules or develop new ones, has long been a focus of IL scholarship.[97] The "practice turn" in international law studies can broadly be categorized into two distinct strands of scholarship. The first strand, featuring rigorous empirical and often ethnographic

---

2019): 167–90; Dylan M H Loh, "Institutional Habitus, State Identity, and China's Ministry of Foreign Affairs," *International Studies Review* 22, no. 4 (2020): 879–902, https://doi.org/10.1093/isr/viz051.

93 Niels Nagelhus Schia, "Being Part of the Parade – 'Going Native' in the United Nations Security Council," *PoLAR: Political and Legal Anthropology Review* 36, no. 1 (2013): 138–56; Ingvild Bode, "Reflective Practices at the Security Council: Children and Armed Conflict and the Three United Nations," *European Journal of International Relations* 24, no. 2 (June 1, 2018): 293–318; Vincent Pouliot, "The Gray Area of Institutional Change: How the Security Council Transforms Its Practices on the Fly," *Journal of Global Security Studies* 6, no. 3 (September 1, 2021): 1–18.

94 Maïka Sondarjee, "Change and Stability at the World Bank: Inclusive Practices and Neoliberal Technocratic Rationality," *Third World Quarterly* 42, no. 2 (February 1, 2021): 348–365; Galit Sarfaty, *Values in Translation: Human Rights and the Culture of the World Bank* (Stanford University Press, 2012).

95 Deepak Nair, "Saving Face in Diplomacy: A Political Sociology of Face-to-Face Interactions in the Association of Southeast Asian Nations," *European Journal of International Relations* 25, no. 3 (September 1, 2019): 672–697; Rebecca Adler-Nissen, *Opting Out of the European Union: Diplomacy, Sovereignty and European Integration* (Cambridge: Cambridge University Press, 2014).

96 Séverine Autesserre, *Peaceland: Conflict Resolution and the Everyday Politics of International Intervention*, Problems of International Politics (Cambridge: Cambridge University Press, 2014); Christian Bueger, "Experimenting with Global Governance: Learning Lessons in the Contact Group on Piracy," in *Knowing Governance*, ed. Jan-Peter Voß and Richard Freeman (London: Palgrave Macmillan UK, 2016), 87–105.

97 *See* Jens Meierhenrich, "The Practice of International Law: A Theoretical Analysis," *Law and Contemporary Problems* 76, no. 3/4 (2013): 59; Jeffrey L. Dunoff and Mark A. Pollack, "Practice Theory and International Law," in *Research Handbook on the Sociology of International Law*, ed. Mosche Hirsch and Andrew Lang (Edward Elgar Publishing, 2018), 252–272; Nicolas Lamp, "The 'Practice Turn' in International Law: Insights from the Theory of Structuration," in *Research Handbook on the Sociology of International Law*, ed. Mosche Hirsch and Andrew Lang (Edward Elgar Publishing, 2018), 273–295.

work, focuses on the role that professional practices of lawyers played in shaping new domains of international law. In particular, these works highlight how such practices contributed to the emergence of "specialist" international lawyers in fields such as international criminal law, regional law, or commercial arbitration, whose professional orientation is distinct from generalist international lawyers as well as national lawyers.[98] Their self-identification as specialists, prompted by communal practices relating to a shared educational experience or professional engagements, contributed to these lawyers developing new rules (or interpreting existing rules differently) for various domains of international law. A second strand of scholarship highlights what actually happens within specialized institutional bodies, such as international courts or IGOs.[99] To be sure, the focus of this work is mainly on *legal practices* – evidence gathering and docket preparation in international courts and tribunals, practices of legal interpretation, monitoring and evaluation by multilateral institutions of rule of law indices, etc.[100] These studies have offered rich insights into how rule-creation and interpretation is essentially a competitive and strategic interaction between international lawyers and judges within

98 Yves Dezalay and Bryant G. Garth, *Dealing in Virtue: International Commercial Arbitration and the Construction of a Transnational Legal Order* (University of Chicago Press, 1996); John Hagan and Ron Levi, "Crimes of War and the Force of Law," *Social Forces* 83, no. 4 (2005): 1499–1534; Salvatore Caserta and Mikael Rask Madsen, "Between Community Law and Common Law: The Rise of the Caribbean Court of Justice at the Intersection of Regional Integration and Post-Colonial Legacies," *Law and Contemporary Problems* 79, no. 1 (2016): 89–115.

99 Jutta Brunnee and Stephen J. Toope, *Legitimacy and Legality in International Law: An Interactional Account* (Cambridge: Cambridge University Press, 2010); Henry Redwood and Hannah Goozee, "Shifting Accounts of Justice: The Legalization and Politicization of International Criminal Justice," *Social & Legal Studies* 31, no. 4 (August 1, 2022): 623–643; Frédéric Mégret, "International Criminal Justice as a Juridical Field," *Champ Pénal/Penal Field*, no. Vol. XIII (February 29, 2016), https://doi.org/10.4000/champpenal.9284; Nora Stappert, "Practice Theory and Change in International Law: Theorizing the Development of Legal Meaning through the Interpretive Practices of International Criminal Courts," *International Theory* 12, no. 1 (March 2020): 33–58.

100 Thomas Gammeltoft-Hansen and Tanja Aalberts, "Introduction: The Changing Practices of International Law," in *The Changing Practices of International Law*, ed. Tanja Aalberts and Thomas Gammeltoft-Hansen, 1st ed. (Cambridge University Press, 2018), 6, https://doi.org/10.1017/9781108349420.002; Karen J. Alter, Lauren Helfer, and Mikael Rask Madsen., "How Context Shapes the Authority of International Courts", 79 *Law and Contemporary Problems* 1–36 (2016); Frédéric Mégret, "Thinking about What International Humanitarian Lawyers 'Do': An Examination of the Laws of War as a Field of Professional Practice," in *The Law of International Lawyers*, ed. Wouter Werner, Marieke de Hoon, and Alexis Galán, 1st ed. (Cambridge University Press, 2017), 265–296; Galit Sarfaty, *Values in Translation: Human Rights and the Culture of the World Bank* (Stanford University Press, 2012).

these institutions. Their work shines a light on, and contributes to a fuller understanding of the links between profession and discipline – indeed, it strengthens the thesis that international law is indeed the "law of international lawyers".[101] In particular, influential works around why certain legal formulations acquire intersubjectivity through "interactional" practices and induce compliance within specialized settings fall within this category.[102]

While the focus of these two strands of scholarship has largely been on formal-legal institutions and their practices, legal scholars have more recently sought a greater exploration of links between informal law-making and institutional practices.[103] This is an empirical endeavor that is long overdue. International law scholarship has examined in detail whether legal practices are effective in international law at once managing international politics while preserving its own disciplinary autonomy.[104] It is arguably in informal initiatives that the tension between both objectives is most apparent, because such settings also draw in private and governmental actors who are not lawyers, and feature non-legal practices that have *some* discursive impact on international law.

To be sure, the mere identification of practices of recruitment or deliberation by technical experts in informal settings cannot by itself support the claim that they influence international law discourse. Having a seat at the table is no guarantee of being influential. After all, "institutional structures

---

101 Wouter Werner, Marieke de Hoon, and Alexis Galán, eds., *The Law of International Lawyers: Reading Martti Koskenniemi* (Cambridge: Cambridge University Press, 2017), https://doi.org/10.1017/9781108147620.

102 Jutta Brunnee and Stephen J. Toope, *Legitimacy and Legality in International Law: An Interactional Account* (Cambridge University Press, 2010), https://doi.org/10.1017/CBO9780511781261.

103 Nikolas M. Rajkovic, Tanja E. Aalberts, and Thomas Gammeltoft-Hansen, "Introduction: Legality, Interdisciplinarity and the Study of Practices," in *The Power of Legality: Practices of International Law and Their Politics*, ed. Nikolas M. Rajkovic, Tanja E. Aalberts, and Thomas Gammeltoft-Hansen (Cambridge: Cambridge University Press, 2016), 1–26, https://doi.org/10.1017/CBO9781316535134.002; Jakob v. H. Holtermann, Mikael Rask Madsen, and Nora Stappert, "Legal Validity and the importance of epistemology for research on legal norms," iCourts Working Paper Series, no. 268 (2021), 14; Ian Johnstone and Steven Ratner, "Toward a Theory of Legal Argumentation," in *Talking International Law: Legal Argumentation Outside the Courtroom*, ed. Ian Johnstone and Steven Ratner (Oxford University Press, 2021), 339–256, https://doi.org/10.1093/oso/9780197588437.003.0017.

104 Tanja Aalberts and Ingo Venzke, "Moving Beyond Interdisciplinary Turf Wars: Towards an Understanding of International Law as Practice," in *International Law as a Profession*, ed. André Nollkaemper et al. (Cambridge: Cambridge University Press, 2017), 287–310, https://doi.org/10.1017/9781316492802.013.

[and] procedures in the informal realm are slowly becoming 'lawlike'", notes Krisch, but he adds the caveat that actors still consider "informal norms" to be non-binding.[105] It is important firstly to trace how specific institutional practices are owed to deeply held background beliefs within a CoP, and secondly, also to show that those practices have, through their governance outcomes, influenced perceptions of legality within the community. The second is a more challenging task, because the pronouncements of informal institutions on legality of cyber operations can hardly be considered authoritative, much less binding on states. Still, it is possible, through immersive observation in the CoP's discussions as well as interviews with various actors to assess such perceptions, subjective as they are. Both empirical methods have been deployed extensively to answer the questions raised in this book, and I return to a discussion of research methods later in this chapter.

4 Articulating Informal Norms, Advancing International Law: The Logic of "Creeping Expertise"

This book presents the results of such an empirics-driven assessment, offering granular insights into the working of the community of practice involved in cybersecurity governance (hereafter in this chapter and across the book termed "cyber CoP"). It demonstrates not only that informal initiatives can and do influence perceptions of legality in a domain, but also that non-legal actors such as technical experts play a key role in molding those perceptions.

As this chapter has already noted, the main goal of most informal initiatives involved in cybersecurity governance has been to articulate normsof responsible state behavior. The UN GGE as well as multistakeholder initiatives have explicitly characterized these informal cyber norms as "voluntary and non-binding" guidelines. However, this book demonstrates that norms, notwithstanding their non-binding character, have become entwined with discussions on international law over the years. The central claim of the book is that actors involved in international cybersecurity governance – diplomats, lawyers, technology companies, human rights NGOs, etc. – believe discussions on the application of international law to cyberspace can be advanced through the articulation of cyber norms. Paradoxically, norms have

105 Nico Krisch, "The Decay of Consent: International Law in an Age of Global Public Goods," *American Journal of International Law* 108, no. 1 (January 2014), https://doi.org/10.5305/amerjintelaw.108.1.0001.

often borrowed legal vocabulary or referred to specific legal principles,implying they were not merely aspirational statements but cyber-specific interpretations of existing international law. Technical experts, who were key interlocutors in norms-articulation initiatives, were able to influence legal discourse on cybersecurity because the boundaries between norms-articulation and law-interpretation were blurred. I term this phenomenon "creeping expertise" in international cybersecurity law.

This core belief within the cyber CoP, that norms and rules are functionally equivalent tools to advance responsible state behavior, is reflected by the practices of informal initiatives within this community. The entangling of informal norms and existing international law – which critically shaped cybersecurity governance – is owed to geopolitics, the book demonstrates. Cyber norms began referring to legal principles on account of a compromise made between the US and Russia at the 2010 UN Group of Governmental Experts on cybersecurity (UN GGE). While Russia had sought for new, binding constraints on disruptive cyber operations and cyber-enabled espionage by the US and its allies, the US resisted additional obligations beyond those that already existed in international law. As a compromise formulation, the UN GGE adopted new norms or specialized guidelines for responsible conduct in cyberspace, but which often drew from existing legal obligations.

With geopolitical deadlock making it difficult either to develop new binding obligations for states, or clarify how existing international law applied to their behavior, subsequent UN GGEs interpreted and applied international law to specific situations through cyber norms. The book demonstrates that UN GGEs developed everyday practices that reinforced this conflation of norms and rules. These practices pertained to recruitment to GGEs, their rules of procedure and deliberation, and reporting of GGE outcomes to external actors, all of which reinforced the view that norms and international law were intertwined. Adopting practices similar to the GGE, intergovernmental, multistakeholder and private initiatives that also articulated informal norms followed suit in their approach to advancing cybersecurity governance. The book details the practices of six such initiatives: two intergovernmental initiatives (the UN GGE and UN Open-Ended Working Group on cybersecurity); two multistakeholder initiatives (the Global Commission on the Stability of Cyberspace and the Paris Call for Trust and Security in Cyberspace); and two private initiatives (the Tallinn Manuals on International Law applicable to Cyberspace and the Oxford Process on International Law Protections in Cyberspace).

The following chapters illustrate how, despite differences in composition, deliberative procedures, and eventual objectives, the practices of all six initiatives reified the conflation of informal norms and existing rules. As noted previously, this conflation is most apparent in the direct incorporation of legal vocabulary or references to legal principles by voluntary norms articulated by these initiatives. For example, the UN GGE's decades-long practice of issuing reports with a joint section on "norms, rules and principles" strongly facilitated such "borrowing" by norms of existing international law, the book shows. In other cases, multistakeholder initiatives have specifically recruited or set up consultative practices with international lawyers to help them draft the text or commentary for informal norms. The result was that such commentaries would often be based on international law principles, as though presenting a legal justification for norms. In yet other instances, exercises to identify and apply existing international law applicable to cyberspace have been designed in the manner of norms-articulation processes, the book demonstrates. The Tallinn Manuals and Oxford Process are two important initiatives belonging to the cyber CoP. Although they are law-finding initiatives, their working was nevertheless influenced by the CoP's blurring of boundaries between informal norms and rules. They instituted what the book terms "managerial practices" to accommodate the views and interests of state and private actors on the applicability of existing law to ensure their findings elicit agreement, and ultimately, adoption by those actors. In this regard, they do not identify or apply existing rules in a strictly formal-doctrinal sense, but "manage" it in a pragmatic and policy-oriented manner.

The adoption of such practices, the book demonstrates, allowed technical experts who were key interlocutors in articulating norms, to also shape the application of existing international law to cyberspace. The book identifies two main ways by which the cyber CoP's conflation of norms and law facilitated "creeping expertise".

a. *Identification of specific digital infrastructure or technical properties of cyberspace as protected or deserving of protection under international law*: Informal initiatives articulate cyber norms for various reasons. Some of them call on states to exhibit restraint in relation to certain cyber operations, while others seek positive commitments to monitor malicious activity or mitigate cyber attacks in a timely manner. Often, the focus of such norms has a technical component. States, technology companies, and standards bodies all have interests in protecting specific digital assets or class of assets in cyberspace. In other cases, they may want to protect technical properties of global cyberspace – such as its seamless availability and interoperability – from serious and geopolitically motivated cyber operations. The following chapters illustrate how practices of informal initiatives bound together norm-articulation on these assets or properties with the identification and application of existing international law for their protection. Consequently, technical experts not only guided early discussions within these initiatives towards articulating norms around those objects, but also influenced discussions on how international law would apply to them. Examples illustrated in this book include discussions in the UN GGE on the protection of critical infrastructure from serious cyber operations, the GCSC's deliberations on cyber-enabled interference with electoral processes, and the Oxford Process group's considering the protection of vaccine research data from cyber-enabled operations, including espionage.

b. *Guiding discussions on the scope of application of existing rules*: Multistakeholder initiatives like the Paris Call and GCSC developed the practice of annotating their norms with "law-like" memos that drew on existing rules and principles. These memos essentially interpreted how specific rules applied to the norm in question. They were drafted after extensive deliberation among participants in the initiative as well as advisory groups that included technical experts and lawyers. The outcome of such deliberation, the book demonstrates, was that technical experts helped other stakeholders understand whether states could conceivably fulfill their obligations or adapt their cyber operations in line with proposed interpretations of existing rules. Discussions in various groups on the legality of "hack backs" by private companies and cyber "due diligence" by states against malicious operations reflect the influential role of technical experts in this regard. The book also highlights discussions on the implementation of cyber countermeasures by the Tallinn Manual lawyers as one such example.

These illustrations of "creeping expertise" in international cybersecurity emphasize the importance of, and the precise mechanisms by which non-legal arguments and practices shape legal discourse around a domain. This book lends some nuance to the view, cited previously in this chapter, that "law-like norms" are generally not considered binding by states and other interlocutors in a community of practice. My research demonstrates that perceptions of bindingness or legality can in fact emerge through informal norms within a community of practice. Actors within the cyber CoP have, over the years, come to accept informal norms as cognates to international legal principles. These actors, as the chapters of this book show, certainly include states and their international legal advisors. To be sure, states may not consider themselves bound by cyber norms, but the importance of norms and norms-articulation processes lies in their capacity to critically advance legal discourse in cybersecurity governance. Cyber norms do not merely enunciate "soft law" that may crystalize over time into harder obligations, but they are tools of governance that dynamically shape actors' views on how existing international law regulates state conduct in cyberspace.

4.1 Empirics

Any empirical assessment of practices in a global governance institution or community, as scholars have highlighted, faces two main challenges. The main challenge is recovering "inarticulate" background knowledge that the researcher interprets as shaping the beliefs of actors and ultimately the practices of that community.[106] A related concern is ascertaining the social significance of certain practices within the community as reflecting of core beliefs. In interviews, practitioners of diplomacy may often recount the significance of practices with the benefit of hindsight or selectively reflect on some over others upon being requested to do so.[107]

For both reasons, some element of ethnographic enquiry into the community of practice is desirable.[108] Participant observation of discussions between stakeholders, often conducted alongside interviews, enables the researcher to triangulate findings about the meaning attributed to certain practices. Participant observation is also an opportunity to see practices "in the field". Their deployment by various actors in contextual settings offers hints as to the underlying beliefs driving their and the CoP's actions. Admittedly, such close-quarter observation is not always possible, especially in sensitive security-oriented discussions.

This book relies on nine months of participant observation – conducted primarily between November 2020 and September 2021 – in eight sites of negotiation that include a mix of UN intergovernmental and multistakeholder settings. Most of the observed discussions were organized by the six initiatives identified in this book, but some also included standalone meetings within the broader CoP on cyber norms and international law. A full list of observed sites

106 Janice Gross Stein, "Background Knowledge in the Foreground," in *International Practices*, ed. Emanuel Adler and Vincent Pouliot, Cambridge Studies in International Relations (Cambridge: Cambridge University Press, 2011), 89.

107 Vincent Pouliot, "Practice Tracing," in *Process Tracing: From Metaphor to Analytic Tool*, ed. Andrew Bennett and Jeffrey T. Checkel, Strategies for Social Inquiry (Cambridge: Cambridge University Press, 2014), 237–259, https://doi.org/10.1017/CBO9781139858472.013.

108 Jeffrey T. Checkel, "Process Tracing and International Political Economy," in *The Oxford Handbook of International Political Economy*, ed. Jon C. W. Pevehouse and Leonard Seabrooke (Oxford University Press), accessed June 13, 2024, https://doi.org/10.1093/oxfordhb/9780198793519.013.47.

and discussion details is provided in the book's appendix. Participant observation was conducted alongside 67 interviews with practitioners in the cyber CoP – specifically, the list of interviewees includes 29 technical experts, 17 current or former negotiators involved in UN cybersecurity discussions, 16 international lawyers, and five policy analysts. Interviews for the project were conducted between November 2020 and March 2022. A list of interviewees and three sets of questionnaires for different stakeholders are appended along with the book.

5 Structure of the Book

Chapter 2 traces the evolution of the UN Group of Governmental Experts on cybersecurity, and highlights the geopolitical considerations that led the group to advance international law discussions through norms. The GGE is the preeminent entity among informal cybersecurity initiatives, featuring the five permanent members of the UN Security Council. Six GGEs have been convened since 2004, with significant participation from technical experts nominated by respective states. The chapter details how a US–Russia compromise in the 2010 GGE led specifically to cybersecurity norms integrating legal principles. This outcome set in motion the institution of operating practices by future GGEs that conflated "voluntary" norms and rules. The chapter demonstrates how those practices allowed technical experts to shape GGE pronouncements on two crucial legal concerns: the protection of critical infrastructure in international law and the attribution of wrongful cyber operations to states. This chapter argues the GGE's practices were instrumental in incubating a community of actors and institutions bound by practices that similarly conflated norm-articulation and legal interpretation. This chapter covers the period up until 2017, culminating in the failure of the fifth UN GGE to produce a consensus report.

The GCSC and Paris Call were prominent multistakeholder initiatives that were co-founded by technology companies and standards bodies such as Microsoft and internet Society. **Chapter 3** highlights how both initiatives were specifically set up to articulate norms around the technical community's priorities, such as the seamless availability of the global internet and enhancing trust in digital infrastructure among users. These multistakeholder initiatives followed the template set by the UN GGE, and instituted practices that actively sought the counsel of international lawyers into the drafting of their "non-binding" norms. Consequent interactions between technical experts and international lawyers during the articulation of norms, the chapter highlights, shaped the initiatives' views on two legal topics. Firstly, experts helped scope out how the rule of non-interference should apply to protecting election infrastructure such as voting machines and electoral rolls from cyber operations. Secondly, they were able to persuade some states and non-state actors why "hackbacks" by companies should be prohibited in international law. Discussions in the Paris Call even promoted a future model of cybersecurity governance wherein informal, political norms would be used to translate or clarify international legal obligations for states.

The Tallinn Manuals and Oxford Process cannot be considered norm-articulation initiatives. They consist exclusively of eminent international lawyers, who ascertain how existing international law applies to cyberspace. Yet, as **Chapter 4** demonstrates, the impact of the cyber community of practice is discernible on these law-finding initiatives. The Tallinn Manuals and Oxford Process meetings were *managed* like norms-articulation exercises, this chapter highlights, instituting several practices that allowed for their lawyers to absorb inputs from policymakers and technical advisors in their deliberations. The chapter terms these "managerial practices". While claiming to identify existing rules for cyberspace, these initiatives did not simply use legal-doctrinal methods of interpretation or ascertainment. They advanced legal discourse by balancing traditional law-finding with an accommodation of policy and technical concerns, in order to secure wide acceptance for their pronouncements from the cyber community of practice. Their working points distinctly to the future of global law, whereby traditional, state-led development and ascertainment of rules evolves alongside informal, private-led initiatives.

When do actors in a CoP question their closely held beliefs, and what impact does that have on processes of learning? This is a topic that is under-explored in the international relations and international law literature on practices. Drawing on developments in the fifth UN GGE from 2016 onward, **Chapter 5** highlights how heightened geopolitical tensions between US and Russia, the primary protagonists in the UN GGE, led to reflexive thinking within the UN grouping on the status of cyber norms. Whereas GGE negotiators hitherto held the orthodox view that norms articulation and legal interpretation were intertwined, they began questioning it after the failure of the fifth GGE, and seeking consequently a separation of norms and law, I show. Particularly among Western states involved in the UN GGE, there was a more conscious assessment of whether norms were diluting or rendering ambiguous the application of existing international law to cyber operations. On the other hand, Russia and China resisted the introduction of legal tools like countermeasures into the cybersecurity governance framework through norms. As a result, discussions and reports of the sixth UN GGE and the first OEWG, both of which began meeting in 2019, saw states seeking to separate voluntary norms from binding rules. This muted "creeping expertise" in the UN reports, this chapter demonstrates, with states reluctant to let technical considerations shape legal formulations.

Chapter 6 offers a cross-sectional view of "creeping expertise" in the cyber CoP, using the example of the norm to protect core internet infrastructure. Core internet infrastructure, which includes subsea cables and their terrestrial landing stations, satellites, the Domain Name System, and internet Exchange Points, among others, is critical to the smooth and seamless functioning of global digital networks. Promoted first by a Dutch government think tank in 2015, the idea of protecting core internet infrastructure was championed by multistakeholder initiatives like the GCSC and Paris Call, and eventually endorsed by the UN GGE and UN OEWG in 2021. These initiatives articulated slightly varying versions of a voluntary norm that called on states to restrain from targeting core infrastructure through cyber or physical means, with a view to safeguard the stability of cyberspace. What's notable is that the norm, as it "traveled" through the cyber CoP, picked up legal meaning: in other words, various initiatives read the protection of core infrastructure into the existing obligations of states under international law. This chapter demonstrates that technical experts were influential in shaping the scope of those legal obligations. Specifically, they helped define what constitutes "core" infrastructure, and therefore what objects deserve protection from cyber operations under international law. Secondly, they also influenced discussions on what is the quantum of acceptable damage to the internet's core, and the kind of cyber operations that would therefore be proscribed by international law.

Chapter 7 offers concluding thoughts, reviews the book's empirical findings, and analyzes its consequences for the cybersecurity regime as well as contemporary international law-making. Briefly, this chapter makes three claims as to the contribution of the book:

a. Firstly, as global governance increasingly integrates transnational actors, especially subject-matter experts, it is important to study how they influence law-ascertainment. This book offers an in-depth, empirical case study of how technical experts contributed to the development of international cybersecurity law.
b. Secondly, the book demonstrates how communities of practice evolve around rulemaking for specific domains even in the absence of formal governance mechanisms. Studying everyday practices of actors and institutions in cybersecurity throws into relief not only how the business of

governance is conducted for this domain but also in relation to other contemporary global challenges.

c. This book offers a micro-level assessment of how specialized domains of international law develop. If "creeping expertise" leads international lawyers to apply rules to cyberspace differently than how these principles are understood in PIL, it is important to study how experts contribute to fragmentation of PIL.

6 Contribution of the Book

This book contributes in three ways to the literature on international cybersecurity governance, and more generally, international law-making in increasingly informal and specialized domains of global governance. These themes are touched upon in more detail in Chapter 7.

Firstly, it answers the question of whether and how technical expertise shapes the development of international cybersecurity law. This question is of interest not only to practitioners and scholars of cybersecurity governance, but also contemporary global governance. It may seem obvious that technical experts play *some* role in shaping rules for specialized domains, especially highly technical ones like cybersecurity and AI. Private actors have long shaped global governance in such domains, either by exerting *de facto* authority through the development of technical and industry policy standards, or through their epistemic authority in framing governance agendas.[109] In recent decades, they have been instrumental in forging transnational coalitions or advocacy networks of state and private actors that influence the work of formal intergovernmental organizations.[110] But the rise of non-legally binding agreements, and the role especially of multistakeholder and private initiatives in shaping those agreements, bring technical experts to the frontlines of the legal-interpretive process. To be sure, the ILC Special Rapporteur

109 Tim Büthe and Walter Mattli, *The New Global Rulers: The Privatization of Regulation in the World Economy* (Princeton University Press, 2011); Laura DeNardis, *The Global War for internet Governance* (Yale University Press, 2014); Peter M. Haas, "Introduction: Epistemic Communities and International Policy Coordination," *International Organization* 46, no. 1 (1992): 1–35.

110 Thomas J. Biersteker, "The Role of Transnational Policy Networks in Informal Governance: Creating the Office of the Ombudsperson at the United Nations," in *Informal Governance in World Politics*, ed. Kenneth W. Abbott and Thomas J. Biersteker, 1st ed. (Cambridge University Press, 2024), 215–240, https://doi.org/10.1017/9781009180528.014; *See* Liliana B. Andonova, *Governance Entrepreneurs: International Organizations and the Rise of Global Public-Private Partnerships* (Cambridge University Press, 2017).

on non-legally binding agreements has recommended that agreements "concluded with or between non-state entities" should fall beyond the scope of the ILC's work on the topic.[111] However, as this book demonstrates, the outcomes of multistakeholder governance initiatives pertaining to international law can and have been reflected in UN processes as well, making it important to study how the role of private actors in those initiatives. As the following chapters highlight, entities like Microsoft, internet Society, and Kaspersky have sought not only to influence the outcomes of the UN GGE or UN OEWG directly, but also steer norm-articulation by other entities in the cyber CoP. The widespread belief within the CoP that the articulation of norms and legal interpretation can advance interconnectedly and alongside each other has allowed these actors to shape perceptions of legality through cyber norms. The logic of "creeping expertise" may differ from one domain to another, but studying how experts shape legal discourse in critical in this evolving global governance context. Studying the involvement of experts (and private actors, more broadly) in shaping agreements that have legal effects is not only important from an outcomes perspective. The participation of stakeholders with deep pockets and significant convening power also raise legitimacy and accountability concerns about informal governance that merit closer scrutiny.[112] This book does not address all those concerns, but offers a modest theoretical framework and empirical assessment to begin thinking about the pathways by which technical experts can shape legal discourse in contemporary global governance.

Secondly, and on a related note, the book demonstrates using extensive empirical evidence how law-finding occurs within and across ad hoc and informal institutions of global governance. Informality in cybersecurity governance has been pervasive but it is also a study in contrasts. Multistakeholder and private initiatives rise and decline every few years, but informal intergovernmental organizations have been, true to expectations, "remarkably durable".[113] The establishment by the UN GA of a second, five-year UN Open-Ended Working Group on cybersecurity (2021–2025) has meant that *ad hoc* UN

111 ILC, *First report on non-legally binding international agreements, by Mathias Forteau, Special Rapporteur*, n.38, 361.

112 Dr Tim Corthaut et al., "Operationalizing Accountability in Respect of Informal International Lawmaking Mechanisms," in *Informal International Lawmaking*, ed. Joost Pauwelyn, Ramses Wessel, and Jan Wouters (Oxford University Press, 2012), 310–336, https://doi.org/10.1093/acprof:oso/9780199658589.003.0015.

113 Felicity Vabulas and Duncan Snidal, "Cooperation under Autonomy: Building and Analyzing the Informal Intergovernmental Organizations 2.0 Dataset," *Journal of Peace Research* 58, no. 4 (July 1, 2021): 859–69, https://doi.org/10.1177/0022343320943920.

groups will have steered discussions on international cybersecurity for nearly three decades since the topic was first addressed in 1998 by the UN GA First Committee.[114] The longevity of such mechanisms and the high churn of multistakeholder and private initiatives on international cybersecurity governance may be owed to the fact that they are "low-cost", flexible institutions, and less prone to political deadlock than formal mechanisms.[115] Yet, these institutions may also set the template for formal discussions on international cybersecurity rules. As Reinsberg and Westerwinter note, such mechanisms are likely to create "temporal dependence" in institutional design.[116] Such dependence may involve formal institutions of the future emulating practices established by informal initiatives, framing substantive agendas in a manner similar to the latter, or involving the same set of actors from informal initiatives who can claim experience and expertise in evaluating different proposals and rules for international cybersecurity.

Looking ahead, cybersecurity governance is therefore likely to be managed by a "hybrid institutional complex",[117] i.e., a regime marked by the presence of intergovernmental, multistakeholder, and private arrangements which are overwhelmingly informal in character. Formal arrangements, whether multilateral or bilateral in nature, may co-exist alongside these initiatives, simultaneously guiding and learning from informal governance. Informality in the global governance of this domain neither implies the absence of a hierarchy nor are the importance of these institutions likely to dim even if formal mechanisms are instituted. The UN GGE process has been influential in setting a template for discussion by other informal initiatives on norms and international law. It can be considered a first among equals, whose pronouncements have a signaling effect both on substantive outcomes and governance procedures instituted by other informal initiatives. This book offers a working account of how the governance and law-finding template for international

114 "Open-Ended Working Group on Information and Communication Technologies (2021) | United Nations," accessed March 1, 2023, https://meetings.unoda.org/open-ended-working-group-information-and-communication-technologies-2021.

115 Kenneth W. Abbott and Benjamin Faude, "Choosing Low-Cost Institutions in Global Governance," *International Theory* 13, no. 3 (November 2021): 397–426, https://doi.org/10.1017/S1752971920000202.

116 Bernhard Reinsberg and Oliver Westerwinter, "The Global Governance of International Development: Documenting the Rise of Multi-Stakeholder Partnerships and Identifying Underlying Theoretical Explanations," *The Review of International Organizations* 16, no. 1 (January 2021): 59–94, https://doi.org/10.1007/s11558-019-09362-0.

117 Kenneth W. Abbott and Benjamin Faude, "Hybrid Institutional Complexes in Global Governance," *The Review of International Organizations* 17, no. 2 (April 1, 2022): 263–291, https://doi.org/10.1007/s11558-021-09431-3.

cybersecurity has been developed and reinforced by practices of the cyber CoP. Just as importantly, this book helps understand the dynamic between various initiatives within the CoP. Understanding how those initiatives interact with each other, substantively and procedurally, is critical to understanding the development of the overall regime in any domain. This is also an aspect that is relatively understudied in the scholarship on informal global governance.[118]

Thirdly, this book joins the growing literature in international law that has turned to the study of practices to understand how rules are created or interpreted, while also filling a gap in this literature. As this chapter has noted, the "practice turn" in international law has tended to focus mostly on legal practices. The most careful theorizations of the "practice of legality" still view the creation or application of international law as insulated from other disciplines.[119] "Epistemic communities"[120] or "communities of practice" in international law are conceptualized as exclusively comprising lawyers, albeit from different institutional backgrounds or roles such as judges, attorneys, legal officers, or academics.[121] To be sure, international law scholars, especially those who work at the intersection of international relations and international law, acknowledge the importance of practice, as it occurs "outside the courtroom" and "in intergovernmental and expert committees, in diplomatic exchanges, and in various non-compliance mechanisms",[122] to the construc-

---

118 Karen J. Alter, "The Promise and Perils of Theorizing International Regime Complexity in an Evolving World," *The Review of International Organizations* 17, no. 2 (2022): 375–396.

119 *See generally,* Daniel Peat and Matthew Windsor, "An Interpretive Turn to Practice Part II: Interpretation in International Law Symposium," *Cambridge Journal of International and Comparative Law* 3, no. 2 (2014): 444–449; Jean d'Aspremont, "The Professionalization of International Law," in *International Law as a Profession*, ed. André Nollkaemper et al. (Cambridge: Cambridge University Press, 2017), 19–37, https://doi.org/10.1017/9781316492802.003; Friedrich Kratochwil, "Practicing Law: Spoudaios, Professional, Expert or 'Macher'? Reflections on the Changing Nature of an Occupation," in *The Law of International Lawyers: Reading Martti Koskenniemi*, ed. Alexis Galán, Marieke de Hoon, and Wouter Werner (Cambridge: Cambridge University Press, 2017), 225–264; Frédéric Mégret, "Thinking about What International Humanitarian Lawyers 'Do,'" in *The Law of International Lawyers: Reading Martti Koskenniemi* (Cambridge University Press, March 2017).

120 Peter M. Haas, "Introduction: Epistemic Communities and International Policy Coordination," *International Organization* 46, no. 1 (1992): 1–35.

121 Andrea Bianchi, "Epistemic Communities," in *Concepts for International Law*, ed. Jean d'Aspremont and Sahib Singh (Edward Elgar Publishing, 2019), 251–266; d'Aspremont, *The Professionalization of International Law.*

122 Jeffrey L. Dunoff, "Perspectives on the Perils, Promise, Politics – and Practice – of Interdisciplinarity," in *The Power of Legality: Practices of International Law and Their Politics*,

tion of legality. But the study of practices has largely been limited to understanding how "Article 38 of the Statute of the International Court of Justice, with its itemizing of the formal sources of international law, [is] ultimately the product of social interplay between policy, institutional and scholarly practices."[123] In other words, the dominant conception of the practice of international law still remains one of "modes of legal reasoning associated with [its] sources".[124]

I advance the scholarship on practices in international law by demonstrating that "extra-legal expertise", such as technical expertise, does much more than just "supplement" the interpretation of international law.[125] In international cybersecurity governance, the habitual conflation of voluntary norms and existing rules has meant that the same actors who are involved in the articulation of cyber norms are also able to influence what counts as applicable law, and how specific rules apply to the domain. The micro-processes involved in ascertaining the legality of state behavior and developing shared understandings of applicable rules in cyberspace are not shaped by legal practices – because there are few to speak of in the absence of formal processes or mechanisms – but by "everyday" practices of recruitment, deliberation, and reporting that reflect this conflation of norms and rules. The importance of such practices transcends international cybersecurity governance. Actors in other domains of global governance may not similarly conflate norms and rules, that is to say, the vector of "creeping expertise" may not be the same for say, climate change, global health or artificial intelligence. But this book demonstrates that in domains of global governance, particularly those characterized by *ad hoc* and fluid mechanisms of negotiation and deliberation, international lawyers do not rely on their disciplinary "tool-box"[126] alone to apply

ed. Nikolas M. Rajkovic, Tanja E. Aalberts, and Thomas Gammeltoft-Hansen (Cambridge: Cambridge University Press, 2016), 368.

123 Nikolas M. Rajkovic, Tanja E. Aalberts, and Thomas Gammeltoft-Hansen, "Introduction: Legality, Interdisciplinarity and the Study of Practices," in *The Power of Legality: Practices of International Law and Their Politics*, ed. Nikolas M. Rajkovic, Tanja E. Aalberts, and Thomas Gammeltoft-Hansen (Cambridge: Cambridge University Press, 2016), 1–26, https://doi.org/10.1017/CBO9781316535134.002.

124 Samantha Besson and Jean D'Aspremont, "The Sources of International Law: An Introduction," in *The Oxford Handbook of the Sources of International Law*, ed. Jean d'Aspremont and Samantha Besson (Oxford: Oxford University Press, 2018), 7.

125 Rajkovic, Aalberts, and Gammeltoft-Hansen (2016), 20.

126 International Law Commission, "Fragmentation of International Law: Difficulties Arising from the Diversification and Expansion of International Law – Report of the Study Group of the International Law Commission," *UN Doc. A/CN.4/L.682/Corr.1* (Aug. 11, 2006), 256.

rules. Instead, the practices of these institutions help shape how lawyers perceive the applicability of international law to cyberspace, and those practices often allow for technical considerations to tacitly shape intersubjective perception.

CHAPTER 2

UN Cybersecurity Negotiations: Origins of a Community of Practice

1 Introduction

The UN Group of Governmental Experts (GGE) on cybersecurity is arguably the most influential body involved in shaping responsible state behavior for cyberspace. Its preeminence among informal initiatives is owed to the participation of the five permanent members of the UN Security Council, who have nominated Experts to all six groups established between 2004 and 2021. Until 2018, when a parallel UN Open-Ended Working Group (OEWG) was established by the UN General Assembly, the GGE remained the only multilateral grouping on cybersecurity governance that saw participation from the US, Russia, and China. While the UN GGE derived its heft from geopolitics, those geopolitical considerations also contributed to the group's opening a door for private and multistakeholder mechanisms to shape cybersecurity governance. In other words, the UN GGE seeded a community of practice that shaped notions of responsible state behavior in cyberspace, including how international law applied to the domain. This may sound somewhat counterintuitive, since the GGE is not only an intergovernmental initiative, but it is also a closed group whose deliberations are inaccessible to private actors.

This chapter highlights how the GGE's substantive pronouncements were shaped at an early stage by a US–Russia compromise. With limited guidance from the UN General Assembly, the GGE autonomously determined it should advance cybersecurity governance through "norms" of responsible state behavior. The status of those norms in relation to existing international law was left ambiguous. While the US and its partners sought for cyber norms to reflect "legal norms", i.e., norms drawn from existing international law, Russia wanted "additional norms" that would generate new legal obligations on states. The outcome of a compromise to break this geopolitical deadlock was the articulation of lawlike norms, that resembled applications of international law to cyberspace rather than just aspirational guidelines for states to adopt voluntarily.

Practices of early GGEs pertaining to its deliberations and reporting of outcomes reflected this conflation of norms and existing international law. Groups established subsequently continued to adopt those practices, signal-

HTTPS://DOI.ORG/10.1163/9789004737617-003

ing not only to states but also private actors who were closely tracking UN discussions that norms were the "site" of legal interpretation. During GGE sessions, multistakeholder initiatives or private actors articulated cybersecurity norms that were similarly characterized as informal, but drew directly from international law. Among these actors were technology companies like Microsoft, whose influential norms reports sought to draw states' attention to the participation and substantive interests of technology companies in the application of international law to state behavior. In short, private actors mimicked the approach of the UN GGE, and through the articulation of informal norms – which in principle could be done by anyone in the cyber CoP – sought to influence legal interpretation as well. While the practices of various initiatives would be different from one another, they would all reflect the widespread belief that norms and rules were intertwined. This, the chapter notes, is the lasting legacy of the UN GGE in cybersecurity governance. That technical experts were seeking to shape legal discourse through norms was not only evident through Microsoft's efforts, but also within the UN GGE itself. On key issues such as the attribution of wrongful cyber operations and the protection of critical infrastructure, the GGE's technical experts played an important role in framing the application of international law, the chapter demonstrates.

2 Groups of Governmental Experts: A Unique UN Mechanism

The Group of Governmental Experts (GGE) is a series of unique, *ad hoc* UN entities that have been established to address the governance of specialized domains of international security. The first instance of the creation of a GGE was reportedly in 1968, when the UN General Assembly requested the Secretary-General to prepare a report on the "various aspects of the problem of chemical, bacteriological, and biological weapons" with the "assistance of qualified consultant experts" appointed by the SG.[1] Comprising specialized technical experts, including from government, this group submitted its report to both the UNGA as well as the Conference on Disarmament. Since then, over thirty GGEs have been constituted in nearly thirteen domains, with states increasingly relying on such Groups – and through them, subject-matter experts – to clarify issues relating to regime compliance or offer guidance on new developments that complicate such compliance. According to the

1 "2454 (XXIII). Question of General and Complete Disarmament" (UN General Assembly, Twenty-third Session, December 20, 1968), https://www.unoosa.org/pdf/gares/ARES_23_2453E.pdf; "Means to Reinforce Research on Nuclear Disarmament Verification: Report on a Series of Regional Conversations," Matters No. 13 (VERTIC, November 2017), http://www.vertic.org/media/assets/Publications/VM13.pdf.

London-based Verification Research, Training and Information Centre (VERTIC), GGEs have been constituted with respect to the following multilateral regimes:[2]

a. Chemical Weapons Convention
b. Biological Weapons Convention
c. Fissile Material Cutoff Treaty
d. Convention on Certain Conventional Weapons (CCW)
e. Register of Conventional Arms
f. Arms Trade Treaty
g. Small Arms and Light Weapons
h. ICTs in the Context of International Security
i. Committee on the Peaceful Uses of Outer Space

GGEs have also been created to discuss broad and open-ended topics, such as spreading awareness on disarmament and non-proliferation, the growing use of missiles to deliver Weapons of Mass Destruction (WMDs), and the role of the UN in arms control verification.

GGEs may be created in two ways: by a Conference of Parties to an existing treaty, or through the UN General Assembly, which often tasks the UN Secretary-General with setting up a GGE. In either case, the cardinal rule of the GGE's composition – which always includes the five permanent members of the UN Security Council – is that it should reflect "equitable geographic representation".[3] While review conferences and UNGA resolutions can offer broad or specific guidance to the GGE on an issue area, the working of the Group is usually left to its members.[4] The diversity of mandates received by GGEs in the past indicates that such Groups may be created on a range of regime-related issues, be it conducting open-ended studies,[5] offering voluntary and non-binding norms,[6] recommending Confidence Building-Measures,[7] or recom-

2 *Means to Reinforce Research on Nuclear Disarmament Verification: Report on a Series of Regional Conversations*, n.l, 49–55.

3 *Means to Reinforce Research on Nuclear Disarmament Verification: Report on a Series of Regional Conversations*, N.1, 49–55.

4 *Interviews with two negotiators who have participated in GGEs across multiple domains.*

5 "55/33. General and Complete Disarmament" (UN General Assembly, Fifty-fifth Session, January 12, 2001), https://documents-dds-ny.un.org/doc/UNDOC/GEN/N00/561/37/PDF/N0056137.pdf?OpenElement.

6 "Developments in the Field of Information and Telecommunications in the Context of International Security – UNODA," accessed November 23, 2022, https://www.un.org/disarmament/ict-security/.

7 "65/68. Transparency and Confidence-Building Measures in Outer Space Activities" (UN General Assembly, Sixty-fifth Session, January 13, 2011), https://doi.org/10.18356/9789210021753c001.

mending specific measures with a view to their being incorporated in a legally binding instrument[8] negotiated in the future. In at least one case, specifically the 2014 Arms Trade Treaty (ATT), a GGE report has directly contributed to the text of a legally binding instrument.[9] Additionally, the non-binding 2005 International Tracing Instrument (ITI) on small arms and light weapons was also the outcome of a GGE.[10] Some regimes and Conference of Parties have been prolific in the use of GGEs to clarify treaty-related aspects: the High Contracting Parties to the CCW have established GGEs regularly since 2002 to the present day, addressing issues such as cluster munitions, LAWS, and Explosive Remnants of War.[11] Usually comprising between 10 and 25 "Experts", GGEs across specialized domains of international security have been constituted in the belief that small, dedicated groups of subject matter experts can advance shared understandings of governance concerns in specific issue areas, that are subsequently adopted or form the basis of discussions by all states.

Their diversity notwithstanding, some general claims can be made on the practices of informal GGEs based on a review of the groups highlighted in this section. The requirement of geographical representation has already been noted above. GGEs tend to meet three to four times during a year, converging either in New York or Geneva as the parties decide. These meetings, which usually go on for a week, may be interspersed by exchange of preparatory material and draft texts that are then negotiated in-person. Whether established by a review conference or by the UNSG, GGEs usually have secretarial staff that provides research and administrative assistance to their Chairs. And finally, the closed nature of GGE participation is often (but not always) balanced against the requirement that its reports should be adopted by consensus among the Experts.

---

8 "Treaty Banning the Production of Fissile Material for Nuclear Weapons or Other Nuclear Explosive Devices" (UN General Assembly, Sixty-seventh Session, January 4, 2013), https://doi.org/10.18356/9789210021753c001.

9 "Arms Trade Treaty," Reaching Critical Will, accessed November 23, 2022, https://www.reachingcriticalwill.org/disarmament-fora/att.

10 Andrea Edoardo Varisco, Jonah Leff, and Himayu Shiotani, "The International Tracing Instrument: Examining Options to Support Operationalization" (Geneva: United Nations Institute for Disarmament Research, 2018), https://unidir.org/sites/default/files/publication/pdfs//the-international-tracing-instrument-examining-options-to-support-operationalization-en-712.pdf.

11 "Meetings of the High Contracting Parties," United Nations Office for Disarmament Affairs (UNODA), accessed November 23, 2022, https://www.un.org/disarmament/the-convention-on-certain-conventional-weapons/meetings-and-documents/.

3 The Cyber UN GGE: Governance through "Law-Like" Norms

At the time of writing, the UN GGE on cyber security (hereinafter, "the UN GGE" or "the GGE") has been convened six times since 2004 by the UN Secretary-General at the request of the UN GA. The sixth and most recent UN GGE successfully submitted its consensus report to the UN GA in June 2021. The UN GGE's creation is owed in large part to Russia's persistent diplomacy in the UNGA and its First Committee on Disarmament and International Security.[12] Between 1998 and 2003, Russia sponsored successive UN GA resolutions and circulated draft proposals seeking the ban of "information weapons" and preventing the rise of "information technologies [...] whose military applications may be compared to the use of weapons of mass destruction".[13] The first UN GGE was constituted in 2004, with Russia chairing the group. It was mandated by the UN GA to "examine relevant international concepts aimed at strengthening the security of global information and telecommunications systems".[14] However, the UN GGE could not arrive at a consensus report. In his ensuing statement to the UNGA as the UN GGE Chair, Andrey Krutskikh of Russia identified three reasons behind its failure:[15]

a. The relatively short amount of time that the GGE had to meet and discuss its report. The GGE met on three occasions during 2004–2005, meeting twice for five days, and for a final occasion for 10 consecutive days. The process of "elaborating a full text" on "fundamentally new and sensitive problems", the Chair submitted, "will not be brief".
b. The inability of GGE Experts to communicate effectively given the "*lack of unified and generally accepted definitions of key terms and concepts*" [emphasis added] in international cybersecurity. The Chair specifically

---

12 Elaine Korzak, "Russia's Cyber Policy Efforts in the United Nations," Tallinn Papers (NATO CCDCOE, 2021).

13 "International Information Security Legal Acts and Fundamental Documents," accessed November 23, 2022, https://namib.online/wp-content/uploads/2019/03/МИБ_английс кая-версия.pdf.

14 United Nations, "58/32. Developments in the Field of Information and Telecommunications in the Context of International Security" (UN General Assembly, Fifty-eighth session, December 18, 2003), https://doi.org/10.18356/9789210021753c001.

15 "First Committee 13th Meeting| Monday, 17 October 2005, 10 a.m." (UN General Assembly, Sixtieth session, October 17, 2005), https://documents-dds-ny.un.org/doc/UNDOC/GEN/N05/555/42/PDF/N0555542.pdf?OpenElement; Eneken Tikk and Mika Kerttunen, "The Alleged Demise of the UN GGE: An Autopsy and Eulogy" (Cyber Policy Institute, 2017), https://cyber-peace.org/wp-content/uploads/2018/11/Tikk-Kerttunen-2017-The-Alleged-Demise-of-the-UN-GGE-An-Autopsy-and-Eulogy.pdf.

noted that "even" the "use of translation" could not overcome the problem, suggesting the issue was the absence of intersubjective terms to understand state behavior in the nascent cybersecurity regime.

c. Different domestic laws pertaining to cybersecurity, and "different interpretations of current international law" in the domain, which made harmonization of views difficult.

The UN GGE's failure indicated from the outset that states were unclear how "unified and generally accepted definitions" on responsible state behavior would emerge, or the GGE's role in their emergence. The lack of clarity in the GGE's mandate complicated the problem: unlike the GGE on the Arms Trade Treaty, the cyber UN GGE did not have a clear purpose or goal. Unlike GGEs that were established by review conferences, there was neither an umbrella treaty nor Conference of Parties that could offer guidance on the GGE's mandate. The UN General Assembly resolutions that established the first two GGEs simply requested that they "study […] possible cooperative measures" to mitigate cyber threats to international peace and security.[16]

The 2010 GGE's report elaborated the nature and scope of those possible measures. International cybersecurity concerns arose, the Report noted, because of a "lack of shared understanding regarding international norms pertaining to State use of ICTs".[17] The Report highlighted that "existing agreements" contained "norms relevant to the use of ICTs". At the same time, the GGE also noted that "additional norms could be developed over time", given cyberspace's unique attributes.[18]

The GGE report thus identified "norms" as a form of cooperative measure among states, but the exact provenance of those norms remained unclear. On the one hand, references to norms drawn from "existing agreements" as well as the need to develop "shared understandings" around them suggested the GGE was pointing to "legal norms" – i.e., norms drawn from existing international

16 United Nations, "58/32. Developments in the Field of Information and Telecommunications in the Context of International Security" (UN General Assembly, Fifty-eighth session, December 18, 2003), https://doi.org/10.18356/9789210021753c001; United Nations, "60/45. Developments in the Field of Information and Telecommunications in the Context of International Security" (UN General Assembly, sixtieth session, January 6,2006), https://documents-dds-ny.un.org/doc/UNDOC/GEN/N05/490/30/PDF/N0549030.pdf?OpenElement.

17 "Group of Governmental Experts on Developments in the Field of Information and Telecommunications in the Context of International Security" (UN General Assembly, Sixty-fifth Session, July 30, 2010), https://documents-dds-ny.un.org/doc/UNDOC/GEN/N10/469/57/PDF/N1046957.pdf?OpenElement. (hereafter "Second UN GGE report").

18 *Second UN GGE Report*, 8.

law – as the way forward for cooperation. Yet, on the other hand, the GGE also called for "additional norms" that were specific to the cyber domain, suggesting new norms that did not have any basis in "existing agreements" could also shape its governance.

This ambiguity about the precise nature of norms was not coincidental or the outcome of careless drafting. The formulation was a *modus vivendi* to accommodate the interests of two political camps who sought different "cooperative measures" to determine responsible state behavior in cyberspace. The United States and other (mostly) Western European countries who formed a "like-minded group" were principally opposed to a binding international instrument to govern state behavior, because they believed existing international law was sufficient for this purpose. The US in particular did not want its "perceived dominance"[19] in cyberspace to be constrained or the development of new, cyber-enabled military platforms to be foreclosed prematurely by additional binding rules. Therefore, these countries sought for "norms" to be based on existing international law, and common understandings to develop around those legal norms.

Russia, as its persistent efforts at the UN GA since the late nineties indicated, sought a new multilateral treaty precisely to constrain and limit US advantages in cyberspace. Russia also had concerns with the application of existing international law to state behavior in cyberspace. These concerns could be classified broadly into three. First, Russia was concerned about the application of the state responsibility regime to cyberspace and the use of below-the-threshold tools of state response such as countermeasures that had been recognized in the International Law Commission's 2001 Articles on the Responsibility of States for Internationally Wrongful Acts (ARSIWA). It was the Russian Federation's, and prior to its collapse, the Soviet Union's longstanding position that the use of self-help measures were not "authorized by the UN Security Council", and that any reference to measures of Self-defense should be restricted to those under Article 51 of the UN Charter.[20] Even in relation to Article 51, Russia was concerned that the "absence of general prac-

19 Cherian Samuel, *UN Cyber OEWG Ends after Five-Year Run* (Manohar Parrikar Institute for Defence Studies and Analyses, 2025), https://www.idsa.in/publisher/issuebrief/un-cyber-oewg-ends-after-five-year-run.

20 Gaetano Arangio-Ruiz (Special Rapporteur), "Fifth Report on State Responsibility (Extract from the Yearbook of the International Law Commission)" (International Law Commission, 1993), 16, https://legal.un.org/ilc/documentation/english/a_cn4_453.pdf; "YEARBOOK OF THE INTERNATIONAL LAW COMMISSION 1982" (International Law Commission, Thirty-fourth session, 1982), 17, https://legal.un.org/ilc/publications/yearbooks/english/ilc_1982_v2_p1.pdf.

tice in the application of international custom" around the use of ICTs would lead to "abuse" by states of their inherent right of self-defence.[21] Second, Russia pointed out that international humanitarian law pertaining to the treatment of "belligerent" and "non-belligerent" states, the legal status of participants in an armed conflict, and the protection of certain persons and objects during armed conflict were not adequate or clear in relation to the use of ICTs, and therefore a new instrument was needed to address the ambiguities. And finally, Russia wanted an international instrument that would reinforce the sovereignty of states in cyberspace. However, none of its proposals for such a treaty gained traction within the UN, so Russia sought for the GGE to recognize the need for new rules through the formulation of "additional norms".[22]

With both camps vying for their preferred outcomes within the GGE, the 2010 report's eventual formulation read:

> Existing agreements include norms relevant to the use of ICTs by States. Given the unique attributes of ICTs, additional norms could be developed over time.[23]

While some scholars have described this formulation as the "optimal point of balance in the international cyber norms dialogue",[24] Russia itself would term it later as a "hard-won and a fragile consensus formula".[25]

The GGE's compromise formulation suggested norms could not only be a vehicle to interpret existing international law but advance legal discourse in this domain by identifying new obligations. This approach of the UN GGE contrasted with the approach of its "parent" body, the UN GA First Committee.

21 Anatoly A. Streltsov, "Application of International Humanitarian Law to Armed Conflicts in Cyberspace," 2012, 2, https://digital.report/wp-content/uploads/2016/04/169747-Streltsov-ENG.pdf.

22 Elaine Korzak, "National Views on the Application of International Law to Cybersecurity," in *Perspectives on Responsible Behavior in State Uses of ICT* (ICT4Peace Foundation & Cyber Policy Institute, 2017), https://ict4peace.org/wp-content/uploads/2017/02/ICT4 Peace-Book-Draft.pdf.; Tom Gjelten, "Shadow Wars: Debating Cyber 'Disarmament,'" *World Affairs* 173, no. 4 (November 1, 2010): 33–43.

23 *Second UN GGE Report*, 8.

24 Eneken Tikk and Mika Kerttunen, "Parabasis: Cyber-Diplomacy in Stalemate" (Oslo: Norwegian Institute of International Affairs, 2018), https://nupi.brage.unit.no/nupi-xmlui/bitstream/handle/11250/2569401/NUPI_Report_5_18_Tikk_Kerttunen.pdf?sequence=1&isAllowed=y.

25 "Statement by Vassily Nebenzia, Permanent Representative of the Russian Federation to the United Nations, at the 'Arria-Formula' VTC of the UNSC Members on Cyber-Attacks against Critical Infrastructure" (Permanent Mission of the Russian Federation to the United Nations, August 26, 2020), https://kemlu.go.id/download/L1NoYXJlZCUyMER vY3VtZW50cy9SdXNzaWFuJTIwRmVkZXJhdGlvbi5wZGY=.

A review of the First Committee's deliberations from 2009 to 2012 (during the 64th to 67th sessions of the UNGA)[26] indicates UN member states usually invoked "norms" to refer to legal norms – norms deriving from various legal instruments, whether they were non-proliferation norms relating to the Comprehensive Test Ban Treaty or norms established by the Convention on Certain Conventional Weapons or the Convention on Cluster Munitions. In some cases, states expressly contrasted legal norms from "political" or "moral" norms. In fact, even Russia referred, in the 2009 meetings of the First Committee, to "norms of international law" while referring broadly to global trends in arms control.[27] At the 65th annual session of the UN GA First Committee, however, Russia, while presenting the GGE report as its Chair, made no such reference to existing international law. The Russian representative stated only that the GGE had agreed to consider "norms pertaining to the state use of ICTs", while it was the US representative responding to this statement who argued that "existing principles of international law" should be the basis to "identify and analyze" cyber norms.[28]

The UN GGE's formulation on norms had already begun to influence the approach of other stakeholders in the cyber CoP planning to promote informal initiatives of their own. By the summer of 2010, when the second GGE published its report, there was considerable interest from private and governmental actors in tracking discussions on responsible state behavior in cyber-

26 The verbatim records of the UN GA First Committee's plenary sessions from 2009 to 2012 may be found in the following links: "General Assembly First Committee Sixty-Seventh Session (2012) | United Nations," accessed January 30, 2023, https://meetings.unoda.org/meeting/29605/documents?f%5B0%5D=author_documents_%3AGeneral%20Assembly%20First%20Committee; "General Assembly First Committee Sixty-Sixth Session (2011) | United Nations," accessed January 30, 2023, https://meetings.unoda.org/meeting/29604/documents?f%5B0%5D=author_documents_%3AGeneral%20Assembly%20First%20Committee&f%5B1%5D=document_type_meeting%3AVerbatim%20records; "General Assembly First Committee Sixty-Fifth Session (2010) | United Nations," accessed January 30, 2023, https://meetings.unoda.org/meeting/29603/documents?f%5B0%5D=author_documents_%3AGeneral%20Assembly%20First%20Committee&f%5B1%5D=document_type_meeting%3AVerbatim%20records; "General Assembly First Committee Sixty-Fourth Session (2009) | United Nations," accessed January 30, 2023, https://meetings.unoda.org/meeting/29602/documents?f%5B0%5D=author_documents_%3AGeneral%20Assembly%20First%20Committee.

27 "Official Records of the 17th Meeting of the First Committee" (New York: UN General Assembly, Sixty-fourth Session, October 22, 2009), 8, https://documents-dds-ny.un.org/doc/UNDOC/GEN/N09/571/73/PDF/N0957173.pdf?OpenElement.

28 "Official Records of the 15th Meeting of the First Committee" (New York: UN General Assembly, Sixty-fifth session, October 20, 2010), 24 https://documents-dds-ny.un.org/doc/UNDOC/GEN/N10/594/32/PDF/N1059432.pdf?OpenElement.

space. The 2007 Russian cyber attacks on Estonian critical infrastructure played a contributing role in heightening this interest, as stakeholders began to understand the implications of malicious cyber operations. But the GGE's role was key. As one negotiator has noted, "more than the report itself, the 2009–2010 process [of the second GGE] was an important vehicle for forming a nascent international cyber community coalescing" around rules for cyberspace.[29]

The UN GA adopted the second GGE report and requested the UN Secretary General in 2011 to set up a third GGE to examine "norms, rules *or* principles of responsible behavior of states" [emphasis added]. The use of the conjunction "or" suggested norms, rules, and principles were all separate but equivalent categories that served the same function, that is, to advance cybersecurity governance. Another interpretation is that the General Assembly sought clarity from the third GGE on the precise method of "cooperative measures" among states in this domain.

However, the practices of the 2012–2013 GGE reinforced the perception that the articulation of norms and interpretation of existing international law were intertwined. The 2012–2013 GGE report included its pronouncements on both norms and international law under the *same section* titled "Recommendations on norms, rules *and* principles of responsible behavior by States".[30] The UN GGE's report reified the view that norms and rules, even if not the same, were functionally equivalent in shaping responsible state behavior. The phrase "norms, rules and principles" would emerge as a term of art not just adopted by future GGE reports, but also other actors in the cyber CoP.

In this section, the third UN GGE notably affirmed the "applicability of international law and, in particular, the Charter of the United Nations" to state behavior in cyberspace. However, while it noted that "norms derived from existing international law" were important to reduce the risk of cyber conflict, it retained the previous GGE's observation that "additional norms" may be needed over time. It is in the substantive pronouncements within this section that the conflation of norms and international law is most apparent. The 2012–2013 GGE issued three kinds of norms within this section.

---

29 Heli Tiirma-Klaar, "The Evolution of the UN Group of Governmental Experts on Cyber Issues," Cyberstability Paper Series New Conditions and Constellations in Cyber, 5 (The Hague Centre for Strategic Studies, December 2021), https://hcss.nl/wp-content/uploads/2021/12/Klaar.pdf.

30 "Group of Governmental Experts on Developments in the Field of Information and Telecommunications in the Context of International Security" (UN General Assembly, Sixty-eighth session, June 24, 2013), https://documents-dds-ny.un.org/doc/UNDOC/GEN/N13/371/66/PDF/N1337166.pdf?OpenElement. (hereafter "Third UN GGE Report").

First, it included norms that borrowed legal language, and thus seemed to reflect interpretations of existing international law. Specifically, they referred to "internationally wrongful acts" as used by the ILC's articles of state responsibility. What reinforced the perception that they were interpretations of international law was the use of the verb "must" to qualify these norms.

a. States must meet their international obligations regarding internationally wrongful acts attributable to them.
b. States must not use proxies to commit internationally wrongful acts.

Second, the section contained norms that seemed to reflect existing principles of international law, namely the positive obligation of due diligence, but whose application was qualified by the verb "should".

a. States should seek to ensure that their territories are not used by non-State actors for unlawful use of ICTs.
b. States should encourage the private sector and civil society to play an appropriate role to improve [...] supply chain security for ICT products and services

And *third*, the same section contained norms that seemingly reflected political statements.

a. State sovereignty and international norms and principles that flow from sovereignty apply to State conduct of ICT-related activities [...].
b. States should intensify cooperation against criminal or terrorist use of ICTs [...].

The statement on state sovereignty was reportedly included on China's insistence.[31] Although sovereignty is recognized as a general principle of international law, there is hardly an uncontested or unified view of the "norms" and rules that flow from it.[32] Furthermore, reportedly on Russia and China's insistence, the final GGE report removed references made by an earlier draft affirming "verbatim" the applicability of international humanitarian law.[33] This raised the question whether at least some states were using the section on norms, rules and principles to not only advance interpretations of existing rules, but also project others as inapplicable to the domain. As these three

31 Rogier Creemers, "China's Approach to Cyber Sovereignty" (Berlin: Konrad-Adenauer-Stiftung, 2020), https://www.kas.de/documents/252038/7995358/China%E2%80%99s+Approach+to+Cyber+Sovereignty.pdf/2c6916a6-164c-fb0c-4e29-f933f472ac3f?version=1.0&t=1606143361537.

32 Samantha Besson, "Sovereignty," Oxford Public International Law, accessed November 23, 2022, http://opil.ouplaw.com/view/10.1093/law:epil/9780199231690/law-9780199231690-e1472.

33 Michael N Schmitt and Liis Vihul, "The Nature of International Law Cyber Norms," Tallinn Papers, 13 (NATO CCDCOE, 2014).

"categories" of norms illustrate, it is not possible to distinguish whether this section in the GGE's report reflected aspirational statements for state behavior or interpretations of existing international law.

As soon as the UN GGE published its report, major states sought to interpret and promote their own preferred framing of norms and their relationship with international law. Krutskikh, Russia's GGE Expert, welcomed the GGE's consensus report as containing once again a "balanced formula". "It is obvious that not all legal norms formulated in relation to traditional human environments can be 'automatically' applied in the information space", he wrote. "[The] *criteria for the application of international law and methodology for its adaptation* to interstate relations arising in the use of ICT have not yet been developed", he declared, suggesting that "new legal norms" could be considered in their place[34] [emphasis added]. Krutskikh seemed to suggest that it was difficult to discern state practice in this domain and norms articulated by the GGE should emerge as markers of legality, if not substitute existing rules altogether.

The opposing camp pushed back against this view, even before GGE discussions had concluded. In 2011, the UK Foreign Minister William Hague called for cyber norms to be based on the principle that state behavior must be in "accordance with international law".[35] In 2012, while the third GGE discussions were under way, Harold Kongju Koh, then legal adviser to the US Department of State, delivered a landmark speech outlining the US position on international law applicable to state behavior in cyberspace. The speech argued "established principles" of international law apply squarely to the domain. "The more widespread the understanding that cyberspace follows established rules [...] the stronger we can be in pushing back against those who would seek to introduce brand new rules that may be contrary to our interests", argued Koh.[36] The subtext of Koh's speech – "most of its points" were articulated by the United States at GGE negotiations – was that cyber norms had to reflect "established principles" and not "brand new rules". In 2012, the US statement at the UN First Committee's 68th session in 2013,

34 "Архив 11 Номера 2014 Года Международное Право и Проблема Обеспечения Международной Информационной Безопасности," Журнал Международная жизнь, accessed November 23, 2022, https://interaffairs.ru/jauthor/material/1167. [translated using Google Translate].

35 "Security and Freedom in the Cyber Age – Seeking the Rules of the Road," GOV.UK, accessed November 23, 2022, https://www.gov.uk/government/speeches/security-and-freedom-in-the-cyber-age-seeking-the-rules-of-the-road.

36 "International Law in Cyberspace," U.S. Department of State, accessed November 23, 2022, //2009-2017.state.gov/s/l/releases/remarks/197924.htm.

made by the country's GGE Expert, hailed the "historic consensus" of the third group on the applicability of international law, but made no references to "norms".[37] In that same session, the Russian representative pointedly referred to the possibility of "additional norms", using them once again as a heuristic for binding rules.[38]

Meanwhile, the then legal adviser to the Chinese Ministry of Foreign Affairs Huang Huikang outlined his government's position on the matter in a speech at the 2012 Budapest Conference (the successor to the London Conference). "Cyberspace needs both rules *and* norms to follow [...] and the UN is the best forum for [their] elaboration [emphasis added]", Huang argued.[39] That Huang, one of China's senior most international lawyers, and his country's representative to the International Law Commission since 2011,[40] conflated norms and international law in this manner is notable.

As is evident from the positions articulated by senior officials from Russia, the US, the UK, and China, major powers all sought to interpret the nature of norms differently. While Russia and China sought for norms to signal new obligations for states in cyberspace, the US, the UK, and like-minded countries wanted such norms to be closely aligned with existing legal principles. What was not contested, however, is the significance of norms in advancing legal discourse, a belief that would be further reinforced by the practices of the fourth UN GGE.

3.1 The GGE's Approach to Norms: International Lawyers Respond, as Does Microsoft

The third UN GGE's publication of a consensus report represented a landmark moment for the cyber CoP in that it charted a pathway towards international cybersecurity governance. No longer a "nascent" community, more practitioners and legal scholars were paying attention to the work of the UN

37 "Statement by Michele G. Markoff, Delegation of the United States of America," October 30, 2013, https://unoda-documents-library.s3.amazonaws.com/General_Assembly_First_Committee_Sixty-eighth_session_(2013)/united-states_4.pdf.

38 "Statement by Vladimir YERMAKOV, Deputy Director of the Department for Security and Disarmament Affairs, MFA of Russia, Acting Head of the Delegation of the Russian Federation to the First Committee of the 68th Session of the UN General Assembly," October 30, 2013, https://unoda-documents-library.s3.amazonaws.com/General_Assembly_First_Committee_Sixty-eighth_session_(2013)/russian-federation.pdf.

39 "Statement at Budapest Conference on Cyber Issues," accessed November 23, 2022, http://vienna.china-mission.gov.cn/eng/zgbd/201210/t20121009_8848606.htm.

40 "International Law Commission," accessed November 23, 2022, https://legal.un.org/ilc/elections/2021election_outcome.shtml.

group. Among lawyers, the ambiguous nature of UN GGE norms and the lack of clarity regarding their relationship with existing rules generated some discussion. In particular, the UN GGE's recommendations on international law invited comparisons with the work of the Tallinn Manual International Group of Experts on the International Law Applicable to Cyber Warfare. The Tallinn Manual drafters, whose work and practices are highlighted in Chapter IV, began meeting in 2009 under the aegis of NATO CCDCOE. The manual itself was published in 2013, just prior to the publication of the third UN GGE's report, but its work had concluded prior to UN discussions. Consequently, the Manual does not refer to the UN GGE. While the Tallinn Manual purports to identify *lex lata* – i.e., existing law applicable to cyber conflict – it is careful to note that customary law in this domain is "sparse" and therefore is not an "incontrovertible restatement" of the law.[41] But, as the introduction to the 2013 Manual makes clear, every effort was made by this group to doctrinally ascertain the applicability and scope of existing rules to cyberspace.

In this context, the GGE's approach to norms muddied the waters more than it clarified. An international lawyer affiliated with NATO CCDCOE and a member of the Tallinn Manual group criticized the "prevalence of misleading language and 'parallel vocabularies'" with respect to legal terms for international cybersecurity.[42] Michael Schmitt and Liis Vihul, director and project manager respectively of the 2013 Tallinn Manual, argued that "divergent language employed by legal and non-legal communities" in discussions about "international law cyber norms" was a "source of much confusion".[43] In particular, they highlighted the "improper reference" by "various normative communities" to "various norms that reside in different fields of international law" that were not material to specific cases.[44] "Cross-disciplinary confusion" can be avoided by "distinguishing legal norms from non-binding norms", they wrote.

The American Bar Association's working group on "International Law and Cyber"[45] was among the organizers of a multistakeholder workshop at MIT

41 Michael N. Schmitt, ed., *Tallinn Manual 2.0 on the International Law Applicable to Cyber Warfare*, 1st ed. (Cambridge University Press, 2013), 5.

42 Louise Arimatsu, "A Treaty for Governing Cyber-Weapons: Potential Benfits and Practical Limitations," ed. C. Czosseck, K. Ziolkowski, and R. Ottis 2012 4th International Conference on Cyber Conflict (2012).

43 Michael N Schmitt and Liis Vihul, "The Nature of International Law Cyber Norms," Tallinn Papers (NATO CCDCOE, 2014).

44 *Schmitt and Vihul* (2014), 2.

45 "A Call to Cyber Norms: Discussions at the Harvard-MIT–University of Toronto Cyber Norms Workshops, 2011 and 2012," March 2015, https://www.americanbar.org/content/

that expressed reservations against the way informal norms were being positioned vis-s-vis international law. A few participants in this workshop, which published its report in 2012, were formally involved in the then ongoing UN GGE discussions.[46] "[I]nternational relations scholars use the term 'norms' whereas lawyers speak in the language of laws and rules. The two are not the same", the workshop report noted.[47] "By legal norms, we mean legally binding rules."

Even as lawyers criticized the UN GGE for not distinguishing between informal norms and existing international law, they also acknowledged the importance of norms in signaling broad political consensus about legal issues. The MIT workshop report conceded that "applying [sources of international law under Article 38(1)] to factual scenarios [was] very complicated". "*One cannot only look at norms from a legal perspective these days*, because not all norms have yet been tested in practice, it noted"[48] [emphasis added]. Schmitt and Vihul also pointed out that the three kinds of aforementioned norms published by the 2013 GGE – contained in paragraphs 20 to 23 of the Report – "*confirmed the appropriateness* of the law of sovereignty and of state responsibility" [emphasis added]. International lawyers, especially Western legal scholars, were essentially acknowledging that norms had some role to play in advancing legal discourse in cybersecurity in so far as they were key to breaking a geopolitical deadlock around international law. The challenge was in distinguishing the legal attributes of norms from their purported non-legal components, a task made more complicated by the fact that Russian and Chinese diplomats and lawyers were simply using norms as proxies for rules.[49]

The technical community, on the other hand, relied on the UN GGE report and discussion on norms as an opportunity to shape legal discourse in this domain. The publication of Microsoft's landmark report on "cybersecurity norms" a few months after the third GGE's report marked the beginning of a concerted effort by a major player in the technical community to influence the international cybersecurity regime. Microsoft's report, titled "Five Princi-

---

dam/aba/administrative/law_national_security/A_Call_to_Cyber_Norms.authcheckdam.pdf.

46 *Interview with a workshop participant*, April 12, 2022.

47 Catherine Lotrionte and Enekken Tikk, "Panel 3: Applicability of International Law to Cyberspace & Characterization of Cyber Incidents" (Cambridge, MA: Cyber Norms Workshop 2.0, September 2012), https://citizenlab.ca/cybernorms2012/panel3summary.pdf.

48 *Lotrionte and Tikk* (2012), 3.

49 Li Zhang, "A Chinese Perspective on Cyber War," *International Review of the Red Cross* 94, no. 886 (June 2012): 801–7, https://doi.org/10.1017/S1816383112000823.

ples for Shaping Cybersecurity Norms", framed norms as guidelines for state behavior that were drawn from international law.[50] The report expressly defined a norm as "*behavior at the nation-state level codified by international law*" [emphasis added], not only referring to normative conduct drawn from customary international law and treaty law, but also citing specifically Article 38(1) as the source of such norms.[51] At the same time, the report suggested that the articulation of cybersecurity norms should be guided by the need to "build consensus to modify international law", so that it can respond to technological challenges.[52] Microsoft's characterization of norms as cybersecurity-specific guidelines that interpreted and simultaneously advanced international law mirrored the GGE's approach.

Whereas the GGE had articulated lawlike norms for geopolitical reasons, Microsoft's report highlighted reasons why technical and industry considerations should also guide their development. In this regard, the report represents an early illustration of "creeping expertise" in international cybersecurity law. Firstly, Microsoft asserted that private actors should also shape international law discourse in this domain. "Unlike the historical evolution of international norms", i.e., legal norms that drew from customary practice and treaties, "the development of 'cybersecurity norms' should engage the private sector", the report suggested. While acknowledging that only "nation-states can create actual legal norms", the report also noted that private technical actors have influenced agreements such as the "Missile Technology Control Regime, Financial Action Task Force on Money Laundering, and the norms promoted by the International Civil Aviation Organization for civil air travel."[53] Collaboration with the private sector not only had "some precedents in international law", but was also necessary to "develop any norm" or "execute any treaty" given the ownership or management by private actors of global internet resources.[54]

Substantively, the report identified a number of principles that in Microsoft's view should "influence cybersecurity norms". These principles drew directly from the company's experience as a multinational technology company, and sought to prevent destabilizing actions by states in cyberspace, as well as management of global threats. Included among these principles were "risk reduction" and "proportionality", among others. Risk reduction involved

50 "Five Principles for Shaping Cybersecurity Norms" (Microsoft, 2013), https://query.prod.cms.rt.microsoft.com/cms/api/am/binary/REVmc9.

51 *Five Principles for Shaping Cybersecurity Norms*, 5.

52 *Five Principles for Shaping Cybersecurity Norms*, 11.

53 *Five Principles for Shaping Cybersecurity Norms*, 7.

54 *Five Principles for Shaping Cybersecurity Norms*, 10.

states and industry actors engaging in "systematic activities" to identify and mitigate threats, and developing "collective responses" to those threats. Although risk reduction is not a "well-developed concept in international law", the report noted, the global scale of the internet required an alteration of the existing "paradigm". With respect to proportionality, the report noted it was important to states to assess what would be an appropriate response by state in self-defense against a cyber attack. States should "begin to develop interpretations of proportionality in cyberspace under customary international law". Although the report does not specify how those interpretations should be developed, Microsoft's highlighting this principle under its discussion on cybersecurity norms suggested that such discussions should be shaped through norms.

From the report, and Microsoft's efforts at socializing the report with other stakeholders, it was clear the company sought to influence discussions on international law through cyber norms. The company released it at the 2013 Seoul Conference on Cyberspace, the third iteration of the London Process, in whose "pre-workshop" on the applicability of international law Microsoft was also a participant.[55] Whether the company was tacitly mimicking the UN GGE's approach to norms and international law or strategically using norms to insert itself and other private stakeholders into legal discussions is difficult to ascertain. What can be said with more certitude is that the third GGE's template was widely discussed and even accepted among other stakeholders in the CoP.

4 The Fourth UN GGE: A Landmark Report on Norms

The report of the fourth UN GGE, constituted in 2014 with an expanded membership of 20 "Experts", was a landmark document in advancing responsible state behavior in cyberspace.[56] This GGE articulated eleven norms of respon-

55 "Foreign Ministry to Hold the Pre-Workshop on International Security for Seoul Conference on Cyberspace 2013 | Ministry of Foreign Affairs, Republic of Korea," accessed November 24, 2022, https://www.mofa.go.kr/eng/brd/m_5676/view.do?seq=312480&srchFr=&amp%3BsrchTo=&amp%3BsrchWord=&amp%3BsrchTp=&amp%3Bmulti_itm_seq=0&amp%3Bitm_seq_1=0&amp%3Bitm_seq_2=0&amp%3Bcompany_cd=&amp%3Bcompany_nm=.

56 "Group of Governmental Experts on Developments in the Field of Information and Telecommunications in the Context of International Security" (UN General Assembly, Seventieth session, July 22, 2015), https://documents-dds-ny.un.org/doc/UNDOC/GEN/N15/228/35/PDF/N1522835.pdf?OpenElement. (hereafter "Fourth UN GGE Report").

sible state behavior in cyberspace, which included norms of restraint against states' targeting certain types of actors and digital infrastructure as well as positive commitments to protect ICT supply chains, respect human rights on the internet, and prevent the launching of cyber operations from their territories.[57]

The articulation of norms of state behavior was a significant step forward in cybersecurity governance by the GGE, given they were endorsed by the US, Russia, and other permanent members of the UN Security Council. The GGE's report suggests the group discussed the status of norms in relation to international law. This may have been partly in response to the UN General Assembly, which had tasked the fourth GGE not only to study "norms, rules or principles" of responsible state behavior but this time also to study "how international law applies to the use of ICTs by states".[58] The GGE report consequently created two sections, one on "Norms, rules, and principles", continuing the practice of its predecessor GGE, and a second new section, titled "How international law applies to the use of ICTs". Further, the report declared that cyber norms were "voluntary and non-binding", and that they did not "prohibit or limit action" that was "otherwise consistent with international law".

This formulation ironically deepened the ambiguity over norms rather than clarify their status. Some of the eleven "voluntary norms" articulated by the GGE continued to refer to "obligations" of states under international law, including their responsibility not to conduct or knowingly allow their territory to be used for "internationally wrongful acts". "One can only speculate why Experts have offered as voluntary something that by the majority of states is considered legally binding", a commentator has observed in relation to the GGE's references to the state responsibility regime.[59] The invocation of legal language in these norms raised the question: if they referred to existing international law, were these norms genuinely "non-binding"?

What reinforced the view that norms and international law were not conceptually different was also the similarity in the GGE's pronouncements in the section on norms as well as in that on international law. One of the norms articulated by the GGE read:

---

57 *Fourth UN GGE Report*, 7–8.

58 "68/243. Developments in the Field of Information and Telecommunications in the Context of International Security" (UN General Assembly, Sixty-eighth session, January 9, 2014), https://doi.org/10.18356/9789210021753c001.

59 Jason Jolley, "Recommendation 13(f)," in *Voluntary, Non-Binding Norms for Responsible State Behaviour in the Use of Information and Communications Technology: A Commentary*, ed. Eneken Tikk (New York: United Nations Publication, 2017), 171, https://www.un.org/disarmament/wp-content/uploads/2018/04/Civil-Society-2017.pdf.

> States should not knowingly allow their territory to be used for internationally wrongful acts using ICTs.

In the international law section, the UN GGE meanwhile declared in similar terms:

> States must not use proxies to commit internationally wrongful acts using ICTs, and should seek to ensure that their territory is not used by non-State actors to commit such acts.

With little distinction in substantive terms between the language of norms and interpretations of existing rules, the GGE further noted that "additional norms" could be developed over time, leaving open the question whether those could contravene or replace existing rules.

Ultimately, this continued conflation of norms and rules reflected the group's collective dilemma. The US and Western partners, who sought a re-assertion of the applicability of existing international law to cyberspace, acknowledged that standalone discussions on existing rules were unlikely to progress, given Russian and Chinese positions. Norms were therefore the "site" for legal discourse, and the like-minded countries strove for norms to reflect existing legal language to the extent possible. At the same time, creating law-like norms raised the possibility of Russia and China advocating for new norms that created new obligations. Asked in an interview with *Kommersant* whether the outcomes of the GGE are "rules, principles or norms", Krutskikh indeed argued that Russia had taken a "non-standard diplomatic move [to] write all three terms into the report". "Wine is judged by the drink, not by the bottle it is poured into", he said. "In our business, the main thing is the content of the document."[60] With Russia seeking in this manner to remove any distinction between norms and rules, the like-minded countries had no option other to assert that norms were voluntary and non-binding, something Krutskikh alluded to in his interview.[61] At the same time, Russia's emphasis on norms as a potential source of additional legal obligations meant Moscow too would have to concede some existing rules were confirmed as applicable through those norms. This uneasy compromise meant that while both negoti-

60 Daniel Paltiel, "Russian Newspaper Kommersant Interviews Special Representative Krutskikh on UN GGE Cyber Arrangements," Center for Strategic and International Studies, accessed November 24, 2022, https://www.csis.org/blogs/strategic-technologies-blog/russian-newspaper-kommersant-interviews-special-representative.

61 *Russian Newspaper Kommersant Interviews Special Representative Krutskikh*, n.60.

ating blocs in the GGE sought for norms to have some signaling effects on international law, but neither could fully lay claim to those effects.

5 Creeping Expertise in the UN GGE

The following section highlights two areas where technical experts were able, through the norm-articulation process, to influence discussions on international law within the GGE. These two topics, namely, the attribution of wrongful cyber operations to states, and the protection of critical infrastructure from malicious attacks, are among the foremost concerns of the cyber CoP. As the previous section suggests, norms articulated by the UN GGE on both topics were closely aligned with existing international law and referred to states' obligations. However, the framing of those norms in turn was done with the help of technical experts within the group. Ultimately, the inclusion of technical formulations on the presentation of evidence and threshold of acceptable damage respectively shaped legal discourse on attribution and CI protection in cyberspace.

Prior to illustrating these instances of "creeping expertise" in the GGE, it is worth pointing out that external private actors too were trying to influence the group's law-like norms. This included Microsoft, which by this period had emerged as an influential interlocutor from within the technical community. During the fourth GGE negotiations, Microsoft released a second report that detailed six cybersecurity norms to "limit conflict in cyberspace".[62] The report categorized these norms into "offensive" and "defensive" norms. The former category of norms sought to avoid escalation or restrain states from offensive actions that could have a "catastrophic" impact. Defensive norms referred to those around risk reduction and information sharing.

These norms were characterized by Microsoft as voluntary, as the UN GGE would in its final report. Yet, it made numerous references to international law, and analogized Microsoft's role as a norm entrepreneur to private actors like the Dutch jurist Hugo Grotius as well as non-profit entities that helped craft rules on maritime law, international labor standards, and chemical weapons. Commentaries on three of these norms expressly referred to legal principles from domains of state responsibility, international humanitarian law, and non-proliferation were presented as interpretations of international

62 Angela McKay et al., "International Cybersecurity Norms: Reducing Conflict in an internet-Dependent World" (Microsoft, December 14, 2014), https://query.prod.cms.rt.microsoft.com/cms/api/am/binary/REVroA.

law.[63] For example, one "offensive norm" called on states to develop and use cyber weapons that adhered to the IHL principle of distinction, but framed "distinction" as the use of weapons that were "controllable, precise and not reusable by others". While the voluntary norm was broadly about exercising restraint in offensive operations, the associated commentary offered a technical understanding of how an IHL principle applied to cyber conflict. Another norm articulated by Microsoft called on states to restrain from cyber operations that created "mass events" during armed conflict. Highlighting the IHL principles of necessity and proportionality, the norm commentary suggested that these principles were to be evaluated based on their impact on the confidentiality, integrity, and availability (C-I-A) of ICT systems. In a separate table, Microsoft clearly laid down the technical parameters to evaluate the C-I-A criteria: economic or reputational damage through unauthorized access (confidentiality); loss of trust in data even if it is still accessible (integrity); and loss of access to data for finite or indefinite amounts of time (availability).[64]

These norms were not addressed by the UN GGE, given the application of IHL was itself a contested matter in the group, but Microsoft's report illustrated the mechanism of "creeping expertise". Microsoft adopted practices that were different from that of the fourth UN GGE. If UN GGE norms expressly adopted legal vocabulary, Microsoft's norms featured legal interpretation in the commentary to those norms. This practice, as Chapter III highlights, would be adopted by multistakeholder initiatives like the GCSC and Paris Call. The effect, however, was similar to norm-articulation by the GGE. Microsoft sought to influence legal discourse using norms in two ways: first, the report affirmed that certain legal principles, such as IHL principles were indeed applicable, and the norms clearly illustrated how they would be applicable using concrete illustrations. Second, the company used the norms commentaries to introduce technical principles that would inform the application of existing rules. These technical principles were of course aligned with its commercial interests around the stability of digital platforms and the general internet.

5.1 The Wicked Problem of Attributing Wrongful Cyber Operations to States

The issue of state responsibility, as the previous section noted, was first raised in the third UN GGE. The group articulated a norm calling on states to not

63 *International Cybersecurity Norms*, 12–13.

64 *International Cybersecurity Norms*, 8.

commit or allow proxies to commit "internationally wrongful acts". Discussions around this norm illustrate the close involvement of technical experts in how state responsibility was framed by that GGE. Sherif Heshem of Egypt, one of the Experts in the 2012–2013 group who had a technical background, noted technical experts faced "some difficulty" adjusting to GGE discussions in the beginning. "We spent eight to nine working days [in the GGE] arguing whether international law was applicable or not. If international law is not applicable, what is? Alien law?! Then I realized, there were specific aspects of international law that were up for debate."[65] Although the GGE spent a lot of time discussing international law, Heshem noted, it was were not fully sensitive to technical realities. "Some [of the norms] suggested in the 2012–2013 and future GGEs were from successful [arms control] agreements – I support and endorse a few of those articles, but we cannot assume articles from nuclear will be fundamental in cyber." The attribution of cyber attacks and the "responsibility of states to prevent the launch of cyber attacks" were two such issues, said Heshem. "Attribution [and by extension, applying the articles of state responsibility] of cyber attacks is extremely difficult, and you also cannot use the same [principles] of due diligence", he said. "For example, when I spoke with South Korea about the DDoS attacks of 2009 that the country faced, they said the attacks emanated from 59 countries – they have said so publicly in the OECD."

As noted earlier, the third GGE ultimately called on states to meet their international obligations regarding "internationally wrongful acts attributable to them" [emphasis added]. If the GGE's objective was to align this norm with the principles of state responsibility and specifically the language used in the ARSIWA, there was no requirement to include the italicized phrase. The ARSIWA make it amply clear that "internationally wrongful acts" are those that are attributable to a state, and constitute a breach of its international obligation.[66] The additional requirement of attributability in the GGE norm implied – based not only on Heshem's comments but numerous references to the difficulty of technical attribution within the GGE report[67] – that in addition to the legal standard under the ARSIWA, states had to somehow meet a technical threshold. Although that threshold was not specified, it was clear the GGE was concerned mainly about accusations by states leading to heightened

65 *Interview with Sherif Heshem*, November 24, 2020.

66 International Law Commission, "Draft Articles on Responsibility of States for Internationally Wrongful Acts with commentaries" (UN General Assembly, Fifty-third session, December 12, 2001), Article 2. (hereafter "ARSIWA with commentaries").

67 *Third UN GGE report*, 2,6,7.

geopolitical tensions and a deterioration in international security. The risk of "mistaken attribution and unintended escalation", noted the GGE report, made it important to develop "common understandings" on responsible state behavior.

Technical experts like Heshem impressed upon the broader group the challenges in technically attributing cyber operations to states. To be sure, states may have been concerned about the attribution problem in cyberspace even before the third GGE. However, this was the first instance where major cyber powers convened to discuss the issue and framed it as a collective governance concern. The GGE's highlighting of the hard problem of legal attribution was also novel. The 2013 Tallinn Manual, which discusses the application of the state responsibility regime to cyberspace, makes no reference to the technical challenges associated with attribution. The presence of technical experts alongside diplomats and lawyers in the GGE shaped the group's deliberations, and the use of legal vocabulary in that norm meant those experts were in fact influencing legal discourse on "cyber" state responsibility.

The fourth GGE restated the norm and, in its section on international law, expanded it to reflect the exact wording of Article 2(a) of ARSIWA:

> States must meet their international obligations regarding internationally wrongful acts attributable to them under international law.[68]

This formulation may have been inserted to clarify the norm, and align it fully with ARSIWA language. In other words, to suggest that the legal standard of attribution under the customary law of state responsibility remained the same. However, the same paragraph also went on to declare that the fact an ICT activity was "launched or otherwise originated" from the territory of a state "may be insufficient" attribute such operations to the State.[69] Accusations against of "organizing and implementing wrongful acts […] should be substantiated", the paragraph concluded.[70] Read together, the effect of the norm would that the cyber-specific standard of responsibility would not only require attribution under ARSIWA's legal standards but also *demonstrable or documented*[71] *technical evidence.*

68 *Fourth UN GGE report*, 8.

69 *Fourth UN GGE report*, 13.

70 *Fourth UN GGE report*, 13.

71 Martha Finnemore and Duncan B Hollis, "Beyond Naming and Shaming: Accusations and International Law in Cybersecurity," *European Journal of International Law* 31, no. 3 (August 1, 2020): 969–1003, https://doi.org/10.1093/ejil/chaa056.

If the discussion about the concerns associated with cyber attribution was shaped by technical experts, this particular outcome was once again the result of a compromise formulation owed to geopolitical factors. The outcome highlights the instrumental uses of "creeping expertise", where states rely on such expertise for legal argumentation. Russia, which relies extensively on proxies for its cyber operations, arguably sought to insert the technical qualification as a loophole. The Russian negotiator Krutskikh also indicated that the qualification was necessary to prevent "strong cyber powers" – in other words US or NATO countries – from taking retaliatory measures simply through accusations "without any legal basis".[72]

The practices of the GGE facilitated such a compromise. With no clear distinction between norms articulation and legal interpretation, the GGE's subgroup on international law was facilitated by Katherine Getao, the Kenyan Expert with a technical background. "It was a bit of a shock to me", Getao recounted in an interview about being appointed the facilitator by the GGE chair, "because I was not a lawyer, and this was a highly contentious section of the report".[73] "There are one or two articles in the international law section that [could be phrased more clearly]…like the one on attribution", she reminisced. "[The part about] 'should be substantiated' and so on… I thought this would be difficult to implement in practice. But it was done in the spirit of compromise, [because] inclusion or exclusion of a phrase may determine whether the group achieves consensus and produces a report."

Getao reaffirmed that the difficulties of technically attributing cyber attacks to states did shape the GGE's discussion on the rules of state responsibility. "Yes, an appreciation of the technical difficulties of attribution makes one a bit skeptical about the capacity of all states to apply the rules of attribution in context." Knowledge about the challenges of attribution, Getao said, helped GGE negotiators "look at an article or rule that someone is trying to introduce, and say 'OK, we need to tone the language down a little bit to take into account that this is a process which is not completely factual, and driven by knowledge other than [objective] factors'".[74] The geopolitical dynamics of the GGE pushed the group to make those subjective considerations explicit, giving the ARSIWA language a cyber-specific interpretation.

Would having an international lawyer as a facilitator, as opposed to a technical expert, had made a difference to the GGE's pronouncements on attribution? This is unlikely to have been the case. Getao's technical expertise was

72 *Russian Newspaper Kommersant Interviews Special Representative Krutskikh*, n.60.

73 *Interview with Katherine Getao*, August 16, 2021.

74 *Interview with Katherine Getao*, August 16, 2021.

arguably crucial to GGE interlocutors outside the sub-group understanding and accepting the compromise formulation, which was ultimately essential for the group to have a successful outcome. However, this formulation also triggered the beginning of a protracted discussion on the importance of technical attribution to establishing state responsibility in cyberspace, which would continue right up to the sixth GGE that concluded discussions in 2021.[75]

5.2 Critical Infrastructure: An Object of Protection in International Cybersecurity Law?

The protection of critical infrastructure (CI) from cyber operations has long been an issue of concern to states and private actors. A 2011 report by the Centre for Strategic and International Studies for the UN Institute for Disarmament Research (UNIDIR) identified more than 30 states that had published military doctrines or strategies around cyberwarfare or the role of cyber operations in national security matters.[76] Most, if not all of these states accorded high priority to the protection of CI, recognizing their vulnerability against major, nation-state attacks. In so far as international law was concerned, the 2013 Tallinn Manual had addressed the possibility that attacks on CI could violate existing rules – especially, and in relation to operations with catastrophic consequences, rules on the use of force.[77] By and large, the Manual's focus was on attacks that cause debilitating or incapacitating damage to CI.

Nevertheless, it is the UN GGE process that first contributed to the framing of CI as an object of protection under international law. The second GGE (2009–2010) recommended the creation of norms around the protection of "critical national and international infrastructure".[78] Nine of the fif-

75 Andraz Kastelic, "Non-Escalatory Attribution of International Cyber Incidents: Facts, International Law and Politics" (Geneva: United Nations Institute for Disarmament Research, 2022), https://unidir.org/files/2022-01/UNIDIR_Non-Escalatory_Attribution_International_Cyber_Incidents.pdf.

76 James A. Lewis and Katrina Timlin, "Cybersecurity and Cyberwarfare: Preliminary Assessment of National Doctrine and Organization," UNIDIR Resources (Washington D.C: Centre for Strategic and International Studies, 2011), https://unidir.org/files/publication/pdfs/cybersecurity-and-cyberwarfare-preliminary-assessment-of-national-doctrine-and-organization-380.pdf.

77 Michael N. Schmitt, ed., *Tallinn Manual 2.0 on the International Law Applicable to Cyber Warfare*, 1st ed. (Cambridge University Press, 2013), Rule 9, Rule 18.

78 Group of Governmental Experts on Developments in the Field of Information and Telecommunications in the Context of International Security" (UN General Assembly, Sixty-fifth session, July 30, 2010), 8 https://documents-dds-ny.un.org/doc/UNDOC/GEN/N10/469/57/PDF/N1046957.pdf.

teen Experts, i.e., delegation heads, in that GGE were technical experts and belonged to national institutions such as CERTs. Evidently, the issue was a priority for those from the technical community. The goal of articulating a norm around CI protection was realized when the fourth UN GGE included it among the 11 norms for responsible state behavior. Norm 13(f) read:

> State should not conduct or knowingly support ICT activity **contrary to its obligations under international law** that intentionally damages critical infrastructure or otherwise impairs the use and operation of critical infrastructure to provide services to the public. [emphasis added][79]

Norm 13(f) is not articulated as an aspirational guideline. It refers to existing international law, indicating states can violate say, the rule of non-intervention or the use of force, by targeting CI through cyber operations. By itself, this is not a unique claim. As the Tallinn Manual pointed out, targeting CI could violate *jus ad bellum* rules if the effects of such cyber operations on a state's territory are significant. However, Norm 13(f) also goes on to prescribe a *de minimis* standard for cyber operations that would be in breach of a state's international obligations. It refers simply to the intentional "damaging" or "impairment of the use and operation" of CI, noting further that impairment can also be brought about through the unintended consequences of cyber operations. Any quantum of damage wrought to CI by a targeted cyber operation, whether incapacitating or not, would therefore violate a state's legal obligations. The stringency of the standard is apparent from its urging states to be mindful about the spillover impact of cyber operations on the functioning of CI.

Such an expansive interpretation of the scope of obligations towards CI is only possible because rule interpretation on state responsibility in cyberspace was entwined with the articulation of a norm championed by technical experts. Norm 13(f) triggered a discussion on whether CI – as a general class of assets or in relation to specific critical sectors – have special or protected status under international cybersecurity law.[80] Indeed, some states have

---

79 *Fourth UN GGE report*, 8.

80 Samuli Haataja, "Cyber Operations against Critical Infrastructure under Norms of Responsible State Behaviour and International Law," *International Journal of Law and Information Technology* 30, no. 4 (December 31, 2022): 423–443, https://doi.org/10.1093/ijlit/eaad006; "Arria-Formula Meeting on Cyber-Attacks Against Critical Infrastructure," *What's In Blue | Security Council Report* (blog), August 25, 2020, https://www.securitycouncilreport.org/whatsinblue/2020/08/arria-formula-meeting-on-cyber-attacks-against-critical-infrastructure.php.

addressed this concern in their legal positions, pointing out that the critical "nature of the target" of a cyber operation can invoke state responsibility.[81] As Chapter III and IV note, private and multistakeholder initiatives like the GCSC and the Paris Call, and even law-finding exercises like the Tallinn Manuals and the Oxford Process have sought to identify and scope applicable rules for specialized critical infrastructure pertaining to elections, healthcare research, and supply chains. The UN GGE's invocation of legal obligations around CI protection has been invoked by many of these initiatives in support of their own norms.

6 The UN GGE, Cybersecurity Governance, and International Law-Making

In the final analysis, the UN GGE's contribution lies in articulating a unique template for governance in international cybersecurity. Certainly, the GGE seeded a substantive agenda for international cybersecurity governance. Blessed as they were by major powers, consensus reports of the early GGEs were important markers of what states identified as banner strategic and economic concerns pertaining to cybersecurity. States that did not have the opportunity to nominate Experts to the GGE as well as private actors like companies and standards bodies benefited from this high-level framing of the cybersecurity agenda. However, the UN GGE's signaling of the importance of norms to legal discourse may be its most consequential legacy to global governance in this domain. The "framework of responsible state behavior" articulated by the GGE encompassed norms and interpretations of international law in similar measure. The defining characteristic of informal cyber norms was that they shared a porous relationship with international law, drawing on or referring directly to specific legal principles in various cases.

This conflation of norms and rules by the UN GGE was driven by the need to break geopolitical deadlock. However, it was also reinforced by the practices of deliberation and reporting in the third and fourth GGEs, as this chapter has shown. Notably, every GGE after the 2009–2010 grouping had a section on "norms, rules and principles" which facilitated the integration of international law concepts into informal norms. Practices adopted after the publication of

81 "INTERNATIONAL LAW APPLIED TO OPERATIONS IN CYBERSPACE – Paper shared by France with the Open-ended working group established by resolution 75/240," August 2021, https://documents.unoda.org/wp-content/uploads/2021/12/French-position-on-international-law-applied-to-cyberspace.pdf.

the fourth GGE report also reflected this view. The eleven norms in that report are widely referred to by diplomats as well as lawyers and technology companies involved in cybersecurity governance as the "*acquis*" of the GGE.[82] The term *acquis communitaire* is specifically used in EU law parlance to denote the corpus of binding community rights and obligations between states.[83] Despite the GGE's declaring that norms were non-binding, practitioners in the cyber CoP continue to describe the eleven norms as *acquis*, implying they have some precedential value.

The practice of describing UN GGE norms as the *acquis* of the group – it is arguably to practitioners in the cyber CoP what Vauchez terms a "legal artefact"[84] – reflects the core belief within the community that norms and binding rules are functionally equivalent. It is prevalently used outside the UN context, including by companies and technical actors, such as Microsoft and the Cyber Peace Institute.[85] Contrast this practice in the cyber CoP to references made by the UN GGE on Lethal Autonomous Weapons Systems (LAWS) specifically to the "international legal *acquis*" while referring to applicable international law for LAWS.[86] The practice of calling the UN cyber GGE "*acquis*" signals their importance to the CoP, but also the widespread belief that norms can have the effect of shaping legal obligations with respect to state actors.

Indeed, if UN GGEs conflated norms and rules for geopolitical reasons, it has since become an accepted way of developing the framework of responsible behavior in the cyber CoP. The GGE's approach to cybersecurity governance opened a path for private actors, especially industry and standards bodies, to try and influence the behavior of states, and advance legal discourse in this domain.

---

82 "UN OEWG in 2025 – DW Observatory," *Geneva internet Platform – DigWatch*, n.d., accessed September 7, 2025, https://dig.watch/processes/un-gge.

83 Jan Klabbers, "Safeguarding the Organizational Acquis: The EU's External Practice," *International Organizations Law Review* 4, no. 1 (January 1, 2007): 57–89.

84 Antoine Vauchez, *Brokering Europe: Euro-Lawyers and the Making of a Transnational Polity*, Cambridge Studies in European Law and Policy (Cambridge: Cambridge University Press, 2015), 175.

85 CyberPeace Institute, "Statement on the Cyber Programme of Action," *CyberPeace Institute* (blog), July 11, 2023, https://cyberpeaceinstitute.org/news/statement-cyber-programme-of-action/; Microsoft's submission for the second substantive session of the Open-Ended Working Group on security of and in the use of information and communications technologies, April 22, 2021, https://documents.unoda.org/wp-content/uploads/2022/04/Second-Microsoft-Submission-to-the-OEWG-Chair-March-2022.pdf.

86 "Chairperson's Summary, Group of Governmental Experts on Emerging Technologies in the Area of Lethal Autonomous Weapons Systems", April 19, 2021, https://documents.unoda.org/wp-content/uploads/2020/07/CCW_GGE1_2020_WP_7-ADVANCE.pdf.

6.1 GGEs in the Cyber Community of Practice after 2016

The UN GGE's profile would itself dim in years following the heady success of the fourth group, resulting in multistakeholder and private norms-articulation initiatives becoming more visible and relevant. The GGE's decline in prominence after 2016, and the impact that had on both the pronouncements of the group as well as on "creeping expertise" in those pronouncements, is elaborated in detail in Chapter 5. Nevertheless, a brief summary is in order here. In December 2015, a few months after the fourth GGE's report was adopted by the UN GA, the General Assembly requested the UN Secretary General to constitute a fifth group with a similar mandate.[87] Through a fifth group, UN member states sought an elaboration of the original eleven cyber norms, and for the GGE to articulate new norms that further guided state behavior. However, geopolitical tensions that always simmered in the background of GGE discussions came to a head in 2016 with Russian interference in the US presidential elections that year. US-Russia tensions greatly diminished prospects for a consensus outcome at the GGE, but the group's failure can be specifically attributed to come to an agreement on the application of international law.[88]

Even before the fifth UN GGE formally acknowledged its inability to deliver a consensus report, major state and private actors in the cyber CoP had begun to look at alternative initiatives. The Netherlands, which had nominated an Expert to the GGE for the first time in 2016, championed simultaneously the creation of a multistakeholder commission called the Global Commission on the Stability of Cyberspace (GCSC) to articulate new norms for state behavior in cyberspace.[89] As the next chapter highlights, the GCSC's founders accounted for the possibility that the GGE process "may come to an end" in 2017, and the Commission indeed acquired heightened prominence in the aftermath of the fifth Group's failure. The Dutch government also lent its formal support to the Tallinn Manual 2.0 discussions on the international law applicable to peacetime cyber operations, convening consultative discus-

87 "70/237. Developments in the Field of Information and Telecommunications in the Context of International Security" (UN General Assembly, Seventieth session, December 30, 2015), https://documents.un.org/doc/undoc/gen/n15/457/57/pdf/n1545757.pdf.

88 Arun M. Sukumar, "The UN GGE Failed. Is International Law in Cyberspace Doomed As Well?," *Lawfare* (blog), July 4, 2017, https://www.lawfaremedia.org/article/un-gge-failed-international-law-cyberspace-doomed-well.

89 HSD Foundation, "Launch of Global Commission on the Stability of Cyberspace," HSD SecurityDelta.nl, March 7, 2017, https://securitydelta.nl/news/interviews/launch-of-global-commission-on-the-stability-of-cyberspace.

sions in 2016 between key states and the Manual's drafters under the "Hague Process".

France, meanwhile, began efforts to convene a multistakeholder norms initiative that resulted in the 2018 Paris Call for Trust and Security in Cyberspace. The GCSC and the Paris Call became magnets for the technical community, actively participating in their deliberations on, *inter alia*, the application of rules to cyberspace. Microsoft was a champion and co-sponsor of the GCSC, even as it worked with the French government as a partner to evangelize the Paris Call norms, recruit signatories, and deepen discussions on the precise scope of those norms.

The GGE's failure in June 2017 to produce a report thus provided further impetus to these initiatives whose conceptualization and planning were already in advanced stages. With the involvement of more private actors and a proliferation of multistakeholder initiatives that articulated norms, the GGE's own closed nature would come before the spotlight.

7 2019–2021: UN Negotiators Revisit Their Approach

The GGE's exclusive nature was arguably one of the main reasons why UN member states in 2018 voted to support two parallel processes – a sixth UN GGE, that would resemble its predecessors, but also an Open-Ended Working Group (OEWG) that was open to all UN member states.[90] In contrast to the GGE process, the OEWG would also allow limited participation by private actors. Both groups were initially meant to conclude their discussions within a year, but delays caused by the onset of the COVID-19 pandemic meant their terms were extended by the year. The UN GGE and OEWG began negotiations in 2019, and submitted their consensus reports in the summer of 2021.

These parallel mechanisms were established to help implement existing UN GGE reports and advance the "framework of responsible state behavior" in cyberspace. However, as Chapter 5 of this book demonstrates, negotiations in the sixth UN GGE and 2019–2021 UN OEWG were characterized by a conscious effort to decouple the articulation of norms and the interpretation of existing rules. Put differently, UN negotiators sought to address voluntary cyber norms separately from any discussion on international law. What explains their reflexive re-evaluation of what was hitherto an established and taken-for-

90 Louise Marie Hurel, "The Rocky Road to Cyber Norms at the United Nations | Council on Foreign Relations," *Net Politics* (blog), September 6, 2022, https://www.cfr.org/blog/rocky-road-cyber-norms-united-nations-0.

granted approach to advancing cybersecurity governance? Chapter 5 demonstrates how changes that had been afoot in the UN GGE for years – namely, its gradual "professionalization", with arms control diplomats replacing technical experts, as well as the constant pressure to deliver consensus reports to the UN General Assembly – played an important role in negotiators becoming more attuned to the geopolitical dynamics within their group. If early UN GGEs focused on building a nascent framework for responsible state behavior – whether it was through norms or international law – later groups were more occupied with managing the deteriorating relationship between the US and Russia. Norms or applications of international law to cyber operations were evaluated on the touchstone of whether they favored, say the Western camp over the Russia-China camp, and vice-versa. With the application of international law becoming a sensitive issue and entirely separated from norms discussions, states were more cautious in letting technical considerations shape legal formulations. Consequently, the effect of "creeping expertise" was muted in the reports of the sixth GGE and 2019–2021 OEWG.

Following the conclusion of the 2019–2021 OEWG, a second group was established by the UN General Assembly, this time with a five year term. At the time of writing, it is unclear whether the second OEWG (2021–2025) will lead to yet another one, or yield to a permanent, regularized mechanism for discussion of international cybersecurity issues, as many states have sought.[91]

The deliberations and outcomes of GGEs over the years generated a strong, widespread belief that norms of cyber state behavior could advance discussions on the application of international law. This belief, reflected in the practices of the UN negotiations, guided the work of the broader CoP as well. Stakeholders such as technical experts were consequently able to shape the legal interpretive process through the articulation of informal norms. After the fifth GGE stalled, the work of advancing the framework of responsible cyber behavior would be carried on by multistakeholder initiatives. As sensitivities over binding commitments on states heighten, it is unclear whether and how much UN mechanisms will continue to focus on norms in the coming years. Indeed, the final substantive session of the OEWG in July 2025 is slated to discuss a permanent mechanism that will have a "thematic group" on international law, but envisages no further consultations on norms. It may be the case that the UN OEWG's revised approach to legal interpretation will also be reflected in the practices of other initiatives in the cyber CoP. However, the

91 "Resolution on the Programme of Action (PoA) on Cybersecurity Adopted | Digital Watch Observatory," November 3, 2022, https://dig.watch/updates/resolution-on-the-programme-of-action-poa-on-cybersecurity-adopted.

influence that informal cyber norms have hitherto had in shaping legal discourse around cyber operations – as well as the role of technical experts in crafting those norms – cannot be understated. In June 2025, the chair of the OEWG released a draft Final Report that proposed the creation of a dedicated thematic group on international law. The draft report specifically called for the participation of technical experts in this dedicated group. Although the proposal for a dedicated group on international law was abandoned in the OEWG's Final Report, the proposal is indicative of the influence of such experts.[92] The UN GGE not only seeded the cyber community of practice, but also charted a framework of governance that allowed non-legal stakeholders like technical experts to shape the evolution of international cybersecurity law.

92 Burhan Gafoor, "Letter from the OEWG Chair dated 25 June 2025", https://docs-library.unoda.org/Open-Ended_Working_Group_on_Information_and_Communication_Technologies_-_(2021)/Letter_from_OEWG_Chair_25_June_2025.pdf.

CHAPTER 3

Multistakeholder Cyber Norms Initiatives: GCSC and the Paris Call

As the previous chapter highlighted, the UN GGE process charted a unique approach to identifying and framing responsible state behavior in cyberspace. If the conflation of cyber norms and international legal principles in UN GGE reports was initially meant as a compromise formula to address American and Russian concerns, it became an established way of thinking about and advancing international cybersecurity governance. Practices of the UN GGE – specifically, the second, third, and fourth GGEs – ingrained the belief that the application of international law to cyber operations could be advanced through the articulation of norms. Even though the GGE's clubbing together of norms and rules first generated discussion among international lawyers, notable actors like Microsoft were soon mimicking UN reports by articulating cyber norms of their own. Consequently, when discussions in the fifth UN GGE stalled due to sharp geopolitical differences between its main players, other actors in the cyber CoP stepped up by promoting multistakeholder initiatives on international cybersecurity. The cast of actors that incubated such initiatives included powerful states, major technology companies, global civil society organizations, and internet standards bodies.

This chapter highlights the work of two such prominent multistakeholder initiatives: the Global Commission on the Stability of Cyberspace (GCSC) and the Paris Call for Trust and Security in Cyberspace. Although both initiatives featured a few common promoters and participants and had overlapping terms, their methods of operation were quite different. In fact, practices around agenda-framing, participation, and deliberation differed substantially between the GCSC and the Paris Call. Yet, as this chapter demonstrates, the practices of both initiatives further blurred the boundaries between informal norm articulation and legal interpretation. The GCSC and the Paris Call developed practices which clearly indicated they shared the UN GGE's belief that informal norms and legal principles were functionally equivalent tools to advance the framework of responsible state behavior in cyberspace.

HTTPS://DOI.ORG/10.1163/9789004737617-004

1 "Frameworks" and "Principles": Synthesizing Cyber Norms and International Law

In comparison to the UN GGE, the GCSC and Paris Call were not open-ended multistakeholder initiatives and had clearly defined objectives. The UN GGE process, over the course of several years of negotiations and iterations of the group, had developed a general "framework of responsible state behavior" of "norms, rules and principles" in cyberspace. As the previous chapter notes, this was an autonomously developed framework with little guidance from the UN General Assembly, which had initially asked the GGE simply to "study concepts" pertaining to international cybersecurity.

The GCSC, meanwhile, was set up specifically to advance a "cyber stability framework". Critical to "cyber stability" in the view of the GCSC's promoters was the protection of core internet infrastructure such as subsea cables, satellites, the Domain Name System, and internet Exchange Points. But cyber stability was about states exercising a degree of restraint, both against executing certain kinds of cyber operations as well as targeting certain critical, cyber-enabled infrastructure, such as election infrastructure. Although the GCSC in this manner was set up to meet a more specific objective, what's remarkable is that the Commission, like the UN GGE, conceived of the "cyber stability framework" as encompassing both "voluntary norms" and "adherence to international law".[1] Beyond stating that its framework would "reduce the potential for significant disruptions of cyberspace", the Commission did not clarify the relationship between norms and legal principles, and how their interplay would result in responsible state behavior.[2] Indeed, the GCSC said at the outset that it would focus "primarily" on multistakeholder engagement, norms, and principles,[3] presumably leaving international law discussions to states. However, as this chapter demonstrates, its norms and principles freely cited international legal instruments and obligations. On occasion, the GCSC even sought state accountability and "collective action" to remedy the "violation" of norms, indicating the extent to which norm articulation was conflated with the interpretation of existing rules.

As for the Paris Call, its main output was the nine Paris Call "principles", which were articulated in the manner of informal norms but were heavily

1 "Advancing Cyberstability – Final Report | Global Commission on the Stability of Cyberspace" (The Hague Centre for Strategic Studies and East-West Institute, November 2019), 8, https://hcss.nl/wp-content/uploads/2019/11/GCSC-Final-Report-November-2019.pdf. (hereafter "GCSC Final Report").

2 *GCSC Final Report*, 10.

3 *GCSC Final Report*, 14.

foreshadowed by assertions from France and Microsoft, its chief promoters, on the need for rules for cyberspace. Further, one of the nine principles itself was the advancement of "international norms of responsible behavior", which called into question the precise status and provenance of the "principles" as well as the norms which they sought to advance. Were at least some of the Paris Call principles legal principles or were they political in nature? The answer is unclear. Paris Call signatories were required to "reaffirm" that "international law together with voluntary norms of responsible state behavior [...] is the foundation for international peace and security in cyberspace".

The practices of both initiatives reinforced the thinking of participants and observers that informal norms were in some manner linked to international law. With respect to the GCSC, firstly, this chapter details its practices pertaining to the recruitment of international lawyers not only for the Commission but also for its research advisory groups. Secondly, it highlights how Requests for Proposals (RfPs) routinely put out by the GCSC often solicited international law scholarship or required international legal expertise to expound on such topics as offensive cyber operations and hack backs that would be taken up by the Commission's norms. Thirdly, this chapter notes the crucial function played by the Commission's annexing a "background paper" and "additional note" to its norms respectively on electoral interference and private "hack backs", explicitly grounding these norms in international law.

The practices of the Paris Call also conflated norm-articulation and rule-interpretation. This chapter examines the discussions of Working Group 3 and Working Group 4 of the Paris Call, tasked respectively with promoting multistakeholder participation in UN cybersecurity negotiations and advancing interpretations of the Paris Call norms. The practices of these two groups – specifically, frequent briefings by noted international lawyers, and the practice of interspersing "memo-like" notes on international law principles among their commentary on norms – played an important role in conflating non-binding norms with existing rules.

Then, drawing on norms and explanatory statements published by the GCSC and Paris Call, this chapter highlights how such conflation of norms and rules facilitated "creeping expertise". Both the GCSC and Paris Call were initiatives that prominently featured technical experts, whether they were directly involved in the articulation of some norms or emerged as influential interpreters of norms through working groups and research advisory bodies. Participant observation and interviews with actors from both initiatives indicate that the articulation and interpretation of cyber norms involved extensive discussions with various stakeholders. As can be expected, the norms-articulation process was designed to elicit views from a broad spectrum of stakeholders on what responsible behavior by states and non-state actors should look like in cyberspace.

Technical experts were, in this vein, consulted to explain or clarify how the operational realities of cyberspace clashed with, constrained, or facilitated norms of responsible behavior. However, the practices of both groups – the recruitment of Commissioners and research advisors with formal training in international law, briefings and presentations by invited legal scholars to the GCSC and Paris Call working groups – reinforced the perception that these norms were connected to existing rules or principles. Indeed, several of the norms published by these initiatives were tied to existing international law through their commentary. Technical or technically adjacent concepts used in GCSC norms or Paris Call principles such as "active cyber defence", "electoral infrastructure", or "supply chain integrity" were linked to international law concepts related to state responsibility and measures of self-help, coercive intervention, and due diligence. The work of the GCSC and Paris Call lent intersubjective legal meaning to technical formulations – i.e., practitioners in the cyber CoP began associating technical terms in these norms with evoking or triggering certain rules or principles.

The deliberations of the Paris Call Working Groups highlight another dimension of "creeping expertise": technical experts not only influenced the application of legal principles to international cybersecurity but also how the cyber CoP thought about future models of compliance frameworks for this domain. WG3 of the Paris Call, which was tasked with articulating multistakeholder models of international cybersecurity discussions, gravitated towards global governance regimes that "clarified" or "translated" existing legal obligations of states through non-binding norms. As the chapter notes, there is no evidence to suggest that the technical community, alongside other stakeholders in WG3, was reflexively forum-shopping to promote frameworks where private actors would have a say in international law interpretation. It would appear in fact that these participants endorsed frameworks and non-binding instruments such as the Montreux Document/International Code of Conduct for Private Security and Military Companies (PMSCs) and the Programme of Action for Small and Light Weapons (PoA SALW)/International Tracing Instrument because those forums best reflected how the cyber CoP already conflated norms and law.

2 The Global Commission on the Stability of Cyberspace: Origins and Background

The GCSC was a multistakeholder initiative set up to promote the continued availability and resilience of the global internet, in light of increasing state or state-sponsored cyber operations that targeted core internet infrastructure like subsea cables and the Domain Name System (DNS). The initiative was flagged off by the government of the Netherlands in 2016, with an announcement by then Foreign Minister Bert Koenders at the Munich Security Conference. In his speech, Koenders argued the Commission could address "cyber stability" both by concentrating on the "stability of international relations between states and other actors in cyberspace", and the "stability of the cyber ecosystem as a whole […], especially the internet's backbone".[4] From the outset, therefore, the GCSC was tasked with a dual mandate to flag political and strategic considerations that underpinned "cyber stability" as well as to highlight the technical elements of the internet that needed protection from destructive cyber operations.

Following the Minister's announcement, the Netherlands government worked with the Hague Centre for Strategic Studies (HCSS), a Dutch think tank, to set up the Commission. The GCSC was based on two important pillars, which were explicitly identified in the early discussions leading up to the Commission's creation. Firstly, the GCSC was modeled along the lines of other international commissions, whose members while retaining their "capacity to act as high-profile and significant carriers of ideas" ultimately formed a "collective agency able to pursue a shared sense of the mental map or common vision" for global governance.[5] Secondly, the promoters of the GCSC were concerned about how the Commission would fit within the "regime complex" of institutions that governed cyberspace.[6] Mindful that extant discussions on cyber stability were driven by states, the GCSC understood the importance of being considered a helpful initiative by major powers. The Commission there-

4 *Speech by Foreign Minister Bert Koenders at the Munich Security Conference, February 12, 2016.*

5 *Correspondence with a GCSC Commissioner*; John English and Andrew F. Cooper, "International Commissions and the Mind of Global Governance," in *International Commissions and the Power of Ideas*, ed. Ramesh Thakur, Andrew F. Cooper, and John English, 1st ed. (United Nations University Press, 2005), 11.

6 *See generally*, Joseph S. Nye, Jr, "The Regime Complex for Managing Global Cyber Activities," Paper Series No.1 (Global Commission on internet Governance, May 2014), https://www.cigionline.org/sites/default/files/gcig_paper_no1.pdf.

fore pursued, as one of its main goals, a "vertical awareness"[7] of the cyber regime complex – i.e., helping states understand how high-level norms or rules would fit within the broader landscape of cybersecurity and internet governance, where key security and resilience functions were already being addressed through bottom-up participation from technical standards bodies and industry.

These founding tenets already created a conducive environment for "creeping expertise" within the GCSC. On the one hand, the Commission's dual political-technical mandate and its goal of creating a high-profile body to address this mandate necessitated the participation of reputed technical experts, international lawyers, scholars, and practitioners of international relations. On the other hand, its desire to bridge vertical silos of the cybersecurity regime complex also prompted the GCSC to bring in commissioners who were involved both in political discussions on cybersecurity governance and standard-setting discussions in technical internet governance bodies. As a result, the GCSC's work would be characterized by frequent and intensive discussions between, *inter alia,* technical experts, diplomats, and international lawyers.

The GCSC's work began with the setting up of an Inception Group, comprising individuals from the United States, the Netherlands, Australia, India, and Germany. This group, chaired by James Lewis of the United States, was tasked with identifying and recruiting commissioners, refining the objectives and terms of the GCSC, and, crucially, along with the HCSS and the East-West Institute in New York, sounding out governments for their views and potential engagement with the commission.[8] While HCSS and EWI comprised the GCSC Secretariat, the Commission was also supported by a Research Advisory Group. The Inception Group sought to balance three considerations in the composition of the GCSC: expertise, regional representation and gender balance. A third of the Commission, according to initial plans, was to be selected from among scholars and professionals involved in international cybersecurity policy. The remaining commissioners would be selected from technical experts, international lawyers, and representatives from internet governance bodies. The eventual objective of the GCSC, according to its Terms of Reference, was to "formulate and advance norms in an agenda common to all the affected stakeholders of international peace and security in

7 *Correspondence with a GCSC Commissioner.*

8 *Terms of Reference on the Inception Group for the Global Commission on the Stability of Cyberspace,* July 12, 2016.

and of cyberspace".[9] In addition to the government of the Netherlands, the Commission was able to secure initial funding from the internet Society (ISOC) and Microsoft, further entrenching the voice and participation of technical actors in its work.[10] The preparatory work of the Inception Group and the GCSC Secretariat eventually led to the formal launch of the Commission in January 2017, once again by the Dutch Foreign Minister Koenders at the Munich Security Conference. The first Full Commission Meeting – comprising the 28 commissioners, funders, and the RAG – was held for the first time in June 2017.

2.1 Practices of the Cyber Stability Commission

The previous chapter noted how the GCSC's creation was owed at least partly to the Dutch government's concern that the UN GGE, deadlocked between the US and Russia, would not be able to advance the "framework of responsible state behavior" in cyberspace. UN GGE reports and practices, as the chapter argued, were crucial to the CoP conflating norm-articulation and rule-interpretation. Following the failure of the 2016–2017 UN GGE to agree on a consensus report, the GCSC and other multistakeholder initiatives stepped in, articulating "voluntary norms"[11] that often borrowed the language of existing legal principles or were expressly grounded in international law.

The GCSC's "stepping in" to fill the vacuum left by the UN GGE process may appear smooth with the benefit of hindsight. Nonetheless, it needs emphasizing that the Commission, as a multistakeholder body, did not have a specific model or template to follow. The GCSC's decision to be an initiative that articulated cybersecurity norms is therefore as notable as the substance of the norms themselves. At the time of its establishment, the only comparable initiative to the GCSC was the Global Commission on internet Governance (also known as the Bildt Commission, after its chairman and former prime minister of Sweden, Carl Bildt). The Bildt Commission, whose term coincided with the work of the fourth UN GGE, offered broad commentary on norms that mir-

---

9 *Terms of Reference*, n.8.

10 "Global Commission on the Stability of Cyberspace – About," The Hague Centre for Strategic Studies (HCSS), accessed November 26, 2022, https://hcss.nl/global-commission-on-the-stability-of-cyberspace-about/.

11 "ADVANCING CYBERSTABILITY FINAL REPORT FACT SHEET" (Global Commission on the Stability of Cyberspace, November 2019), https://hcss.nl/wp-content/uploads/2022/08/GCSC-Fact-Sheet.pdf.

rored the debates in the GGE.[12] However, it refrained from articulating new cybersecurity norms. In contrast, the GCSC was not only clear from the time of its conceptualization that it intended to articulate new norms of behavior, but also expressly recognized the linkages between its work and that of the GGE. The Inception Group's deliberations coincided with those of the fifth GGE, and acknowledging that the 2016–2017 GGE could be the last such group, it sought to understand what could replace the process, and explore the GCSC's future role in the cybersecurity regime complex.[13] Indeed, the final GCSC report even lists the norms articulated by the 2014–2015 GGE, and argues that the goal of the Commission was to "supplement and not duplicate" the work of other norm-setting institutions.[14] A draft concept note published by the Commission in 2016 argued that "without further norms on state behavior in cyberspace, [offensive cyber operations] can lead to inadvertent escalation and disproportional response."[15]

Therefore, it is clear that the GCSC compared itself to the GGE process and, in doing so, also reinforced the GGE's own conflation of norms and existing international law. Whereas the GGE sought through its reports to club "norms, rules and principles" together in its framework for "responsible state behavior" in cyberspace, the GCSC did the same through its "cyber stability framework". The "development and implementation of voluntary norms" was a core aspect of this framework but so was "adherence to international law".[16] However, the Commission did not clarify how these two pillars of the "cyber stability framework" interacted with each other. Moreover, the GCSC's final report also argued that "there must be meaningful consequences for violations of norms *and* international law"[17] [emphasis added], which cast the "voluntary" nature of norms into doubt, but also compared them to applications of international law to cyberspace. For example, the Commission suggested that the "principle of due diligence may [prove] helpful in defining the level of care required from states" for implementing norms.[18] Additionally, the GCSC report hinted that the customary law of state responsibility could help frame the "accountability"

12 "Global Commission on internet Governance | One internet" (Centre for International Governance Innovation and The Royal Institute for International Affairs, 2016), 69–77, https://www.cigionline.org/static/documents/gcig_final_report_-_with_cover.pdf.

13 *Interview with Samir Saran*, October 26, 2022.

14 GCSC Final Report, 8.

15 *Correspondence with a GCSC Commissioner.*

16 GCSC Final Report, 14.

17 GCSC Final Report, 24.

18 GCSC Final Report, 24.

of states for norms violations.[19] Thus, the GCSC identified and presented itself before the cyber CoP as a multistakeholder entity offering a "framework" of responsible behavior that included both voluntary norms and binding international law.

2.1.1 Needed: "A Strong Knowledge of International Law"

What were the practices of the Commission that led to its own conflation of norms and existing international law? The recruitment practices of the GCSC and its Research Advisory Group (RAG) offer some insights. Norm articulation may have been the focus of the GCSC's work, but in the early stages of planning, the GCSC's promoters earmarked some "seats" in the Commission to be represented by legal academics, policy professionals, and policymakers with a background in international law. Its eventual composition included the three camps: the GCSC's first chair, Marina Kaljurand, was a politician with formal training in international law;[20] her successor and co-chair, Michael Chertoff, the former US Secretary of Homeland Security, was also a lawyer;[21] and the Commission also included Jonathan Zittrain, a professor of international law at Harvard University.[22] If the Chair of the RAG, Sean Kanuck, was a policy professional trained in international law, the Deputy Chair for Law – deputy chairs of the RAG were "acknowledged experts in specific fields" – Liis Vihul, was not only a recognized international cybersecurity lawyer, but was also the managing director of the Tallinn Manual 2.0 project.[23]

The presence of international lawyers among the GCSC's membership and RAG likely influenced the Group's "request for proposals (RFP)" for memos and working papers from external researchers and analysts. On two occasions, the GCSC issued RFPs for researchers to submit papers that would be presented to the Commission during its scheduled meetings. Each RFP advertised four to five themes of interest to the Commission: the first RFP invited papers that mapped cyber norms and diplomatic initiatives, and the extent to which

19 GCSC Final Report, 24.

20 "Curriculum Vitae | Marina KALJURAND | MEPs | European Parliament," MEPs | European Parliament, https://www.europarl.europa.eu/meps/en/197491/MARINA_KALJURAND/cv.

21 "Michael Chertoff – Co-Founder and Executive Chairman," *The Chertoff Group*, January 1, 2022, https://chertoffgroup.com/michael-chertoff-co-founder-and-executive-chairman/.

22 "Jonathan L. Zittrain," Harvard Law School, accessed September 18, 2025, https://hls.harvard.edu/faculty/jonathan-l-zittrain/.

23 *Global Commission on the Stability of Cyberspace – About*, n.10.

such initiatives dealt with critical information infrastructure. The second RFP addressed specific, substantive concerns such as:[24]

a. discussion formats that could continue the work of the GGE; and
b. defining and categorizing offensive cyber capabilities, and determine what constitutes a "cyber weapon".

Some of these RFPs specifically solicited contributions from applicants "who show that they have a strong knowledge of international law", while others such as the one on offensive cyber capabilities required candidates to have "experience in, or aptitude for, understanding the procedures of international institutions and the application of international law".[25] The latter RFP related to an effort by the Commission to inform its deliberations on a norm against offensive cyber operations by non-state actors. The RFP clearly stated that the "purpose [of memos and working papers] would be to identify existing frameworks [on 'hack backs' and countermeasures] and then provide critical analysis that builds upon those taxonomies". By inviting the contribution of international lawyers in this manner to guide its own work, the GCSC's norms arguably became intertwined with legal concepts and principles. This despite the Commission's own caveat that it did not focus primarily on international law.[26] The GCSC sought to articulate voluntary norms that identified and plugged gaps in the "framework of responsible state behavior" but by grounding them in existing rules, it arguably contributed to the development of international cybersecurity law. "When I was first approached by the Dutch government [to join the GCSC], I think they did not have a full picture what they wanted, but later we had detailed discussions with the two co-chairs of the GCSC secretariat, and it was clear that we wanted to work on norms," said Kaljurand.[27] "***Because we felt that international law was still far away, and it wasn't realistic*** [***to address them***]***. The GGE was doing something, and had its very good norms, but there was something missing. So, we thought we will look at the picture that we have and try to*** **fill in some of the norms** ***that are critical and needed***" [emphasis added].

24 "GCSC Request for Proposals: Call for Research [Closed]," GCSC [Archived], accessed June 23, 2021, https://web.archive.org/web/20210423120218/https://cyberstability.org/wp-content/uploads/2017/12/GCSC_Request_For_Proposals_2018.pdf.

25 *GCSC Request for Proposals*, n.24.

26 GCSC Final Report, 14.

27 *Interview with Marina Kaljurand*, October 7, 2021.

2.2 Creeping Expertise in the GCSC Norms

With the GCSC linking its articulation of norms with the application of international law to cyberspace, technical experts were able to influence the development of international cybersecurity law through the Commission's norms. The following paragraphs explain the underlying mechanism of "creeping expertise" within the GCSC.

At the outset, it is important to highlight the intensive involvement of technical experts in the GCSC norms-articulation process. The technical community, which included technology companies, standard-setting and internet governance bodies, and cybersecurity agencies, was especially well-represented through eight GCSC commissioners. At least one technical expert associated with the Commission, who did not wish to be identified for reasons of confidentiality, was an active participant (through their country's nominated delegation) in concurrent UN GGE negotiations.[28] These technical experts were not only ambassadors of the GCSC to their respective communities, but also became conduits for the Commission and its Research Advisory Groups to learn from the work of other, external technical experts. For instance, the GCSC hosted a lunch at the IETF 102 meeting in Montreal, where three technical expert-Commissioners presented two of the Commission's proposed norms to the engineering standards community.[29] Just as importantly, these Commissioners helped orchestrate GCSC meetings alongside other important gatherings of technical experts. Such gatherings included:

- CyCon, Tallinn, May 2017
- Black Hat USA, Las Vegas, July 2017
- Israel Cyber Week, Tel Aviv, June 2018
- Singapore International Cyber Week, Singapore, September 2018
- ICANN 64 Meeting, Kobe, March 2019
- ICANN 65 Meeting, Marrakesh, June 2019
- Global Forum for Cyber Expertise Annual Meeting (hosted by the African Union), Addis Ababa, October 2019

Many of these meetings were "Full Commission meetings", which involved not only the GCSC Commissioners, but also RAG members as well as external

28 *Interview with a technical expert*, November 19, 2020.

29 Megan Kruse, "At IETF 102: The Global Commission on the Stability of Cyberspace – Cyber Diplomacy Meets InfoSec and Technology," *internet Society* (blog), June 26, 2018, https://www.internetsociety.org/blog/2018/06/at-ietf-102-the-global-commission-on-the-stability-of-cyberspace-cyber-diplomacy-meets-infosec-and-technology/.

researchers, including international lawyers.[30] Alongside face-to-face interactions between technical experts and international lawyers under the aegis of these conferences and gatherings, the GCSC's RAG also maintained a mailing list for the technical community to offer its feedback on specific Commission proposals.[31]

Unsurprisingly, therefore, all GCSC norms – the Commission published a total of eight norms – had a technical component.[32] As noted previously, one of the main goals of the GCSC was itself the protection of core, technical infrastructure key to the continued availability of the internet, otherwise called the "public core of the internet". In other cases, those norms addressed state and non-state actor behavior on key technical issues such as the disclosure of ICT vulnerabilities or tampering with ICT products in the development and production stages. The precise formulation and technical scope of each norm were often subject to multiple rounds of correspondence between the Commissioners.[33] This appears very much to have been intended. Reflecting on the nature of norms-articulation in its final report, the GCSC notes that "finding the most appropriate language to express a norm can be challenging".[34] Worded too precisely, norms may not "achieve consensus" and may leave "significant gaps in coverage". On the other hand, vague drafting would come at the cost of clear guidance to states and non-state actors. The Commission specifically noted that it sought to draft norms to "encourage common behavior in the future" and not "codify existing practice".[35]

While it reflected on the need to articulate aspirational norms and turn "desirable" behavior into "normative" behavior by encouraging their adoption, the GCSC did not refer to the role international law played in the norms-articulation process. While discussions at the GCSC on norms focused on political and technical aspects of cybersecurity governance, some of these norms were connected tacitly and habitually to international law through

---

30 For a list of the GCSC's Full Commission Meetings, *see*, "MEETING WITH ICANN GOVERNMENTAL ADVISORY COMMITTEE | ICANN 65, Marrakesh" (Global Commission on the Stability of Cyberspace, June 27, 2019), https://gac.icann.org/presentations/public/ICANN65-13.1-GCSC.pdf?language_id=1.

31 "The GCSC Research Advisory Group Is Recruiting," HCSS, June 26, 2017, https://hcss.nl/news/the-gcsc-research-advisory-group-is-recruiting/.

32 "Global Commission on the Stability of Cyberspace – Norms," HCSS, accessed November 27, 2022, https://hcss.nl/gcsc-norms/.

33 *Six GCSC commissioners, one member of an RAG of the Commission, and three individuals associated with institutions promoting or sponsoring the GCSC were interviewed for this chapter.*

34 GCSC Final Report, 22.

35 GCSC Final Report, 23.

"background" papers and "additional notes". Even in the absence of a formal law-identification or interpretation exercise – drawing on Kaljurand's interview, it would seem the GCSC did not want to engage in international law interpretation *per se*, given political sensitivities at the 2016–2017 GGE – international law was freely referenced in such commentary to these norms. And because some norms in which technical experts played a key role as drafters and interpreters came thus to be defended on the basis of existing rules, technical experts came indirectly to shape the evolution of international cybersecurity law.

Specifically, I present evidence of "creeping expertise" in the following three norms published by the Commission:

a. Norm on non-interference with the public core;
b. Norm to protect electoral infrastructure;
c. Norm against offensive cyber operations by non-state actors.

2.2.1 Norm on Non-interference with the Public Core

The "public core" of the internet refers to critical infrastructure resources that are transnational in character, and essential to maintaining the general availability and integrity of the internet.[36] These resources include physical infrastructure such as root servers and Domain Name System (DNS) resolvers, subsea cables facilitating the transcontinental flow of data, satellite internet services, key internet organizations such as regional internet registries and internet Exchange Points, as well as intangible, universal technical protocols such as TCP/IP and SSL that lay down specifications for the flow and security of data packets across digital networks. The protection of the "public core" – a term coined by the Netherlands Scientific Council for Government Policy – from destructive cyber operations has been among the diplomatic priorities of the Dutch government since 2016.[37] One of the primary objectives of the GCSC was to explore the scope of public core protections, and frame a norm governing state behavior around it. The protection of the public core is addressed in Chapter 6 as a standalone illustration of "creeping expertise", given that the GCSC norm was itself based on, and evolved from

36 *See*, "The Public Core of the internet. An International Agenda for internet Governance – Report – The Netherlands Scientific Council for Government Policy," rapport (Ministerie van Algemene Zaken, October 1, 2015), https://doi.org/10/01/the-public-core-of-the-internet.

37 Alexey Trepykhalin and Veni Markovski, "Country Focus Report: The Netherlands and the 'Public Core of the internet'" (ICANN, 2021), https://www.icann.org/en/system/files/files/ge-008-28may21-en.pdf.

prior deliberations outside the Commission, and was subsequently deliberated by the UN GGE and OEWG, as well as the Paris Call Working Group 4 on Advancing International Norms. It suffices to note here that the scope of this norm and its basis in international law was the outcome of extensive deliberations between technical experts and international lawyers.

2.2.2 Norm to Protect Electoral Infrastructure

In June 2018, GCSC published a norm against the disruption of elections through cyber operations. The norm read:

> State and non-state actors should not pursue, support, or allow cyber operations intended to disrupt the technical infrastructure essential to elections, referenda, or plebiscites.[38]

The norm is notable for the precise and somewhat limited scope of protection it seeks to afford for electoral processes. The GCSC's background note to the norm emphasizes that "the actual conduct of elections or participatory processes at the regional, local or federal level is firmly the remit of states, to be carried out in accordance with their respective national laws".[39] The norm's focus is instead only on the protection of the technical infrastructure meant to implement those processes.

Why did the GCSC choose thus to limit the scope of its norm to technical electoral infrastructure? In an interview, a GCSC commissioner said, "[the norm] was good, but it was low-hanging fruit. I mean, it was addressed [only] for election machines, infrastructure, etc. We had a debate about this: 'Is this really in our mandate?' Our mandate was critical infrastructure and cyber stability – is [election interference] really part of that, or are we biting off a large issue [that we can't chew]? And we decided, you know, that election infrastructure was critical infrastructure. That fit the mandate, and we also figured that it would be impossible to come to any real conclusion about disinformation operations [which could count as election interference]."[40]

---

38 "Norm Proposal | Global Commission Urges Protecting Electoral Infrastructure," HCSS, accessed November 27, 2022, https://hcss.nl/report/norm-proposal-global-commission-urges-protecting-electoral-infrastructure/. (Disclosure: this author provided some background inputs to the drafting of this norm.)

39 "CALL TO PROTECT THE ELECTORAL INFRASTRUCTURE" (Bratislava: Global Commission on the Stability of Cyberspace, May 2018), https://hcss.nl/wp-content/uploads/2022/08/GCSC-Call-to-Protect-Electoral-Infrastructure.pdf.

40 *Interview with Christopher Painter*, August 30, 2021.

The decision by the GCSC to interpret its mandate narrowly was, as noted above, likely influenced by political and technical considerations. The previous chapter highlighted how discussions at the UN GGE since 2015 were shaped by Great Power rivalry, especially as US–Russia relations worsened in the aftermath of cyber-enabled Russian interference in the 2016 US presidential elections. By the time the GCSC began deliberations on this norm, and eventually published it, the fifth GGE had failed to arrive at a consensus report. Election interference, an underlying political factor that restricted room for compromise within the GGE, was therefore a fraught subject. The GCSC's background note for the norm seems to suggest that the Commission was mindful of these sensitivities, and consciously avoided an expansive treatment of the topic.

Technical expertise also played an important role in shaping the GCSC's decision. A survey conducted among the technical community in late 2017 by the GCSC's Working Group on Critical Infrastructure Assessment saw respondents overwhelmingly qualify election infrastructure as critical infrastructure.[41] In this survey, respondents were asked to "consider the internet-accessible and ICT-enabled aspects of these sectors and systems [and tell the GCSC] whether [...] they are or are not worthy of protection in a cybersecurity norm." "Systems supporting the functioning of government and democratic institutions [such as] citizenship databases and voter rolls, voting systems, the public and private communications of electoral candidates" could definitely be considered critical infrastructure, respondents agreed. The response of technical experts arguably affirmed the Commission's view that the norm on protecting electoral infrastructure was within its remit, despite political sensitivities.

The GCSC's "background" paper to the norm provides a striking example of how the articulation of voluntary norms and the interpretation of existing rules were conflated. On the one hand, an introductory footnote to the paper declares: "Norms are voluntary, non-binding commitments. Over time they can crystallize into international law."[42] This statement gives the impression, which is supported by the GCSC Final Report, that GCSC norms do not reflect existing international law, but are aspirational statements from the Commission that may become part of binding rules down the road. However, the background paper also notes at the end that its norm to protect technical electoral infrastructure "merely affirms the numerous international legal pro-

41 "Report of the GCSC Critical Infrastructure Assessment Working Group" (New Delhi: Global Commission on the Stability of Cyberspace, November 20, 2017), 21.

42 *CALL TO PROTECT THE ELECTORAL INFRASTRUCTURE*, n.39.

tections already afforded against external interference in the internal affairs of another state". The lack of clarity on the precise status of norms in relation to international law leaves the door open as to whether the Commission's commentary on the protection of technical election infrastructure is an interpretation of the non-intervention rule in the case at hand. Indeed, the paper could be read as making the case for why external interference against elections should be interpreted specifically and narrowly as the Commission has done.

In this manner, the GCSC arguably interpreted (and made the case for interpreting) cyber election interference differently from "traditional" or physical forms of external interference. The customary rule on prohibited interventions has two elements: the intervention must bear on "matters in which each State is permitted, by the principle of State sovereignty, to decide freely", and secondly, there must be an element of coercion involved.[43] While there is no doubt that the conduct of elections falls within the *domaine reserve* of a state, it is questionable whether all cyber-enabled election interference would qualify as "coercion".[44] The GCSC's formulation suggested that cyber operations on technical electoral infrastructure, regardless of their political consequences, would qualify as coercive measures prohibited under international law. Indeed, all operations that "intended to disrupt" technical infrastructure for elections would be covered by this norm – even actual technical disruption was not necessary.

To understand the significance of the GCSC's pronouncement, it is important to evaluate it alongside other views on the legality of cyber-enabled foreign election interference by states and legal scholars. At the time of the GCSC's publication of this norm, only a handful of states and scholars had offered their views on the topic. The United States, for instance, noted in 2017 that "a cyber operation by a State that interferes with another country's ability *to hold an election* or that manipulates another country's *election results* would be a clear violation of the rule of non – intervention" [emphases added].[45] The United Kingdom, which published its views on the topic almost at the same time as the GCSC, declared that "the use by a hostile state of cyber

43 *Military and Paramilitary Activities in and Against Nicaragua* (Nicaragua v. U.S.), 1986 ICJ 14, 205 (hereafter "*Nicaragua case*").

44 Chapter 4 summarizes in detail the debate among international lawyers on this topic in the context of the Oxford Process statement on foreign election interference, which was published in 2022, four years after the GCSC articulated this norm.

45 Brian Egan, "Remarks on International Law and Stability in Cyberspace," U.S. Department of State, November 10, 2016, https://2009-2017.state.gov/s/l/releases/remarks/264303.htm.

operations to manipulate the electoral system *to alter the results of an election* in another state" would breach the non-intervention rule [emphasis added].[46] The US and UK thus weigh the coercive nature of a cyber operation on electoral infrastructure against its impact on the outcomes of the electoral process or the ability of a state to hold it altogether. This is arguably a high threshold to meet. The Tallinn Manual 2.0 International Group of Experts (2017) defined coercion as an "affirmative act designed to deprive another State of its freedom of choice, that is, to force that State to act in an involuntary manner or involuntarily refrain from acting in a particular way".[47] The Tallinn Manual arguably offered a broader lens from which to interpret coercion, although the Manual's Experts also focused only on election-altering cyber operations. To be sure, the director of the Tallinn Manual 2.0 project, Michael Schmitt had previously argued that "cyber operations [that] manipulated the process of elections and therefore *caused them to unfold in a way that they otherwise would not have*" [emphasis added] could be considered coercive.[48] In contrast, the GCSC's norm takes a stricter view of non-intervention, prohibiting attempted disruptions to the technical infrastructure itself, irrespective of the impact of such disruptions on the overall electoral process.

Has the GCSC's view been adopted by states or scholars? Since the publication of the GCSC's norm, more states have offered their views on the topic, and indeed, on the broader topic of coercion in cyberspace. While the Australian position appears to be closer to that of the UK – linking coercive cyber interference to the altering of electoral outcomes[49] – the Israeli view is aligned with that of the United States, which includes interference in a country's "ability to hold an election".[50] Finland, meanwhile, acknowledges that not all methods of

---

46 The Attorney General's Office, "Cyber and International Law in the 21st Century," GOV.UK, May 23, 2018, https://www.gov.uk/government/speeches/cyber-and-international-law-in-the-21st-century.

47 Michael N. Schmitt, ed., *Tallinn Manual 2.0 on the International Law Applicable to Cyber Operations*, 1st ed. (Cambridge University Press, 2017), 317 (hereafter "TM 2.0").

48 Michael N. Schmitt, "Grey Zones in the International Law of Cyberspace," *Yale Journal of International Law Online* 42, no. 2 (2017), https://cpb-us-w2.wpmucdn.com/campuspress.yale.edu/dist/8/1581/files/2017/08/Schmitt_Grey-Areas-in-the-International-Law-of-Cyberspace-1cab8kj.pdf.

49 "Annex B: Australia's Position on How International Law Applies to State Conduct in Cyberspace | Australia's International Cyber and Critical Tech Engagement," Australian Government, accessed November 27, 2022, https://www.internationalcybertech.gov.au/our-work/annexes/annex-b.

50 Roy Schöndorf, "Israel's Perspective on Key Legal and Practical Issues Concerning the Application of International Law to Cyber Operations," *International Law Studies* 97 (2021), 403.

electoral interference display the element of coercion, but "serious" operations such as "hacking of voter databases or manipulation of vote counts *in order to alter the election results* count as coercive" [emphasis added].[51] The Finnish view, again, emphasizes the purported political objective of the operation in order to evaluate its coercive nature.

Germany, on the other hand, notes that the "disabling of election infrastructure and technology" through cyber means could violate the non-intervention rule, including where such disruptions "prevent the holding of an election".[52] The German position does not take the same view as the GCSC – the mere targeting or disruption of election infrastructure is not enough – but comes close to acknowledging the importance of such infrastructure and the legal consequences of disabling it.

So, the GCSC view appears at first blush to be a minority view, but significant nonetheless because of the involvement of the technical community in articulating this norm. Furthermore, as the next chapter shows, the view that coercion in cyberspace and coercive cyber interference in electoral processes should be interpreted broadly is gaining traction. "If a state assumes control over another state's governmental systems [...] and manipulates their operation, this would amount to coercion to the extent that the systems operate counterintuitively to how they were programed to operate by the victim state, and produce actions and effects desired by the intervener," writes Nicholas Tsagourias in the context of election interference.[53] Similarly, in a more recent article, Schmitt distinguishes between cyber operations that "affect the State's *ability* to conduct an election from those that target voter *attitudes*". He argues that targeted operations that hamper the state's ability to conduct the

51 "International Law and Cyberspace | Finland's National Positions" (Ministry of Foreign Affairs, Finland), accessed November 27, 2022, https://um.fi/documents/35732/0/Cyber±and±international±law%3B±Finland%27s±views.pdf/41404cbb-d300-a3b9-92e4-a7d675d5d585?t=1602758856859.

52 "Official Compendium of Voluntary National Contributions on the Subject of How International Law Applies to the Use of Information and Communications Technologies by States Submitted by Participating Governmental Experts in the Group of Governmental Experts on Advancing Responsible State Behaviour in Cyberspace in the Context of International Security Established Pursuant to General Assembly Resolution 73/266" (UN General Assembly, Seventy-sixth session, July 13, 2021), 35, https://front.un-arm.org/wp-content/uploads/2021/08/A-76-136-EN.pdf.

53 Nicholas Tsagourias, "Electoral Cyber Interference, Self-Determination, Non-Intervention," in *Governing Cyberspace: Behavior, Power and Diplomacy*, ed. Dennis Broeders and Bibi van den Berg, 1st ed. (London: Rowman & Littlefield, 2020), 53.

electoral process smoothly are "almost always coercive".[54] The Oxford Process on International Law Protections in Cyberspace dedicated two workshops specifically to foreign election interference and information operations, and the subject of what constitutes "coercive" cyber behavior was among its most discussed points.

The UK government in a re-calibration of its earlier position on the applicability of international law to cyberspace, has gone further than most. In a speech delivered by the Attorney General at Chatham House in May 2022, the UK declared that "a cyber operation to *delay* another State's election" is "certainly [a form] of coercion"[55] [emphasis added]. Moreover, the UK position asks states to consider "whether disruptive cyber behaviors are coercive *even where it might not be possible to point to a specific course of conduct which a State has been forced into or prevented from taking*" [emphasis added]. The UK position therefore reflects a crystallization of the GCSC norm, insofar as attempts to disrupt the functioning of election infrastructure alone could themselves be considered in breach of the non-intervention rule. The UK's focus on the "coercive effect on the target of the [cyber] operation" rather than the "target state's choice" through such an operation may not be agreeable to all other states. Still, the fact remains that the GCSC was among the first institutions to articulate a distinct view to this effect, and the role of technical experts in helping the Commission articulate it is notable.

Mindful perhaps of the ongoing debate among states on coercion and non-intervention in cyberspace, the Commission itself walked back its views in its final 2019 report. "Experts have debated whether the type of cyber-related election interference recently seen amount [to] an unlawful intervention," the Commission noted, citing prominent international law scholars. "In recommending this norm, the Commission merely affirms that election interference is intolerable whether it is considered to be a violation of international law or not."[56] While this confusing statement does not clarify the Commission's position on what constitutes a prohibited cyber intervention vis-à-vis election interference, the norm can be considered an example of "creeping expertise" in international cybersecurity law.

54 Michael N Schmitt, "Foreign Cyber Interference in Elections," *International Law Studies* 97 (2021): 746.

55 The Attorney General's Office, "International Law in Future Frontiers," GOV.UK, May 19, 2022, https://www.gov.uk/government/speeches/international-law-in-future-frontiers (hereafter "2022 UK statement").

56 *Global Commission on the Stability of Cyberspace – Norms*, N.32.

2.2.3 Norm against "Hack Backs" by Non-state Actors

In November 2018, the GCSC released a "package" of six norms, which included a norm on the prohibition of offensive cyber operations by non-state actors.[57] The norm read:

> Non-state actors should not engage in offensive cyber operations and state actors should prevent and respond to such activities if they occur.[58]

The context surrounding the norm's development and articulation is important. Like the norm on election interference, the one on "hack backs" was driven also by technical and political considerations. The norm against "hack backs" found support among the technical community and industry, given the risks of involving private actors as parties to geopolitical conflict or potentially destabilizing conduct in cyberspace. In particular, Microsoft – a key sponsor of the GCSC that was also represented in the Commission – had been an advocate for greater self-restraint in cyberspace by the private sector, and through private initiatives like the Cybersecurity Tech Accord, sought commitments from technology companies to "not help governments launch cyberattacks against innocent citizens and enterprises from anywhere".[59] Microsoft and other corporations that "signed" the Tech Accord had legitimate self-interests in championing this norm: as global technology companies operating across jurisdictions, they not only sought to avoid being targets of serious state-sponsored cyber attacks, but were also wary of states requesting their platforms or networks as attack surfaces for cyber operations during armed conflict. Being caught in the crosshairs of such conflict would seriously undermine consumer trust in the products and services of such companies. In 2017, Microsoft advocated the creation of a "Digital Geneva Convention", calling for global technology companies to be treated as "Digital Switzerlands", i.e., "trusted and neutral" platforms that could "protect the internet and customers everywhere

57 "Norm Package Singapore | Global Commission Introduces Six Critical Norms Towards Cyber Stability," HCSS, accessed November 27, 2022, https://hcss.nl/report/norm-package-singapore-global-commission-introduces-six-critical-norms-towards-cyber-stability/.

58 *Ibid.*

59 "Cybersecurity Tech Accord," *Cybersecurity Tech Accord* (blog), accessed November 27, 2022, https://cybertechaccord.org/accord/.

from nation-state attacks".[60] "[Technology companies] should pledge that we'll continue to take no efforts to assist in offensive actions anywhere," wrote Brad Smith, Microsoft's President and Chief Legal Officer.

Microsoft's views resonated not only with several global technology companies but also among independent technical experts,[61] including those responsible for the development of internet standards. "When I heard a presentation from [a] professional in a global company saying we have the right to hack back… that [often results in] a preemptive strike in technical terms," said Sherif Heshem a former UN GGE Expert and technical expert.[62] "Now, not just countries are talking about it, but a lot of global companies. So instead of 190-plus countries, you [will] have thousands of companies across the globe who [claim] the right to hack back. [This will result in] a chaotic environment." ISOC, another key sponsor of the GCSC, also voiced its opposition to private hack backs. "'Hacking back' laws are a recipe for major international disputes, even if they are only authorized within a country", said an ISOC representative at the time. "It's practically impossible to effectively restrict the effects of 'hacking back' to national borders, and there's the risk that a private entity could be inadvertently hacking a foreign nation's networks or systems, an act that could be regarded as an attack against the nation, its interests or its citizens."[63]

Legislative proposals on hack backs by major cyber powers also lent urgency to the need for such a norm. In 2017, a US Congressman introduced a draft bill – titled the Active Cyber Defense Certainty (ACDC) Act[64] – that sought to exempt companies from criminal liability for unauthorized intrusions into a third party's networks for the purposes of:

a. attributing its criminal activity and sharing such information with law enforcement agencies;
b. disrupting ongoing cyber operations undertaken by that party; or
c. monitoring malicious cyber activity to prevent future intrusions.

---

60 Brad Smith, "The Need for a Digital Geneva Convention," Microsoft On the Issues, February 14, 2017, https://blogs.microsoft.com/on-the-issues/2017/02/14/need-digital-geneva-convention/.

61 Sara Sorcher, "Influencers: Companies Should Not Be Allowed to Hack Back," *Christian Science Monitor*, April 1, 2015, https://www.csmonitor.com/World/Passcode/Passcode-Influencers/2015/0401/Influencers-Companies-should-not-be-allowed-to-hack-back.

62 *Interview with Sherif Heshem*, November 24, 2020.

63 UDT, "US 'Hacking Back' Law Could Create a Cyber Wild West of Vigilantism," *UDT* (blog), July 3, 2018, https://udtonline.com/us-hacking-back-law-could-create-a-cyber-wild-west-of-vigilantism-jeff-engle/.

64 Tom Graves, "Active Cyber Defense Certainty Act," Pub. L. No. H. R. 4036 (2017), https://www.congress.gov/bill/115th-congress/house-bill/4036/text?q=%7B%22search%22%3A%5B%22Active±Cyber±Defense±Certainty±Act%22%5D%7D&r=1.

Similarly, the German government in 2017 reportedly considered introducing policy measures permitting hack backs by law enforcement and intelligence agencies against serious criminal activity in cyberspace.[65] Although the proposal reportedly limited such powers to government entities, it envisaged active cooperation from the private sector, including their introduction (for potential exploitation by law enforcement) of backdoors in their products and services.[66] With policy proposals of this sort being considered by advanced digital economies, experts from the technical community and industry recognized the need for a global effort to proscribe hack backs by private actors. Furthermore, the consideration of draft laws on hack backs by their respective legislatures also likely constrained diplomats from committing to intergovernmental norms on the precise role of the private sector vis-à-vis cyber operations. As a result, to expect the (already politically deadlocked) UN GGE to address this topic would have been unrealistic.

To be sure, the technical community/industry was not alone in advocating a norm against hack backs by private actors. They found a powerful supporter in France, which has been outspoken on the topic, and who, alongside ISOC and Microsoft, was also a sponsor of the GCSC.[67] As a result of these factors, and in part due to the advocacy of technical experts, the GCSC became the first prominent norms initiative to articulate a prohibition on hack backs by private actors.

Remarkably, the norm not only included a background note explaining its contents, but also an "additional note" grounding the norm in international law.[68] Although, as this section has underlined, some of the norms published

65 "Reports: Berlin Plans Cyberattack 'hackback' – DW – 04/20/2017," dw.com, accessed November 27, 2022, https://www.dw.com/en/reports-german-government-plans-cyberattack-hackback-ahead-of-election/a-38506101.

66 Pierluigi Paganini, "German Government Prepares Law for Backdoors and Hacking Back," Security Affairs, December 5, 2017, https://securityaffairs.co/wordpress/66370/digital-id/german-government-backdoors-law.html.

67 Glyn Moody, "France Says 'No' to Company Hack-Backs Following Online Attacks – But Wants to Keep the Option Open for Itself," Techdirt, February 20, 2018, https://www.techdirt.com/2018/02/20/france-says-no-to-company-hack-backs-following-online-attacks-wants-to-keep-option-open-itself/.

68 "NORM PACKAGE SINGAPORE" (Singapore: Global Commission on the Stability of Cyberspace, November 2018), 19, https://hcss.nl/wp-content/uploads/2022/08/GCSC-Singapore-Norm-Package-3MB.pdf; "ADDITIONAL NOTE TO THE NORM AGAINST OFFENSIVE CYBER OPERATIONS BY NON-STATE ACTORS (Archived)" (Singapore: Global Commission on the Stability of Cyberspace, August 7, 2022), https://web.archive.org/web/20220807221137/http://cyberstability.org/wp-content/uploads/2018/11/

by the GCSC referred to international law, this was the only norm had a separate note on international law appended to it. The practice of appending such a note provided a good opportunity for technical experts to help expound the substantive scope of this norm as well as the legality of private hack backs. The following paragraphs analyze the background note and the additional note on international law in detail.

The background note to the norm observed "states have a monopoly on the legitimate use of force, strictly bound by international law", but that some non-state actors have advocated for the "right to conduct offensive cyber operations across national borders, potentially claiming that it constitutes 'self-defense'". "These non-state actors' offensive cyber operations are sometimes euphemistically referred to as 'active cyber defense,' including but not limited to so-called 'hack-backs,' as they are conducted for defensive purposes." While noting that some states have proposed "legitimizing" hack-back operations, the Commission emphasized that such offensive operations "undermine the stability of cyberspace" and were likely to "trigger complex international legal disputes" with injured third parties. Offensive measures should be "reserved solely to states", and "if states permit such action, they may [be] held responsible under international law", the note concluded.

The additional note on international law focused on state responsibility for allowing or orchestrating private hack backs. It scopes out a maximalist position, arguing any hack backs by companies could trigger the obligations of states in most cases. Such an approach is likely to have been prompted by the realization that the actions of private actors themselves are unregulated by public international law, and the Commission would have run into difficulty outlining the scope of a rule where none existed. For instance, the Tallinn Manual argues that "non-State actors are not entitled to take countermeasures [because] there is no underlying international law basis for the private entity's operations".[69] However, were a private actor to hack back against a state adversary's network, it would "have violated no customary rule of general international law", the Manual notes.[70] Therefore, the only feasible option available to the GCSC was to define private hack backs in such a way that it would almost always lead to the responsibility of states. The GCSC's definition of private hack backs – or more precisely, "active cyber defense" – is a technical one, which the Commission then uses as the

Additional-Note-to-the-Norm-Against-Offensive-Cyber-Operations-by-Non-state-Actors-Norm-Package-Singapore.pdf.

69 *TM* 2.0, 39.

70 *TM* 2.0, 130.

baseline for invoking the legal obligation of states with respect to such operations. In short, what the GCSC sought to do was not so much interpret the legality of private hack back operations under international law, but define it in such a way that most such operations would be impermissible under state-centric legal regimes.

The GCSC arguably offered a more expansive approach to regulating "hack backs" under international law, than in comparison to the Tallinn Manual 2.0, which also addressed the topic. TM 2.0 notes through the example of the 2014 Sony hack that Sony had no recourse to hacking back against North Korea, the alleged perpetrator of the cyber attack. Had Sony hacked back, "it might have raised the issue of due diligence on the part of the United States", the Manual notes. In this regard, both the GCSC and TM 2.0 tie the issue of hack backs to the responsibility of states. But the devil may be in the detail, or specifically, in the definition by both groups of "active cyber defense" and hack backs. The GCSC's additional note defined "active cyber defense" as a set of "measures ranging from self-defense on the victim's network to destructive activity on the attacker's network". "Offensive cyber operations within this continuum imply for the defender to act outside of its own network *independently of their intention (offense or defense) and the legal qualification of their acts*", the note read [emphasis added]. The Tallinn Manual 2.0 glossary, on the other hand, defines active cyber defense as the "taking of proactive defense measures outside the defended cyber infrastructure".[71] Hack backs are operations to mitigate, stop, or gather evidence for the sake of attributing an "identified source" of malicious cyber operations.[72] The GCSC's definition is arguably broader in scope and covers a wider range of intrusive measures. More importantly, the GCSC note explicitly rejects any possibility that "legal qualifications" within domestic law could be used to justify hack backs. The Tallinn Manual, which is more conservative in its judgment of hack backs, could be interpreted as more accommodating of state practice in this regard.

The Commission's note indeed went on to argue that such offensive cyber operations by private actors should be "prohibited by states in their domestic legislation". If the state "granted such possibilities to a non-state actor, it may lead to a violation of [the state's] international obligations". Specifically, the GCSC invoked both the rules on state responsibility and due diligence in this regard. Where states decided to "involve" non-state actors to "act on their behalf", the actions of those private actors would "generally be considered as the acts of the states". Similarly, where a state "permitted" non-state actors to

71 *TM 2.0*, 563.

72 *TM 2.0*, 565.

engage in offensive cyber operations, the note argued, it could result in a situation where the state is in breach of its due diligence obligation. The application of the state responsibility and due diligence regimes by the GCSC in this context is interesting. The responsibility of a state can be invoked only when it is in breach of an international obligation. Mindful perhaps of the possibility of states (like the US and Germany proposed to do in 2017) validating hack backs through domestic legislation, the GCSC seems to imply that hack backs are effectively "internationally wrongful acts" most of the time. Similarly, the due diligence obligation of states is triggered only when the non-state actor engages in conduct that causes "significant transboundary harm" or is generally "contrary to the rights of states". Through its note, the GCSC seemed to suggest that hack backs on the "continuum" of offensive cyber operations could meet these substantive thresholds. This is hardly a settled matter. Given the widely held view that private hack backs cannot be considered regulated by international law, the GCSC's norm and interpretation is certainly unique. It offers an illustration of "creeping expertise" within the Commission's pronouncements, whereby a technical definition of cyber operations was used to influence perceptions of what constitutes lawful state behavior in cyberspace.

2.3 The GCSC in the Cyber Community of Practice

Although the term of the GCSC concluded in 2019, the Commission has continued to engage the wider community of practice that articulates cybersecurity norms and interprets rules for cyberspace. Members of the GCSC have been active participants in the UN norms processes, with some Commissioners briefing the UN OEWG during its intersessional meetings.[73] The GCSC has also engaged with other multistakeholder initiatives – the Commission is itself a supporter of the Paris Call,[74] which addresses a number of similar topics such as the protection of the public core and hack backs by private actors. The GCSC Secretariat has also briefed the Paris Call Working Groups on the subject

73 "Updated List of Experts for the Presentations on the Six Areas Outlined in Paragraph 5 (a)-(f) of the Provisional Agenda of the OEWG (A/AC.290/2019.1) as of 28 August 2019" (Open-ended Working Group on Developments in the Field of Information and Telecommunications in the Context of International Security, August 2019), https://front.unarm.org/wp-content/uploads/2019/09/280819-Updated-list-of-experts-first-substantive-session-OEWG-on-developments-in-the-field-of-information-and-telecommunications.pdf.

74 "Supporters – Paris Call," accessed November 27, 2022, https://pariscall.international/en/supporters.

of public core protections.[75] Finally, the Commission has also created a "Cyberstability Paper Series" inviting diplomats and researchers to offer their written views on topics relevant to the Commission's mandate.[76] These channels of interaction create avenues for the GCSC, both collectively and through its individual Commissioners, to influence how its norms are received by the cyber CoP and through those norms, influence the application of international law to cyberspace as well. The 2019–2021 UN OEWG and GGE not only adopted the norm on the protection of the public core – albeit differently phrased than that of the GCSC – but also addressed the issue of election interference for the first time in its consensus reports.[77] As norms and terms of art developed by the GCSC "travel" through the cyber CoP, it remains to be seen whether legal interpretations advanced by the Commission will also be picked up by other forums.

3 The Paris Call for Trust and Security in Cyberspace

The Paris Call for Trust and Security in Cyberspace is a prominent multistakeholder declaration on international cybersecurity that was announced by French President Emmanuel Macron at the internet Governance Forum in November 2018. The Paris Call sought to articulate a set of shared principles that would not only guide responsible state behavior in cyberspace, but also outline responsibilities of the private sector, which owns or operates critical internet resources across the world. The Paris Call was conceived as a joint initiative between the government of France and Microsoft, and represents a successful effort at multistakeholder diplomacy, given that over 80 states, 30 sub-national governments, and 700 companies have "signed" this non-binding instrument at the time of writing.

Conceptualized against the backdrop of the 2016–2017 UN GGE's failure to arrive at a consensus report, the Paris Call was explicitly framed as an initiative that would advance cybersecurity governance without being drawn into Great Power rivalry. At the announcement of the initiative, Macron decried the emergence of "two kinds of internet: [a] Californian cyberspace and Chinese cyberspace", likening them to two polar opposite models of minimal and

75 A member of the GCSC Secretariat briefed the Paris Call Working Group 4 on this topic on September 9, 2021 [*via Participant Observation*].

76 "Cyberstability Paper Series: New Conditions and Constellations in Cyber," HCSS, accessed November 27, 2022, https://hcss.nl/report/cyberstability-paper-series-new-conditions-and-constellations-in-cyber/.

77 Sixth GGE Report, 13; OEWG Report, 4.

maximalist regulation by the state respectively of data governance and cybersecurity.[78] The Paris Call, presented as a platform to forge an alternative to these models, emphasized a "collegial method" of cooperation between states and non-state actors to ensure "confidence, stability, and security" in cyberspace.[79] The initiative itself dovetailed into France's efforts to develop a model of "strategic autonomy" for Europe, in which its interests would not be subsumed by the priorities of geopolitical conflict between the United States, Russia, and China.[80]

Like the GCSC, the Paris Call also focused heavily on technical considerations relevant to international cybersecurity. Macron's speech at the IGF itself was unusually technical in nature, coming as it did from a head of state. It addressed several internet governance topics in granular detail, including internet neutrality, platform responsibilities, election interference and disinformation campaigns, data governance issues such as portability, internet fragmentation, and finally, the stability of cyberspace. Macron even proposed, in collaboration with Canada and other G7 partners, an "IPCC" – modeled along the Intergovernmental Panel for Climate Change, a highly technical, specialized body comprising scientific and policy experts – to deal with "technical, scientific, and ethical dimensions" of artificial intelligence.[81]

The launch of the Paris Call at the IGF was itself an invitation to technical experts gathered at the Forum to join the "community" coalescing around its norms.[82] Well before its formal announcement, technology companies and cybersecurity experts played a crucial role in rallying support for the Paris Call. Nearly a hundred technology companies, *internet* service providers, and network/infrastructure organizations were enlisted to support the Paris Call at the time of its launch through the Cybersecurity Tech Accord (CTA) and Charter of Trust, two umbrella initiatives that were led by Microsoft and Sie-

78 "IGF 2018 Speech by French President Emmanuel Macron," Text, internet Governance Forum, November 14, 2018, https://www.intgovforum.org/multilingual/content/igf-2018-speech-by-french-president-emmanuel-macron.

79 *Speech by French President Emmanuel Macron*, N.78.

80 *See*, Ministère de l'Europe et des Affaires étrangères, "Guaranteeing Cybersecurity," France Diplomacy – Ministry for Europe and Foreign Affairs, accessed November 28, 2022, https://www.diplomatie.gouv.fr/en/french-foreign-policy/digital-diplomacy/france-s-international-digital-strategy/article/guaranteeing-cybersecurity.

81 *Speech by French President Emmanuel Macron*, N.78.

82 "Cybersecurity: Paris Call for Trust and Security in Cyberspace," France ONU, accessed November 28, 2022, https://onu.delegfrance.org/Cybersecurity-Paris-Call-for-Trust-and-Security-in-Cyberspace.

mens, respectively.[83] While the CTA offered an avenue for private industry to articulate their views on cybersecurity principles, Microsoft found that it was insufficient without active participation and leadership from states, who ultimately had the prerogative to define responsible behavior in this domain. Following an invitation by Macron for ideas to "strengthen democracy and multilateralism in the 21st century", Microsoft began discussions with the French foreign ministry to articulate a multistakeholder initiative. "It took strong French leadership and months of careful conversations around the world", to formally launch the Paris Call, wrote Brad Smith, President and Chief Legal Officer of Microsoft, and Carol Anne Browne, in their assessment of the initiative.[84]

Ultimately, the launch of the Paris Call was piloted by France, which reportedly undertook a "major rewriting" of the statement owing to differences with Microsoft's original version of the document.[85] The Call is centered around nine principles, which, among others, call on states and non-state actors to protect critical infrastructure and the global, "public core" of the internet, defend electoral processes, prevent intellectual property theft, address the proliferation of malicious cyber tools, prevent hack backs by non-state actors, and implement norms of responsible state behavior and confidence-building measures in cyberspace.[86] In 2020, the French foreign ministry announced the creation of working groups to advance the agenda of the Paris Call by consolidating support for multistakeholder participation in cyber norms creation and implementation, as well as clarifying the scope of the nine Paris Call principles.[87] Six working groups were created to specifically address the following topics:

83 "The Cybersecurity Tech Accord Endorses the Paris Call; Strengthening Our Commitment to Ensuring Trust and Stability in Cyberspace," *Cybersecurity Tech Accord* (blog), November 12, 2018, https://cybertechaccord.org/endorses_paris_call/.

84 Brad Smith and Carol Ann Browne, *Tools and Weapons: The Promise and the Peril of the Digital Age* (Penguin, 2019), 123.

85 "La France veut relancer les négociations sur la paix dans le cyberespace," *Le Monde.fr*, November 8, 2018, https://www.lemonde.fr/pixels/article/2018/11/08/la-france-veut-relancer-les-negociations-sur-la-paix-dans-le-cyberespace_5380571_4408996.html *c.f.* Arthur P. B. Laudrain, "Avoiding A World War Web: The Paris Call for Trust and Security in Cyberspace," *Lawfare* (blog), December 4, 2018, https://www.lawfareblog.com/avoiding-world-war-web-paris-call-trust-and-security-cyberspace.

86 "The Call and the 9 Principles," Paris Call, November 12, 2018, https://pariscall.international/en/principles.

87 Ministère de l'Europe et des Affaires étrangères, "Cybersecurity: Paris Call of 12 November 2018 for Trust and Security in Cyberspace," France Diplomacy – Ministry for Europe and Foreign Affairs, accessed November 27, 2021, https://www.diplomatie.gouv.fr/en/

1. Expanding the community of supporters to the Paris Call;
2. Engaging stakeholders in emerging countries;
3. Promoting a multi-stakeholder approach in UN cyber negotiations;
4. Advancing international norms;
5. Creating a cyberspace stability index; and
6. Developing practical tools for implementation for Paris Call supporters

3.1 High-Level (Legal) Principles? Unpacking the Paris Call

As the section on the GCSC noted, the Commission had presented itself as a multistakeholder initiative to help develop a "cyber stability framework" of rules and norms. In doing so, the GCSC had reflected the GGE's conflation of "norms, rules and principles" as functionally equivalent tools in governing the conduct of states in cyberspace. The Paris Call takes a similar approach with respect to its mandate. The Call is officially described as a "high-level declaration" and a "framework" for state and non-state actor behavior in cyberspace. Although Microsoft alluded, at the launch of the Paris Call, to the need to "move these norms forward",[88] France does not make any reference to the Call being a cyber norms initiative. Even if its prescriptions are worded similar to norms published by the GGE or other multistakeholder initiatives, the use of the term "principles" to describe the goals of the Paris Call leaves their precise character ambiguous, and open to the inference that they may refer to legal or political principles that inform state behavior in cyberspace. One of the nine Paris Call principles is itself the "[strengthening of] international norms of responsible behavior", implying that the other eight principles are not of the same status as norms.

What lends credence to this theory is the French MFA's practice of housing the Paris Call within its diplomatic agenda of strengthening multilateralism. French efforts at championing the Call should be seen in the context of its larger program and objective to support an "international system based on rules" and "protecting international standards, agreements and institutions".[89]

french-foreign-policy/digital-diplomacy/france-and-cyber-security/article/cybersecurity-paris-call-of-12-november-2018-for-trust-and-security-in.

88 "'Paris Call': 51 States Vow Support for Global Rules on Cyberweapons," *France24*, November 11, 2018, https://www.france24.com/en/20181112-france-internet-paris-call-51-states-support-cybersecurity-rules-cyberweapons-peace-forum.

89 Ministère de l'Europe et des Affaires étrangères, "Paris Call for Trust and Security in Cyberspace," France Diplomacy – Ministry for Europe and Foreign Affairs, accessed June 17, 2021, https://www.diplomatie.gouv.fr/en/french-foreign-policy/united-nations

Furthermore, the launch of the Paris Call itself was foreshadowed by statements on international law from its founders. At the 2018 IGF launch, Macron made no reference to cyber norms. He declared, instead, that the Paris Call was "the first declaration to call on states, international organizations [and private actors] to work together to uphold international law in cyberspace […]".[90] If Microsoft considered the Paris Call to be a multistakeholder norms initiative, the company too publicized it as a precursor to binding rules on state behavior in cyberspace. A week before the IGF launch, Brad Smith addressed a gathering of international lawyers and researchers at the International Court of Justice during a reception jointly hosted by Microsoft and the City of Den Haag.[91] Smith highlighted the imminent announcement of the Paris Call, and the collaborative efforts of France and Microsoft to launch it against the backdrop of the 100th anniversary of the WWI armistice. Smith, a trained lawyer himself, would have been aware of the implications of situating the Paris Call in an international legal context. "We need governments […] to ultimately do what has always been done in this very building, and that is to move norms *and* international law forward" [emphasis added], said Smith at the Peace Palace event.[92] From the beginning therefore, the Paris Call always presented itself to the cyber CoP as an initiative whose pronouncements addressed or clarified international law.

The text of the Call, as well as declarations by signatories to the Call, conflate norms and existing rules. The Paris Call requires signatories to "reaffirm that international law, including the United Nations Charter in its entirety, international humanitarian law, and customary international law is applicable to the use of information and communication technologies (ICT) by States".[93] The significance of a commitment by states to this effect is appreciable, but is unclear why the Paris Call also elicits the "reaffirmation" by private actors of the applicability of public international law, given that they are neither subjects of PIL nor do they play a role in the identification or evolution of customary law. Further, it is also not clear why specific multilateral instruments and domains of international law such as the UN Charter or

/multilateralism-a-principle-of-action-for-france/alliance-for-multilateralism/article/paris-call-for-trust-and-security-in-cyberspace.

90 *Speech by French President Emmanuel Macron*, N.78.

91 "November 6 2018 – The Need for Digital Peace, The Hague, The Netherlands," *I4ADA Institute* (blog), November 6, 2018, https://i4ada.org/november-6th-18-the-need-for-digital-peace-the-hague-the-netherlands/.

92 MicrosoftNL, *The Need for Digital Peace at the Peace Palace, The Hague*, 2018, https://www.youtube.com/watch?v=rMXJMMcHjYs.

93 "The Paris Call," Paris Call, November 12, 2018, https://pariscall.international/en/call.

international humanitarian law were highlighted to the exclusion of others. The Paris Call recognizes the UN Charter to be applicable "in its entirety": a notable and revealing claim, given the backdrop of the fifth UN GGE failing to agree on a consensus report over the inclusion, *inter alia*, of states' right to self-defense against cyber armed attacks. The phrase was first adopted by the 2014–2015 GGE, which noted "the inherent right of States to take measures consistent with international law" in an apparent nod to Article 51 of the UN Charter. In modeling its language and declaration after the GGE, however, the Paris Call statement gives the impression that it too is a norms initiative identifying certain rules as applicable to cyberspace, and much like the GCSC, is carrying forward the work of the GGE.

Furthermore, the Call also asks signatories to "reaffirm that international law, *together with the voluntary norms of responsible State behavior during peacetime* [...] developed within the United Nations, is the foundation for international peace and security in cyberspace"[94] [emphasis added]. This framing is significant. The Paris Call does not claim that voluntary UN GGE norms are part of international law – adopted by the General Assembly, UN GGE reports can certainly be considered as *opinio juris* – but gives the impression that the adoption of norms serves the same purpose as the "reaffirmation" of existing international law. This framing of norms by the Call is in line with the UN GGE's grouping together of "norms, rules and principles" of responsible state behavior in its reports.

Declarations by states that endorsed the Paris Call also conflate norms and international law. In 2022, the United States endorsed the Call, noting that the US and France had long "championed a global framework of responsible state behavior in cyberspace, underpinned by the *applicability of international law* [*and*] *adherence to voluntary peacetime norms of state behavior in cyberspace*", among others [emphasis added]. Signing the Call, the US declared, reflected its "continuing commitment to this *framework*"[95] [emphasis added]. Similarly, the EU's statement on its signing of the Paris Call also compared the initiative to supranational EU legislation around cybersecurity and data protection.[96] Australia announced its support for the Paris Call as being consistent with its international cyber security strategy, which seeks "high-level reaffirmations

94 *The Paris Call.*

95 "The United States Supports the Paris Call for Trust and Security in Cyberspace," *United States Department of State* (blog), accessed November 28, 2022, https://www.state.gov/the-united-states-supports-the-paris-call-for-trust-and-security-in-cyberspace/.

96 "Speech by the President at the Paris Peace Forum," Text, European Commission – European Commission, accessed November 28, 2022, https://ec.europa.eu/commission/presscorner/detail/en/speech_21_5977.

from states that they will act in accordance with international law *and* identified norms of responsible state behavior in cyberspace"[97] [emphasis added]. In committing to the Paris Call, these key states and actors seemingly acknowledged the importance of Paris Call principles in developing a framework that binds international law and cybersecurity norms together.

3.2 International Law Briefings, Legal Memos: Practices of Paris Call Working Groups

If the Paris Call and its key state signatories blurred the boundaries between the articulation of norms and the application of international law to cyberspace, the practices of the Paris Call Working Groups (WGs) further entrenched this view. While the text of the Paris Call and especially its nine principles are important, the WGs have played an equally influential role in advancing common understandings around those principles. Of the six WGs, the mandates of WG3 and WG4 are particularly relevant: while WG3 sought to "promote a multi-stakeholder approach to UN cyber negotiations", WG4 was tasked with developing the substantive scope of "international norms", which the group tellingly took to be the Paris Call principles.[98] Participation in these groups was open to all interested – their meetings were held throughout 2021.

In particular, two practices of the Paris Call WGs are notable in this context. The first is the working group briefings by international lawyers on the invitation of the chairs respectively of WG3 and WG4 on the nature of private sector participation in norms initiatives and the legal basis of international cybersecurity norms. The first meeting of WG3 in May 2021 saw Anne-Marie Buzatu, an international lawyer with the ICT4Peace Foundation, brief participants on "examples of multistakeholder governance and discuss their applicability to the UN negotiations on cyber".[99] Similarly, WG4 invited Joanna Kulesza, Professor of Law at Lodz University and the author of a well-received book on the principle of due diligence, to make a presentation to its participants on the applicability of due diligence in cyberspace.[100] The participation of these lawyers was not simply formal or nominal in nature. The final reports of WG3 and

97 "Australia's International Cyber Engagement Strategy" (Australian Government, October 2017), 50, https://www.internationalcybertech.gov.au/sites/default/files/2020-11/The%20Strategy.pdf.

98 *Paris Call of 12 November 2018 for Trust and Security in Cyberspace*, N.87.

99 "First Session of Paris Call Working Group 3 Moderated by Anne-Marie Buzatu, ICT4-Peace," *ICT4Peace Foundation* (blog), May 25, 2021, https://ict4peace.org/activities/first-session-of-paris-call-working-group-3-moderated-by-anne-marie-buzatu/.

100 Paris Call Working Group 4 meeting, July 8, 2021 [*participant observation*].

WG4 make several references to international law, alluding both to multilateral instruments that facilitate multistakeholder participation as well as international legal principles that could concretize obligations specified in the Paris Call principles. Other processes aimed exclusively at identifying and clarifying international cybersecurity law have also engaged with the Paris Call. For example, the Oxford Process on International Law Protections in Cyberspace, an initiative jointly promoted by Oxford University, MFA Japan, and Microsoft, acknowledges that representatives of the Process were "regularly invited to present at various events [...] including those associated with the Paris Call".[101]

The second relevant practice relates to the interspersing of memo-like notes on international law by WG4 between its commentary on the Paris Call norms. While two of these notes in the WG4 report were written by lawyers, another discussed the application of the due diligence principle. These notes were not randomly interspersed, but directly followed the discussion of a related norm. For example, the note on due diligence penned by a WG4 participant was positioned between the WG4's commentary on the norm of non-proliferation and the norm relating to supply chain integrity, both of which specifically highlighted the responsibility of states to prevent malicious cyber activity emanating from their territory.[102] Another note on "dealing with IP theft" by a lawyer followed the WG4's commentary on the Paris Call norm to "prevent ICT-enabled theft". The note suggested that developing a common understanding of what constituted theft was important. "Legal tools could be [...] used as appropriate" for the implementation of the norm, which would benefit from a "mapping of the international legal framework and a gap analysis", the note concluded. At a minimum, these notes reinforced the view that the Paris Call norms corresponded to issues that were ill-addressed by international law. More likely, they gave the impression to WG4 participants that the obligations specified by the norms corresponded to those already existing under various regimes.

3.3 Creeping Expertise in the Paris Call

With Paris Call WGs having nine months to complete their work – they were launched in March 2021 and submitted their reports ahead of the Paris Peace

101 "The Oxford Process on International Law Protections in Cyberspace: A Compendium" (Oxford, UK: Oxford Institute for Ethics, Law and Armed Conflict (ELAC), 2022), 22 https://www.elac.ox.ac.uk/wp-content/uploads/2022/10/Oxford-Process-Compendium-Digital.pdf (hereafter "Oxford Process Compendium").

102 Paris Call WG4 meeting, 15–20.

Forum in December of the same year – most scheduled recurring discussions invited the same set of registered participants to discuss topics related to the Groups' mandate. The agenda for those meetings was driven by the Chairs of the Group: WG3 was chaired by the Cybersecurity Tech Accord, while WG4 was jointly chaired by Microsoft, the Finnish cybersecurity company F-Secure, and the University of Florence. With some of the WG Chairs themselves being influential members of the technical community and industry, technical experts were not only participants but also penholders who critically influenced the final reports of the group.

How did the conflation of norms and international law in the formulations of the Paris Call, as well as the practices of the WGs allow for technical experts to influence the development of international cybersecurity law? The following sections highlight two different aspects of creeping expertise. WG3, chaired by the Cybersecurity Tech Accord, made their case for greater multistakeholder participation in the UN cyber negotiations drawing partly on briefings by invited international lawyers. The instruments that WG3 held up as models for UN cyber processes to follow, namely the Montreux Document on Pertinent International Legal Obligations and Good Practices and International Code of Conduct for Private Military and Security Companies (PMSCs) as well as the Programme of Action on Small and Light Weapons (PoA SALW) and the International Tracing Instrument (ITI), were notable. To the extent that these instruments or platforms had clear rules for the participation of private actors in the regime creation and development process, it seems obvious why WG3 would favorably highlight them. However, there is another aspect to this "choice". The Cybersecurity Tech Accord and WG3 arguably gravitated towards the Montreux Document/ICoCA and PoA SALW/ITI because they established compliance frameworks that similarly conflated the creation of binding rules and articulation of new norms. The Montreux Document – adopted by states but not binding on them – "clarified" existing legal obligations and established "good practices" for states to regulate the activities of PMSCs.[103] ICoC "translated existing rules into principles that companies [could] apply in their operations".[104] PoA SALW similarly established a permanent institutional mechanism to "develop common

103 Nelleke Van Amstel and Tilman Rodenhäuser, "THE MONTREUX DOCUMENT AND THE INTERNATIONAL CODE OF CONDUCT: Understanding the Relationship between International Initiatives to Regulate the Global Private Security Industry," Public Private Partnerships Series (Geneva: DCAF – Geneva Centre for Security Sector Governance, 2016), 5, https://www.dcaf.ch/sites/default/files/publications/documents/DCAF_PPPs_Series_Paper_The_MD_and_ICoC_Understanding_the_Relationship.pdf.

104 Van Amstel and Rodenhäuser (2016), 7.

understandings of basic issues and the scope of the problems" related to "illicit brokering in small arms and light weapons". "Technical specialists" have played a formal and important role in clarifying SALW-related concepts through expert groups established under this PoA.[105] The scope of the PoA SALW is also a matter of debate – while major powers did not want at the time of the PoA's establishment for it to have the power to establish legally binding instruments, there is some room for discussing the "bindingness" of instruments negotiated by the Programme. For example, the PoA SALW produced the International Tracing Instrument, which has been described as a "politically binding" document, although it imposes no commitments on states.[106] However, it is open to the PoA SALW to review periodically whether the ITI should be elevated into a legally binding instrument. I demonstrate that technical experts and WG3 participants were drawn towards such compliance frameworks because of the fluid nature of politically binding norms and legally binding commitments articulated by them. Their gravitation towards the Montreux Document or PoA SALW was not a case of strategic forum shopping but a tacit decision shaped by the overall approach of the CoP towards cybersecurity governance. The following section highlights how WG3 participants, and especially the Cybersecurity Tech Accord, sought to influence the modalities of participation in both the 2021–2025 UN OEWG and the proposed "cyber" PoA in a manner resembling that of the PoA SALW.

As far as WG4 of the Paris Call was concerned, its practices resembled those of the GCSC. Just as the GCSC invited participation from international lawyers through in-person briefings and papers curated by its Research Advisory Group on law, the Paris Call WG4 too had briefings and presentations by international lawyers. But beyond these set pieces, there were seldom any specific discussions on international legal principles. What's remarkable is that participants in WG4 were, on the face of it, not particularly keen to engage in a debate on how international law applied to specific instances. Microsoft pointed out in a WG4 meeting on July 8, 2021, that, along with the consulting firm KPMG, it had conducted a survey "among Paris Call signatories on challenges and best practices in implementing Paris Call Principle 1".[107] This norm related to the protection of critical infrastructure from malicious

105 "Small Arms and Light Weapons – UNODA," UN Office for Disarmament Affairs, accessed January 25, 2023, https://www.un.org/disarmament/convarms/salw/.

106 "2005 International Tracing Instrument | Weapons Law Encyclopedia," accessed January 25, 2023, https://www.weaponslaw.org/instruments/2005-international-tracing-instrument.

107 Paris Call WG4 Meeting, July 8, 2021 [via participant observation].

cyber operations. Among the "takeaways" of this survey was that respondents wanted for states to "clarify a direction" and to get "enough consensus on how to approach 'agreement' [on what constituted responsible state behavior]". They could do this "through norms *or* through a convention enforced under international law", respondents noted [emphasis added]. An international lawyer in that same discussion observed that "there is so much ambiguity, and different states want different outcomes [of interpretation], so I don't really want to call cyber operations [on critical infrastructure] an 'attack' – taxonomy matters [given the legal implications of the term] – [...] let's just focus on what we call a norm in its principle mode, and [could be] well accepted among states". Yet, even as discussions on norms proceeded on their technical and political aspects, the final report of the WG4, like that of the GCSC made several references to specific legal principles or other reports that drew from international law. This is particularly evident in the memos interspersed between the commentary on norms, as well as references to the Compendium on Countering Election Interference, which addressed the international legal dimensions of "coercive" intervention. Thus, references to international law in the WG4 report that addressed technical dimensions and explanations of Paris Call norms appeared, once again, to be tacit and habitual.

3.3.1 Working Group 3: Promoting Multistakeholderism in UN Cyber Negotiations

WG3 served two broader objectives of the Paris Call: *first*, to advance multistakeholder participation in UN cybersecurity negotiations, and *second*, to promote the Programme of Action (PoA) initiative which was championed by France in the 2019–2021 UN GGE and OEWG. WG3 held three discussions over the course of its term. The first meeting highlighted examples of multistakeholder governance, and sought in particular to examine how international regulations on private security providers could offer an analogy for cybersecurity. The meeting, as noted earlier, was led by Buzatu from ICT4-Peace Foundation. Buzatu, who at the time of writing is the Executive Director of the ICT4Peace Foundation, is a recognized legal expert in human security, and specifically on the legal responsibilities of global, private security providers.

According to Buzatu, the widespread use and deployment of private security companies in theaters of wars in Afghanistan and Iraq in the mid-2000s led to states asking the question, "how should international law be applied to these companies, and what do we do about the fact that international law does not apply to private actors?"[108] This problem, she said, was compounded by the fact that attribution of the conduct of these parties to states was not always clear. Further, many of them operated across states and involved personnel from multiple nationalities, leading to a situation where it was not always possible for a state to exert jurisdiction over them, especially if they were no longer operating in its territory. "Private actors were such a big part of this equation that [there was agreement among states] it needed a multistakeholder framework [for governance]", she said. The governance response of states was the 2008 Montreux Document on Pertinent International Legal Obligations and Good Practices for States Related to Operations of PMSCs During Armed Conflict that sought to "clarify" existing international legal obligations into this domain. Such obligations included: the application of international humanitarian law to PMSCs' conduct; delineation of the responsibilities of contracting states, territorial states, and home states of PMSCs; the reaffirmation of customary international law on state responsibility for actions committed by non-state actors. Notably, Buzatu highlighted that the Montreux Document, which had been endorsed by 57 states, even specified a special standard of "superior responsibility" of government officials *and* directors of PMSCs for actions of these companies under international criminal law acting under their "effective *authority and* control" [emphasis added] – in contrast to the "effective control" test used to determine attribution of non-state conduct to states.[109]

The Montreux Document led to the development of an International Code of Conduct Association for Private Security Providers (ICoCA), a multistakeholder document that "articulated specific principles" around the use of force and conduct of PMSCs vis-à-vis detainees during armed conflict.[110] ICoCA delineated the responsibilities of states, PMSCs and civil society organizations, with states being responsible for setting regulations and policy on the topic, while civil society would undertake monitoring and supervision functions. An important lesson for international cybersecurity governance from the Montreux Document and ICoCA, Buzatu concluded, was that stakeholder participation delineated according to specific areas of expertise could "help translate

108 Buzatu's consent to identify her and use quotes from her statement was taken on March 2, 2023.

109 "The Montreux Document on Pertinent International Legal Obligations and Good Practices for States Related to Operations of Private Military and Security Companies during Armed Conflict" (Montreux: Swiss Federal Department of Foreign Affairs and International Committee of the Red Cross, September 17, 2008), 15.

110 "The Code," *ICoCA – International Code of Conduct Association* (blog), accessed November 28, 2022, https://icoca.ch/the-code/.

existing international law" to cyberspace. Cybersecurity governance could follow a combination of "contractual, policy, and legal measures that harden soft law normative frameworks" into binding commitments. In particular, companies crucially involved in the ICT supply chain had to be members of such a framework for its effectiveness.

Buzatu's presentation resonated with many WG3 participants[111] – the Montreux Document/ICoCA was also referenced in the final WG3 report – arguably for two reasons. Firstly, by drawing participants' attention to the Montreux Document and ICoCA, Buzatu suggested that cybersecurity rules *and* norms could be part of the same institutional, compliance framework. The Montreux Document, as noted above, affirms and describes how international legal principles would apply to PMSCs. While not legally binding on signatory states, it is nevertheless an influential source of "guidance" on how international law regulates the conduct of PMSCs.[112] The multistakeholder ICoCA, described as the "second phase"[113] of the Montreux Document, reflects an endorsement of the latter's principles by the private sector. This formulation corresponded to practitioners in the cyber CoP seeing "norms, rules and principles" of responsible state behavior as functionally equivalent. Alongside legal norms created by states (as in the Montreux Document), private companies and technical standards organizations could articulate and implement norms under an ICoCA-like framework that would carry the same weight as interpretations of existing international law, and even advance it.

Secondly, Buzatu's framing of this governance model also responded to technical considerations that had been flagged as potential hurdles to an effective cybersecurity regime. The Montreux Document model of cybersecurity governance, her argument implied, could address concerns such as the difficulty of attributing cyber operations and enforcing state responsibility and due diligence obligations with respect to malicious cyber activity originating or transiting through a state's territory, by involving the private sector and technical community both in the "translation" of legal obligations to cyberspace, and enforcing such obligations through a mix of private/public con-

111 *Notes from Session 1 of the WG3 meeting*, May 26, 2021. [*via participant observation*].

112 "The Montreux Document," Federal Department of Foreign Affairs FDFA, accessed January 23, 2023, https://www.eda.admin.ch/eda/en/home/foreign-policy/international-law/international-humanitarian-law/private-military-security-companies/montreux-document.html.

113 Rebecca DeWinter-Schmitt (ed.), "Montreux Five Years On: An Analysis of State Efforts to Implement Montreux Document Legal Obligations and Good Practices" (American University Washington College of Law), accessed November 28, 2022, 13, https://www.wcl.american.edu/index.cfm?LinkServID=B1E626D9-095E-4A28-94A94551CEA3488E.

tracts, national law, and international law. This approach appears to have resonated with the technical community in particular, which in turn emphasized a "structured approach" to multistakeholder involvement in the articulation and implementation of norms and rules. "[B]eyond supplying technical expertise, the technology industry has become more active in offering support concerning international cybersecurity norms development and implementation", the WG3 report read.[114] Among WG3's recommendations was "regular engagement [with] the private sector through, for example, the Private Sector Forum [of the] UN Global Compact [or] perhaps even newly developed ones, if required, and with other established multistakeholder forums".[115] The influence of Buzatu's presentations extended beyond the report of the Paris Call as well. In response to a request-for-inputs published by the UN Office of the High Commissioner on Human Rights on the provision of services by private "cyber mercenaries" and their impact on human rights, a technical expert involved with WG3 later submitted a co-authored report, along with international lawyers, arguing that the Montreux Document may not "explicitly mention the activities [of mercenaries] in cyberspace", but their "clauses could be extended to online activities in addition to real-world activities".[116]

The discussion on the Montreux Document illustrates another dimension of "creeping expertise". Technical experts did not simply influence the substantive scope of international law principles applied to cyberspace, but also how the CoP approached *processes* that developed such rules and norms. In furthering this objective, the technical community drew not only on the Montreux Document, but also on other compliance frameworks that could serve as analogous models for cybersecurity governance. The Cybersecurity Tech Accord and the final report of WG3 both highlighted the Programme of Action on Small Arms and Light Weapons (PoA SALW) as a possible model of multistakeholder governance in cyberspace.[117] Like the Montreux Document and ICoCA, the PoA SALW also established a compliance framework of norms in

114 "Multistakeholder Participation at the UN: The Need for Greater Inclusivity in the UN Dialogues on Cybersecurity," November 2021, 10, https://pariscall.international/assets/files/10-11-WG3-Multistakeholder-participation-at-the-UN-The-need-for-greater-inclusivity-in-the-UN-dialogues-on-cybersecurity.pdf. (hereafter "WG3 report").

115 WG3 Report, 27.

116 Noëlle van der Waag-Cowling, Brett van Niekerk, and Trishana Ramluckan, "Submission to the Call for Inputs: Report on the Provision of Military and Security Cyber Products and Services by 'Cyber Mercenaries' and Its Human Rights Impact," (2021) https://www.ohchr.org/sites/default/files/Academia-van-der-Waag-Cowling.docx.

117 "A Statement on the Programme of Action: A Standing UN Body to Uphold International Expectations Is the Best Hope for Stability in Cyberspace," *Cybersecurity Tech Accord* (blog), October 18, 2021, https://cybertechaccord.org/a-statement-on-the-programme-of-

whose development and implementation non-state actors, especially technical experts, have played a key role. The precise status of those norms is somewhat open-ended. While some states saw the PoA SALW as a vehicle for "[...] negotiating legally binding treaties",[118] the UN Small Arms Conference that established it was collectively unable to agree on such a mandate.[119] Nevertheless, the PoA SALW has resulted in instruments such as the International Tracing Instrument (ITI) – a "framework of cooperation" on illicit weapons tracing – which is not legally binding on states, but whose implementation has been sought by the UN GA.[120] Civil society organizations play an important role in monitoring the implementation of the ITI and jointly, biannual national reports under the PoA. Notably, the ITI is open to review by the PoA SALW's review conferences, including of its "legal or political character". The UN Office of Disarmament Affairs notes that the ITI and PoA SALW "constitute the *normative framework* on small arms and light weapons, which *all UN member states have agreed upon*" [emphases added]. This formulation somewhat confusingly gives the impression that the framework is binding on states, when it is not.

The report of WG3 highlighted the PoA SALW as an example of "direct participation [by] multistakeholder actors in international negotiations and agreements, either written or oral".[121] The PoA SALW was certainly endorsed both by WG3 and the Cybersecurity Tech Accord because it recognized the "necessary" involvement of private actors in the work of the UN GA's First Committee on Disarmament and International Security. "The technical expertise required to address disarmament at the global level ensures that [private actors] are directly included in the participation of these discussions", the WG3 report noted.

But there's arguably more to this "selection" of a preferred forum by the working group. WG3 discussions indicate how participants, especially the technical community, were drawn towards instruments and frameworks such as the Montreux Document where legal and political norms sat alongside each

action-a-standing-un-body-to-uphold-international-expectations-is-the-best-hope-for-stability-in-cyberspace/; WG3 Report, 15–16.

118 Matt Schroeder and Rachel Stohl, "Small Arms, Large Problem: The International Threat of Small Arms Proliferation and Misuse | Arms Control Association," *Arms Control Today*, June 2006, https://www.armscontrol.org/act/2006-06/features/small-arms-large-problem-international-threat-small-arms-proliferation-misuse.

119 Schroeder and Stohl (2006), N.118.

120 "Programme of Action on Small Arms and Its International Tracing Instrument – UNODA," United Nations Office for Disarmament Affairs (UNODA), accessed November 28, 2022, https://www.un.org/disarmament/convarms/salw/programme-of-action/.

121 WG3 Report, 15–16.

other as equivalent tools to govern state behavior. As the preceding paragraphs note, the precise nature of norms articulated by the Montreux Document/ ICoCA and the PoA SALW/ITI is ambiguous. Paris Call WG3 participants, as with other practitioners in the cyber CoP who conflated norms and rules, gravitated towards forums that engaged both in norm-articulation and law-interpretation or instruments such as the ITI whose legal and political bindingness was left open-ended.

The characterization of these forums and instruments in the WG3 report reinforces the claim that the working group's "choice" of models was more a tacit reflection of the CoP's core beliefs than an attempt at forum shopping. The WG3 report variously terms the 2011 UN Conference Report that established the PoA SALW as a "treaty" and as a "protocol" in different sections.[122] The landmark UN conference on SALW cannot be considered as a treaty-making body, and the PoA SALW, as noted earlier, is not a legally binding instrument. The WG's projection of "bindingness" on the SALW's institutional and normative framework is consistent with how UN GGE reports have come to be seen as binding "acquis" by practitioners in the cyber CoP: the effect ultimately of the dominant perception that norms do as much to regulate state behavior as interpretations of existing international law.

3.3.2 Impact of the Paris Call WG3 Report on UN Negotiations

The technical community's support of the PoA SALW arguably influenced discussions around multistakeholder participation in the 2021–2025 UN OEWG. Several states and NGOs were dissatisfied with the working procedures of the 2019–2021 OEWG with respect to multistakeholder participation. Of particular concern was the fact that the participation of NGOs not accredited by UN ECOSOC was contingent on a no-objection from all states, but states were under no obligation to justify their objections. Indeed, the requests of most NGOs without ECOSOC accreditation to participate in the 2019–2021 OEWG were summarily rejected.[123] WG3 and the Cybersecurity Tech Accord in particular sought for the UN OEWG to adopt a more formal mechanism for the inclusion of NGOs in the norms process, and the PoA SALW served as a model. The Rules of Procedure of the UN Conference that established the PoA SALW in 2001 – which has been applied *mutatis mutandis* by subsequent

122 WG3 Report, 15,16.

123 Raman Jit Singh Chima, "As States Discuss Global Cybersecurity at U.N., We Must Act to Protect Users," *Access Now* (blog), February 13, 2020, https://www.accessnow.org/as-states-discuss-global-cybersecurity-at-u-n-we-must-act-to-protect-users/.

meeting of states under the PoA framework[124] – allows "interested non-governmental organizations relevant and competent to the scope and the purpose of the Conference" to participate in the discussions, provided that they submit a request with their organizational details and purpose of participation to the President of the conference.[125] The President is required to then offer the list of interested NGOs to states for "consideration on a no-objection basis".[126] Importantly, the rules of procedure stipulated that NGOs shall be provided documents relating to the Conference upon request, which presumably included those relating to their participation as well.[127]

The WG3 report specifically cited these rules, and the group's deliberations on the topic have since been cited by technical community coalitions such as the Cybersecurity Tech Accord to "regularize multistakeholder inclusion" of in the 2021–2025 OEWG.[128] When the Chair of the 2021–2025 OEWG suggested that the second Group also follow the same rules of procedure as its predecessor, a group of stakeholders led by the Tech Accord Secretariat, Microsoft and the multistakeholder "Let's Talk Cyber" initiative responded with an open letter that called for greater transparency in the no-objection process and avenues for NGOs that were denied accreditation to express their views.[129] To marshal support for this open letter, they cited the Paris Call WG3 report. In response, the OEWG – acting on the Chair's proposal – eventually agreed that "objecting Member State(s) will make known [their] objection to the Chair of the OEWG and, on a voluntary basis, make known to the Chair of the OEWG

124 "Informal Australian Research Paper | What Next for Advancing Responsible State Behaviour at the United Nations?," April 2021, https://www.internationalcybertech.gov.au/sites/default/files/2021-04/australian-research-paper-what-next-advancing-responsible-state-behaviour-united-nations_1.pdf.

125 Rule 63(b), "Provisional Rules of Procedure of the Conference" (United Nations Conference on the Illicit Trade in Small Arms and Light Weapons in All Its Aspects, June 14, 2001), https://documents-dds-ny.un.org/doc/UNDOC/GEN/N01/410/92/PDF/N0141092.pdf?OpenElement.

126 Rule 63(b), *Provisional Rules of Procedure of the Conference*, N.125.

127 Rule 63(e), *Provisional Rules of Procedure of the Conference*, N.125.

128 WG3 Report, 16; "A Statement on the Programme of Action: A Standing UN Body to Uphold International Expectations Is the Best Hope for Stability in Cyberspace," *Cybersecurity Tech Accord* (blog), October 18, 2021, https://cybertechaccord.org/a-statement-on-the-programme-of-action-a-standing-un-body-to-uphold-international-expectations-is-the-best-hope-for-stability-in-cyberspace/.

129 "Multi-Stakeholder Letter for OEWG Chair on Modalities: Let's Talk Cyber," Let's Talk Cyber, accessed October 28, 2022, https://letstalkcyber.org/resources/multi-stakeholder-letter-for-oewg-chair-on-modalities.

the general basis of its objections".[130] Furthermore, the OEWG also agreed that the Chair "will share any information received [on objections] with any Member State upon its request".

The unique modalities of participation adopted by the 2021–2025 OEWG – tasked, *inter alia*, with determining how international law applies to state behavior in cyberspace – could be considered an example of "creeping expertise", given that the technical community played a key role in influencing the group's rules of procedure through the Paris Call working group and report. WG3 and the Tech Accord secretariat in particular used the rules of procedure of the SALW as a focal point to advance preferred outcomes for multistakeholder participation in the OEWG. In the end, the modalities of participation adopted by the OEWG can be considered even more accommodating than the PoA SALW, where NGOs are simply informed of the results of their accreditation request. The agreed procedure was adopted for the July 2022 meeting of the OEWG, ahead of which Ukraine and Russia objected respectively to the accreditation of several NGOs. Ukraine reportedly offered its reasoning for the objections, but Russia did not.[131]

3.3.3 From WG3 to the UN Cyber Programme of Action

The WG3 report also assumes relevance in light of the joint proposal put forward by France and Egypt, and supported by over 50 countries, for a Programme of Action for Advancing Norms of State Behavior in Cyberspace (cyber PoA).[132] The cyber PoA proposal, which was tabled in October 2020, was pitched as an effort to bring the parallel tracks of the GGE and OEWG together. The cyber PoA would have regular "working level meetings, focused on implementation" as well as "Review Conferences [...] that could consider if additional norms were needed [given the unique attributes of ICTs]". Thus, it was already envisaged as a permanent mechanism, much like the PoA SALW, that could clarify key aspects of international cybersecurity law as well as develop new norms. The PoA found reference in both the GGE and OEWG reports, and the proposal appears at the time of writing to have been accepted

---

130 Burhan Gafoor, "Letter from the Chair," April 22, 2022, https://documents.unoda.org/wp-content/uploads/2022/04/Letter-from-OEWG-Chair-22-April-2022.pdf.

131 Allison Pytlak, "Cyber Peace & Security Monitor," July 31, 2022, https://www.reachingcriticalwill.org/disarmament-fora/ict/oewg-ii/cyber-monitor/16310-cyber-peace-security-monitor-vol-2-no-7.

132 "The Future of Discussions on ICTs and Cyberspace at the UN," August 10, 2020, https://front.un-arm.org/wp-content/uploads/2020/10/joint-contribution-poa-future-of-cyber-discussions-at-un-10-08-2020.pdf.

and formally established by the UN First Committee.[133] The French foreign ministry pitched the cyber PoA to the Paris Call WG3 in its third and final meeting, and in particular highlighted the PoA's advantages to the technical community.[134] France's ambassador for digital affairs Henri Verdier, who briefed the WG3, acknowledged that countries had made progress on identifying international law applicable to cyberspace. However, several challenges remained. "On due diligence, we need a very precise and technical conversation", he said. "Deterrence [in cyberspace] does not always work – the 'tech' guys in the room know that the same weakness are [often] exploited in our IT systems."[135] Verdier also said that a "lot of cybersecurity protections are not about norms, it is about resources and finances, and [implementation concerns] are why the PoA is needed".

Members of the technical community who participated in that WG3 session responded differently to Verdier's presentation. A representative of a regional internet governance organization said that many "ICT practices are not being used their full potential", and called, as an example, the integration of procurement and supply chain standards into the PoA's plans for the implementation of cybersecurity norms.[136] A representative of an ICT company supported the cyber PoA proposal and called for greater accountability of vendors in the supply chain. However, a representative of a standards organization argued the cyber PoA "risked creating yet another process that [added] to the arguments of those in favor of a treaty mechanism",[137] and instead, the focus should be on building capacity and securing funding resources for developing countries.

In response to the cyber PoA proposal and specifically, the WG3 presentation, the Tech Accord published a note outlining recommendations for the PoA to "aim to accomplish".[138] In particular, the note pointed out that the cyber PoA could help illuminate "*how* states understand international law governs behavior online" by "prompting states to state their own opinions and then tracking these contributions will help to recognize where consensus

---

133 France-Désarmement [@FR_Desarmement], "The Resolution on PoA Cyber, Co-Sponsored by 74 States and Adopted with 157 Votes in Favour, Supports a Future Programme of Action to Strengthen Capacity-Building to Address #cyber Attacks and Advance Responsible Behaviour in the #cyberspace #77unga @francediplo_ASD https://T.Co/FAYLqwUonw," Tweet, *Twitter*, November 3, 2022, https://twitter.com/FR_Desarmement/status/1588195825968156673.

134 WG3 Report, 7.

135 Presentation by Henri Verdier, September 10, 2021. [*participant observation*].

136 Notes from WG3 meeting, September 10, 2021. [*participant observation*].

137 Notes from WG3 meeting, September 10, 2021. [*participant observation*].

138 *A Statement on the Programme of Action*, N.128.

exists" [emphasis original]. Further, the cyber PoA "would be well-positioned to provide updates" on how "technological innovation" and the corresponding evolution of cyber threats "impacts the meaning and implementation of existing [UN] norms". Finally, the cyber PoA "should also include an avenue by which *new norms* could be negotiated and established", given that it is "hubristic to assume" the agreed UN norms would sufficiently regulate state behavior in cyberspace, the note argued [emphasis added]. The Tech Accord's response and recommendations make it quite clear that it sought from the cyber PoA a compliance framework that interpreted how international law applied to states' conduct in cyberspace *as well as* norms of responsible behavior. Specifically, its reference to "new norms" leaves open the question of whether the PoA's norms would replace or alter existing international legal obligations articulated by the same forum. Such an interpretation of the role of norms is encouraged by the role of instruments such as ITI within the PoA SALW framework that aim to become binding commitments over time.

3.3.4 Working Group 4: Advancing International Cyber Norms

WG4, tasked with clarifying the scope of the Paris Call principles, met five times during the course of 2021. A full list of WG4 participants was not available to those who registered to attend its discussions. However, based on observing three of its sessions and electronic correspondence among group members, I assessed participation in WG4 to include over 160 individuals, including international lawyers and technical experts. Most WG4 meetings had over 60 participants, and all meetings saw robust discussion between the presenters of specific topics and the participants. Each meeting focused on one or two Paris Call principles. The meetings would often begin with a presentation on the principle itself and comparable norms articulated by UN or multistakeholder initiatives. The co-chairs of WG4 asked participants to be guided by the following questions in each of their meetings:[139]

1. What should be WG4's key recommendation to the 2021 Paris Peace Forum?
2. What "priority norms areas" should WG4 address?
3. How can WG4 facilitate better implementation of the nine Paris Call principles and "mainstream them into the norms-related discussions of other international fora"?

---

139 *Notes from participant observation*, 2021.

4. How can WG4 help elevate the significance of the Paris Call as the "baseline document for multistakeholder diplomacy" on cybersecurity norms?
5. How can WG4 help position the Paris Call as a "complementary [and] multi-stakeholder" initiative on cybersecurity norms vis-à-vis other multilateral discussions?

The remit of WG4, as these questions indicate, was confined to non-binding cybersecurity norms. There were, as noted previously, briefings by international lawyers made to the group, but discussions within WG4 indicated a reluctance to engage in law interpretation or application to state behavior in cyberspace. Technical experts were also invited to brief the group on specific Paris Call principles, such as the one on non-proliferation. The final report of WG4 however made numerous references to international law. In some cases, the WG4 report directly referred to legal principles in its commentary as well as "memos" that interspersed such commentary. In others, the report referred to discussions on international law principles that had been taken up by law-finding initiatives. This referencing of international legal principles, despite the absence of any in-depth discussions within WG4 on how those rules applied to specific contexts, was arguably habitual. The conflation of norms and international law – notwithstanding exhortations by WG4 of the voluntary nature of those norms – was reflected and reinforced by practices such as the inclusion of memos on international law.

Principle 1 of the Paris Call called on states and non-state actors to "prevent and recover" from cyber operations that caused "significant, indiscriminate or systemic harm to individuals and critical infrastructure". In its report, WG4 sought normative protections afforded to be critical infrastructure (CI) from malicious cyber operations to be grounded in international law. First, the report declared that cyber norms on CI were "currently 'fuzzy'", and in need of greater clarity, precision, and common understanding.[140] This outcome was directly derived from the KPMG-Microsoft survey of Paris Call participants, referred to earlier in this chapter, that sought for CI protections to based either on concrete norms or binding international agreements. The 2014–2015 UN GGE had called on states to "not conduct or knowingly support ICT activity contrary to its obligations under international law that intentionally damages critical infrastructure or otherwise impairs the use and operation of critical infrastructure to provide services to the public".

As a commentary on this norm has noted, the UN GGE "failed to specify whom the state must knowingly support" and "to elucidate a standard of sup-

140 WG4 Report, 5.

port that a state must meet in order for it to violate it".[141] Although the norm seeks to apply international law protections to CI, the GGE also did not elaborate on the nature of those "obligations", as Chapter 4 highlighted. Critically, the GGE also did not define or specify what constitutes CI, and it also explain what impairment of CI meant. The WG4 report argued that "consensus should be fostered" regarding the "precise, intended meaning" of CI protections.[142] As an example, the group pointed to the then draft of the EU's Network and Information Security Directive (NIS2), which was a CI-focused legislation that entered into force in January 2023. NIS2 applies, *inter alia,* to cybersecurity risk management by "essential" and "important" entities, which are not only listed by the draft legislation, but also defined in terms of their functionality.[143] Further, NIS2 offers sophisticated, technical definitions of what constitutes a cybersecurity "incident" as well as technical descriptions of measures that should be in place to mitigate such risks. NIS2 directives do not form international law, but they apply across the European Union, binding member states. WG4 appeared in this vein to be recommending an NIS2-like directive on critical infrastructure that would bind signatories globally.

Additionally, WG4 sought a "consolidation" of the "'top' [cybersecurity] norms", and consensus on their interpretation and application.[144] The UN GGE does not make any reference to a hierarchy among its 11 norms. The WG4 report highlights the work of the Oxford Process on International Law Protections in Cyberspace – an initiative in which Microsoft is also a co-sponsor – as an effort to "articulate points of consensus under international law on pressing global issues". In particular, the report refers to the Oxford Process statements on critical infrastructure protection relating to the healthcare sector, democratic institutions and processes, and vaccine research. The WG4 report's emphasis on "top norms" appear, in this vein, to be a call to highlight norms for specific CI sectors whose international law protections have been clearly identified and elucidated, as the Oxford Process has sought to do.

Secondly, WG4 also sought to highlight the application of specific rules of international law to CI protections. The report asserted that "cyber attacks [against CI] often do not qualify as armed attacks [under Article 51 of the UN

141 Jason Jolley (2017), n.59, chapter 2, 177.

142 WG4 Report, 5.

143 *See*, "Proposal for a DIRECTIVE OF THE EUROPEAN PARLIAMENT AND OF THE COUNCIL on Measures for a High Common Level of Cybersecurity across the Union, Repealing Directive (EU) 2016/1148" (2020), https://eur-lex.europa.eu/legal-content/EN/TXT/?uri=celex:52020PC0823.

144 WG4 Report, 5.

Charter]", and therefore it was important to consider how international law would treat below-the-threshold attacks on such infrastructure. In particular, the report pointed to how "norms relating to proxy operations" can "increase accountability for [the actions of] non-state actors", without offering any prescriptions.[145] While this is an example of norms and existing law being conflated, the report does not prescribe any specific "norm" that could advance the application of the state responsibility regime to conduct by non-state actors.

Principle 2 of the Paris Call relates to the protection of the "public core" of the internet. Multistakeholder initiatives such as the GCSC and Paris Call ascribed legal consequences to cyber operations targeting core internet infrastructure, although they did so through norm-articulation. Deliberations in WG4 around the protection of the public core are detailed in Chapter 6.

Principle 3 of the Paris Call deals with protections against foreign election interference. The principle calls for the prevention of "malign interference by foreign actors aimed at undermining electoral processes through malicious cyber activities". As the language suggests, this principle is more broadly framed than the GCSC norm, which is limited to protecting technical election infrastructure. The Paris Call, on the other hand, seeks to prevent and mitigate cyber operations targeting electoral *processes*. The WG4 report specifically points out that vulnerabilities in the electoral "ecosystem" have to be considered "holistically".[146] As a result, it used the term "interference" which the report explains as encompassing both "cyber interference" as well as acts or campaigns of "disinformation".[147] "Election interference [has] three components – physical, virtual, and psychological", noted the report.[148] This Paris Call principle, unlike the GCSC norm on the topic, is not explicitly grounded in international law, and the report of WG4 also does not refer to international legal principles vis-à-vis election interference. However, the report refers prominently to "A Compendium on Countering Election Interference", which was developed jointly in 2021 by the government of Canada, Microsoft, and the Alliance for Securing Democracy, which addressed in detail the scope of "coercion" required for a cyber operation to be in breach of the non-intervention rule.[149] The findings contained in the Compendium, the report

145 WG4 Report, 5.

146 WG4 Report, 9.

147 WG4 Report, 10.

148 WG4 Report, 10.

149 "Multi-Stakeholder Insights| A Compendium on Countering Election Interference" (Microsoft; Canada; Alliance for Securing Democracy, April 2021), https://www.canada.ca/content/dam/di-id/documents/compendium-eng.pdf.

notes, were "mirrored in discussion among WG4 participants".[150] In fact, the report's view of treating election interference holistically – i.e., including processes and physical infrastructure – is borrowed verbatim from the Compendium.

The WG4 report's emphasis on election "interference" also draws from the Compendium, which addressed at length the scope of the term. The Compendium highlighted the use of the term in the policy context, noting that the US and Australian government had executive measures to counter "foreign interference" and "foreign influence" activities respectively. It also cited academic debates on the lawfulness of "influence operations", pointing out that the scale and effects of the operation were a crucial consideration for such evaluation.[151] Ultimately, the Compendium recommended that "interference" should be distinguished from other related concepts such as "foreign influence" or "coordinated inauthentic behavior", suggesting that all disinformation campaigns do not constitute election interference. The Compendium elevated "interference" into a separate category comprising more serious acts involving "coercion" and "deception". Coercion, the Compendium defines referring to its dictionary meaning, is "forcing [states] to do what [they] are unwilling to do", but should also account for the "power divide among states [that] force the other into taking a particular action."[152] Deception, on the other hand, was defined as the use of covert and opaque means to hide destabilizing operations against democratic processes. The Compendium appears *prima facie* to frame "coercion" narrowly: for instance, an influence operation orchestrated by a major cyber power against another may not necessarily count as election interference, because of a lack of "power divide" between those countries. On the other hand, the Compendium widened the scope of "interference" itself by suggesting it need not be a "singular" event, but the "cumulative effects of individual acts that in the aggregate add up to an impactful act".[153] This understanding of election interference was also adopted by the WG4 report.[154]

The WG4 report and Compendium thus appear to move in the opposite direction of the GCSC in defining protections for election interference. The GCSC limited the scope of its norm to technical electoral infrastructure, but framed coercion widely. The result was a legal interpretation of the rule on

---

150 WG4 Report, 10.

151 *A Compendium on Countering Election Interference,* N.149, 11.

152 *A Compendium on Countering Election Interference,* N.149, 12.

153 *A Compendium on Countering Election Interference,* N.149, 4.

154 WG4 Report, 9.

prohibited intervention that restricted any serious attack on technical electoral infrastructure. On the other hand, the Paris Call WG4 favored a limited interpretation of coercion, but acknowledged the possibility of election "interference" being understood more broadly, including as the cumulative effect of related cyber operations or campaigns. A supplementary event organized by the WG4 on election interference even noted that states should consider when "espionage, which is traditionally permissible under international law crosses the line into being harmful and worth prohibiting". The framing of prohibited interventions (below the *jus ad bellum* threshold) as encompassing cumulative acts is a novel interpretation of international law. The ICJ's jurisprudence suggests the threshold of "armed attack" under Article 51 of the UN Charter may be breached by a series of activities and their "cumulative effects".[155] Indeed, this position has also been considered applicable to cyberspace by some states and scholars.[156] However, the ICJ has not made such observations with respect to "low-level attacks",[157] either under Article 2(7) of the Charter or customary international law. While Article 15 of the ARSIWA refers to composite acts, i.e., breaches of an international obligation through a "series of actions or omissions defined in aggregate as wrongful", the ILC's commentary notes some of the most "serious wrongful acts in international law are defined in terms of their composite character".[158] Specifically, the ILC Commentary refers to breaches of "obligations concerning genocide, apartheid or crimes against humanity, systematic acts of racial discrimination, systematic acts of discrimination prohibited by a trade agreement, etc." It would arguably be difficult to classify disinformation operations in the context of an election among such "composite acts". The practical consequence of such an interpretation would be that an isolated disinformation campaign or influence operation may not qualify as a prohibited intervention, but states could

155 Michael N. Schmitt, Louise Arimatsu, and Tim McCormack, eds., *Yearbook of International Humanitarian Law (2010)*, vol. 13 (TMC Asser Press, 2010); Andrew Garwood-Gowers, "Case Concerning Oil Platforms (Islamic Republic of Iran v United States of America) – Did the ICJ Miss the Boat on the Law on the Use of Force?," *Melbourne Journal of International Law* 5, no. 1 (2004), http://classic.austlii.edu.au/au/journals/MelbJIL/2004/10.html.

156 *See*, Yoram Dinstein, "Computer Network Attacks and Self-Defense," *International Law Studies* 76, no. 1 (June 1, 2002), https://digital-commons.usnwc.edu/ils/vol76/iss1/20; "Brussels Summit Communiqué Issued by NATO Heads of State and Government (2021)," North Atlantic Treaty Organization, accessed November 29, 2022, https://www.nato.int/cps/en/natohq/news_185000.htm.

157 Nicholas Tsagourias, "Cyber Attacks, Self-Defence and the Problem of Attribution," *Journal of Conflict and Security Law* 17, no. 2 (2012): 233.

158 ARSIWA with commentaries, 63.

claim such a violation if they are part of a broader operation or series of events, including but not limited to instances of hybrid operations.

Principles 5 and 6 of the Paris Call relate respectively to non-proliferation of malicious ICT tools and the strengthening of digital supply chains and "life-cycle services". These norms were primarily aimed at technology companies and private businesses that were involved in the ICT supply chain, but also highlighted the importance of states' articulating predictable and clear guidelines around the two issues. The WG4 report emphasized the importance of Coordinated Vulnerability Disclosure (CVD) in its commentary to Principle 5 – the Group was given a comprehensive briefing on vulnerabilities disclosure by a technical expert in one of its meetings[159] – and also called on states to develop domestic policies that encourage the timely and proactive disclosure of exploits and other flaws by companies. While recognizing that existing CVD guidelines have not been adopted widely, the Group also suggested the development of export control regimes to deal with the problem. Specifically, WG4 mooted a "carrot and stick" approach, "whereby inadequate CVD is met with sanctions".[160] However, the report did not clarify whether it was proposing a multilateral initiative towards developing such sanctions, or whether it simply sought them under existing or new domestic law. The report makes an analogous reference to the GDPR as a catalyst for stronger data protection compliance, and suggests the matter of CVD should be addressed at the EU and global levels, with "harmonization" of national laws.[161] The GDPR itself hints at penalties on companies where vulnerabilities left unpatched by ICT products and services leads to data breaches,[162] and the draft NIS2 directive too encourages CVD policies at the national level.[163] The WG4 report did not discount the possibility of an international legal effort to promote CVD, and suggested it would be "helpful to draw relevant lessons from *frameworks pertaining to physical weapon non-proliferation*"[164] [emphasis original].

In the absence of further guidance on the specific provisions or aspects of non-proliferation treaties or other export control initiatives that WG4 consid-

---

159 Paris Call WG4 meeting, July 8, 2021 [*via participant observation*].

160 WG4 Report, 16.

161 WG4 Report, 16.

162 Alana Maurushat and Kathy Nguyen, "The Legal Obligation to Provide Timely Security Patching and Automatic Updates," *International Cybersecurity Law Review* 3, no. 2 (December 1, 2022): 437–465, https://doi.org/10.1365/s43439-022-00059-6.

163 "Coordinated Vulnerability Disclosure Policies in the EU," News Item, ENISA, accessed November 29, 2022, https://www.enisa.europa.eu/news/enisa-news/coordinated-vulnerability-disclosure-policies-in-the-eu.

164 WG4 Report, 16.

ered comparable, it would not be fruitful to speculate what an analogous framework for cybersecurity would look like. That said, technical expert-international lawyer interactions on this issue have led to similar conclusions. Herbert Lin and Joel Trachtman have jointly argued, as an example, for a "carrot-stick" approach to export controls on dual-use, "intrusion" software. Referring to the US Bureau of Industry and Security (BIS) standards on "verified end users" of dual use software, they made the case for a multilateral regime predicated on a formal role for the private sector.[165] Such a regime would balance inducements for states (technology sharing) with sanctions for their non-participation or non-compliance with the regime (refusal to transfer intrusion software). A vulnerabilities disclosure regime could work the same way: states could be offered, via a formal regime, inducements to enact policies requiring CVD from ICT companies (for example, timely international assistance against major cyber incidents like WannaCry or NotPetya) which are balanced against threats of non-cooperation or sanctions on software sales if such policies are not enacted. Lin and Trachtman argue the "carrot-stick" regime would be taken seriously by states if it is based on "formal law", i.e., a legally binding treaty, rather than "soft" regimes such as the Wassenaar Arrangement on Export Controls for Conventional Arms and Dual-Use Goods and Technologies.[166]

Whether or not WG4 contemplated a similar approach, its commentary on Principle 6 too calls on states to explore "governments' obligations and restraints in the supply chain space". Interestingly, the report's commentary on Principles 5 and 6 is interspersed by a brief note on the due diligence principle, penned by a WG4 participant. The note makes no reference to either principle or the subject of non-proliferation and supply chain security, but asks the question: "does the general due diligence duty apply in cyberspace, and what measures does it require states to take?"[167] The WG4 report is marked by similar "notes" by lawyers, usually succeeding the Group's commentary on specific principles. While they cannot be considered the unanimous view of the working group, it is reasonable to attribute a high degree of support among the group's participants to such opinions. As noted previously in this chapter, the Group was already briefed on the due diligence principle by an international lawyer.

165 Herbert Lin and Joel Trachtman, "Diagonal Export Controls to Counter Diagonal Transnational Attacks on Civil Society," *European Journal of International Law* 31, no. 3 (August 1, 2020): 917–939, https://doi.org/10.1093/ejil/chaa053.

166 Lin and Trachtman (2020), N.165 r.

167 WG4 Report, 17.

This evaluation of the due diligence principle in the context of non-proliferation and supply chain integrity throws up interesting possibilities. The due diligence principle requires states to not "knowingly allow" their territories to be used for acts "contrary to the rights of other states". The application of this principle to cyberspace, as the next chapter outlines, has itself been influenced considerably by technical considerations. It is suffice to note at this stage that states differ in their positions as to the existence of a "cyber due diligence" rule, and the scope of its application given especially the technical investments required of governments to monitor and inspect digital networks on their territory.[168] What is also not settled is the scope of the transboundary harm or violation of rights of other states that would operationalize the due diligence obligation. The adoption of policies or laws that enforce sound data protection and cybersecurity practices from private actors would arguably allow a state to claim performance of due diligence, if such a rule exists. However, the WG4 report seems to imply – by positioning this note between Principles 5 and 6 – that the due diligence obligations of a state should extend to policies on CVD as well as supply chain integrity. With the notable exception of China, no state at the time of writing has adopted national policies requiring the disclosure of vulnerabilities, although several major powers have progressively developed guidelines on "responsible" reporting of such flaws by ICT players.[169] Including CVD policies, especially with compulsory reporting requirements, within the ambit of due diligence obligations in cyberspace would be an expansive interpretation of the rule – for reference, the Tallinn Manual 2.0 acknowledges that if a cyber due diligence rule does exist, it is likely limited to a duty to *stop* harmful activities that are ongoing, but not to *prevent* or detect such harms proactively.[170] Further, such an interpretation of the cyber due diligence rule could also open the door for the involvement of the private sector in the setting of rules in export control regimes. Many ICT companies and states would prefer for a multilateral regime to set predictable rules or guidelines that can be adopted nationally, rather than increasing uncertainty and compliance burdens through fragmented CVD policies. Purely for reasons of self-interest, states may thus "tolerate" the creation of a multistakeholder regime on CVD.

---

168 *See*, "Due Diligence," International cyber law: interactive toolkit, September 12, 2022, https://cyberlaw.ccdcoe.org/wiki/Due_diligence.

169 Devin Thorne, "China's Vulnerability Disclosure Regulations Put State Security First," The Strategist, August 31, 2021, https://www.aspistrategist.org.au/chinas-vulnerability-disclosure-regulations-put-state-security-first/.

170 *TM* 2.0, 45–47.

Principle 8 calls on states to "prevent non-State actors, including the private sector, from hacking-back, for their own purposes or those of other non-State actors". Although some common interlocutors were involved in the drafting and commentary on the GCSC norm against "hack backs" and this Paris Call principle – namely, Microsoft, France, and the GCSC itself, which is a signatory to the Paris Call – the latter's framing as well as the corresponding commentary of WG4 differs substantially from its GCSC counterpart. Firstly, the scope of the Paris Call is different in that it targets "hack backs" by private actors for their own purposes or other non-state actors. The WG4 report confirms this by defining hack backs as "offensive actions by private sector organizations – i.e., *independent of governments* – in response to a cyberattack in order to [...] cause harm to the computer systems or networks of attackers"[171] [emphasis added]. In contrast, the GCSC norm referred more broadly to all manner of private hack backs, including those which were supported or sponsored by the state. Secondly, and unlike the GCSC norm, the WG4 report does not base this principle in international law, but nevertheless acknowledge that "discouraging such behaviors is essential to a rules-based order".

Instead, the WG4 report is notable for its scoping of hack backs, which could potentially be adopted by states as they articulate their views on the legality of such actions. As stated previously, the report defines hack backs as those actions taken by non-state actors to "steal" data or "harm" an attacker. As a result, a "range of appropriate active cyber defense measures" are excluded from this definition, protecting what the report calls "legally legitimate actions" and those "that take place in environments *owned or operated* by an organization or their customers with consent"[172] [emphasis added]. This is a broad exception to active cyber defense measures. The "environment" in which companies and their customers operate could easily overlap with that of the attackers: a classic example would be cloud computing or other "multi-tenant" environments.[173] The GCSC on the other hand had defined ACD along a continuum of cyber operations, whether on the victim's own network or the attacker's network. While most offensive cyber operations undertaken by private actors are likely to meet the GCSC's definition, the Paris Call WG4's definition excludes many of these. The definition used by the WG4 is taken from a report on hack backs by the Cybersecurity Tech Accord, making it an instance

171 WG4 Report, 24.

172 WG4 Report, 24.

173 "What Is Multitenancy? | Multitenant Architecture | Cloudflare," accessed November 29, 2022, https://www.cloudflare.com/learning/cloud/what-is-multitenancy/.

where technical experts have sought to influence the intersubjective meaning of hack backs and by extension, its legal implications.

3.4 Paris Call in the Cyber CoP

With the Working Groups submitting their final reports in 2021, there does not appear at the time of writing to be further efforts to articulate or develop the nine principles contained in the original Paris Call. Whether the interpretations advanced by WG4 on issues like election interference, due diligence obligations of states, and private hack backs will be adopted by other institutions or actors within the broader cyber CoP remains to be seen. Given that France and Microsoft have been the sponsors and most prominent champions of the Paris Call, they may push aspects of the WG reports – for example, WG3 recommendations on the participation of private actors in cybersecurity norms negotiations or WG4 conclusions on borrowing attributes of non-proliferation regimes for international cybersecurity governance – into forums at the UN and the EU where they are active participants.

Given France's robust participation in the 2019–2021 OEWG, and continuing efforts to secure agreement among states on its PoA proposal, the UN could be its preferred destination for the WG recommendations. Since Microsoft has been an active participant in multistakeholder EU forums such as the European Cyber Agora,[174] it may seek to convince European interlocutors to adopt the WG recommendations in the implementation of the EU's Cyber Diplomacy Toolbox, especially in relation to the participation of private and technical actors in its collective attribution and sanctions process.[175]

In May 2022, the European Council decided to extend further by three years its "framework for restrictive measures", i.e., sanctions, against perpetrators of cyber attacks against the EU. The imposition of sanctions follows the technical attribution of cyber attacks, and the presentation (confidentially or publicly) of such evidence to EU member states, or in other cases, to third states, to secure their agreement for collective action. Private actors, especially companies, could play an important role in presenting or strengthening such evidence. Further, EU-based companies and technical actors are also likely to

174 "European Cyber Agora, June 14–16 2022 – Microsoft," accessed November 29, 2022, https://www.microsoft.com/en-eu/cyber-agora/.

175 *See generally*, Annegret Bendiek and Matthias Schulze, "Attribution: A Major Challenge for EU Cyber Sanctions," SWP Research Paper 2021 (Berlin: Stiftung Wissenschaft und Politik (SWP), November 16, 2021), https://www.swp-berlin.org/en/publication/attribution-a-major-challenge-for-eu-cyber-sanctions.

advocate for the bloc's CVD policies that give private actors a greater agency in how vulnerabilities are identified, prioritized, and disclosed.

4 Reflections on the Work of the GCSC and Paris Call

This chapter has sought to highlight the practices of the GCSC and Paris Call that reflected and reinforced the conflation of voluntary norms and existing international law by the cyber CoP. With respect to the GCSC, this chapter has pointed to practices of recruitment to the Commission and its research advisory groups that sought engagement from international lawyers and legal scholarship on various norms, as well as unique practices that involved the articulation of background notes and additional papers that sought to defend the basis of "voluntary norms" in existing international law. The Paris Call Working Groups, meanwhile, instituted practices such as organizing briefings by international lawyers not only on responsible state behavior but also on developing institutional mechanisms to advance cybersecurity governance. Such briefings were crucial to Paris Call Working Group 3 gravitating towards frameworks like the Montreux Document and PoA SALW where non-binding norms and existing rules had a porous relationship. Working Group 4's practices of appending "legal-like" memos to its commentary on norms was another unique practice that reinforced this conflation between norms and rules. To the extent that these initiatives were specifically established to carry forward the work of the UN GGE in the aftermath of its failure in 2017, their adoption of such practices is not surprising. If the GGE process broke down owing to Great Power politics in 2017, multistakeholder entities like the GCSC and Paris Call continued to advance the "framework of responsible state behavior" in the same way that the GGE sought to do, i.e., through "norms, rules and principles".

Through these practices that conflated norms-articulation and rule-interpretation, technical experts who were prominent interlocutors in both groups were also able to shape international cybersecurity law. If in the GCSC, technical and industry bodies were strongly represented in the Commission and its RAG, the Paris Call WG3 and WG4 were chaired by industry associations and cybersecurity companies, who were also penholders on its reports. Through their influential roles in these multistakeholder initiatives, and on account of their aforementioned practices, technical experts were often in a position to help determine what rules or regimes applied to certain cyber operations. In other cases, the technical formulations that they helped articulate – "electoral infrastructure", "electoral processes", "active cyber defense", "hack backs", "responsible/coordinated vulnerabilities disclosure" – became intersubjective terms of art that were grounded in legal concepts. As the chapter on the Tallinn Manual and Oxford Process initiatives highlight, at least some of these concepts were picked up and their legal basis further debated by eminent international lawyers.

CHAPTER 4

International Cybersecurity Law Initiatives: The Tallinn Manuals and Oxford Process

1 "Aren't You a Bit Quick to Elevate the Tallinn Manual into a 38(1)(d) Source?"

Analyzing the role of the Tallinn Manuals and the Oxford Process on International Law Protections in Cyberspace, two prominent institutions within the cyber CoP, in advancing international cybersecurity law is important but challenging. On the one hand, the Tallinn Manuals and Oxford Process statements can arguably be classified within Article 38(1)(d) of the ICJ Statute as a "subsidiary means" for the determination of international cybersecurity law, given that they include pronouncements of the "most highly qualified publicists of the various nations". "Expert manuals" like Tallinn Manual 1.0 and 2.0 fit this bill.[1] Interestingly, the question of whether the Tallinn Manuals could qualify as a source under Article 38(1) of the ICJ's statute arose in the Championship Round of the 2022 Jessup Competition, with ICJ judges Bruno Simma and Hillary Charlesworth reportedly suggesting that the Manual had some ways to go before being accepted as an authoritative determination.[2] On the other hand, such a ready categorization would beg the question. For pronouncements of the Tallinn Manuals and Oxford Process to gain acceptance or legitimacy among international lawyers the world over, they first have to be evaluated and pass muster as credible sources of rules within the cyber CoP. In other words, the practitioners in this community which include states, companies, technical standards and governance bodies, academics, and NGOs should debate, invoke, and cite these pronouncements, which in turn elevates their

---

1 Sandesh Sivakumaran, "The Influence of Teachings of Publicists on the Development of International Law," *International & Comparative Law Quarterly* 66, no. 1 (January 2017): 1–37, https://doi.org/10.1017/S0020589316000531; Luke Chircop, "Territorial Sovereignty in Cyberspace after Tallinn Manual 2.0," *Melbourne Journal of International Law* 14, no. 20(2) (2019): 349.

2 *2022 Jessup World Championship*, 2022, https://www.youtube.com/watch?v=JuPWCUqBsxA; Asaf Lubin [@AsafLubin], "Judge Simma during the Championship Round of @The_Jessup, Asking the Applicant on the Use of @TallinnManual as a Source of Law: 'Aren't You a Bit Quick to Elevate the Tallinn Manual into a 38(1)(d) Source.. Is @Schmitt_ILaw Really like Grotius or Brownlie of Our Time?,'" *Twitter*, April 9, 2022, https://twitter.com/AsafLubin/status/1512790447374094338.

acceptability and importance not only to the CoP but to practitioners and scholars outside it. To some extent, this has already happened: as previous chapters and sections in this chapter note, the Tallinn Manuals and Oxford Process have been routinely referenced by various institutions within the CoP, including by states within the UN GGE,[3] even if practitioners may not all agree with their interpretations.

Yet, if practitioners within the cyber CoP have sought to advance international legal discourse on cybersecurity through norms, as chapters in this book have noted, where do these two initiatives fit in relation to the broader community? The Tallinn Manuals and Oxford Process explicitly identify themselves as initiatives to interpret and clarify the scope of existing obligations for states in cyberspace, so the claim that these initiatives conflate voluntary norms and existing rules may seem improbable. As for technical experts, they certainly played an important role in both processes, as the following sections note. However, could technical considerations really have influenced their pronouncements through norms – the underlying mechanism behind "creeping expertise" – if these initiatives only interpreted rules and did not articulate norms in the first place?

This chapter argues that the core, background beliefs of the cyber CoP did in fact shape the practices and outcomes of the Tallinn Manuals and the Oxford Process. Even as these initiatives sought to clarify existing legal obligations of states in cyberspace, they did not rely solely on doctrinal reasoning to ascertain the application and scope of certain existing rules. Leaders and stewards of these initiatives also sought to "manage" their drafting processes so that they would address political, commercial, and technical considerations pertaining to various aspects of international cybersecurity through their pronouncements. In other words, their own characterization as initiatives engaged in law-identification and interpretation notwithstanding, the Tallinn Manuals and the Oxford Process behaved in ways similar to processes within the cyber CoP that articulated norms. Through the orchestration of such a managerial exercise, whose practices were not reflexively evaluated, they looked more like norms-articulation processes than initiatives engaged strictly with rule-interpretation.

In the case of the Tallinn Manuals, the commentaries to its black-letter rules were the site of such management. Commentaries in both Manuals delved into hypothetical scenarios and illustrations of cyber operations –

3 See generally, Niccolò Lanzoni, "The Role of Expert Groups in Shaping International Cyberlaw: A Case Study of the Tallinn Manuals and International Law-Making," *Journal of Conflict and Security Law*, September 26, 2025, kraf013, https://doi.org/10.1093/jcsl/kraf013.

often involving complex technical aspects – to elucidate how specific rules applied to state behavior. The managerial process around the drafting of these commentaries involved consultations with states to get their political buy-in for the Manual, vetting substantive aspects of these hypothetical scenarios with in-house technical experts, and of course, securing consensus from within a room full of distinguished lawyers who often disagreed on the scope of a black-letter rule. In the final analysis, the Tallinn Manuals' commentaries were akin to normative guidelines of responsible state behavior whose basis was drawn equally from international law – in some cases, critics of the Manuals have even pointed out that the legal basis of their interpretation was thin – as they were from political, technical, and even reputational considerations. In this manner, the Manuals could be understood as engaging in norms creation. In at least one important case, the Tallinn Manual expressly borrowed a formulation from a norm that had been negotiated by the UN GGE, revealing its acceptance of political sources. Technical considerations that shaped the Tallinn Manuals' commentaries through these "norms-like" practices thus influenced the development of international cybersecurity law.

This chapter highlights how the Oxford Process adopted a similar managerial approach. In the Oxford Process' case, its promoters acknowledged more openly the policy, business, and technical priorities underpinning their decision to dedicate specific meetings to international law protections for sectors such as healthcare, vaccine research, and supply chains, or regulation of cyber-enabled behavior such as influence operations and ransomware. The Oxford Process also accommodated policy considerations that shaped (and sometimes thwarted) its consensus statements on international cybersecurity law applicable to specific contexts. Relevant practices highlighted in this chapter include briefings by cybersecurity experts, representatives of technology companies, and intelligence officials who often framed the agenda for ensuing discussions by international lawyers on the applicability and scope of specific principles, and the process of consensus-building by which Oxford Process statements were negotiated. Signed almost exclusively by international lawyers – some statements even begin with the phrase "we, the undersigned public international lawyers" – the Oxford Process statements convey the impression that it is a law-interpretation exercise. Based on an assessment of its practices and specific discussions, however, I argue that the Process, much like the Tallinn Manual, did not rely on legal argumentation alone to articulate its statements. In balancing other considerations pertaining to political and technical dimensions of cybersecurity, it too resembled a norm-articulation process in which technical experts played influential roles.

2 The Tallinn Manual International Groups of Experts

2.1 Origins and Background

The Tallinn Manual project was conceived in 2009 by a group of academics based in Europe and the United States, with a view to "answering the [hard] questions" regarding the application of international law to state behavior in cyberspace.[4] The project was put in motion by Michael Schmitt, Thomas Wingfield, and Eneken Tikk – all lawyers – with the latter serving at the time as the legal advisor to the NATO Cooperative Cyber Defence Centre of Excellence (NATO CCDCOE) in Tallinn, Estonia. Tikk invited Schmitt and Wingfield to house the project within the NATO CCDCOE, with the Centre providing the necessary funding and support to what would become the International Group of Experts.[5] Tikk and Wingfield were already academic collaborators at the time. Notably, they argued in a 2010 article co-authored with James Bret Michael, professor of computer science and electrical engineering at the US Naval Postgraduate School, that "the type of operation and the potential damage [cyber operations] cause to a nation's defenses make it vital that international lawyers and computer technologists collaborate to identify lawful thresholds for operational action".[6] Tikk would go on to become the project coordinator for the first Tallinn Manual, while Michael would serve as its principal technical advisor.[7] Wingfield and Michael both served on the editorial committee of the first Manual, and Schmitt became its director, and indeed, the project's most recognizable face.

The Tallinn Manual 1.0 (TM1) on the International Law Applicable to Cyber Warfare was modeled explicitly along the lines of other international law manuals in existence, notably the San Remo Manual on Armed Conflicts at Sea, the Manual on Non-International Armed Conflict (NIAC), and the Harvard University-incubated Manual on International Law Applicable to Air and Missile Warfare (AMW).[8] TM1, as its title indicated, addressed primarily the *jus in bello* framework applicable to state behavior in cyberspace, although the Manual also dealt with *jus ad bellum* questions regarding the threat or use of "cyber" force, and, very briefly, "international cyber security law", which it

4 *CyCon 2012 | Michael Schmitt: Tallinn Manual Part I*, 2012, https://www.youtube.com/watch?v=wY3uEo-Itso.

5 *CyCon 2012 | Michael Schmitt*, n.4.

6 James Bret Michael et al., "From Chaos to Collective Defense," *Computer* 43, no. 8 (August 2010): 91–94, https://doi.org/10.1109/MC.2010.228.

7 *TM 1.0*, x, xii.

8 *CyCon 2012 | Michael Schmitt*, n.4.

understood to be concepts of "public international law that relate to the hostile use of cyberspace". The International Group of Experts comprised international lawyers who were categorized as "legal group facilitators" and "legal experts" in addition to those in the editorial committee.[9] The Group also comprised "technical experts" as well as "observers" from the International Committee of the Red Cross, US Cyber Command, and NATO.[10] The drafters of TM1 emphasized that the Manual was a restatement of the law, and not an effort to progressively develop it. In other words, the Tallinn Manual was an identification of *lex lata*, but not *lex ferenda*.[11] "When TM1 started out, it was purely an academic effort to state the law as it is", said Wingfield, "we brought the 'law of war' experts, and then we moved them into cyber with some technical experts and advisors, [and] this turned out to be the right way to do it".[12]

Following its publication in 2013, TM1 was widely debated among practitioners and scholars of international law, although states themselves appeared to adopt a "wait-and-see"[13] approach before announcing their positions vis-à-vis the Manual. While its rigor and comprehensive approach was widely acknowledged, criticism of the Manual tended to fall into three categories: that the Manual's rules and commentary, however defensible, were hardly the only interpretation of cyber rules pertaining to armed conflict, and therefore could not definitively be identified as *lex lata*;[14] TM1's drafters were legal and technical experts who hailed exclusively from Western countries, and the Manual itself reflected "NATO-centric" views;[15] and finally, that the Manual's focus – i.e., cyber warfare – came at the expense of "below-the-threshold"

9 *For a list see, TM 1.0*, x-xi.

10 *TM 1.0*, xi.

11 "It is a restatement of the law. It does not make the law. There is no effort to progressively develop the law." *CyCon 2012 | Michael Schmitt*, n.4.

12 *Interview with Thomas Wingfield*, April 8, 2022.

13 *Interview with Michael N. Schmitt*, September 13, 2022.

14 *See generally*, Nicholas Tsagourias, "The Tallinn Manual on the International Law Applicable to Cyber Warfare: A Commentary on Chapter II – The Use of Force," in *Yearbook of International Humanitarian Law Volume 15, 2012*, ed. Terry D. Gill et al. (The Hague: T.M.C. Asser Press, 2014), 19–43, https://doi.org/10.1007/978-90-6704-924-5_2; Lianne J. M. Boer, "Restating the Law as It Is: On the Tallinn Manual and the Use of Force in Cyberspace," *Amsterdam Law Forum* 5, no. 3 (2013): 4–18; Dieter Fleck, "Searching for International Rules Applicable to Cyber Warfare – A Critical First Assessment of the New Tallinn Manual," *Journal of Conflict and Security Law* 18, no. 2 (July 1, 2013): 331–51, https://doi.org/10.1093/jcsl/krt011; Kubo Mačák, "Military Objectives 2.0: The Case for Interpreting Computer Data as Objects under International Humanitarian Law," *Israel Law Review* 48, no. 1 (March 2015): 55–80, https://doi.org/10.1017/S0021223714000260.

15 *See generally*, Kristen E. Eichensehr, "Review of Tallinn Manual on the International Law Applicable to Cyber Warfare. Edited by Michael N. Schmitt. Cambridge, New York: Cam-

cyber operations that were far more common, but increasing in severity and sophistication.[16] "There were two things that we learnt from TM1", said Wingfield.[17] "Our mental mindset in 2007, 2008, 2009, was entirely high-end cyber activities, but after the Russians came into the two provinces of Georgia in 2008, we learned that serious cyber activity is rarely a standalone, and often simply another column of advance in a military operation. […] Another thing was that most people did not really know the 'gray area' [of international cybersecurity law] was going to explode. TM1 addressed what an 'attack' was, and what the rules of armed conflict were when states were at war in cyberspace, but now we know that is very secondary to the much greater need to clarify rules around say, 'what about the sanctity of diplomatic communications?', 'what about using cyber means to surveil consular properties', 'what about cyber threats to human rights, and potential remedies', 'what about countermeasures', and finally 'what about sovereignty'?", he said.

Responding to these concerns, the second iteration of the Tallinn Manual (TM2) addressed international law applicable to cyber operations, i.e., operations below the *jus ad bellum* threshold. While several lawyers who participated in TM1 joined the TM2 International Group of Experts, lawyers from Japan, Israel, China, and Thailand were also invited to participate as drafters in the exercise.[18] Notably, TM2 not only included legal and technical experts, but also (legal) "contributors" and "technical peer reviewers" in addition to

---

bridge University Press, 2013. Pp. Xix, 282. Index. $120, Cloth; $58.99, Paper," *The American Journal of International Law* 108, no. 3 (2014): 585–589, https://doi.org/10.5305/amerjintelaw.108.3.0585; Oliver Kessler and Wouter Werner, "Expertise, Uncertainty, and International Law: A Study of the Tallinn Manual on Cyberwarfare," *Leiden Journal of International Law* 26, no. 4 (December 2013): 793–810, https://doi.org/10.1017/S0922156513000411; Lauri Mälksoo, "The Tallinn Manual as an International Event," ICDS, August 8, 2013, https://icds.ee/en/the-tallinn-manual-as-an-international-event/ *c.f.* Priyanka R. Dev, "Use of Force and Armed Attack Thresholds in Cyber Conflict: The Looming Definitional Gaps and the Growing Need for Formal U.N. Response Notes," *Texas International Law Journal* 50, no. 2–3 (2016 2015): 381–402; Papawadee Tanodomdej, "The Tallinn Manuals and the Making of the International Law on Cyber Operations," *Masaryk University Journal of Law and Technology* 13, no. 1 (2019): 67–86; Ashley Deeks, "Tallinn 2.0 and a Chinese View on the Tallinn Process," *Lawfare* (blog), May 31, 2015, https://www.lawfareblog.com/tallinn-20-and-chinese-view-tallinn-process.

16 *See generally*, Ido Kilovaty, "Cyber Warfare and the *Jus Ad Bellum* Challenges: Evaluation in the Light of the Tallinn Manual on the International Law Applicable to Cyber Warfare," *National Security Law Brief* 5, no. 1 (2014): 91–124; Dan Efrony and Yuval Shany, "A Rule Book on the Shelf? Tallinn Manual 2.0 on Cyberoperations and Subsequent State Practice," *American Journal of International Law* 112, no. 4 (October 2018): 583–657, https://doi.org/10.1017/ajil.2018.86.

17 *Interview with Thomas Wingfield*, April 8, 2022.

18 For a list of experts, observers, and technical advisers, *see* TM 2.0, xii-xviii.

legal peer reviewers. The production of TM2 also involved extensive consultations with states – three consultative meetings on the draft Manual were organized by the Dutch Foreign Ministry under the so-called "Hague Process" – and the drafters took into account the inputs from various delegations. "We started talking to the Dutch MFA, and came up jointly with the idea of having state engagement", said Schmitt.[19] "This was [an] invaluable [process]. We intended to meet once, but ended up doing three meetings, because the states were so enthused. One delegation had seven people! Anyway, many of those delegations included technical experts, or they had consulted technical experts." Thematically, while TM2 trained the lion's share of its attention on issues such as state responsibility and due diligence, as well as the interaction of cybersecurity law with those of air, space, maritime, and human rights law, among others, the Manual also updated some of its commentary from TM1 on LoAC questions.

Even if TM2 focused on cyber operations that were more commonplace, the reception to the Manual was no less different from its first iteration. In addition to voices from academia that robustly debated (and often disagreed) with its interpretations and claims of identifying *lex lata* for below-the-threshold operations, states too joined the debate on this occasion. TM2 was published in February 2017, which coincided with the final stages of the contentious and ultimately unsuccessful fifth UN GGE. "The Tallinn Manual was quoted and discussed all the time, repeatedly [during negotiations]", said Karsten Geier, Germany's nominated expert and chair of the fifth GGE in an interview.[20] The UK's evolving position on the international law applicable to cyber operations and contrasting approach to sovereignty from that of the TM2 is perhaps the most visible example of a dialogue between states and the drafters of the Manual. States became active interlocutors with the TM2 process not only on account of the Hague Process, but also the failure of the UN GGE. The fifth GGE's inability to address the question of international law's application to the domain would prompt several states to articulate their national, legal positions in the following years, and TM2, on this count, was doubtless a frame of reference for those pronouncements. This aspect is discussed further in the following section.

In 2021, the CCDCOE commenced work on Tallinn Manual 3.0, conceived as a project to "update all chapters" of TM2, in addition to "accurately reflecting the state of interpretive play [on international cybersecurity law] in the

19 *Interview with Michael N. Schmitt*, September 13, 2022.
20 *Interview with Karsten Geier*, February 8, 2021.

international community".[21] A key effort of the project will be to consolidate and reflect state practice and *opinio juris* in this still nascent field. At the time of writing, TM3 is slated for completion in 2025.

2.2 Practices of the Tallinn Manual International Groups of Experts

To what extent did the practices of the Tallinn Manuals reflect the core beliefs of the cyber CoP? As the introduction to this chapter highlighted, it might seem unrealistic to argue that the Tallinn Manuals conflated voluntary cyber norms and binding international law. The Tallinn Manuals' promoters, as noted above, have repeatedly emphasized the manuals are restatements of the law, as applicable to cybersecurity. Nevertheless, practices of the Tallinn Manuals demonstrate how the process was *managed* in such a manner that resembled norms-articulation processes within the cyber CoP. Legal argumentation and reasoning were only one, albeit critical, determinant of the Manuals' pronouncements. Equally relevant was the accommodation of technical, political, and as I detail later in this section, reputational concerns of the International Group of Experts as well.

The Tallinn Manuals' commentaries, arguably their most important part, was the "site" of such management. The Manuals are divided into "black-letter rules" and their commentaries. This is not an unusual practice: in offering "rules" and commentaries on those "rules", the Tallinn Manuals follow the footsteps of similar academic products like the San Remo Manual or AMW Manual. However, unlike the San Remo and AMW Manuals, which list rules and commentaries or "explanations" separately in different sections,[22] TM1 and TM2 combine them – a significant practice adopted by the drafters purportedly to "set forth" the "terminology and the *legal rationale* for finding that [a rule] represents *lex lata*"[23] [emphasis added]. Moreover, if other manuals drew from state practice and indeed, overt pronouncements of states, drafters

---

21 Charlie Dunlap and J.D., "International Law and Cyber Ops: Q & A with Mike Schmitt about the Status of Tallinn 3.0," *Lawfire* (blog), October 3, 2021, https://sites.duke.edu/lawfire/2021/10/03/international-law-and-cyber-ops-q-a-with-mike-schmitt-about-the-status-of-tallinn-3-0/.

22 *See*, Louise Doswald-Beck, ed., *San Remo Manual on International Law Applicable to Armed Conflicts at Sea* (Cambridge: Cambridge University Press, 1995), https://doi.org/10.1017/CBO9780511622052; *HPCR Manual on International Law Applicable to Air and Missile Warfare* (Cambridge: Cambridge University Press, 2013), https://doi.org/10.1017/CBO9781139525275.

23 Michael N. Schmitt, "Tallinn Manual 2.0 on the International Law of Cyber Operations: What It Is and Isn't," Just Security, February 9, 2017, https://www.justsecurity.org/37559/tallinn-manual-2-0-international-law-cyber-operations/.

of the Tallinn Manuals had to rely extensively on hypothetical scenarios or illustrations to depict cyber operations and their legal consequences. To the extent that commentaries interpret "preexisting rules", both refer to "rules, decisions and discussions that predate the Manual", notes Werner.[24] But the question of how those rules and principles apply to cyberspace is "answered, not by recourse to the past, but through an endless number of fictitious cases and scenarios", he writes – these hypothetical scenarios determine the relevance or irrelevance of specific legal rules to state behavior.[25] The following paragraphs outline, by shining a light on the Manuals' practices, how these scenarios and more broadly, its commentaries, were shaped by a managerial exercise that accommodated political and technical considerations. Put differently, the Tallinn Manuals may claim that the commentaries offer a "legal rationale" for its black-letter rules, but it is also the result of an orchestrated dialogue between legal, political, and technical constituencies.

The TM1 process began first with five individuals coming together in Tallinn for three days to "brainstorm" a table of contents (ToC) for the Manual, and subsequently identified other international lawyers with the necessary expertise to address those issues listed in the ToC.[26] Each member was handed "a list of topics" and told to "draft a 'black-letter rule' [on that topic] and its [corresponding] commentary".[27] The International Group of Experts then worked in plenary format to "redesign the Manual based on inputs" received from individual members.[28] Following suggestions from the plenary, the drafts were returned to those members for revisions. Then, following a small-group review, the plenary reconvened – every "black-letter" rule had the approval of the full group, said Schmitt – to further polish the inputs. Finally, a "drafting committee" that included Schmitt, Wingfield as well as technical experts, put the finishing touches on the Manual. "We had technical experts because we knew we did not understand 'cyber' well enough to do it alone. They were with us every step of the way", said Schmitt in a public presentation about the Manual.[29]

Wingfield offered greater detail in an interview, addressing specifically the contribution of James Bret Michael, TM1's technical advisor in the commentary drafting process. "Up front, we talked about 'okay, for this doctrine of law, this would probably involve [scenario X], and there would be a small educa-

24 Wouter Werner, *Repetition and International Law*, 1st ed. (Cambridge University Press, 2022), 101. https://doi.org/10.1017/9781009039666.

25 Werner (2022), 114.

26 *CyCon 2012 | Michael Schmitt*, n.4.

27 *CyCon 2012 | Michael Schmitt*, n.4.

28 *CyCon 2012 | Michael Schmitt*, n.4.

29 *CyCon 2012 | Michael Schmitt*, n.4.

tional piece where [Bret] would say, 'this is how the cloud works, or this is how emails get to where they're going, or, here are the five or six different types of cyber attack, and here are the things – confidentiality, availability or integrity – that are attacked despite the attack vector'. [These lessons] were of educational value to the 'law of war' professors and oriented them to the domain. Then, as we went on, as the professors were playing out scenarios [arguing] 'what if a country tried to do this, but this happened instead?', then the technologists would say, 'you really couldn't do that, that's not how that works, this is pretty much automatic', and so that the back-and-forth was very helpful in *sharpening where the actual fault lines were for the legal issues*", he said[30] [emphasis added]. This is a critical aspect to the practice and working of the Tallinn Manual. "When we had a question, we knew it was technologically relevant. We could either get consensus or if we failed, then a majority-minority opinion on a *relevant issue* [*of law*], that was not unconnected to technological reality" [emphases added].

Wingfield's comments indicate the extent to which technical experts crucially influenced, in a Dworkinian sense, the "pre-interpretive" stage of the Tallinn Manual process.[31] Technical experts helped generate shared understanding among Tallinn Manual lawyers on what was "roughly the same data" around which legal interpretation should be based, i.e., consensus on what were the banner themes of international cybersecurity, and what were broadly the "rules and standards" for state behavior on those banner themes.[32]

If technical attributes of cyberspace were thus managed in this manner through the Tallinn Manual, what about political considerations? Did states engage with TM1 in any manner, and how did it change after the Manual's publication? While it is public knowledge that the first Manual had no formal process of engagement with states, Schmitt acknowledges that a "number of states approached me, and I had some one-on-one discussions with some of them".[33] "We were kind of flying solo with my backchannel discussions, but after the first Manual, where states were freaked out and held us at arm's length, they embraced us for the second one!"

Its extensive consultation with states stands out as a key distinction between TM2 and its predecessor. TM2 followed a similar preparatory process

30 *Interview with Thomas Wingfield*, April 8, 2022.

31 Ian Johnstone, *The Power of Deliberation: International Law, Politics and Organizations* (Oxford University Press, 2011), https://doi.org/10.1093/acprof:oso/9780195394931.003.0003.

32 Ronald Dworkin, *Law's Empire*, 1st ed. (Cambridge, MA: Harvard University Press, 1986), 91 *c.f.*. Johnstone (2011), n. 31.

33 *Interview with Michael N. Schmitt*, September 13, 2022.

with a bigger and slightly more diverse group – individual authors contributed specific portions of the draft, which were examined by the TM2 editorial committee, while the process of revising and finalizing the draft was once again done in plenary format.[34] Prior to the drafts being considered by the International Group of Experts in plenary, its sections were also sent out for review to subject-matter specialists in specific domains of international law. Interspersed among plenary sessions were the meetings of the so-called "Hague Process" co-organized by TM2 and the Dutch government. The Hague Process meetings held in 2015 and 2016 were usually organized over the course of a day at the headquarters of the Dutch MFA, and hosted nearly fifty countries who were invited to pore over the draft and submit oral and written responses to it. Schmitt specifically highlighted the practice of states submitting written inputs to TM2. "While [the Hague Process] meetings got all the attention, that is not in fact, where the greatest input came from – that came from written submission by states", he said. "Rather than a [standalone input] document [on legal positions], we gave states the draft, and said, 'do margin notes and use track changes. *Change anything you want.*' Then, Liis [Vihul, TM2's project manager] and I would go through them. We had thousands of pages of input! One country, I think, had 97 suggestions for changes [to the draft]"[35] [emphasis added].

What explains greater state engagement with TM2? Ultimately, the Hague Process was an important part of the broader law-ascertainment exercise, in that it brought together distinguished lawyers from various states to debate TM2 rules in the Netherlands. That said, the Manuals' promoters also arguably saw in the Hague Process a valuable opportunity to enhance the acceptability of TM2 within the cyber CoP. As Schmitt's "change anything you want" comment indicates, the Hague Process was as much about recording states' views of *lex lata* as it was about ensuring the Manual reasonably accommodated their diverging policy and strategic considerations. This view is confirmed not just from the comments of the Tallinn Manual experts but also the Dutch government. An international lawyer in the Legal Affairs Department of the Dutch MFA has acknowledged that the Hague Process was "an initiative by the Netherlands to further the debate on how international law applies in cyber space and *to increase the level of agreement*"[36] [emphasis

34 *Tallinn Manual Experts Meet for Intense Drafting Session*, 2015, https://www.youtube.com/watch?v=pu1ZuCbqOeo.

35 *Interview with Michael N. Schmitt*, September 13, 2022.

36 Wieteke Theeuwen, "Attribution for the Purposes of State Responsibility," *Netherlands Military Law Review*, August 17, 2018, https://puc.overheid.nl/mrt/doc/PUC_248325_11/.

added]. How could states "change anything [they wanted]" or "increase the level of agreement" if they were simply restating international law as it applied to cyberspace? Besides, it was not as if states were divulging details of their covert or overt cyber operations in Hague Process consultations, thereby offering a glimpse into emerging state practice. The objective of such consultations, therefore, was equally to ensure the Manual was invoked and cited by the most important practitioners within the cyber CoP: states.

The Hague Process meetings coincided with end of the fourth UN GGE and the beginning of the fifth GGE, and to most governments involved in the UN process, the difficulties in arriving at an agreement on international law issues were apparent. "[There was] very strong disagreement about formalizing some kind of legal arrangement from very early on [in the GGE]", said the fifth GGE chair Karsten Geier.[37] "The conversation began by some states saying: 'oh, we need a legally binding instrument'; others responded saying 'that is taking us too far', and so we decided to meet in the middle and come up with political norms." On the other hand, TM2 offered through the Hague Process the same avenues for negotiations as with political norms, but pitched itself strictly as a process to identify and interpret international law. Put differently, the Hague Process meetings were signaled as a practice that "legalized" and "diminished"[38] political differences over international cybersecurity governance. In an interview to the Estonian Ministry of Defence given in 2015, Schmitt argued that "politics stays out of the room in which [the TM2 group experts] are working". "Politics has confounded the discovery of how international law applies to cyber operations", he declared, noting that TM2 sought to address this problem.[39]

Indeed, upon the fifth GGE's failure to produce a consensus report, Schmitt and Vihul argued that the Hague Process was among the "most promising initiatives" to address the void left by the GGE.[40] There is ample evidence to suggest that this managerial process was successful. States' approaches to TM2 could arguably be divided into two camps: if some (e.g., European states) wanted for TM2 to be forum that articulated rules that the GGE could not, others (e.g., the United States, Israel, and possibly the UK) possibly sought to engage with it in order to limit overly unfavorable interpretations that would limit their actions with respect to cyber operations. The US was among the major cyber powers that, to borrow Schmitt's words, kept TM1 at arm's length.

37 *Interview with Karsten Geier*, February 8, 2021.
38 Aalberts and Gammeltoft-Hansen (2017), 9.
39 *Tallinn Manual Experts Meet for Intense Drafting Session*, n.34.
40 Schmitt and Vihul (2017), n.46, chapter 5.

"Having been in it up to my elbows, I knew that there was almost nothing [in TM1] that would keep the US for doing any lawful military thing it needed to do", said Wingfield. "I'll say this on the record, I was a little bit surprised that the United States was less supportive than I had hoped."[41] However, the US government was an enthusiastic participant in the Hague Process, probably because it knew that the fifth GGE was unlikely to succeed, and saw its engagement with TM2 as essential to retaining some agency over the process of identifying and applying international law to this domain. Perhaps, the most supportive evidence for the claim that the UN GGE and TM2's fates were intertwined comes from China's participation in the Hague Process. If China officially criticized TM1 for ushering in a "'military paradigm' of response to cyberattacks, [...] aggravating cyberspace militarization and arms race", it was an active participant in the Hague Process meetings, often providing line-by-line inputs to the group on their draft.[42] Even as China continued to be strident in its opposition to discuss the applicability of rules, in particular of international humanitarian law, within the GGE, it attended and offered comments on TM2 drafts based on "careful preparation".[43] However, evidence suggests the engagement of states with the Tallinn Manual process was a two-way street. TM2 may have benefited from the fifth UN GGE's political deadlock. As the next section highlights, states also brought the norms discussion with them to TM2 discussions, resulting in the Manual borrowing language from the UN GGE to interpret the due diligence obligation as applied to cyberspace.

Similarly, TM2 continued the practices of its predecessor manual to ensure that its commentaries accurately reflected technical considerations. To aid their work, the drafting committee of TM2 sought the CCDCOE's help in securing a technical expert who understood "law and cyber".[44] The NATO center deputed Bernhards Blumbergs, a Latvian engineer, for this purpose. "Whereas technical experts were not [physically] present when we were polishing the first Tallinn Manual – often we would e-mail our queries to them – there was almost never a moment [in TM2] where the lawyers were in the room, and Bernhards was not", said Schmitt.[45] Blumbergs, who was nicknamed "Moun-

41 *Interview with Thomas Wingfield*, April 8, 2022.

42 [*via participant observation*] This author was among the participants present at a Hague Process consultation organized by the Dutch MFA on July 12, 2016.

43 Zhixiong Huang and Kubo Mačák, "Towards the International Rule of Law in Cyberspace: Contrasting Chinese and Western Approaches," *Chinese Journal of International Law* 16, no. 2 (June 1, 2017): 271–310, https://doi.org/10.1093/chinesejil/jmx011.

44 *Interview with Michael N. Schmitt*, September 13, 2022.

45 *Interview with Michael N. Schmitt*, September 13, 2022.

tain Flower" by the TM2 drafting committee, sat at the top of table with the director and project manager, "reading multiple times drafts and redrafts".[46] Even after the committee's work was done, Schmitt and Vihul sat with Blumbergs to read through the states' inputs, and jointly address how best to reflect their concerns in the Manual.

In addition to political and technical considerations, the Tallinn Manual also had to address reputational factors. During the interview, Schmitt highlighted the difficulty in securing consensus among the International Group of Experts. In response to whether TM1 and TM2 could have followed the model of the International Law Commission, and leave a topic unaddressed where was no clear agreement among its members about the existence of a rule, Schmitt said "it was an option" but that the Manual's drafters instead sought to make rules "as narrow as possible".[47] "If people understand 'this was the consensus view' [of the TM drafters], that means it was the least common denominator", he said. "For example, I've heard many times [from critics] that the Tallinn Manual took the approach that you *have to* have physical damage [for sovereignty violations] – no we didn't! It's just that the group we had, the over-30 individuals we had, this was all we could agree on. But my own view [in this case] happens to be much broader." The underlying argument here is that the "consensus" view of reputed international lawyers was also a crucial factor in the Tallinn Manual's securing policy purchase from practitioners in the cyber CoP (as well as international lawyers outside it). The Manual had staked its authority on the credentials of its distinguished lawyers, so it was important for them to agree broadly on interpretations of its "black-letter rules".[48] Even the "least common denominator" approach proved to be difficult, as the commentaries frequently note divisions between a "majority" and "minority" of experts, or in other cases highlight that "some of the experts took a position", while others did not endorse it. Schmitt emphasizes the reputation of legal experts in the preface of TM1 as well. The "mix" of "[practitioners and] world-class [academic] experts on the *jus ad bellum* and *jus in bello* [is] crucial to the credibility of the product", he wrote.[49] Schmitt repeatedly emphasized that the role of these reputed experts was to accommodate all "reasonable points" in the commentaries, and the views of the Manual should not be seen as the individual views of legal experts.[50]

46 *Interview with Michael N. Schmitt*, September 13, 2022.
47 *Interview with Michael N. Schmitt*, September 13, 2022.
48 *Kessler and Werner (2013)*, 804.
49 TM 1.0, 9.
50 TM 1.0, 6.

In the final analysis, at least some practices of the Tallinn Manual processes resembled those of norms-articulation processes in the cyber CoP. From interviews and public statements, it does not appear to be the case that the Tallinn Manual's drafters reflexively evaluated how their *managing* of political interlocutors, technical expertise, and the reputational authority of their own drafters, would sit alongside claims that the Manuals were simply identifying existing legal obligations. The Tallinn Manual's managerial practices were driven not only by the need to correctly ascertain existing law but also acceptance and adoption of its commentaries within the cyber CoP, much like voluntary norms of state behavior. To secure legitimacy within the CoP, the Manuals needed not only to defend their legal reasoning but also to ensure that key political and technical constituencies accepted, or at the very least, engaged with its commentaries seriously. The hypothetical scenarios and illustrations that the Manuals drew on needed to be sound, realistic, and convincing to technical and political practitioners in the CoP. And to get them on board, the Tallinn Manuals had to engage in negotiations with these practitioners, in the same way as the UN GGE or GCSC would articulate its norms. The Manual's adoption of such practices was not reflexively evaluated because discussions on the "framework of responsible state behavior" within the cyber CoP conflated norm-articulation and rule-interpretation. And to the extent that technical considerations shaped the commentaries of the Tallinn Manuals through these managerial, "norms-like" practices, they can be considered to be examples of "creeping expertise".

2.3 Creeping Expertise in the Tallinn Manuals

Following an overview of the practices of TM1 and TM2, as well as the underlying mechanisms of "creeping expertise" in both Manuals, this section highlights examples where technical considerations decisively influenced the International Groups of Experts' application of international law to state behavior. The section highlights three specific instances or areas of international law taken up by the Manuals where "creeping expertise" is evident: sovereignty violations, the use of cyber countermeasures by states in response to internationally wrongful cyber operations, and the application of the due diligence principle to cyberspace. Here, a caveat is necessary. These are the "hard cases" of international cybersecurity law, where states' views sharply diverge and where doctrinal ascertainment of existing law is extremely challenging. Not only did TM2 drafters have limited insights into state's cyber operations – nearly a decade on, at the time of writing, such data is difficult to come by – but they also did not many declared "national positions" on international law to go by. Most of these positions would be published a year or so after the publication of TM2, and ironically, be influenced by the structure and substance of the Manual itself. Therefore, judging a Manual's managerial approach to law-finding through just three "rules" – out of a total of 154 in TM2 – may not reveal a fuller picture. Nevertheless, these three rules or themes truly cut to the core of international cybersecurity governance, and are essential to advancing responsible state behavior in the domain.

2.3.1 Sovereignty Violations in Cyberspace: Intent v. Effects

The Tallinn Manuals tie sovereignty in cyberspace to the notion of territoriality. "Cyber activities occur on territory and involve objects, or are conducted by persons or entities, over which States may exercise their sovereign prerogatives", notes TM2.[51] Rule 4 of TM2 declares that states should not conduct cyber operations that violate the sovereignty of others.[52] The drafters of the Manual emphasize an "effects-based" approach, categorizing sovereignty violations into three: cyber operations that cause (a) physical damage; (b) loss of functionality of target systems or services; and (c) interfere or usurp "inherently governmental functions".[53] TM2 notes the drafters *could not agree* whether cyber operations that neither caused damage nor loss of functionality – for instance, the installation of malware or Distributed Denial of Service Attacks that caused temporary loss of functions[54] – constituted a violation of sovereignty. At the same time, the Manual also emphasizes that "intent is not a constitutive element of a breach of sovereignty".[55] The spillover effects of cyber operations and cyber espionage, whether intended or not, could result in violations of sovereignty, including of third countries.

TM2 neither justifies its qualification of effects nor its position regarding the intent of states through legal sources. Indeed, TM2's effects-based approach has been criticized on the one hand as setting too high a technical, violative threshold for cyber operations,[56] and on the other, as being bereft of legal

51 TM 2.0, 12.
52 TM 2.0, 17.
53 TM 2.0, 20.
54 TM 2.0, 21.
55 TM 2.0, 24.
56 Przemysław Roguski, "Layered Sovereignty: Adjusting Traditional Notions of Sovereignty to a Digital Environment," in *2019 11th International Conference on Cyber Conflict (CyCon)*, vol. 900, 2019, 1–13, https://doi.org/10.23919/CYCON.2019.8756900.

methodology.[57] As for the motive or intent of states, ILC's commentary on ARSIWA admittedly notes that absent "any specific requirement of a mental element in terms of the primary obligation, it is only the act of a State that matters".[58] Yet, in classifying sovereignty as a primary rule of obligation for states in cyberspace, TM2's decision to cast aside their intent arguably warranted an explanation. TM2's position is notable because the key distinction between sovereignty violations as envisaged by the Manual and prohibited interventions under international law is the element of coercion. While some international lawyers have argued that states' coercive behavior too should be considered independent of their intent,[59] international tribunals have been careful not to wade into this thicket, noting simply that the actions of states in cases before them had demonstrably coercive effects. Indeed, Schmitt himself has classified TM2's position on sovereignty *per contra* the rule on non-intervention, arguing that the latter requires coercive intent.[60]

Balancing thus between the high threshold required for sovereignty violations and the doing away of intent appears to be a delicate compromise struck by TM2 acknowledging the technical realities of cyberspace. Cyber operations would violate the sovereignty of states only if they caused physical damage or loss of functionality of digital infrastructure, but should such effects materialize, not only would perpetrator states be responsible irrespective of their intent to cause such damage/loss but also be responsible for sovereignty violations in each territory where those effects manifested.

This "intent v. effects" juxtaposition of TM2 is arguably owed to its managerial practices that allowed technical experts to impress upon the Manual's drafters the interconnected nature of digital networks and the potentially extraterritorial impact of cyber operations that targeted cloud infrastructure in particular. The compromise formulation is also owed to TM2's efforts to secure the acceptance of states, based on the premise that sovereignty violations would not require for accusers to establish the intent of perpetrator states unlike the non-intervention rule, which had to demonstrate coercive intent on their part.

TM2's formulation on sovereignty is ultimately a balancing act because it acknowledges that states often intrude into network and infrastructure on

---

57 Jack Goldsmith and Alex Loomis, "Defend Forward and Sovereignty," Aegis Series Paper (Hoover Institution, 2021), 7, https://doi.org/10.1093/oso/9780197601792.003.0008.

58 *ARSIWA with commentaries*, 36.

59 *See*, Ido Kilovaty, "The Elephant in the Room: Coercion," *AJIL Unbound* 113 (2019): 87–91, https://doi.org/10.1017/aju.2019.10.

60 Michael N. Schmitt, "In Defense of Sovereignty in Cyberspace," *Just Security* (blog), May 8, 2018, https://www.justsecurity.org/55876/defense-sovereignty-cyberspace/.

other territories, not least for the purpose of surveillance or intelligence collection. This is unlikely to stop anytime soon, and to categorize all such cyber operations as sovereignty violations would be impractical. Hence, TM2's requirement of a high threshold of damage or loss of functionality owing to such operations. On the other hand, the permissibility of such intrusive operations had to be balanced against the risks of seriously impairing networked digital infrastructure, especially those that run on cloud services. Thanks to briefings by technical experts, the implications of cloud computing seem to have weighed in particular on Tallinn Manual lawyers. Cloud computing refers to the offloading of data processing, storage, and increasingly, even networking and cybersecurity functions to a third party, often located outside the borders in which the client operates.[61] Cloud computing has become ubiquitous: most internet businesses are likely to have adopted cloud services at some point during their operations simply because it is cheaper and less resource-intensive to delegate critical processing and networking functions to dedicated vendors. For domestic and international cybersecurity, the popularity of cloud computing raises two main concerns. First, with cloud infrastructure based abroad, governments often do not have adequate visibility over threats and potential vulnerabilities that could affect digital networks and services on their territory.[62] Second, with the rise in adoption of cloud services, they have also become conduits for sophisticated cyber operations by state and non-state actors with serious spillover consequences, given that these services control critical functions of multiple platforms and corporations, presenting a lucrative attack surface.

It is clear from interviews and public statements of the Tallinn lawyers that technical experts briefed them on various aspects of cloud computing. Not only did Wingfield allude to it,[63] but Schmitt himself has noted that he "embarrassingly" did not understand the concept of cloud computing at first – "I didn't think it was actually a cloud, OK, but I did think it was somehow connected to radio waves!".[64] When Bret Michael continued to invoke the term during his briefings, Schmitt said TM1 drafters sought an explanation of the concept.

61 *See*, "What Is Cloud Computing," Amazon Web Services, Inc., accessed December 1, 2022, https://aws.amazon.com/what-is-cloud-computing/.

62 Arun Mohan Sukumar, "'Responsibility to Detect?': Autonomous Threat Detection and Its Implications for Due Diligence in Cyberspace," in *2022 14th International Conference on Cyber Conflict: Keep Moving!* (*CyCon*), vol. 700, 2022, 173–87, https://doi.org/10.23919/CyCon55549.2022.9811012.

63 *Interview with Thomas Wingfield*, April 8, 2022.

64 *International Law and Cyber Operations – Launch of the Tallinn Manual 2.0*, 2017, https://www.youtube.com/watch?v=riP4kStBBJs.

Knowing that cloud computing was all about "networks and routers" enforced the drafters' view that states had sovereignty over such infrastructure on their territory, even if it had extraterritorial use.[65] Operations against cloud infrastructure would "generally" not violate the sovereignty of third states, TM2 declares.[66] However, should such operations lead to loss of functionality or physical damage on another territory, such an operation would have breached the sovereignty of all impacted states. The perpetrator state, as noted previously, cannot claim that such damage was unintentional or unforeseen. The proliferative potential of cyber attacks, as evidenced by banner cases like Stuxnet or WannaCry, is well known.[67] Increasingly, cyber operations have targeted cloud-based vulnerabilities in order to attack third-party services – most notably, Albania's severing of its ties with Iran pertained to the latter's alleged exploitation of a cloud-related vulnerability to target Albanian services[68] – the adoption of TM2's approach to sovereignty violations offers states a plausible argument against the exploitation and weaponization of key multi-service platforms.

The implications of TM2's formulation on sovereignty in so far as cloud computing is concerned seems to have struck a chord with states, even those who have not fully embraced the Manual's position that sovereignty is a "rule". In 2020, Israel – which has distinguished between the "general concept" of sovereignty and the "international legal rule" of "territorial sovereignty" – suggested that a state's "legitimate sovereign interests" extended to the data stored by its government abroad through private, cloud-based services.[69] There is a clash between states' "legitimate interests" and territorial sovereignty, noted Israel, raising the question whether attacks on cloud infrastructure could result in sovereignty violations of third states, even if its effects were not manifested in their physical territory. Such an interpretation would go further than the TM2's formulation.

---

65 *Launch of the Tallinn Manual 2.0*, n.64.

66 TM 2.0, 25.

67 Peter W Singer, "Stuxnet and Its Hidden Lessons on the Ethics of Cyberweapons," *Case Western Reserve Journal of International Law* 47 (2015), 79–86; Adam McNeil, "How Did the WannaCry Ransomworm Spread? | Malwarebytes Labs," Malwarebytes, May 19, 2017, https://www.malwarebytes.com/blog/news/2017/05/how-did-wannacry-ransomworm-spread.

68 "Iranian State Actors Conduct Cyber Operations Against the Government of Albania | CISA," United States Cybersecurity and Infrastructure Security Agency (CISA), September 21, 2022, https://www.cisa.gov/uscert/ncas/alerts/aa22-264a.

69 Roy Schöndorf, "Israel's Perspective on Key Legal and Practical Issues Concerning the Application of International Law to Cyber Operations," *International Law Studies* 97 (2021), 402.

Similarly, the Netherlands has noted that the nature of "cloud-based systems" means it would not be "always possible to establish whether a cyber operation involves a cross-border component and thus violates a country's sovereignty".[70] The Dutch position notes that these kinds of operations may not have a "direct physical or tangible impact", but that it "generally endorses" the position of TM2 on sovereignty.[71] Brazil, which also aligns its position with that of TM2, notably suggests that "cyber operations against information systems located in another State's territory or causing extraterritorial effects" may constitute a sovereignty violation.[72] Both the Dutch and Brazilian statements seem to indicate agreement with TM2's doing away with the intent of perpetrator states, given the increasing likelihood that cyber operations may involve extraterritorial effects due to the nature of cloud computing.

TM2's "intent v. effects" formulation has also been justified by its drafters as one way to avoid the onerous requirement of demonstrating coercive intent for potential violations of the non-intervention rule. In other words, that states should accept its position on sovereignty because violations of the "rule" of sovereignty are easier to establish than breaches of the non-intervention rule. TM2's drafters have articulated this justification through a public and presumably private, managerial dialogue with states, the UK being the most notable example.

In 2018, the UK became the first major cyber power to disagree with TM2's formulation on sovereignty when it declared it was not possible to "extrapolate from [the] general principle [of sovereignty] a specific rule or additional prohibition for cyber activity beyond that of a prohibited intervention [under customary international law]".[73] Yet, in a 2022 statement, the UK too appears to have calibrated its interpretation of the non-intervention rule, meeting TM2's position half-way at least.[74] The 2022 statement expanded the UK's view on what constituted "coercive" behavior in cyberspace. "While the precise boundaries of coercion are yet to crystallize in international law", the statement read, "we should be ready to consider whether disruptive cyber

70 "Official Compendium of Voluntary National Contributions on the Subject of How International Law Applies to the Use of Information and Communications Technologies by States Submitted by Participating Governmental Experts in the Group of Governmental Experts on Advancing Responsible State Behaviour in Cyberspace in the Context of International Security Established Pursuant to General Assembly Resolution 73/266" (UN General Assembly, Seventy-sixth session, July 13, 2021), 56, https://front.un-arm.org/wp-content/uploads/2021/08/A-76-136-EN.pdf.

71 *Official Compendium of Voluntary National Contributions*, N.70, 56.

72 *Official Compendium of Voluntary National Contributions*, N.70, 18.

73 *The Attorney General's Office* (*2018*), n.55, chapter 3.

74 *The Attorney General's Office* (2022), n.55, chapter 3.

behaviors are coercive even where it might not be possible to point to a specific course of conduct which a State has been forced into or prevented from taking". This dilution of *the role of intent*, coupled with a nod to the "overall scale and effect" of a cyber operation arguably brings the UK and TM2 positions closer to each other, albeit with minor differences. It is reasonable to conclude that the UK's shift was prompted by an ongoing dialogue, public and possibly private, with the TM2 drafters. Writing in 2018, barely days before the UK formally announced its position, Schmitt pitched TM2's position on sovereignty *per contra* the rule on non-intervention, arguing that the latter involves the difficult task of establishing coercive intent.[75] The "sovereignty as a principle" approach is "apparently championed by a number of government agencies, including some abroad, that wield significant power in cyber operational and policy circles", wrote Schmitt, hinting that those government agencies had an interest in maintaining "high thresholds and ambiguity" to facilitate offensive cyber operations.

Even after the *modus vivendi* offered by the UK in 2022, Schmitt did not let up: "it has long been anticipated that the United Kingdom would seek to soften the coercion requirement to counterbalance its rejection of the sovereignty rule".[76] The UK's determination of "coercive intent" based not on the perpetrator's "choice" but its "target", is an "oversimplification" of the non-intervention rule and goes against "traditional understanding", he argued, stressing once again the need to accept TM2's position on sovereignty. This dialogue may seem confined to the UK and TM2 but it is also a managerial practice adopted by the Manual's drafters to emphasize that its "intent v. effects" formulation is a balanced one, grounded in technical realities.

2.3.2 Countermeasures in International Cybersecurity Law

In 2015, NATO CCDCOE's annual conference on cyber conflict CyCon hosted a presentation by Paul Walker, then an international lawyer with the US Navy's Fleet Cyber Command. Cdr. Walker in his presentation noted that countermeasures were the "most viable international law tools" for states to respond to internationally wrongful acts that did not breach the *jus ad bellum* thresh-

75 Michael N. Schmitt, "In Defense of Sovereignty in Cyberspace," *Just Security* (blog), May 8, 2018, https://www.justsecurity.org/55876/defense-sovereignty-cyberspace/.

76 Michael Schmitt, "The United Kingdom on International Law in Cyberspace," *EJIL: Talk!* (blog), May 24, 2022, https://www.ejiltalk.org/the-united-kingdom-on-international-law-in-cyberspace/.

old.[77] Organizing his presentation specifically around two major cyber incidents, the 2013 Iranian DDoS attacks on US banks[78] and the 2014 Sony hack,[79] Cdr Walker noted that such non-forcible operations were likely to become more common, necessitating urgent and effective responses from states. However, the law of countermeasures needed "modification", he argued. Specifically, he pointed to three "conditions [of the customary law of countermeasures] that raised problems" for its viability as an effective "cyber" response:

a. Countermeasures could only be taken against the state committing internationally wrongful acts, which presented a challenge in cases like the Iranian DDoS attacks where infrastructure distributed across 120 states were used as launch pads for the whole operation;
b. Countermeasures were permissible only if the wrongful act was ongoing: what did this mean for cyberspace? Some operations were indeed discrete in nature (Sony), but many other attacks started, stopped, and then continued over weeks, sometimes months.
c. Countermeasures, as contemplated in ARSIWA, required an "extended period of negotiations", he noted. In cyber, "this [was] not very feasible, not very realistic", he argued, pointing to the need for swift implementation of cyber countermeasures to remedy the wrongdoing. The notice of intent to take countermeasures would be another hurdle, he said, noting that the only exception available to the notification requirement was in the case of "urgent countermeasures". This "exception should be the norm" in cyberspace, he concluded.

To remedy all three concerns, which were rooted in technical realities, the law of countermeasures had therefore to be modified.

In the ensuing Q&A session with Walker, Schmitt, the director of the team that had by then begun work on TM2, commended his "interesting and provocative" points. "But your whole presentation begs the biggest question: how are you going to do this? The law of state responsibility from which countermeasures originate is not treaty law but arguably customary in nature", he said. Given the extensive debates and difficulties the ILC itself faced in codify-

77 *Law of the Horse to Law of the Submarine: The Future of State Behavior in Cyberspace*, CyCon 2015, 2015, https://www.youtube.com/watch?v=rFeK4jAQvE0.

78 "Denial of Service Attacks against U.S. Banks in 2012–2013," Cyber Operations Tracker | Council on Foreign Relations, accessed January 28, 2023, https://www.cfr.org/cyber-operations/denial-service-attacks-against-us-banks-2012-2013.

79 "Sony Pictures Entertainment Attack (2014)," International cyber law: interactive toolkit, June 9, 2021, https://cyberlaw.ccdcoe.org/wiki/Sony_Pictures_Entertainment_attack_(2014).

ing the exact parameters of this custom, "how in the world [are these modifications] going to come into law?" asked Schmitt.

As it turns out, some of those modifications would emerge from TM2 itself, and presented as an interpretation of existing obligations on the law of countermeasures under the state responsibility regime. Its section on countermeasures displays vividly the influence of the Tallinn Manual's managerial practices, as TM2's drafters attempted to adapt aspects of an already contentious body of international law for cyberspace. The interaction with, and learning of Tallinn lawyers, through TM2's managerial practices, with important technical, political, and legal constituencies within the cyber CoP is evident in the case of countermeasures. The CyCon interaction referenced above is itself one such managerial practice.

During and after the publications of both Tallinn Manuals, CyCon emerged as an important venue for engagement between drafters and other members of the CoP on their rules and commentaries. Operational technical agencies from NATO countries, such as the US Navy Cyber Command that Cdr Walker then represented, are almost always represented in good numbers at CyCon. Feedback from practitioners in the cyber CoP offered during CyCon was arguably valuable to TM2 drafters. At the same edition of CyCon in 2015, Schmitt said during a presentation on TM2: "I'd like to go through three topics [sovereignty, state responsibility, and due diligence], and the challenges we are encountering [while drafting TM2] in terms of interpretation of the law, and then, I would welcome your feedback. *We are at the point of time where if you tell me something, I can fold it into the Manual before it is presented [for discussion] to the International Group of Experts*"[80] [emphasis added].Countermeasures, including what "urgency" meant in the context of cyberspace, were classified as an "open question" before the group of drafters, noted Schmitt.

In this case, the arguments offered by the US Navy lawyer clearly left an impact on Schmitt as well as other lawyers from the group of Tallinn drafters who were present in the audience.[81] By January 2017, with just a few weeks to go for the formal launch of TM2, Schmitt was hinting that TM2 would present a more permissive interpretation of the law of countermeasures that reflected technical realities, and the need for states to engage in effective responses against "below-the-threshold" cyber operations. At the 2017 edition of Suits

80 *Tallinn Manual 2.0 Approach to State Responsibility* (CyCon 2015, 2015), https://www.youtube.com/watch?v=108uuZsPvms.

81 Paul Ducheine @ducheine@mastodon.social [@paulducheine], "@Schmitt_ILaw to Paul Walker on His Proposal on the Law of Countermeasures: How Would That Have to Be Change, given the Customary Status?", *Twitter*, May 27, 2015, https://twitter.com/pauldu cheine/status/603517003354214400.

and Spooks in Washington D.C., a conference well attended by intelligence officers and private cybersecurity contractors, Schmitt held forth on the law of countermeasures, noting specially that there was "vigorous debate among scholars about whether [Russian election interference in US presidential elections] constituted an 'internationally wrongful act' – which would in turn open Russia up to the possibility of U.S. countermeasures".[82]

If managerial practices like CyCon presentations offered TM2 drafters an opportunity to learn from operators *how* the law of countermeasures could be shaped as an effective instrument in cyberspace – the following paragraphs illustrate "creeping expertise" with respect to TM2's commentary on the subject – their engagement with states and policymakers through practices like the Hague Process underlined *why* the law should be interpreted permissively. With the fifth UN GGE (2016–2017) holding its meetings concurrently, tension between major cyber powers, especially the US, Russia, and China on the scope of applicability of international law was apparent to all practitioners in the cyber CoP. A workshop organized by UNIDIR and CSIS for UN GGE delegations and other states in Geneva in April 2016, just before the GGE commenced its work, noted that the "application of the right to self-defence or countermeasures by injured States" was a "re-occurring issue of contention".[83] The report of the workshop also noted:

> There was some discussion of countermeasures, an element of international law that has yet to figure in a GGE report. Some suggested that the next GGE should consider a norm that would read: "the victim State may take actions not involving the use of force in response (or retaliation) to a malicious cyber action by another State".[84]

Four out of five presenters who were part of the specific workshop panel in which the discussion on countermeasures arose were part of the TM2 drafting team.[85] Through the UNIDIR workshop and meetings of the Hague Process, TM2 drafters were able to gauge the views of different states with respect to

---

82 "U.S. Can Respond to Cyberattacks without Showing Proof First, Legal Expert Says," *CyberScoop* (blog), January 11, 2017, https://cyberscoop.com/us-evidence-proof-on-hacking/.

83 "Report of the International Security Cyber Issues Workshop Series" (Geneva: UNIDIR/Center for Strategic and International Studies, April 2016), 15 https://unidir.org/sites/default/files/publication/pdfs/report-of-the-international-security-cyber-issues-workshop-series-en-656.pdf.

84 *Ibid.*

85 *Report of the International Security Cyber Issues Workshop Series*, 26.

the topic – that there were a group of states, especially NATO countries, which were keen to utilize cyber countermeasures as a lawful option, but also that many states, including China and Russia, were opposed to their implementation. By the time of the UNIDIR workshop, TM2 had completed its final session of in-person discussions, but it would not be until June 2016 that the drafters would adopt the final text.[86]

In sum, the practices of engagement adopted by TM2 shaped its technical and political thinking on the need for a "modified" law of countermeasures for cyberspace. In response to a question on how much TM2's pronouncements on countermeasures and the subsequent debate on "collective countermeasures" in international law were influenced by the unique technical attributes of cyberspace, Schmitt said its "absolutely crystal clear that technology is causing us to focus on [these] rules".[87] These modifications, which can be highlighted therefore as examples of "creeping expertise", are illustrated below.

Countermeasures, which refer to "self-help" responses by states to internationally wrongful acts, serve to induce compliance by wrongdoing states with their "obligations of cessation and reparation".[88] Although states have long been adopting such responses, their characterization as "countermeasures" – Delerue notes the ICJ used this term for the first time in the *Tehran Hostages* case in 1980[89] – and the codification of rules around their use is more recent. The ILC's pronouncements on countermeasures were themselves the product of much debate and controversy, not only among individual members, but also states. In particular, the existence of countermeasures as a remedy in international law was itself challenged by a number of countries, especially those of the Global South.[90] The ARSIWA commentary on the topic concedes that it "aims to *establish* an operational system, taking into account the exceptional character of countermeasures as a response to internationally wrongful conduct"[91] [emphasis added]. The Tallinn lawyers, as noted previously, appear

86 "Tallinn Manual 2.0 to Be Completed in 2016," NATO CCDCOE, accessed January 29, 2023, https://ccdcoe.org/news/2015/tallinn-manual-2-0-to-be-completed-in-2016/.

87 *Interview with Michael N. Schmitt*, September 13, 2022.

88 See, *ARSIWA with commentaries*, Arts. 49–54, 128–139.

89 François Delerue, *Cyber Operations and International Law*, 1st ed. (Cambridge University Press, 2020), 435, https://doi.org/10.1017/9781108780605.

90 For a critical survey of the ILC debate on countermeasures and views of developing countries towards this debate, see, Separate Opinion of Judge Cançado Trindade, *Appeal relating to the Jurisdiction of the ICAO Council under Article 84 of the Convention on International Civil Aviation (Bahrain, Egypt, Saudi Arabia and United Arab Emirates v. Qatar)*, Judgment, I.C.J. Reports 2020, 122–133.

91 *ARSIWA with commentaries*, 128.

to have been conscious that the customary law of countermeasures, while not *terra nova*, presented considerable gray areas around the identification and interpretation of rules in cyberspace.

Rules 20 to 25 of TM2 outline the scope of cyber and non-cyber countermeasures, with the "black-letter" rules largely restating the articles on state responsibility, especially Articles 22, 49, 50, and 51 of ARSIWA.[92] However, TM2's commentary around those rules carve out a number of exceptions for the deployment of cyber countermeasures from the procedural safeguards enshrined in the ARSIWA commentary. The difference in the framing of both commentaries is itself notable. The ARSIWA commentary begins by noting that it applies equally to "reciprocal" countermeasures – those "that correspond to, or are directly connected with, the obligation breached" – as it does to any other form of countermeasures.[93] In fact, the ILC pointed out that tit-for-tat measures are often precluded by "considerations of good order and humanity".[94] The possibility that states may still resort to reciprocal measures, the commentary goes on to highlight, was one of the ILC's main considerations behind identifying procedural safeguards for their implementation.

In contrast, TM2's commentary on the topic goes further than reciprocal measures and leads by highlighting the possibility that countermeasures "may directly achieve compliance with an international legal obligation breached by the responsible States".[95] It is clear that the Manual here is contemplating cyber countermeasures and not offline measures. This assertion is illustrated through the post-war example of a victim state hacking and copying a database of refugees and displaced persons maintained by another state – which it has refused to share, contravening the law of armed conflict – using it to reunify families along border areas.[96] The victim state's cyber operations, including the continued exfiltration of information from said database, "are permissible as a countermeasure even though not designed to compel the first to provide the information itself", notes TM2. Such remedial actions, which Cannizzaro terms "executive countermeasures", represent the "extreme border of the instrumental conception of countermeasures".[97] "Understandably,

92 TM 2.0, 111–134.
93 *ARSIWA with commentaries*, 129.
94 *ARSIWA with commentaries*, 129.
95 TM 2.0, 117.
96 TM 2.0, 117.
97 E. Cannizzaro, "The Role of Proportionality in the Law of International Countermeasures," *European Journal of International Law* 12, no. 5 (December 1, 2001), 911, https://doi.org/10.1093/ejil/12.5.889.

international law looks at this hypothesis with caution", notes Cannizzaro.[98] In other words, TM2 adopts a more permissive approach to countermeasures on account of the possibility that in cyberspace, states can undertake direct measures to remedy another wrongful cyber operation.

This permissive approach is evident throughout TM2's treatment of the procedural safeguards applicable to countermeasures. For example, on the issue of whether states should adopt a countermeasure that is "most easily reversed" or simply "reversible" – another question that was prompted largely on account of the technical possibilities of cyber operations, given that the ILC's commentary makes no such granular distinction – TM2 notes that a majority of lawyers left it to the choice of states.[99] Only a minority argued that countermeasures must be easily reversed in order not to "exacerbate relations between states". TM2 also expanded considerably the leeway available to states regarding prior notification before the implementation of countermeasures. While ARSIWA relaxes the requirement of notification when "urgent countermeasures" are "necessary", those envisaged in this category include "temporary stay orders, the temporary freezing of assets, and similar measures".[100] On the other hand, TM2 notes, without qualification, that situations warranting urgent countermeasures are "highly likely", given "the speed with which the consequences of a cyber operation manifest".[101] Further, TM2 also does away with the requirement of notification in instances where it is likely to "render a countermeasure meaningless".[102] The drafters offer no additional justification in support of such an interpretation, but note that the "same logic applies" as in the case of urgent countermeasures. TM2's prescription is precisely the same as the "modification" that Cdr Walker sought in his CyCon presentation.

Additionally, TM2 also rejects the view of the ILC – although a minority of lawyers noted it reflected customary international law – that states should also offer to negotiate before implementing countermeasures.[103] The majority rejected the requirement to negotiate based solely on the position of the United States in the *Air Service Agreement* case, and the award of the Arbitral Tribunal in that case.[104] The tribunal's decision in *Air Services* did not com-

98 *Cannizzaro* (2001), N.97, 911.

99 *TM* 2.0, 119.

100 *ARSIWA with commentaries*, 136.

101 *TM* 2.0, 120.

102 *TM* 2.0, 120.

103 *TM* 2.0, 120.

104 TM 2.0, 121. *Case concerning the Air Service Agreement of 27 March 1946 between the United States of America and France*, RIAA, 9 December 1978, Volume XVIII, pp. 417–493.

ment on the need to engage in good faith negotiations *prior* to the adoption of countermeasures – indeed, there was no need for such a decision, given the US-France air services agreement already included several provisions for consultations – but simply rejected the view that they could not be taken while negotiations had commenced.[105] TM2, meanwhile reasoned that a negotiation requirement would allow the wrongdoing state "to control the duration and impact of its breach" by instrumentally conducting its negotiations accordingly.[106]

TM2's permissive interpretation is also evident in its treatment of obligations that may not be impaired by countermeasures. The ARSIWA in Article 50(1)(b) notes that states undertaking countermeasures still have an obligation to "protect fundamental human rights". A significant issue regarding the implementation of some cyber countermeasures – especially hack backs – is their potential violation of privacy of citizens in the territory of the wrongdoing state, and even third states. However, TM2 could "achieve no consensus" on whether the right to privacy is fundamental, although the Manual notes elsewhere the "customary international law character" of the right.[107] Further, it notes complications owing to the "extraterritorial applicability of human rights norms".[108] The debate on the extraterritorial applicability of human rights, especially in the context of the state responsibility regime, is not new, but TM2 cast aside any detailed assessment of this practical and important consideration.

All this is not to say TM2 ignores the prescriptions of the ILC's commentary on countermeasures *in toto* – notably, the treatment by the Manual of what constitutes a "proportionate" cyber countermeasure is careful and considered. TM2 defers questions of proportionality, as the ILC did, to the primary obligation in question rather than offering prescriptive recommendations on technical thresholds or requirements for proportional countermeasures.[109] Yet, TM2's commentary on countermeasures can, in the final analysis, be considered a deviation from the letter and spirit of the ILC's pronouncements on the topic. Whereas the ILC was concerned that its pronouncements should not legitimize physical, non-forcible measures to the detriment of peaceful settlement of disputes in international relations, TM2 works towards making the countermeasures regime "stick" in cyberspace. And its interpretation, going by

105 *Air Services arbitral award*, N.104, 444–445.
106 *TM* 2.0, 120.
107 TM 2.0, 124, 189.
108 *TM* 2.0, 124.
109 *TM* 2.0, 128.

Schmitt's own admission at the 2015 CyCon exchange, would constitute a "modification" of the customary law of countermeasures, because the legal basis of many of the majority/minority opinions of TM2 drafters on the topic is extremely thin. Those interpretations, I have sought to argue, are not the result of legal argumentation alone, but the result of practices of engagement and dialogue with technical experts and states.

2.3.3 Due Diligence and State Responsibility: The Twain Shall Meet in Cyberspace

Perhaps among the more remarkable interpretations of TM2 – made even more so because it has gone relatively unchallenged – pertain to the conflation of the due diligence and state responsibility regimes in their applicability to cyberspace by the Manual. Both TM1 and TM2 endorse the applicability of a due diligence rule to cyberspace. Rule 5 of TM1 declares that states shall not "knowingly allow" cyber infrastructure located in its territory or exclusively controlled by the government to be used for acts that "adversely and unlawfully affect other states".[110] Rule 7 of TM2, as scholars have noted,[111] revises this formulation to declare that states should not allow their "territory, or territory or cyber infrastructure under its governmental control" to be used for cyber operations "that affect the rights of, *and* produce serious adverse consequences" for other states[112] [emphasis added].

In this manner, TM2 lays down a "cumulative requirement" for the applicability of the due diligence rule.[113] The cyber due diligence rule seemingly applies to actions or omissions by states that breach their international obligations *and* cause serious harm, but may not otherwise be wrongful in international law.[114] However, this formulation is confusing, as the same conduct cannot be unlawful and lawful at the same time. It is more likely that TM2 sought dual standards of harm, not a "cumulative" requirement for due diligence. The commentary to Rule 6 (due diligence) suggests TM2 intended to cover both unlawful acts or omissions by state *as well as* cyber operations that caused serious effects, even if they were not prohibited by international law – for example, some actions of non-state actors. The operative phrases "affect the rights of" and "serious adverse consequences" used by TM2 appear to be

110 *TM 1.0*, 26.
111 Delerue (2020), N.89, 358.
112 *TM 2.0*, 43.
113 *TM 2.0*, 34.
114 *TM 2.0*, 34–35.

used as cognates for established legal standards drawn respectively from the *Corfu Channel* case,[115] and the *Trail Smelter* case[116] as well as the ILC Draft Articles on the Prevention of Transboundary Harm from Hazardous Activities.[117] However, to add to the confusion, TM2 also notes that the due diligence obligation applies "*only* when the cyber operation [...] amounts to an *internationally wrongful act*", definitively adopting the standard of state responsibility as articulated in ARSIWA.[118] [emphases added]

The origins and implications of TM2's formulation – at a 2022 symposium on international cybersecurity law, Schmitt candidly referred to it as "kind of sloppy"[119] – are worth noting in detail. During the interview, Schmitt conceded that the "'internationally wrongful act' part was problematic". "So, you have zeroed in on something. Maybe I overstated the law [*lex lata*] piece a little bit! *We had to get to something*, and it was hard to articulate the rule [on due diligence] without being overly broad." Schmitt recalled that there were lawyers within the TM2 group who wanted to cyber due diligence to mean "stopping harmful activities from your territory", but others, and some consulted states, argued this would not be practical for all manner of hostile cyber operations. "That's where the stolen phrase from *Trail Smelter*, 'serious adverse consequences', came in, [...] but then we had the problem of calling it 'internationally wrongful acts'...", Schmitt said[120] [emphasis added].

Its due diligence formulation clearly illustrates how the managerial practices of TM2 led to its consideration of technical factors relevant to the application of the rule. The Manual's drafters did not want to ignore the due diligence principle – "*we had to get to something*", said Schmitt – because the question of how the rule applied was important to the cyber CoP. If it was to be taken seriously by states, TM2 could not skirt important legal issues, no matter how controversial. At the same time, to get to an agreement, the drafters had to forge a compromise between themselves that was, by Schmitt's own admission, unwieldy in legal terms. It was instead grounded in technical reality:

115 *Corfu Channel case*, Judgment of April 9th, 1949, I.C. J. Reports 1949, 22.

116 *Trail smelter case* (*United States, Canada*), RIAA, 16 April 1938 and 11 March 1941, Volume III, 1965.

117 "Draft Articles on Prevention of Transboundary Harm from Hazardous Activities, with Commentaries (as Submitted to the UN General Assembly)" (Dordrecht: International Law Commission, Fifty-third session, 2008), https://doi.org/10.1007/978-1-4020-8367-9_23. (hereafter Draft Articles on Transboundary Harm).

118 TM 2.0, 34.

119 *TLS – Day 2 – Roundtable 5 – Get Your House in Order – What Diligence Is Due?* (Washington D.C: American University Washington College of Law, 2022), https://media.wcl.american.edu/Mediasite/Play/999ce17eb3f04fe3ab28559de68fff0d1d.

120 *Interview with Michael N. Schmitt*, September 13, 2022.

some drafters did not think it practical for the cyber due diligence to cover all kinds of cyber operations emanating from a state's territory. The phrases "serious adverse consequences" was therefore added to ensure states were not burdened to monitor all malicious cyber operations on their territory.

What about the phrase "internationally wrongful acts", which appears in TM2's commentary to the due diligence rule? Here too, the practices of engagement between TM2 and states arguably sensitized the drafters to important political and technical considerations that ultimately swayed their interpretation.

By referring to "internationally wrongful acts", TM2 borrowed a specific legal formulation that not only referred to Article 2 of ARSIWA, but was used by the third UN GGE to describe the norm of due diligence in cyberspace. Norm 13(c) of the 2014–2015 UN GGE report declared:[121]

> States should not knowingly allow their territory to be used **for internationally wrongful acts** using ICTs. [emphasis added]

Why did the GGE in turn use this unique formulation to describe the due diligence norm? The simple answer is politics: Norm 13(c) was the result of a compromise within the like-minded countries in the third GGE – countries like the US, UK, and Australia have not embraced the due diligence rule in cyberspace – that became entrenched over time. Arguably, those states which did not recognize due diligence as a primary obligation were more comfortable attaching the language of state responsibility to this norm. "Norm 13 (c) uses 'internationally wrongful acts', whereas under the *Corfu Channel* case, it should have been acts 'contrary to the rights of other states'", said Takeshi Akahori, a prominent international lawyer and senior negotiator in the 2019–2021 round of UN negotiations.[122] "That was a compromise [from the earlier GGEs]." As the next chapter notes, UN negotiators would begin to reflexively evaluate the relationship between norms and existing international law after the failure of the fifth GGE, and the 2019–2021 OEWG would reject attaching state responsibility language to the due diligence norm. However, the 2019–2021 UN GGE, which arguably felt bound to its own previously formulation retained the norm. "There was a quiet but important game that took place on due diligence in the GGE", said Akahori. "France and Japan pointed to the UK, Australia, etc, and said this was a compromise formulation and that we should not change it". Akahori noted that it was an imperfect compromise.

121 *Fourth UN GGE Report*, 8.
122 *Interview with Takeshi Akahori*, August 6, 2021.

It is reasonable to conclude that TM2 was influenced by the GGE's compromise formulation through its consultative practices, which gave the Manual's drafters a sense of what would and would not be acceptable commentary to major powers. Certainly, circumstantial evidence suggests so, given that the fourth UN GGE coincided with the initial preparation of TM2, and took place alongside consultations with states as part of the Hague Process. Schmitt's abovementioned reference to the inclusion of the phrase upon consulting on the due diligence rule with states is telling, although there is just not enough evidence to suggest if any or all of the same states involved in the GGE compromise also persuaded TM2's drafters to adopt their preferred formulation. That the UN GGE was an influential document for TM2 is not in doubt: in fact, TM2 debates the use of "should" (rather than "must") in Norm 13(c) to evaluate whether the due diligence obligation reflected existing law or simply a normative guideline for states to consider.[123]

There could be another reason why TM2 sought to link the cyber due diligence rule to the state responsibility regime: the lack of effective remedial measures against the breach of due diligence.[124] The due diligence obligation, as is now commonly understood, is an obligation subjectively of conduct, and not objectively of result.[125] Consequently, the standard for non-performance of due diligence in cyberspace – if such a rule exists for the domain – is arguably high, given that states could simply claim they had put in place legal-institutional measures to monitor malicious cyber activity but nevertheless could not stop a specific operation, or that they lacked the technical capacity to adequately safeguard against cybersecurity threats.[126] The issue of consequences owing to non-performance of due diligence has been the subject of controversy and debate among legal practitioners and scholars, including within the ILC, when the Commission discussed the draft articles for prevention of transboundary harm. While James Crawford acknowledged that "due diligence standards were more flexible than obligations of result", they did not

123 TM 2.0, 31.

124 *See generally*, Attila Tanzi, "Liability for Lawful Acts," Oxford Public International Law, January 2021 (last updated), http://opil.ouplaw.com/view/10.1093/law:epil/9780199231690/law-9780199231690-e1065.

125 Timo Koivurova and Krittika Singh, "Due Diligence," Oxford Public International Law, August 2022 (last updated), http://opil.ouplaw.com/view/10.1093/law:epil/9780199231690/law-9780199231690-e1034?prd=OPIL.

126 Russell Buchan, "Cyberspace, Non-State Actors and the Obligation to Prevent Transboundary Harm," *Journal of Conflict and Security Law* 21, no. 3 (December 2016), 444–445, https://doi.org/10.1093/jcsl/krw011; TM 2.0, 46.

want for "regional or particularist exemptions" from such an obligation.[127] Bruno Simma was sympathetic to this view, arguing that it was within the Commission's remit to address the link between the state responsibility regime and non-performance of due diligence.[128] Some other ILC members, including Special Rapporteur P.S. Rao, were keen that "no *a priori* principles be laid down for all situations", and that the special regime in question address the topic of remedies.[129] Yet others like Ian Brownlie argued that addressing the legal consequences around non-performance of due diligence would require clarity on the "final form" of the draft articles themselves.[130] If the ILC sought to progressively develop the law on this count (which was within its scope), it could simply submit a declaration to the UN General Assembly, and hope that they would eventually "acquire the status of principles of customary international law", Brownlie argued. But the ILC had to be clear of its purported goal.

Owing to a lack of consensus as well as "acute" differences among states on the topic, the ILC did not address further the consequences of failing to comply with due diligence. "State responsibility as it related to the operator's [i.e., private actor] liability raised a very interesting question, but would have to be analyzed further in the light of current-day realities", the Commission concluded.[131] Where the ILC could not agree, TM2 pointed to "self-help" measures under the state responsibility regimes to victim states affected by the non-performance of due diligence by another. TM2 argues that "if a State is *unwilling to terminate* harmful cyber operations encompassed by the due diligence principle as opposed to *unable to do so*, the injured State may be entitled to resort to countermeasures[132]" [emphases added].

It is probable that TM2 afforded states the availability of cyber countermeasures in order to ensure timely, technical redressal of the damage caused by cyber operations from abroad. The due diligence obligation traditionally contemplates redressals such as compensation or peaceful dispute settlement mechanisms, which may be impractical in the context of cybersecurity, given that the transboundary effects of cyber operations can cause serious and often

127 "Yearbook of the International Law Commission 1998 Volume 1 | Summary Records of the Meetings of the Fiftieth Session 20 April-12 June 1998 27 July-14 August 1998" (International Law Commission, Fiftieth session, 2000), 68, https://legal.un.org/ilc/publications/yearbooks/english/ilc_1998_v1.pdf.

128 *Yearbook of the International Law Commission 1998 Volume* 1, n.127, 82.

129 Yearbook of the International Law Commission 1998 Volume 1, n.127, 82.

130 Yearbook of the International Law Commission 1998 Volume 1, n.127, 82.

131 Yearbook of the International Law Commission 1998 Volume 1, N.127, 86.

132 TM 2.0, 50.

irreversible harm to digital infrastructure. It is plausible that TM2 sought also to include the phrase "internationally wrongful acts" to make explicit the link to state responsibility, *with a view* to permitting the use of countermeasures against non-performance of due diligence. Both TM1 as well as Schmitt's own work on due diligence prior to the publication of TM2 had endorsed the use of countermeasures in the event of non-performance. Seriously harmful cyber operations are often likely to be "internationally wrongful acts", and unlike the requirements of legal attribution and the need to prove "grave and imminent" threats to "essential interests" that respectively qualify the application of countermeasures under the state responsibility and necessity regimes, due diligence has no such procedural hurdles, Schmitt has previously argued.[133] Rejecting the due diligence rule in cyberspace, Schmitt cautioned states, would be to reject "operationally viable" responses to cyber operations. This view has resonated with some international lawyers, who have argued that the technical complexities associated with attribution should result in countermeasures being available to states through the back door, i.e., as a tool to address non-performance of due diligence obligations.[134]

The unique formulation of TM2 on "cyber due diligence" is thus owed to its managerial practices that sought to ensure on the one hand, a commentary on the rule that was broadly acceptable to its own distinguished group of drafters and on the other, states who were reluctant to recognize it as a primary rule while still wanting to retain a tool of response against wanton refusal by states to monitor malicious activity on their territory. The concerns of both states and scholars were of a technical nature, and hardly based on legal arguments around the precise scope of the customary law of due diligence (if one exists) or state responsibility. The explicit borrowing of the GGE norm's formulation – itself an "imperfect" political compromise – by TM2 is perhaps the most revealing aspect of such management: it emphasizes how the practices of negotiation and consultation within and outside the Tallinn Manual drafting

133 Michael N. Schmitt, "In Defense of Due Diligence in Cyberspace," *The Yale Law Journal Forum* 125 (2015), 78, https://www.yalelawjournal.org/forum/in-defense-of-due-diligence-in-cyberspace.

134 *See*, Luke Chircop, "A Due Diligence Standard od Attribution in Cyberspace," *International & Comparative Law Quarterly* 67, no. 3 (July 2018): 643–668, https://doi.org/10.1017/S0020589318000015; Tomohiro Mikanagi, "Application of the Due Diligence Principle to Cyber Operations," *International Law Studies* 97 (2021): 21. For arguments caution such an approach, *see* Eric Talbot Jensen and Sean Watts, "A Cyber Duty of Due Diligence: Gentle Civilizer or Crude Destabilizer? Symposium: Tallinn Manual 2.0 on the International Law Applicable to Cyber Operations," *Texas Law Review* 95, no. 7 (2017 2016), 1555–1578; Rebecca Crootof, "International Cybertorts: Expanding State Accountability in Cyberspace," *Cornell Law Review* 103, no. 3 (2018 2017), 565–644.

groups resembled a norms articulation process rather than an exercise to identify and interpret existing international law.

Equally interesting and revealing is the fact that leading legal scholars within the cyber CoP have internalized the differences between this "norm-like" formulation of TM2 and existing law. In response to Schmitt's admission at the 2022 symposium that the due diligence formulation of TM2 had been "sloppy" and an effort to accommodate the drafter's perspectives, Yuval Shany noted in response that he did not have "the same reading [as Schmitt on 'serious adverse consequences']", and that it opened a "new front" of debate.[135] Shany has been critical of the Manual in the past, writing in a seminal 2018 article with Dan Efrony that the "threshold of 'serious adverse consequences' [was] unclear" but that it was "safe to assume" that it covered operations undertaken by non-state actors, which, if they were instead conducted by states, would breach international law thresholds on the use of force and non-intervention.[136] Talita Dias and Antonio Coco have perceptively noted all actions that "affect the rights of other states" are not "internationally wrongful" in nature but accept TM2's formulation as a "cyber-specific articulation of the *Corfu Channel* principle".[137] In fairness, some lawyers have also acknowledged the compromises that were made by TM2 to get to a formulation acceptable to important practitioners in the cyber CoP. "I do not see a big difference between the UN GGE norms and the Tallinn Manual", said Dan Efrony, who has previously critiqued the Manuals, in an interview.[138] "Both are examples of soft law that will likely be the source of binding rules developed later in the future." However, it does not take away from the fact that lawyers like Efrony have in the past critiqued TM2's formulations on the basis of legal methodology, which arguably reflects the tacit acceptance of the conflation between negotiated norms and existing rules.

135 *TLS – Day 2 – Roundtable 5*, N.119.
136 Shany and Efrony (2018), 643.
137 Antonio Coco and Talita de Souza Dias, "'Cyber Due Diligence': A Patchwork of Protective Obligations in International Law," *European Journal of International Law* 32, no. 3 (August 1, 2021), 771–806, https://doi.org/10.1093/ejil/chab056.
138 *Interview with Dan Efrony*, September 28, 2022.

3 The Oxford Process on International Law Protections in Cyberspace

3.1 Origins and Background

The Oxford Process on International Law Protections in Cyberspace (OPC) is a more recent, albeit influential exercise that aims to "[identify and clarify] rules of international applicable to cyber operations across a variety of contexts".[139] At the time of writing, OPC is in its fourth year of existence – its first meeting was held in May 2020 – having held seven consultative workshops with international lawyers, diplomats, technical experts, and companies on specific aspects of international cybersecurity law as well as outreach meetings with the wider cyber CoP to disseminate its findings. OPC is driven by three prominent international lawyers with deep experience in academia and government: Dapo Akande, Duncan Hollis, and Harold Kongju Koh. The initiative is hosted by the Oxford Institute for Ethics, Law, and Armed Conflict (ELAC), which is affiliated to the Blavatnik School of Government at Oxford University. A team of international lawyers at ELAC help coordinate and guide OPC discussions by providing background papers, briefings, and research assistance.[140]

OPC was initially conceived as a "periodic conference where international lawyers meet and discuss [the application of international law to state behavior in cyberspace]."[141] The onset of the COVID-19 pandemic was decisive in influencing the format and substance of OPC meetings away from a general, open-ended conference to issue-oriented workshops meant to generate consensus statements on respective topics. Referring to the background of the first OPC meeting in May 2020 that focused on "cyber operations targeting the healthcare sector", Hollis noted the influence of the pandemic.[142] "We [Akande and himself] were planning the [first] conference, when the pandemic hit. Then hospitals started getting hit [with cyber operations]." With the help of the International Committee of the Red Cross (ICRC), which was already involved in identifying international law protections for the healthcare sector, ELAC convened the first meeting on the subject, and since then, has focused on specific issues in the same manner.

---

139 *Oxford Process Compendium*, 9.

140 "The Oxford Process | People," Oxford Institute for Ethics, Law and Armed Conflict, accessed December 2, 2022, https://www.elac.ox.ac.uk/the-oxford-process/people/.

141 *Interview with Duncan Hollis*, September 15, 2022.

142 *Interview with Duncan Hollis*, September 15, 2022.

TABLE 4.1 Outcomes of Oxford Process meetings

Topic	Date	Outcome
Cyber operations targeting the healthcare sector	May 2020	Consensus statement
Healthcare sector during COVID-19: Safeguarding vaccine research	July 2020	Consensus statement
Foreign electoral interference through digital means	October 2020	Consensus statement
Integrity of ICT supply chains	March 2021	Workshop report
Information operations and activities	June 2021	Consensus statement
Ransomware operations	October 2021	Consensus statement
Countermeasures in cyberspace	May 2022	Workshop report

The seven OPC meetings that have been convened at the time of writing are listed in Table 4.1, along with the outcomes of those meetings.

As the table indicates, OPC has been an intensive and prolific affair, often convening three meetings during a calendar year. Two OPC meetings – on supply chain integrity and cyber countermeasures – did not generate the consensus required to put out a statement, but deliberations from those meetings were released as workshop reports (as with other meetings).

Despite its recent origins, OPC has had high visibility within the cyber CoP. The Process was cited at the UN Security Council's Arria formula discussions on cybersecurity in 2020,[143] and the meetings themselves have increasingly seen participation from legal advisers of influential states. In India – which sent a delegation to The Hague Process consultations of the Tallinn Manual 2.0 – the foreign minister was asked in Parliament "whether the policy experts of the Government of India [planned] to engage" with OPC.[144] The Process is

143 Dapo Akande, Antonio Coco, and Talita de Souza Dias, "The Second Oxford Statement on International Law Protections of the Healthcare Sector During COVID-19: Safeguarding Vaccine Research," *EJIL: Talk!* (blog), August 11, 2020, https://www.ejiltalk.org/the-second-oxford-statement-on-international-law-protections-of-the-healthcare-sector-during-covid-19-safeguarding-vaccine-research/.

144 "List of Questions for WRITTEN ANSWERS" (Lok Sabha, February 11, 2022), https://loksabhadocs.nic.in/questionslist/MyFolder/11022022.pdf.

attractive to policy planners, as Hollis himself acknowledged, partly because it offers "off-the-shelf" statements on specific issues that states, companies or NGOs can highlight in their own statements on international cybersecurity law. The policy-oriented focus of OPC appears to have been by design: "at the time [of the first meeting in May 2020], we kind of knew there was a Security Council meeting coming up, and the part of the reason the statement [on healthcare protections] happened was so we could put a two-pager in front of UNSC representatives at the Arria-style meeting", said Hollis. Following the UNSC meetings and increasing interest from states, "we realized that if [OPC meetings] were short enough and topical enough, we can get the attention of principals than would otherwise be the case for an academic project".[145]

3.2 Practices of the Oxford Process

As the previous paragraphs already indicate, OPC meetings are designed and topics are chosen to elicit interest and participation from key actors in the cyber CoP, and ultimately, their approval of OPC statements. In its own words, OPC offers "clarity on the protective reach of international law, via its prohibitions, permissions, and requirements" in order to "*exercise a pull towards compliance by all actors*"[146] [emphasis added]. Consequently, the managerial practices of the Process that aim to get states, technical experts, and businesses on board are more apparent than with the Tallinn Manual initiatives.

OPC and its founders themselves have shone light on this methodology. "The Tallinn Manual [process] is a deductive exercise", said Hollis.[147] "It takes general rules of international law and applies them to cyber operations. The Oxford Process is more an inductive process. [We first ask:] what are the main cybersecurity threats? Then, let's figure out how the object is protected by international law or what are the methods that international law can regulate [in relation to that threat]." In the selection of topics that are addressed in its meetings, therefore, OPC remains open to the influence of stakeholders other than international lawyers, such as technical experts, businesses, or even the political or policy priorities of important states. In fact, OPC emphasizes its role as a "neutral, capacity-building initiative",[148] signaling that it is a

145 *Interview with Duncan Hollis*, September 15, 2022.
146 *Oxford Process Compendium*, 12.
147 *Interview with Duncan Hollis*, September 15, 2022.
148 *Oxford Process Compendium*, 12.

managerial exercise meant to accommodate the interests of all relevant stakeholders. Notably, OPC is sponsored both by Microsoft and the government of Japan – stakeholders from different constituencies that have independently emphasized the importance of clarifying international cybersecurity law – reflecting this multi-disciplinary approach.[149]

What is the role of international lawyers themselves in OPC? To be clear, OPC statements still formally claim to identify existing international law. In particular, the practice of some OPC statements invoking the phrase "we, the undersigned public international lawyers" suggests the OPC, like the Tallinn Manuals, relies on the reputation of its eminent legal group of signatories to establish the authoritative character of its interpretations. Reports from OPC meetings, as well as participant observation in two of them indicate the debate among lawyers prominently involved legal reasoning. However, OPC statements were not decided on legal-methodological considerations alone. An important factor was consensus within the group. "We were looking for what John Rawls termed 'overlapping consensus'[150] or Cass Sunstein called 'incompletely theorized agreements' – we wanted people to say 'we agree attacking hospitals is off limits, *even if we can't agree why*'", said Hollis[151] [emphasis added]. Therefore, the drivers of this initiative were open to any sound methodological consideration that formed the basis for a "justificatory discourse"[152] – i.e., offered sufficient precision, clarity, and normative direction about rules to generate a "sense of obligation" among states and other relevant actors to comply with them.[153] Indeed, OPC takes pride in the fact that it was able to secure consensus among lawyers on a number of contentious issues that have been deadlocked at the UN. "Even in a virtual room filled

---

149 "Behind the Scenes," Oxford Institute for Ethics, Law and Armed Conflict, accessed December 2, 2022, https://www.elac.ox.ac.uk/the-oxford-process/behind-the-scenes/.

150 "[…] an overlapping consensus is not a mere *modus vivendi*. The object of consensus […] is itself a moral conception [and not] merely a consensus on accepting certain authorities, or on complying with certain institutional arrangements, founded on a convergence of self – or group-interests. […] The stability of [overlapping consensus also] does not depend on happenstance and a balance of relative forces [between those who strike such consensus]." John Rawls, "The Idea of an Overlapping Consensus," *Oxford Journal of Legal Studies* 7, no. 1 (1987): 1–25.

151 *Interview with Duncan Hollis*, September 15, 2022.

152 Abram Chayes and Antonia Handler Chayes, *The New Sovereignty: Compliance with International Regulatory Agreements, The New Sovereignty* (Harvard University Press, 1998), 26, https://doi.org/10.4159/9780674262638.

153 Ian Johnstone, "Security Council Deliberations: The Power of the Better Argument," *European Journal of International Law* 14, no. 3 (June 1, 2003), 441, https://doi.org/10.1093/ejil/14.3.437.

with international lawyers – each with their own take on the existence and content of particular rules – agreement emerged in substance", the OPC compendium notes about its first meeting on healthcare protections.[154] "*Despite differences on the precise legal route taken*, there was widespread agreement on the nature of the prohibited acts and the coverage of international legal protection" [emphasis added]. "The practice of international law" within the OPC, to paraphrase Johnstone, was "indicative of th[e] sense of being bound and gives specific content to the legal rules'" about protections of objects in cyberspace.[155] OPC places faith in its interpretive community to self-regulate, by determining through dialogue both the "types of arguments" and the "styles of reasoning" that can be accepted, as well as the validity of legal claims made through such reasoning.[156] The OPC compendium expressly notes the importance of "garnering consensus by its own distinctive methodology, through which an epistemic community is established and continuously expanded through repeated dialogue".[157] As a minor point of difference, the group of international lawyers, technical experts, diplomats and other stakeholders that OPC meetings have brought together is not an "epistemic community" because they do not have "shared causal beliefs",[158] but an interpretive community[159] for the reasons highlighted above.

This unique methodological approach of OPC draws heavily from the core beliefs of the cyber CoP vis-à-vis norm-articulation and rule-interpretation, and its practices reinforce those beliefs. The failure of the UN norms processes in the past to clarify the applicability of international law, and ongoing attempts by states to address how international law applies through the UN GGE and OEWG were clearly motivations for the directors and sponsors of OPC to take up such an initiative. "As *a norm-identification and interpretation process* in a critical and fast-moving area, [the Oxford Process] *complements* other important initiatives, such as the UN GGE, OEWG, and the Tallinn Manuals", notes the OPC compendium[160] [emphasis added]. If the OPC wanted to highlight that its norms were "legal norms", there was no reason to invite comparisons with the work of the UN processes, which clearly include voluntary norms of state behavior. Fashioning itself as an interpretive community

154 *Oxford Process Compendium*, 14.
155 Johnstone (2003), 441.
156 *Ian Johnstone* (2011), n.31, 25.
157 *Oxford Process Compendium*, 12.
158 Peter M. Haas, "Introduction: Epistemic Communities and International Policy Coordination," *International Organization* 46, no. 1 (1992), 3.
159 *Ian Johnstone* (2011), n.31, 33–54.
160 *Oxford Process Compendium*, 22.

that was open to any sound methodology of identifying and applying international law – including political, normative, legal-doctrinal, and of course, technical considerations – meant that the OPC deliberations in crucial respects were managed like norms-processes to secure consensus and approval. This brings us to the issue of what those managerial practices looked like.

The managerial nature of OPC was evident from the nature of the first meeting itself. The first OPC meeting on healthcare protections specifically co-opted the ICRC as a partner, because the ICRC was simultaneously involved in championing a norm on the subject at the 2019–2021 UN OEWG. The background paper for the OPC meeting was penned by the ICRC.[161] The text of the ICRC's proposed norm read: "States should not conduct or knowingly support [cyber] activity that would harm medical services or medical facilities, and should take measures to protect medical services from harm."

The objective of the ICRC-led discussion was less about aligning the norm's language with existing international law, and more about eliciting a statement about healthcare protections that would be accepted by practitioners in the cyber CoP, including states who were concurrently weighing precisely this proposal at the UN norms processes. The ICRC background paper itself asked whether the "norm [on healthcare protections] proposed by the ICRC strengthened or weakened the existing international law framework", implying flexibility about its legal grounding.[162]

Even in terms of its schedule and timing, OPC meetings mirrored norms discussions. For example, the OPC meeting on foreign election interference was organized just a few months after the UN GGE and OEWG, somewhat unexpectedly, referred to the need for regulating "malicious ICT activities against Critical Infrastructure and Critical Information Infrastructure that undermine trust and confidence in political and electoral processes". Admittedly, the UN statement and OPC meeting may have both been motivated by the US presidential elections of November 2020 to pronounce on the topic, but OPC also used the language of the OEWG/GGE, and before it the Paris Call, to refer to "electoral processes" as broadly encompassing both infrastructure and information serviced by such infrastructure.

Hollis' personal reflection in the interview on the relationship between cyber norms and international law shines some light on why the Process may have been organized like a norms-articulation process. "Although I'm

161 Kubo Mačák, Laurent Gisel and Tilman Rodenhäuser, "International Law Protections against Malicious Cyber Operations Targeting the Healthcare Sector" (The Oxford Process on International Law Protections in Cyberspace, May 6, 2020), https://www.elac.ox.ac.uk/wp-content/uploads/2022/10/Oxford-Process-Compendium-Digital.pdf.

162 Mačák, Gisel, and Rodenhäuser (2020), 75.

an international lawyer first and foremost, I think norms are more important. Norms as social expectations and standards of behavior for a given community are what actually results in conduct – the goal of a law is to be normative! In cyberspace, norms are really important because you internalize norms – my identity as a responsible state in cyberspace is to do this or do that even when no one is watching me. [...] Given that so much of cyber activity is covert, norms can have real power because they may be the one way to restrain state behavior apart from carrots and sticks, which by the way we've seen to be [ineffective]."[163] For international cybersecurity law to be normative in character, i.e., internalized by states, practitioners should be able to understand and make generalizable conclusions about the mechanisms and effects of cyber operations, much of which are secretive. In other words, for international law to lay down "expected standards of behavior", lawyers must know what 'good' and 'bad' behavior in cyberspace looks like. "One of the things is that international [cyber] law needs is transparency, it needs public behavior. So much of cyber activity is *sub rosa* – so that does elevate the [Oxford Process] because this is [a platform] where you can articulate views, as opposed to classic customary international law [ascertainment] where views were articulated through questions such as 'did you exercise your right of free navigation through the archipelago strait, and did you get away with it or was there a protest?'", said Hollis. Having a process like OPC is important, Hollis noted, because "law by analogy", i.e., applying principles of international law to cyberspace based on state behavior in other domains, does not always work, given that "cyber" behavior can be truly novel.

The practices of OPC meetings thus arguably reinforced the norm-like development of its statements. How did those managerial practices facilitate "creeping expertise"? While background papers for OPC meetings were invariably written by international lawyers, most OPC meetings began with a briefing by technical experts, framing the issue at hand.

A table of technical experts who briefed OPC meetings is provided in Table 4.2.

The role of the technical experts in OPC meetings was carefully orchestrated, in that they did not simply present technical assessments of cybersecurity threats, but often aligned their briefings to reflect debates on international cybersecurity law. For example, Graham Ingram addressed at length issues around attribution of cyber operations as well as the importance of information integrity, especially in case of healthcare and clinical data, implying that "scale and effects" may not often be the most appropriate test to

163 *Interview with Duncan Hollis*, September 15, 2022.

TABLE 4.2 Technical experts who briefed Oxford Process meetings

Oxford Process meeting	Technical expert
Healthcare protections	None
Safeguarding vaccine research	Graham Ingram, Chief Information Security Officer, University of Oxford
Foreign election interference	Josh Benaloh, Senior Cryptographer, Microsoft Research
ICT supply chains	Tom Burt, Corporate Vice President, Customer Security & Trust, Microsoft
Information operations and activities	Olga Belogolova, Security Policy Lead, Influence Operations, Meta;
Ransomware attacks	Chris Krebs, Partner, Krebs Stamos Group LLC
Countermeasures in cyberspace	None

frame prohibitions on state behavior.[164] Josh Benaloh's technical presentation pointed to the specific ways in which election interference could occur, which arguably was useful to international lawyers in framing protections around key voting processes.[165] Tom Burt's briefing highlighted the precise method used by the SolarWinds hackers, pointing specifically to harms caused by cyber operations, including espionage, that attack critical elements of the ICT supply chain.[166] He argued any "compromise of a vendor's update process" – the *modus operandi* of SolarWinds hackers – "should be inherently a violation of international law". Olga Belogolova's presentation, as the next section notes, was influential in shaping how OPC lawyers viewed "coercion" vis-à-vis information operations.[167] Chris Krebs emphasized, among others, the role of host nations in allowing ransomware grounds to operate with impunity – although he avoided any references to a cyber due diligence obligation.[168] In other words, technical experts often framed the debate for international lawyers in the OPC meetings, allowing them to peg legal interpretations and principles to contemporary cybersecurity concerns. Some of these meet-

164 *Oxford Process Compendium*, 140–141.
165 *Oxford Process Compendium*, 191–192.
166 *Oxford Process Compendium*, 282–284.
167 *Oxford Process Compendium*, 376–380.
168 *Oxford Process Compendium*, 462–463.

ings also featured briefings by officials from intelligence agencies and representatives from technology companies who would provide their perspective on respective topics.

In sum, OPC meetings unfolded in the same way a norms articulation process would: identifying first a specific topic which had policy purchase, and around which consensus could be generated, and subsequently inviting different stakeholders to frame their concerns on the topic. By inviting the participation of technical experts, including those from key intelligence agencies and technology companies, to frame the debate for international lawyers, the "norm-like" managerial methodology of OPC lend itself to "creeping expertise". Following presentations or technical briefings, OPC meetings focused largely on the interpretation or applicability of specific international law principles, much like the drafting and review sessions of the Tallinn Manual group of experts. According to Hollis, a draft statement would generally be circulated among eight to ten attendees following the meeting.[169] A polished version would subsequently be sent to the workshop participants for their approval.

3.3 Creeping Expertise in the Oxford Process

I identify three instances that best illustrate "creeping expertise" in the deliberations and outcomes of OPC meetings. As with the Tallinn Manuals, here too a caveat is in order. The optics of a singular technical expert "briefing" international lawyers in an OPC meeting may give rise to the impression of that expert's singular influence. It is prudent therefore to caution against the view that all technical experts were equally influential over international lawyers in each of these meetings. A plausible explanation for having a few technical experts in OPC meetings is that the organizers wanted those with in-depth experience on a particular topic, the availability of high-profile experts to join particular sessions, and ultimately the organizers themselves becoming comfortable with a set-piece briefing and choosing to adopt that as a "format" for OPC sessions.

3.3.1 Protecting Data Integrity: Going Down the Rabbit Hole of Espionage

Perhaps the more interesting and notable discussions among international lawyers in OPC meetings pertain to international law protections available for the integrity of data. Whereas the Tallinn Manuals focus mainly on the scale and effects of cyber operations – only to the extent that cyber operations

169 *Interview with Duncan Hollis*, September 15, 2022.

on data result in physical damage (improbable), loss of functionality (probable), or usurp inherently governmental functions (probable), would they be regulated by international law – OPC discussions evaluate the integrity of data as an object of protection itself. "Data integrity", according to one technical definition, refers to the "property whereby data has not been altered in an unauthorized manner since it was created, transmitted, or stored".[170]

Data integrity features in two OPC statements, and was a key theme of discussion in a third meeting that did not result in a consensus statement.

The second OPC statement on vaccine research states:[171]

> International law prohibits cyber operations by States that have significant adverse or harmful consequences for the research, trial, manufacture, and distribution of a COVID-19 vaccine, including by means that damage the content or **impair the use of sensitive research data, particularly trial results** [...] [emphasis added].
>
> [...]
>
> States must take all feasible measures to **prevent, stop and mitigate malicious cyber operations against the data** or technologies used for **COVID-19 vaccine research, trial**, manufacture or distribution which they know or should have known emanate from their territory or jurisdiction [emphasis added].

The third OPC statement on election interference states:[172]

> International law applies to cyber operations by states, including those that have adverse consequences for the electoral processes of other states.

"Adverse consequences" in the electoral context is defined as:[173]

---

170 "Data Integrity – Glossary," NIST COMPUTER SECURITY RESOURCE CENTER, accessed December 2, 2022, https://csrc.nist.gov/glossary/term/data_integrity.

171 "The Second Oxford Statement on International Law Protections of the Healthcare Sector during Covid-19: Safeguarding Vaccine Research," Oxford Institute for Ethics, Law and Armed Conflict, accessed December 2, 2022, https://www.elac.ox.ac.uk/the-oxford-process/the-statements-overview/the-second-oxford-statement/.

172 "The Oxford Statement on International Law Protections Against Foreign Electoral Interference Through Digital Means," Oxford Institute for Ethics, Law and Armed Conflict, accessed December 2, 2022, https://www.elac.ox.ac.uk/the-oxford-process/the-statements-overview/the-oxford-statement-on-international-law-protections-against-foreign-electoral-interference/.

173 *Ibid.*

> [...] actions [...that] include but are not limited to intrusions into digital systems or networks that **cast doubt on the integrity of election data**, such as votes and voter registers [...] [emphasis added].

Lastly, the fourth OPC meeting on ICT supply chains also focused on integrity, albeit not of data, but of lines of code. Organized as the meeting was in the backdrop of the SolarWinds hack, much of the discussion focused on the integrity of software in the supply chain – such as critical updates or "patches" to fix vulnerabilities – and international law protections for it.[174] "Data" could broadly be interpreted to include code as well, but even otherwise, the logic of protecting its integrity is the same as that of human-readable information in the healthcare and election contexts.

Data integrity came to occupy an important place in OPC discussions and interpretations of international law primarily on account of the role of technical experts. This issue was tabled before OPC directly through Ingram's briefing at the second OPC meeting on vaccine research. The confidentiality of data in vaccine research by itself was "less of a consideration", Ingram told participants, indicating that the threat in question was not data breaches or exposure. The "integrity and availability" of clinical data was more important. If cyber operations were "successful in damaging the integrity of the [COVID-19 vaccine] trials data, then approvals for use of vaccine may have been delayed or the credibility of therapeutics findings questioned", said Ingram.[175] This assertion stayed with OPC international lawyers long after the briefing was over. "This was a lightbulb moment for all of us", said Hollis. "Whatever else we [international lawyers] may think of state cyber espionage, in the case of clinical trials, the mere fact that the data has been accessed without authorization affects the integrity of results. This is the sort of observation that you don't hear made much in state cyber espionage/international law discussions, which tends to focus on [questions like] 'is it [espionage] prohibited or is it extra-legal?' At least in this discrete context, here was evidence that breach of integrity [brings in] a bunch of international law questions."[176]

Indeed, during the discussions among international lawyers that followed the briefing, some mooted the idea of "declaring legal 'no fly' zones, whereby any cyber operation against particular objects and sectors, regardless of any discernible adverse effect, would be considered illegal".[177] "Even operations

174 *Oxford Process Compendium*, 279–296.
175 *Oxford Process Compendium*, 141.
176 *Interview with Duncan Hollis*, September 15, 2022.
177 *Oxford Process Compendium*, 146.

with the sole aim of espionage can do damage to vaccine research", a participant in the group noted.[178] The discussions even took a technical character, with some suggesting that confidentiality and integrity should be treated separately – the availability of data and protected objects should be the primary focus of rules. This would allow international law to "bypass" the espionage problem and focus solely on the integrity of the object which may enjoy protection. In this manner, "beneficial espionage" – done with care for data integrity, and which contributed to speedy development of vaccines – would also be still permitted in certain scenarios.[179] This proposal was, however, contested, as others argued the integrity of clinical data was not often separable from breaches of confidentiality. In this manner, the second OPC meeting confronted the issue of espionage head-on.

The negotiated consensus outcome of this meeting – as highlighted in the excerpt above – was that the second OPC statement identified negative and positive obligations on states to protect the integrity of clinical trial data. The statement declared that cyber operations that impaired the use of sensitive research and trials data was prohibited in international law. Although the prohibition pertains only to cyber operations that cause "significant adverse or harmful consequences", notes from the aforementioned OPC meeting clearly indicate that such consequences could be caused without actual harm by way of physical damage or loss of functionality. Additionally, the statement declared that states have a due diligence obligation to take "all feasible measures to prevent, stop and mitigate malicious cyber operations against [clinical trial and research] data". This assertion presumably covers instances of cyber espionage for commercial purposes undertaken by non-state actors from a host country. The OPC statement is a significant departure from the approach of international lawyers towards cyber espionage. The Tallinn Manual, as well as most legal scholars who have commented on this issue, consider cyber espionage to be "*per se* not regulated" by international law, although many acknowledge that the methods of espionage matter.[180] It is possible that cyber espionage operations could breach primary norms of international law – e.g., the rules of sovereignty or non-intervention – if they generate the necessary effects upon which such rules are triggered. TM2 in particular noted that its drafters could achieve no consensus of a "threshold of severity" that, when breached, would make remote cyber espionage operations unlaw-

178 *Oxford Process Compendium*, 146.

179 *Oxford Process Compendium*, 148.

180 TM 2.0, Rule 32, 168–172.

ful.[181] In contrast, the OPC formulation is significantly broader and addresses the very action of espionage, and going by the second statement, even prescribes a *de minimis* threshold of illegality in relation to highly sensitive objects such as vaccine research data. "Hearing from the officer in charge of the cybersecurity of the Oxford/Astra Zeneca vaccine"[182] arguably made all the difference in this instance.

The third OPC statement on election interference is also relevant in this context. This statement sought to define what constituted "adverse consequences" as including "intrusions into digital systems or networks that cast doubt on the integrity of election data". It also outlined negative and positive obligations on states. States had a duty to refrain from "conducting, authorizing or endorsing cyber operations" that affected the integrity of election data, the statement declared. States also had a due diligence obligation "all feasible measures to prevent, stop and mitigate any harms ***threatened or generated***" by such cyber operations [emphasis added]. As its formulation indicates, the scope of the due diligence obligation laid out by the third OPC statement is very broad indeed, and requires states to address even the threat of harm caused by cyber operations on election integrity. Despite these articulations, the OPC meeting on election interference did not go into greater detail on espionage. It is conceivable that election data of a country – whether it pertains to voter rolls or ballots – might be the target of cyber espionage by an adversary, with the intention not of disrupting elections, but to gain valuable demographic or political insights. Despite having defined "election interference" widely so as to include potential threats to the integrity of election data and ballots, the third OPC meeting focused largely on whether such interference constituted a violation of the rule on non-intervention.[183] The workshop report of this meeting suggests participants did indeed discuss the "core of the wrong" with respect to election interference, and at least some "favored a prohibition that would encompass any interference", whether or not it was "intentionally manipulative".[184]

The issue of data integrity and espionage nevertheless was a central theme of discussion in the fourth OPC meeting on supply chain protections. This meeting did not result in a consensus statement. However, the workshop report suggests that the technical expert's briefing was once again key to framing the discussion among OPC international lawyers. Microsoft's Tom Burt

181 TM 2.0, 170.

182 *Interview with Duncan Hollis*, September 15, 2022.

183 *Oxford Process Compendium*, 192–197.

184 *Oxford Process Compendium*, 203.

first laid out the *modus operandi* of the SolarWinds hack, highlighting how the perpetrators "incorporated" malware into a security update of the SolarWinds' Orion software. The update was then downloaded by Orion users/clients: once inside, the attackers subsequently used a "variety of techniques" to steal data from compromised systems. The SolarWinds hack did not cause physical damage or loss of functionality – except when vendors had to take systems offline to fix them upon discovering the hack – but it was a classic instance of cyber espionage that likely resulted in the breach of data of critical public as well as private systems. Burt emphasized in his presentation that the technique of corrupting the integrity of the update process made this a "unique and problematic" attack. Attacking the software supply chain, "regardless of the aim of the attacker", had a very "wide blast radius", he cautioned.[185] He concluded by arguing that customers' trust in security updates was so "fundamental" that any compromise of it should "be inherently a violation of international law".[186] The question for international lawyers at the OPC meeting was therefore whether the software supply chain was protected under international law from any manner of cyber operations, including those aimed at espionage.

The discussions following Burt's briefing threw up different viewpoints from international lawyers. One lawyer cautioned that the "urgency on the ground", i.e., the imperative of addressing supply chain attacks targeting the integrity of code, should not result in "short-cuts being taken".[187] It is not possible, she argued, to discern from state practice and *opinio juris* a customary international law prohibiting espionage operations. Another acknowledged that the "target set" of espionage has been broadened with IT supply chains, and they pose a risk of "collateral impacts".[188] Therefore, a useful question would be whether the "law needs to change". Yet another called for a rejection of the "stringently formalistic and positivist account of the international law of intelligence", and to adopt "interdisciplinary viewpoints" on the role of intelligence.[189]

Unsurprisingly, the prevalence of strong and opposing perspectives meant this OPC meeting could not result in a consensus statement. Yet, the workshop notes indicate there was "broad agreement that the label 'espionage' does not preclude a finding of a violation where the means, methods and effects of espionage operations fall foul of international legal rules".[190] And

185 *Oxford Process Compendium*, 284.
186 *Oxford Process Compendium*, 284.
187 *Oxford Process Compendium*, 285.
188 *Oxford Process Compendium*, 286.
189 *Oxford Process Compendium*, 287.
190 *Oxford Process Compendium*, 288.

ICT supply chains, some participants noted, were a "clear vulnerability sector" that "may allow a finding of illegality on the means, methods or effects plane". However, in the absence of further clarification, it is not possible to deduce whether or how OPC participants meant for the integrity of code/updates to be evaluated along this plane.

Taken together, the OPC's statements and discussions on data integrity are novel and influential, in that they provoke states as well as legal scholars to think more deeply about the legality of cyber-enabled espionage in certain cases. The managerial practices of the OPC, which brought cybersecurity experts from key companies involved in vaccine research and ICT supply chain software, were crucial to OPC lawyers in ascribing or thinking about ascribing special protections for the integrity of data and code from unauthorized intrusions for any purpose, including espionage. As these meetings themselves noted, it is difficult to discern a customary rule in general international law prohibiting or even regulating espionage. Perhaps anticipating the lack of consensus on the issue in its third meeting on supply chain protections, the OPC team understandably tried to shoehorn the status of cyber espionage into other rules on sovereignty, non-intervention, and due diligence, arguing that espionage operations that resulted in loss of functionality, coercive measures, and transboundary harm, respectively, could be prohibited in international law. But the second and third OPC meetings are categorical: their statements prompt the cyber CoP to seriously consider whether in some cases, the integrity of data is so sacrosanct that any manner of cyber operation – whether to disrupt, deceive, or simply discover – would be considered unlawful.

3.3.2 Cyber Coercion and "Coordinated Inauthentic Behavior"

Coercion has been defined as constituting "the very essence" of prohibited interventions in international law by the ICJ in the *Nicaragua* case, yet the scope of the term and the activities that could be termed "coercive behavior" has remained ambiguous. The ICJ in *Nicaragua* noted that the element of coercion is "particularly obvious" when the intervention in question uses force or in the "indirect form of support for subversive or terrorist armed activities" in another state.[191] Less obvious is its application to the domain of cyberspace, which has seen a significant rise in recent times of influence operations and specifically, operations meant to disrupt or interfere with elections in other states. The 2022 UK statement, cited earlier in this chapter, waded

191 *Nicaragua case*, 108.

into this debate by calling for a flexible standard of "cyber" coercion, one which does not necessarily account for a "causal nexus"[192] between the intervention in question and its outcomes.[193] The UK position, this section argues, is partly the result of a robust debate within the OPC community of international lawyers, technical experts, and negotiators who addressed the topic of coercion extensively in its third and fifth meetings on foreign electoral interference and information operations respectively.

To be sure, the debate on coercive behavior in the cyber context started well before these OPC meetings. As the previous section noted, the dialogue between the Tallinn Manual drafters and the UK on the issue of sovereignty was an important factor. Also notable is TM2's important role in triggering a debate about the precise threshold of coercion, given that there were no pronouncements by states before 2017 (the year TM2 was published) on what constituted prohibited intervention in cyberspace.[194] TM2 defined coercion as any "affirmative act designed to deprive another state of its freedom of choice", i.e., "forcing" it to act or refrain from acting in an involuntary manner.[195] Although TM2 cites the 1970 Declaration on Principles of International Law concerning Friendly Relations and Cooperation among States in accordance with the Charter of the United Nations in support of this definition, the Declaration itself takes a narrower view of coercion. The Declaration links coercion to the "subordination of the exercise of [a state's] sovereign rights *and* [so securing] from it advantages of any kind"[196] [emphasis added]. Importantly, a majority of TM2 drafters said the "coercive effort must be designed to influence outcomes" in relation to a matter within the *domaine réservé* of another state.[197] But there was a difference of opinion within the group on this matter, with others noting that it was "enough that an act has the effect of depriving the State of control" over the said activity.[198] A majority of drafters, as noted previously, also held the view that there had to be a "causal nexus"

192 *TM 2.0*, 320.

193 *2022 UK statement.*

194 *See*, Brian Egan (2016), "Remarks on International Law and Stability in Cyberspace," Chapter 3, n.45, calling on states to "do more work to clarify how the international law on non-intervention applies to States' activities in cyberspace".

195 TM 2.0, 317.

196 "Declaration on Principles of International Law Concerning Friendly Relations and Cooperation among States in Accordance with the Charter of the United Nations," (UN General Assembly, Twenty-fifth session, 1970), 123, https://digitallibrary.un.org/record/202170.

197 TM 2.0, 318.

198 TM 2.0, 318.

between the act in question and the infringement upon a state's *domaine réservé*.

In 2019, the Netherlands became the first state to articulate its views specifically on the requirements of prohibited "cyber" intervention, defining coercion to mean "compelling a state to take a course of action [...] that it would not otherwise voluntarily pursue".[199] This definition tracked that of TM2 and stated the "goal of the intervention must be to effect change in the behavior" of another state.

TM2 and the Dutch statement laid down an influential marker to evaluate "cyber coercion": should cyber operations result in, or compel states to change their behavior or is it sufficient for the coercive behavior simply to disrupt the ability of states to control and pursue an action to its ordinary end? Recent legal scholarship has taken opposing views on the subject. One approach notes that following a "consequentialist logic" for coercion results in "subjective results" – it is not always possible, the argument goes, to demonstrate a causal link between a purportedly coercive act and its impact on state behavior.[200] Rather than examining the intensity or outcome of cyber operations, therefore, any cyber operation "intended to disrupt, deny, degrade, or destroy information" pertaining to *domaine réservé* activities of a state should be considered coercive in nature.[201] Another approach argues that "coercion" is of little legal significance because "states have not reached a consensus regarding its meaning".[202] Further, international courts and tribunals have also been reluctant to set a definitive standard. In such a scenario, the argument goes, only "actual forms of intervention" should be evaluated for their legality.[203] This essentially doctrinal approach finds that most cyber operations would not breach the rule of prohibited intervention, unless they cause physical destruction and/or death. Yet another approach calls, on the other hand, for an expansive interpretation of coercion, considering the "diversity of threats, methods, and scale" posed by cyber operations.[204] "Milder" forms of intervention such as election manipulation would also fall within this expanded defi-

199 *Official Compendium of Voluntary National Contributions*, N.70, 57.

200 Mohamed Helal, "On Coercion in International Law," *NYU Journal of International Law and Politics* 52 (2019), 6, https://doi.org/10.2139/ssrn.3357513.

201 *Helal (2019)*, 112.

202 Ori Pomson, "The Prohibition on Intervention under International Law and Cyber Operations," *International Law Studies* 99 (2022), 217.

203 *Pomson (2022)*, 217.

204 Ido Kilovaty, "The International Law of Cyber Intervention," in *Research Handbook on International Law and Cyberspace*, ed. Nicholas Tsagourias and Russell Buchan (Edward Elgar Publishing, 2021), 106, https://www.elgaronline.com/view/edcoll/9781789904246/9781789904246.00014.xml.

nition.[205] This approach too notes that the "causal nexus" test of TM2 is problematic and likely impractical to adopt given the landscape of evolving technologies that allow obfuscation of any traceable links to perpetrators.

The OPC meetings arguably moved the needle towards interpreting "cyber coercion" as including manipulative influence operations that limited or disrupted the ability of a state to control *domaine réservé* activity. The timing of its meetings – from the first one in May 2020 to the fourth meeting on information operations in June 2021 – was critical, as it coincided with a number of states articulating generally their position on the applicability of international law to cyberspace,[206] and specifically on the scope of the rule of non-intervention as it pertained to the domain. OPC meetings were arguably convened to influence the positions of these states, a conclusion circumstantially strengthened by the fact that some of their legal advisors were invited workshop participants.

As early as the May 2020 meeting on healthcare protections, OPC flagged the issue of coercion in cyberspace. "Some participants questioned", the workshop report notes, "whether the element of coercion necessarily implies an action taken to force another State into pursuing, or abstaining from pursuing, a particular line of conduct".[207] Given the potentially disastrous consequences of a state "losing control" of its healthcare system, acts that "disrupted" or "inhibited" *domaine réservé* activity "without advancing any demands"[208] should also be considered coercive behavior, they argued. There was no consensus among the OPC lawyers on this point, with others pointing out that it was difficult to find practice "supporting the existence of coercion" beyond the use of force.

This question was debated extensively in the meeting of October 2020 on foreign election interference. Notably, the background paper for this meeting from the OPC team argued that most scholars believed "coercion must be set at a high threshold, requiring pressure or compulsion on the part of the coercing State", and that most disinformation operations "would fall outside the scope of non-intervention".[209] One international lawyer pointed out that an appropriate test for coercion would be to see whether "deceptions" result in

---

205 *Kilovaty (2021)*, 108–111.

206 To be sure, these positions were articulated likely to coincide with the final stages of the UN GGE and OEWG negotiations, and were not directly connected to the Oxford Process as such.

207 *Oxford Process Compendium*, 49.

208 *Oxford Process Compendium*, 49.

209 Talita Dias and Tsvetelina van Benthem, "Online Electoral Disinformation: A Human Rights Law Perspective" (The Oxford Process on International Law Protections in Cyber-

states "losing [their] ability to conduct [their] electoral processes", and not simply influence the opinions of individual voters.[210] Such an interpretation would arguably leave room for an expansive interpretation of "coercion" but still tie it to consequences for the state as a whole. Another lawyer pointed out that "manipulation, as a term, casts a wider net than the intentional spreading of false information", and that it was important to "draw lines" between "acceptable persuasion" and "unacceptable manipulation".[211] Specifically, she argued that "coordinated inauthentic behavior" should be understood as an example of such manipulation. The term "coordinated inauthentic behavior" is a technical label that was first used by Meta (then Facebook) in 2018 to refer to orchestrated influence operations that are intentionally "misleading" or deceptive, and has since evolved into a term of art used by social media platforms and cybersecurity companies.[212] Although these observations were made at the OPC meeting, the international lawyers in attendance do not seem to have arrived at a consensus on the precise threshold for coercion. Nevertheless, the notion that "intentional [cyber] manipulation" regardless of its outcome could be considered as coercive behavior was seeded at this meeting.

With the fifth OPC meeting of June 2021 focused on "information operations", the topic of coercive behavior was thrown into even greater relief among participants. Olga Belogolova's presentation to workshop participants is especially notable, given the aforementioned background.[213] Belogolova, Meta's security policy lead on influence operations, made two important points. First, she defined "inauthentic behavior" as any operation whose goal is to "intentionally mislead" people. Second, she emphasized that companies like Meta were not examining "inauthenticity" from the lens of content but from the "patterns of behavior" – digital footprints, coordination, etc. – established by perpetrators.

These observations were key to generating a "particularly robust discussion"[214] on coercion at the OPC meeting. It is clear the technical expert's brief-

---

space, 2022), 252, https://www.elac.ox.ac.uk/wp-content/uploads/2022/10/Oxford-Process-Compendium-Digital.pdf.

210 *Oxford Process Compendium*, 193.

211 *Oxford Process Compendium*, 201.

212 Evelyn Douek, "What Does 'Coordinated Inauthentic Behavior' Actually Mean?," *Slate*, July 2, 2020, https://slate.com/technology/2020/07/coordinated-inauthentic-behavior-facebook-twitter.html; Bond Huberman Emery David, "Snopestionary: What Is 'Coordinated Inauthentic Behavior'?," Snopes, September 4, 2021, https://www.snopes.com/articles/366947/coordinated-inauthentic-behavior/.

213 *Oxford Process Compendium*, 376–380.

214 *Oxford Process Compendium*, 391.

ing had left an impact, even if international lawyers did not all agree on whether Meta or another digital platform's approach should be relevant considerations for determining coercive behavior. For instance, one lawyer reflexively dismissed "coordinated inauthentic behavior" as a technical term bereft of legal meaning.[215] Still, the presentation arguably led international lawyers to consider whether "deception" in influence operations could be a determinant of coercive behavior. Another participant opined that "fake news and lies" in the context of election interference could be classified as coercive behavior in some cases.[216] The "focus ought to be on the *behavior* of the outside power", this lawyer said, and the intention with which it sought to intervene.[217] This is directly analogous to the method of evaluation that Meta's Belogolova highlighted. It would also be reasonable to conclude that the evaluation of "behavior" is essentially a technical determination, driven by analysis of digital footprints, modes of operation, and such like.

The OPC meeting on information operations ultimately could not come to an agreement on how to characterize coercive behavior in cyberspace. "More work is needed", the workshop report noted, "on determining whether coercion entails an elimination of choice or the reduction of a state's menu of options".[218] On the question of deception itself, the report made no categorical assertions.

The OPC meetings of 2020 and 2021 provided a platform to evaluate the nature and threshold for coercive behavior in cyberspace. The OPC statements themselves do not reflect them – most simply affirm the high-level applicability of the rule against non-intervention to the protected object in question – but the workshop reports point to a robust and often contested debate on the topic. The meetings were an opportunity to probe further what had hitherto been considered a minority view expressed by TM2: can inauthentic behavior designed to disrupt or deprive a state of its control over *domaine réservé* activities also be considered coercion? At least some of the international lawyers in attendance seemed to agree, and some even closely aligned their views with the technical approach pursued by major platforms such as Meta.

In 2022, the UK became the first major state to endorse this wider interpretation of coercion in cyberspace. The UK Attorney General called on other states to "consider whether disruptive cyber behaviors are coercive even

215 *Oxford Process Compendium*, 381.
216 *Oxford Process Compendium*, 389.
217 *Oxford Process Compendium*, 391.
218 *Oxford Process Compendium*, 392.

where it might not be possible to point to a specific course of conduct which a State has been forced into […]". Is it possible to trace the UK's position on coercion, articulated in 2022, to the OPC discussions, given the circumstances? While no conclusive evidence exists for such a claim, it is worth nothing that technical experts, intelligence officials, and legal advisors from the UK have all been active participants in OPC. One interviewee, who preferred to speak on background, noted that the UK Foreign and Commonwealth Office (FCO) hosted at least one meeting of international lawyers to discuss the UK's position on sovereignty and non-intervention. Dapo Akande, the OPC co-convenor, is the UK's nominee to the ICJ at the time of writing. So it is possible, based solely on circumstantial evidence, to argue that the UK's position may have been influenced by the OPC deliberations and reports.

Even without tying the UK's position to OPC discussions, it is worth noting that a number of states have begun to put out statements elucidating their position on the rule of non-intervention. This trend began in late 2020 – around the time of OPC's third meeting on foreign election interference – and likely also coincided with states' articulating their views on the overall application of international law to cyberspace before the UN GGE and OEWG. At the same time, the attention that has been paid by states to defining coercion in some of these statements – despite no prior debates on this topic at the UN – suggests the OPC very likely influenced or at least motivated them to articulate their positions. Among those who have adopted a wider view of coercion at the time of writing include the UK, Australia, Canada, New Zealand, and the United States, while Germany, Switzerland, Norway, and Romania appear to favor a high threshold for coercive behavior.[219] Especially noteworthy is the fact that the Five Eyes countries, which differ on other issues such as due diligence, have converged on a broader understanding of coercion, which may correspond to their collective assessment of the risks of influence operations and the threat they pose to democratic processes in particular.

It is too early at the time of writing to conclude if coercive behavior in cyberspace will be interpreted broadly to encompass actions that deprive or disrupt the ability of states to control *domaine réservé* activities. Should that be the case, the rule of non-intervention could conceivably apply to a number of orchestrated influence operations which may not be intended to achieve a specific result, but seriously or irreversibly disrupt the normal functioning of critical activities and services. It would also likely trigger a discussion on the

219 "Prohibition of Intervention," International cyber law: interactive toolkit, September 12, 2022, https://cyberlaw.ccdcoe.org/wiki/Prohibition_of_intervention.

applicability of the rule beyond cases of election interference, and in domains like finance, healthcare, and even education. At least some of the parameters of evaluating coercion widely are technical in nature: states will have to consider, like Meta and other platforms do, the "coordination" and "inauthenticity" involved, and whether "patterns of behavior" reflect the intent of a state to coercively interfere in another.

3.3.3 The Due Diligence Standard for Ransomware Threats

Previously, this chapter highlighted the unwieldy compromise that TM2 offered with respect to the application of the due diligence rule in cyberspace. That compromise was to impose a "cumulative requirement", restricting the due diligence obligation of states to acts from their territory or infrastructure that were "affecting the rights of states" *and* caused "serious adverse consequences". What TM2's drafters sought to do with this compromise was to ensure all manner of "hostile cyber operations" from territorial infrastructure did not trigger due diligence obligations, but only those with the potential to cause serious harm. However, TM2's qualification of due diligence obligations being applicable only against "internationally wrongful acts" was confusing and left the precise scope of this rule unclear. What can be said with certainty is that TM2 drafters meant for the rule to (a) apply only to cyber operations causing serious harm, and (b) sought to include the actions also of non-state actors which may not otherwise be considered wrongful in international law.

OPC meetings, with their focus on specific topics and objects of protections under international law, had an advantage that the Tallinn Manual process did not. TM2 tried with limited success to articulate a catch-all standard for due diligence in cyberspace. OPC, on the other hand, could clarify precise standards of harm relevant to specific sectors such as healthcare, vaccine research, election interference, ransomware, and so on.

Unsurprisingly, therefore, OPC statements reflect differing standards of harm that trigger the "cyber due diligence" rule in different cases. The following Table 4.3 highlights the various standards of harm imposed by respective OPC statements.

The OPC statements on the healthcare sector and election interference call on states to take "all feasible measures" to prevent, stop, or mitigate cyber operations that cause "adverse consequences" on another state's territory. The statement on vaccine research goes even further – for reasons identified above in the section on data integrity – calling on states to address any "malicious cyber operations" that target "data or technologies" using COVID-19 vaccine research and clinical trial data, among others. No due diligence obligation

TABLE 4.3 Due diligence standards in Oxford Process statements

OPC statement	Healthcare	Vaccine research	Election interference	Information operations	Ransomware
Due diligence standard	"adverse consequences"	"malicious cyber operations against the data or technologies used [for COVID-19 research, etc]"	"adverse consequences"	None	"contrary to the rights of other states"

is specified in the OPC statement on information operations. Only the OPC statement on foreign election interference defines "adverse consequences", but makes it clear, as noted above, that even cyber intrusions that cast a doubt on election data's integrity could fall within this definition.

Given this context, it is notable that the fifth OPC statement frames the due diligence obligation on states to prevent or mitigate ransomware attacks differently from previous statements. States must not allow their territory or infrastructure to be used by states or non-state actors for "ransomware operations that are contrary to the rights of other states", reads the statement. The OPC statement thus adopts in entirety the language of the *Corfu Channel* principle, without any reference to "adverse consequences". What explains this formulation, and did "creeping expertise" play a role in shaping it?

The technical inputs on ransomware received from experts were critical to shaping the overall discussion on due diligence, and ultimately, the OPC statement. Briefing the participants at the outset of the meeting, Krebs outlined an "unholy trinity" of factors that allowed for ransomware attacks to succeed: poor cyber defenses of the victim state and its private sector, emergence of cryptocurrencies which makes tracking ransom flows difficult, and "*fertile ground in host nations for ransomware groups to operate with impunity*"[220] [emphasis added]. In this manner, the technical expert – that too, a former head of the US Cybersecurity and Infrastructure Security Agency (CISA) – framed due diligence as an important aspect of international law protections relevant to ransomware attacks. The unique practices of the fifth OPC meeting also contributed to an in-depth discussion on due diligence. Interestingly, the meeting was subsequently divided into two session on the negative and positive obligations of states, respectively. Although the focus on positive obliga-

220 *Oxford Process Compendium*, 462.

tions is not new to OPC meetings – it is in fact a specific goal of the Process to clarify them[221] – this was the first meeting to be organized in such a manner.[222] It permitted a nuanced debate on the scope of the due diligence rule in relation to ransomware attacks. The session on positive obligations was organized around a background memo, which laid out four "case studies" for the participants to evaluate.[223] The case studies were hypothetical scenarios outlining the details of ransomware operations launched by a "hacker group" with "indications" of strong ties to the host state. The technical consequences of these attacks were spelled out in elaborate detail for workshop participants. The ransomware attacks targeted the following sectors in another state:

a. Management software used by critical infrastructure services and government agencies, where the ransomware payload was introduced by exploiting a known vulnerability in its code. The attack led to disruptions in schools and hospitals.
b. A research institute that had been conducting COVID-19 vaccine clinical trials, which were interrupted by the ransomware attack. The trials were consequently delayed by weeks.
c. A water filtration facility whose compromised passwords were exploited to mount a ransomware attack. The attack prompted a "rapid shutdown" of the facility, which in turn caused a poisonous gas leak (without casualties or injuries).
d. The national healthcare provider was targeted in a ransomware attack that led directly to the death of patients. The victim state formally attributed the attack of the hacker group to the host state and threatened to launch a military strike against it.

In particular, the memo noted that the host state has failed to conduct investigations into each of these cyber operations and the hacker group in general. Unfortunately, the workshop proceedings do not indicate how these specific scenarios were evaluated by participants, and if all or any instance was determined to be a violation of the host state's due diligence obligation. Nevertheless, they appear to have sensitized the participants to the broad spectrum of sectors that may be targeted, as well as harms that may be caused by ransomware attacks. This awareness, in turn, seems to have triggered a cautionary approach to due diligence within the group. One international lawyer briefing the group argued that due diligence obligations for ransomware in the OPC statement should not have such a "robust formulation" as to "prompt escala-

221 *Oxford Process Compendium*, 17.
222 *Oxford Process Compendium*, 464–473.
223 *Oxford Process Compendium*, 478–479.

tory measures" such as countermeasures or result in violations of human rights by the host state in the pretext of network monitoring.[224] Another argued that both the *Corfu Channel* principle and no-harm principle could be considered in the OPC statement on ransomware. However, she acknowledged that a "wide range" of harms could be covered by the no-harm principle. In the open discussion that followed, another participant "expressed concern that an expansive view of 'transboundary harm' may swallow the rest of international law",[225] i.e., the application of the no-harm principle to ransomware attacks may result in all manner of economic, political, or social harm being covered within it. It was better, therefore, to analyze whether other harms were subject to "other specific rules of international law".

Likely on account of the lack of consensus in the meeting regarding a threshold of harm for due diligence in relation to ransomware, the OPC statement adopted the *Corfu Channel* language. In effect, this leaves the obligation to be conditioned by *lex specialis* for cyberspace that outlines the rights of states. However, if due diligence is indeed a primary obligation of international law as some states have argued, the interpretation of this OPC statement could also be that there is no *de minimis* threshold of harm that arbitrates its application to cyberspace. Any ransomware attack that contravenes states' rights could be considered under the due diligence rule, irrespective of whether it causes "significant transboundary harm". Indeed, this would achieve the opposite effect of what the OPC drafters likely intended.

4 The Tallinn Manuals and Oxford Process: Bookends of the International Cybersecurity Law Debate

The pronouncements and statements of the Tallinn Manuals and Oxford Process meetings reflect in many respects the enduring influence of the core beliefs of the cyber Community of Practice. Both initiatives were interpretive exercises where technical and policy perspectives of key stakeholders in the cyber CoP arguably influenced the pronouncements of international lawyers as much as legal argumentation over the existence and applicability of certain rules to cyberspace. Those important constituents, which included major cyber powers, were engaged and their opinions accommodated through what this chapter calls "managerial practices", whether they pertained to the selection of high-priority topics, scheduling meetings to coincide with, or on the

224 *Oxford Process Compendium*, 471.

225 *Oxford Process Compendium*, 473.

sidelines of UN negotiations, or orchestrating outreach meetings ranging from conference presentations to formal consultations such as the Hague Process and technical expert briefings. Just as important were reputational considerations to both initiatives in determining the final commentaries of these products. The Tallinn Manuals and OPC statements sought to elicit consensus from as broad a group of distinguished international lawyers as possible so that their pronouncements would be considered authoritative by the cyber CoP. Negotiating between these international lawyers and ensuring that the initiative collectively had *something* to say international cybersecurity law was just as important as the legal reasoning behind specific principles.

At the time of writing, both initiatives also bookend the CoP's debate over the applicability of international law to state behavior in cyberspace. TM1, published in 2013, held its deliberations alongside seminal GGE discussions that confirmed the applicability of international law to the domain. On the other hand, OPC held its first meetings during the final stages of 2019–2021 UN GGE and OEWG negotiations. It is quite likely that the sixth UN GGE was the last of its kind, as the OEWG process and UN Programme of Action emerge as the main intergovernmental platforms for debates on cyber norms and international law. The Tallinn Manuals, as this chapter has noted, played an immensely influential role in structuring debates around the application of international law. The OPC, it would seem, is the preferred venue for lawyers as well as other stakeholders to contemplate the future contours of international cybersecurity law.

CHAPTER 5

The UN GGE's Changing Position within the Cyber Community of Practice

1 2015 and Onward: The UN GGE Breaks Away from the Cyber CoP

As Chapter 2 highlighted, the UN GGE's practices were crucial to the cyber CoP's conflating norm-articulation and rule-interpretation as it developed a "framework of responsible state behavior" in cyberspace. This chapter also noted that the failure of the fifth (2016–2017) GGE to produce a consensus report spurred the creation of multistakeholder initiatives like the GCSC and the Paris Call, which continued to expound on international law through "voluntary norms". These initiatives, whose work has been detailed in Chapters 3 and 4, mimicked the GGE's approach and developed their own practices that facilitated norms-law conflation. Following its deadlock, however, the UN GGE itself gradually became isolated from the broader community of practice. Discussions within the later GGEs, notably those between 2016 and 2021, were marked by debates on the need to separate norms and interpretations of international law. In other words, if there was previously a tacit internalization of the view that law interpretation could be done through norms, GGEs from 2016 sought consciously to separate binding rules and non-binding norms.

Why did the GGE "break" from the cyber CoP? The answer arguably lies in the evolution of CoPs over time. Far from being static entities, communities of practice are characterized by fluid boundaries (in terms of membership) and constant learning (new knowledge and beliefs).[1] While practices of a CoP reinforce its ingrained beliefs, there is always the possibility that actors acquire new knowledge and beliefs that clash with older, deeply held ones. Sociologists who draw on the work of Bourdieu have in this vein identified a "primary"/community and "secondary"/professional *habitus* that often shape individual actions. The secondary or proximate *habitus* reflects dispositions gained by a

1 Emanuel Adler et al., "Communities of Practice in World Politics: Advancing a Research Agenda," *Global Studies Quarterly* 4, no. 1 (2024): 2, https://doi.org/10.1093/isagsq/ksad070.

person through "professional socialization".[2] It is often "grafted" on to the primary *habitus* of childhood through the "pedagogical labor of didactic institutions", such as schools and colleges, professional associations, political organizations, etc.[3] Of note is the relationship between the primary and proximate *habitus*, and its impact on an individual. If a practitioner's proximate *habitus* is disconsonant or misaligned with that of the primary *habitus*, it "raises their consciousness", forcing them to question those beliefs that were previously unquestioned.[4] In other words, this misalignment results in reflexive thinking, prompting the practitioner to challenge the validity of their prior beliefs and dispositions.

A CoP encompasses actors with diverse and often multiple institutional affiliations, and this is especially true for most domains of global governance. Yet, it is not unthinkable that actors' associations with certain institutions that are more cohesive than others (professional backgrounds, exclusive membership, more routine and "formal"-like meetings) can also shape their beliefs. As the following sections highlight, the UN GGE's composition and working style contributed to new beliefs[5] within the group that made its participants question how they had hitherto advanced international cybersecurity governance.

As previous chapters have noted, Great Power rivalry between the United States and Russia was an omnipresent feature of the UN GGE – the GGE's unique approach to cyber norms was indeed a product of a delicate compromise between both camps. In later years, however, this rivalry became so heightened as to define and ultimately deadlock UN negotiations. This did not reduce the relevance of the UN GGE. However, it prompted negotiators to reflexively review the pronouncements of the UN GGE on norms and inter-

2 Claudio E. Benzecry, "Habitus and Beyond: Standing on the Shoulders of a Giant Looking at the Seams," in *The Oxford Handbook of Pierre Bourdieu*, ed. Thomas Medvetz and Jeffrey J. Sallaz (Oxford University Press, 2018), p. 539, https://doi.org/10.1093/oxfordhb/9780199357192.013.25.

3 Loïc Wacquant, "A Concise Genealogy and Anatomy of Habitus," *The Sociological Review* 64, no. 1 (February 1, 2016): 64–72.

4 Yang Yang, "Bourdieu, Practice and Change: Beyond the Criticism of Determinism," *Educational Philosophy and Theory* 46, no. 14 (December 6, 2014): 1522–40, https://doi.org/10.1080/00131857.2013.839375.

5 Although this chapter does not refer to it, of note here is Pierre Bourdieu's concept of "doxa", increasingly used in international relations literature to refer to "taken for granted" beliefs – "what goes without saying" – that can nevertheless "generate conscious struggles" between practitioners in a CoP. Michael James Grenfell, *Pierre Bourdieu: Key Concepts*, 2nd ed, 115 (London: Routledge, 2014). *See generally*, Rebecca Adler-Nissen, *Opting Out of the European Union: Diplomacy, Sovereignty and European Integration* (Cambridge: Cambridge University Press, 2014).

national law through the prism of Great Power politics. Conscious evaluation of the norms-law relationship by UN negotiators limited the possibility of "creeping expertise" in later GGEs, I demonstrate. I highlight the culmination of the fourth UN GGE (2014–2015) as an important moment that marked the beginning of the GGE's break from the cyber CoP. Highlighting reflexive statements and practices seeking to clarify the precise relationship between norms and international law in the 2019–2021 GGE and OEWG drafts, and the rejection in two instances of technical considerations within the text of the UN reports, I conclude that the GGE exists at the time of writing in splendid isolation from the broader CoP that identifies and applies rules to cyberspace.

2 UN GGEs Emerge as Sites of Great Power Rivalry

The 2014–2015 GGE's culmination was an important moment for the Group with respect to its place in the cyber CoP. The US and Russia, the group's most critical interlocutors, had always had an impact on substantive issues and discussions in the GGE. The use of ICT platforms by the United States in the Gulf War had provided the impetus for successive Russian proposals leading up to the establishment of the first GGE,[6] while the second GGE (2009–2010) was constituted in the backdrop of the 2007 Russian cyberattack on Estonian critical infrastructure as well as the Russian invasion of Georgia[7] – but their evolving bilateral dynamic was increasingly dominating those discussions. If the United States merely acquiesced to the norms-articulation efforts of the GGE at first, it subsequently saw those negotiations as an opportunity to develop Confidence-Building Measures (CBMs) with Russia to prevent escalatory scenarios. The policy of rapprochement with Russia followed by the US during the first term of Barack Obama's presidency extended to cooperation on "cyber arms control".[8] This atmosphere of competitive cooperation spilled

6 Camino Kavanagh, "The United Nations, Cyberspace and International Peace and Security: Responding to Complexity in the 21st Century" (Geneva: United Nations Institute for Disarmament Research, 2017), https://unidir.org/sites/default/files/publication/pdfs//the-united-nations-cyberspace-and-international-peace-and-security-en-691.pdf.

7 Eneken Tikk and Mika Kerttunen, "The Alleged Demise of the UN GGE: An Autopsy and Eulogy" (Cyber Policy Institute, 2017), https://cyber-peace.org/wp-content/uploads/2018/11/Tikk-Kerttunen-2017-The-Alleged-Demise-of-the-UN-GGE-An-Autopsy-and-Eulogy.pdf, 10.

8 Tim Maurer, *Cyber Norm Emergence at the United Nations – An Analysis of the Activities at the UN Regarding Cyber-Security* (Belfer Center for Science and International Affairs, Harvard Kennedy School, 2011), https://www.belfercenter.org/sites/default/files/legacy/files/maurer-cyber-norm-dp-2011-11-final.pdf, 23–25.

over into the GGE, and "the conversation became more productive" from 2009.[9]

As the US–Russia dynamic became more prominent within the GGE, the group's practices started evolving in tandem. From the second GGE onwards, the selection of GGE Experts – who technically did not represent their governments but were almost always civil servants – became increasingly politicized, and both camps sought to ensure they had adequate support in the group.[10] The GGE's substantive agenda also became subservient to US–Russia politics. The formulations of the 2009–2010 GGE reflected the concerns around proxies and critical infrastructure that had been the subject of conversations between the US and Russia in the backdrop of cyberattacks in Estonia and Georgia. As Chapter 2 noted, the multiple political compromises in the 2012–2013 GGE and 2014–2015 GGE that led to the conflation of cyber norms and existing international law were all forged between these Great Powers. Significant as the 2014–2015 GGE's report was, the political compromises made in the report finally took their toll on the Group. As one international lawyer noted at the time, "any remaining room for consensus, particularly with regard to the application of international law, [had] been exhausted".[11]

These changing practices of the GGE gradually generated new beliefs within the group. As a result of these practices and beliefs, the Group's own thinking on cyber norms and international law became misaligned from that of the broader CoP. UN negotiators, who conflated the articulation of "voluntary" norms and application of binding international law began to reflexively evaluate the norms-law relationship from the prism of Great Power politics. They were no longer looking to collectively advance "norms, rules and principles" of responsible state behavior, but were evaluating whether specific formulations of norms or interpretations of international law favored one power or bloc over another.

This did not prevent "creeping expertise" altogether but limited the possibility that technical considerations could shape international cybersecurity

9 Tim Maurer et al., "Cyberspace and Geopolitics: Assessing Global Cybersecurity Norm Processes at a Crossroads" (Carnegie Endowment for International Peace, February 26, 2020), https://carnegieendowment.org/2020/02/26/cyberspace-and-geopolitics-assessing-global-cybersecurity-norm-processes-at-crossroads-pub-81110.

10 "With 15 Experts, the GGE had provided a controlled environment for the leading cyber powers' strategic dialogue with marginal oversight from other countries": Tikk and Kerttunen (2017), n.7, 28.

11 Elaine Korzak, "The 2015 GGE Report: What Next for Norms in Cyberspace?," *Lawfare* (blog), September 23, 2015, https://www.lawfareblog.com/2015-gge-report-what-next-norms-cyberspace.

law through norms. The earliest indicators were already present in 2015: at the UN GA's 70th session that took stock of the fourth GGE report, Israel stated that "future groups of governmental experts should [...] maintain a clear distinction between existing international law, on the one hand, and voluntary non-binding norms, on the other, in order to continue to facilitate a broad base for international consensus".[12] If there was no ambiguity over the legal status of norms, then technical formulations or concerns within political statements would simply remain aspirational. The following sections outline how the GGE's changing practices generated beliefs innate to the group, and ultimately changed its own outlook towards the role of norms vis-à-vis international cybersecurity law.

3 Diplomats Reflect: What Really Is the UN GGE?

How did GGEs come to view norm-articulation and rule-interpretation from the prism of Great Power politics? The evolution of two beliefs within the group was responsible for this shift in the overall outlook of the group:

a. "The UN GGE is a 'professional' body"
b. "The UN GGE must work by consensus"

3.1 "The UN GGE Is a 'Professional' Body"

Following the practice of replacing technical experts by arms control diplomats in the third GGE, the Group's participants began to internalize the belief that the Group's work belonged primarily to the political domain.

"The younger diplomats in age [in the GGE] were more senior in profession, more political and diplomatic", said a veteran arms control negotiator involved in recent GGE negotiations, "many of them did not want to leave it to the technical people alone".[13] Another GGE negotiator argued that "lawyers need to do their work before the technical community can do theirs".[14] A diplomat who was part of two GGE delegations was critical of the "wild, wild ideas" of his peers that "were never going to be feasible", but said the "technical community might not be as involved because they don't want to,

12 "Official Records" (UN General Assembly, Seventieth session, October 30, 2015), 20, https://digitallibrary.un.org/record/835423/files/A_C.1_70_PV.21-EN.pdf.

13 *Interview with Guilherme Patriota*, July 29, 2021.

14 *Interview with a diplomat*, June 15, 2021.

or they have no idea what's going on".[15] "The moment they get the impression we diplomats are touching their little toy [the internet], they all suddenly panic and freak out", he said. On the other hand, a technical expert from an advanced digital economy who was part of their GGE delegation seemed to suggest that this belief was self-reinforcing. "The GGE became a lot more politicized [in the early years] and then you saw a lot more states nominating diplomats."[16] Specifically referring to developing countries, she said they did not have the desired level of technical expertise to nominate to the GGE, and therefore sent "MFA officials", further reinforcing the GGE's politicization.

An experienced practitioner of EU cyber diplomacy and Estonia's Expert in the 2019–2021 GGE described the early days of the GGE "as creating 'positive tension' between technical cyber geeks and non-technical policy wonk, helping to show that the wonks also had something valuable to offer to this field".[17] GGE discussions gradually became "professionalized", she argued, referring to shift in the composition of Groups from "technical cyber experts, military officers, academics, and diplomats" to "diplomats with international security and arms control backgrounds".[18] The rise of "cyber diplomat tradecraft" enhanced the quality and substance of negotiations. She quotes another GGE expert suggesting that "subject-matter expertise" in the GGE can be understood as expertise in "cyber as a strategic foreign policy issue".[19]

This new perspective held by diplomats sharpened US–Russia centricism of the GGE in two ways. First, for professionals who cut their teeth in international politics, banner developments surrounding the GGE such as the alleged Russian interference in the 2016 US presidential election became an important cognitive frame of reference. They perceived the work of the GGE in relation to larger geopolitical factors at work. For example, one senior GGE representative noted that the substantive reason behind the failure of the GGE may have been disagreement over the international law section, but that the "geopolitical context" was also relevant. "Two weeks [after the US presidential elections], we met in Geneva, for the GGE", the diplomat said.[20] "Krutskikh

---

15 *Interview with a diplomat*, July 7, 2021.

16 *Interview with a diplomat*, August 3, 2021.

17 Heli Tiirmaa-Klaar, "The Evolution of the UN Group of Governmental Experts on Cyber Issues," Cyberstability Paper Series New Conditions and Constellations in Cyber, 5 (The Hague Centre for Strategic Studies, December 2021), https://hcss.nl/wp-content/uploads/2021/12/Klaar.pdf.

18 Klaar (2021), 11.

19 Klaar (2021), 11.

20 *Interview with a diplomat*, September 17, 2021.

[the Russian Expert] – who is hilarious, by the way, but sometimes he goes a little too far – he showed up at a bilateral with the Americans wearing a 'Make America Great Again' (then US President Trump's campaign slogan) baseball cap. I have a picture of a beautiful moment, so he's doing a thumbs up…let's just say that I found that quite funny. But the Americans did not find it all that funny for reasons you can understand. *That kind of poisoned the well*" [emphasis added]. The anecdote is revealing for the perception of the kind of impact that the bilateral meeting, and by extension, the relationship, had on the group as a whole.

Second, and on a related note, the views of professional diplomats were shaped directly by their interactions with their senior colleagues Andrey Krutskikh and Michele Markoff, the Russian and US Expert respectively, who were the co-owners and drivers of this process. Both are career diplomats who belong to the world of disarmament and arms control. At the time of writing, Krutskikh has stepped down from his role, while Markoff continues to be the lead US cyber negotiator in the UN First Committee. The Estonian Expert cited above herself acknowledged there were "principals among the Experts who provided steadiness and historical memory for the group". "The dynamic between the two senior and experienced cyber experts from two superpowers in the room *often defined the atmosphere of negotiations*. Without the long-standing relationship between them, it would be hard to imagine the GGEs as we know them"[21] [emphasis added]. Interviews with negotiators from the third, fifth, and sixth GGEs corroborated this view: one said "Krutskikh and Markoff were both excellent Experts and they worked really in a very professional way within the group",[22] while another recalled that Markoff's "temper is strong and patience is thin, but she provided the 2019–2021 Group with high quality inputs".[23] A podcast hosted by a veteran member of the secretarial team that supported the UN GGE's work called Markoff the "Mother of Norms".[24] The constant and powerful presence of both senior diplomats, and their role in the negotiations, arguably reinforced the perception of other negotiators that the US–Russia dynamic was indeed central to the group's negotiations.

21 Klaar (2021), 11.

22 *Interview with Sherif Heshem*, November 24, 2020.

23 *Interview with a diplomat*, 2021.

24 James A. Lewis and Christopher Painter, "Discussing the UN OEWG with the Mother of Norms," Inside Cyber Diplomacy, accessed November 25, 2022, https://www.csis.org/podcasts/inside-cyber-diplomacy/discussing-un-oewg-mother-norms.

3.2 "The UN GGE Must Work by Consensus"

The practice of adopting GGE reports by consensus is an understudied but complex topic. The "rule" of consensus in the cyber GGE, which has been followed by all six Groups held thus far, mirrors those of *ad hoc* groups constituted by other disarmament fora of the UN. Some of these fora formally stipulate the requirement of consensus – for example, the Rules of Procedure of the Conference on Disarmament require that the forum "conduct its work and adopt its decisions by consensus".[25] The "consensus rule" of the CD, which has been applied also to its GGEs, has been criticized by several NGOs and analysts as the cause behind the conference's current deadlock and failure to develop a Programme of Work.[26] Similarly, the Rules of Procedure for meetings and conferences of the CCW call for decision-making by those bodies to be in accordance with Article 8 of the Convention, which in turn requires that all amendments to the CCW be adopted by consensus.[27] As with the CD, the "consensus-as-unanimity"[28] rule has trickled down to the GGEs instituted under the CCW. When the 2015 CCW Meeting of States Parties established an "informal group of experts" to discuss how the question of LAWS should be addressed within the Convention, it noted that this group had to agree on its recommendations for further work by consensus.[29] This group in turn recommended to the CCW's Fifth Review Conference of 2016 that a GGE on

25 "Rules of Procedure of the Conference on Disarmament" (Conference on Disarmament, July 28, 2022), https://documents-dds-ny.un.org/doc/UNDOC/GEN/G22/439/18/PDF/G2243918.pdf?OpenElement.

26 Ray Acheson, "Presentation on Consensus, Political Will, Nuclear Disarmament, and the Conference on Disarmament," Reaching Critical Will, October 11, 2012, https://www.reachingcriticalwill.org/resources/statements/7062-presentation-on-consensus-political-will-nuclear-disarmament-and-the-conference-on-disarmament; Paul Meyer, "Does the Conference of Disarmament Have a Future?," *Journal for Peace and Nuclear Disarmament* 4, no. 2 (July 3, 2021): 287–94, https://doi.org/10.1080/25751654.2021.1993632.

27 "Draft Rules of Procedure of the Fifth Review Conference of the High Contracting Parties to the Convention on Prohibitions or Restrictions on the Use of Certain Conventional Weapons Which May Be Deemed to Be Excessively Injurious or to Have Indiscriminate Effects" (UN Office of Disarmament Affairs, September 28, 2016), https://documents-dds-ny.un.org/doc/UNDOC/GEN/G16/215/36/PDF/G1621536.pdf?OpenElement;.

28 Ray Acheson, "The CCW Is Still Standing, but to What End?" (Reaching Critical Will, November 18, 2019), https://reachingcriticalwill.org/disarmament-fora/ccw/2019/laws/ccwreport/14445-ccw-report-vol-7-no-8.

29 "Convention on Certain Conventional Weapons – Informal Meeting of Experts (2016) | United Nations," United Nations Office for Disarmament Affairs (UNODA), accessed November 25, 2022, https://meetings.unoda.org/ccw-ime/convention-certain-conventional-weapons-informal-meeting-experts-2016.

LAWS should be established, and operate by consensus.[30] Similarly, the Sixth Review Conference of 2021, while establishing a second iteration of the LAWS GGE, expressly stated that the rules of the Review Conference applied *mutatis mutandis* to the GGE and that its report had to be adopted by consensus. In yet other cases, the UN GA has itself specified the decision-making procedure of an *ad hoc* body, as it did with the GGE on the Prevention of an Arms Race in Outer Space (PAROS). The UN GA resolution that established the PAROS GGE in 2017 stipulated for the group to "operate by consensus, without prejudice to national positions in future negotiations".[31]

In contrast, there are no formal guidelines around the work and operating practices of the cyber GGEs. Unlike Review Conference decisions or UN GA resolutions on many other GGEs that have specified the dates and even duration of their working sessions, the UN GA has *never* offered guidance with respect to the format and timing of cyber GGE meetings. For example, the cyber GGE's practice of meeting three to four times a year for a week each, often splitting calendar year meetings equally between the UN in New York and Geneva, appears simply to have become institutionalized over time.

The informal requirement of consensus is, however, more than a rule of procedure for the cyber GGE: it represents a practice that has generated and reinforced a new belief among its members. The expectation that its report must be adopted by consensus has influenced not only other practices of the Group but also the actions of its Experts, as well as the substantive pronouncements of the GGE. Most importantly, belief in consensus has played a major role in politicizing the group, accentuating the US–Russia rivalry within it, and isolating the GGE vis-à-vis the larger CoP. I offer below examples to substantiate these claims.

The Chair of a UN GGE played an important role in determining the working procedure of that Group. "I wouldn't call [the GGE's working procedure] rules or practices, it's more like 'culture'", said a veteran GGE negotiator in an interview, "a lot of it boils down to the way the Chair manages the group and the meetings".[32] For GGE chairs, however, the requirement of consensus has been sacred and immutable, although it has no formal basis. Karsten Geier, Germany's Expert and Chair of the 2016–2017 GGE said that within the man-

30 "Report of the 2016 Informal Meeting of Experts on Lethal Autonomous Weapons Systems (LAWS)" (UN Office of Disarmament Affairs, June 10, 2016), https://documents-dds-ny.un.org/doc/UNDOC/GEN/G16/117/16/PDF/G1611716.pdf?OpenElement.

31 "72/250. Further Practical Measures for the Prevention of an Arms Race in Outer Space" (UN General Assembly, Seventy-second session, January 12, 2018), https://doi.org/10.18356/9789210021753c001.

32 *Interview with Katherine Getao,* August 16, 2021.

date of any Group, there are only two restrictions on its chairs – "they cannot determine the composition, and they cannot change the decision-making mode".[33] In fact, the Chairs' conduct was heavily influenced by the expectation that the report must be adopted by consensus. For example, the Chair of the 2014–2015 GGE reportedly determined that if an Expert was not present in the room during a session, and they had not delegated somebody to take their place, the Group would not continue discussions until the Expert arrived.[34] There were reputational and professional considerations for the Chair as well, since the failure of a Group to produce a consensus report could reflect on their leadership, and that of their country. "I convinced my capital that success in the GGE was equal to a [consensus] outcome", said Guilherme Patriota, the Chair of the 2019–2021 GGE.[35] Belief in consensus weighed equally on other Experts. "For some [diplomats], the UN GGE's failing to agree on a report is a career breaker", said an Expert.[36]

Insights from Experts also indicate how the GGE's emphasis on consensus left the Group's substantive formulations vulnerable to political opportunism. "Because we need to get a consensus, there is what I would almost call dishonesty", said an Expert, "because you allow some things which you don't really believe in to pass because you want other things to survive".[37] The expectation of consensus, the same Expert noted, allowed some delegations to come with "prepared statements and not have to listen or negotiate". "They can come and say, everything is rubbish, which can be quite frightening [to hear] if it is your first time in the GGE." Because of this, "the first two weeks of the GGE can be nasty". Then, there was a lot of compromise within the Group. "[Experts] are more willing to be controversial or intransigent in the first three meetings, but there is a lot of pressure in the last meeting – there is a lot of huddling in corners, which adds a degree of pressure, [and] this is, when all that language which people don't really agree to is allowed to pass", the Expert concluded. Although participants in the GGE acknowledge the challenges of producing a consensus report, they also appear to have internalized its necessity. "I don't know how else you can do it, except by consensus", the same Expert said. "Consensus-based decision making is frustrating but good", said another Expert, "otherwise there is a chance of China dominating the G77 group".[38] A negotiator from an ASEAN country – ASEAN is known for its emphasis on,

33 *Interview with Karsten Geier*, February 8, 2021.

34 *Interview with Katherine Getao*, August 16, 2021.

35 *Interview with Guilherme Patriota*, July 29, 2021.

36 *Interview with a diplomat*, 2021.

37 *Interview with a diplomat*, 2021.

38 *Interview with a diplomat*, 2021.

and ability to drive decisions by consensus – acknowledged that the GGE's dynamic was not the "usual one that ASEAN is used to".[39] To get to a GGE consensus, the negotiator said, "one had to work the marvels of the language", creating so broad and ambiguous formulations that "you can always go with either version A or version B" of a draft. The *doxa* of consensus thus played a key role in molding GGE negotiations into overtly political discussions, where legal or technical considerations became subservient to the need to secure compromise.

The pressure to deliver a consensus report decisively shaped the outcome of the 2014–2015 GGE and in particular, reinforced the perception of GGE negotiators that the Group had been captured by Great Power rivalry. In particular, the marginalization of China by a backroom US–Russia bargain underlined this shift. While China had hitherto sent arms control negotiators to GGE discussions, it nominated diplomats identified as "coordinators for cyber affairs" in the Ministry of Foreign Affairs to the fourth GGE.[40] (Their nomination as Experts confirms Beijing too had internalized the view that the GGE needed professionalization.) Convergences between Chinese and Russian positions against expressly identifying principles of existing international law in GGE reports, as well as their recent signing of joint communiques and agreements on information security at the SCO, may have given rise to an impression they were a unified bloc in the GGE. However, the final report of the GGE, which endorsed the applicability of international law, the UN Charter in particular, and even some principles of international humanitarian law, was essentially a compromise between the US and Russia in the final session that kept China out of the loop. "In 2014–2015, Russia threw China under the bus and decided, I don't know for what reasons, to come to the side of the like-minded countries and agree to the language on international law", said a senior Expert who was part of that GGE.[41] Whatever Russia's reasons might be, it is clear China's agreeing to the final GGE report was owed in part to the pressure not to be perceived as spoilers, and to "join the consensus". "The Chinese Expert [in the first and second sessions] did not behave like the other Chinese delegates over the years, you know, he was a good listener", another Expert said.[42] "He spoke perfect English, although he insisted on speaking in Chinese. And he was clearly a person who did not always take the party line, he would think for himself, and so on. He was a big factor in getting to agreement." Given

39 *Interview with a diplomat*, 2021.

40 *Fourth UN GGE report*, 15.

41 *Interview with Marina Kaljurand*, October 7, 2021.

42 *Interview with a diplomat*, 2021.

that US–Russia backroom diplomacy had resulted in a major breakthrough, the "Chinese were left alone, and they had no choice but to acquiesce." "When the same person [Expert in the third and fourth sessions] came to the next GGE they were much more careful", said an Expert.[43] China's marginalization reduced its status as a third pole in the GGE, and thus reinforced the US–Russia centricity of the Group.

In sum, the view held by diplomats around the GGE's professionalization and consensus requirement was critical to the GGE's emergence as an overtly political body, whose dynamic became highly sensitive to the deteriorating relationship between Russia and the United States. When the GGE reconvened for a fifth time in 2016 with 25 Experts, the shadow of alleged Russian interference in the US Presidential Elections loomed large over the Group. As one Expert recounted, "the external influence of cyber incidents" on the Group was notable. "They were referred to in the group, and accusations were going back and forth. At some point, you had a feeling you were in a court of law."[44]

The 2016–2017 GGE failed to produce a report on account of differences between the major cyber powers, led by the US and Russia on either side, over the draft text of the section on international law. This section comprised two paragraphs, numbered 33 and 34 in the GGE's final draft.[45]

The final text of draft paragraph 34, which referred to applicable international law, reads as follows:

> 34. The Group had an intensive exchange on and how international law applies to the use of ICTs by States. The Group noted as of central importance the commitments of States to the UN Charter in its entirety and other sources of international law and legal principles. The Group found that the following apply: sovereign equality; non-intervention in the internal affairs of other States; the settlement of international disputes by peaceful means in such a manner that international peace, security and justice are not endangered; the right to respond to internationally wrongful acts committed through the use of ICTs; the obligation to refrain in international relations from the threat or use of force against the territorial integrity or political independence of any State, or in any other manner inconsistent with the purposes of the United Nations;

---

43 *Interview with Marina Kaljurand,* October 7, 2021.

44 *Interview with Karsten Geier*, February 8, 2021.

45 The text of draft paragraphs 33 and 34 was shared with this author by a UN negotiator on June 24, 2017.

> respect for human rights and fundamental freedoms; the right to self-defence, and the principles of humanity, necessity, proportionality and distinction.

The draft text proposed by the United States and what had by then emerged as the "like-minded group of countries" within the GGE clearly sought to distinguish international cybersecurity law from cyber norms. The text referred specifically to "the commitments of States [to] other sources of international law", elaborating on the previous GGE's assertion of the "general applicability" of international law to the domain. It also invoked state responsibility principles without additional qualifications (such as the requirement of technical attributability). Draft paragraph 33 reaffirmed the conclusion of previous GGEs that international law governed state behavior in cyberspace, but also emphasized that the 2014–2015 Group was guided by the "UN Charter, *other sources of international law*, and its mandate" [emphasis added] in drafting its section on international law. In this manner, draft paragraph 33 represented the work of the fourth GGE as an exercise in legal interpretation, and not the outcome of a political compromise.

As is evident from the formulation, the draft attempted to address the confusion prevalent in the cyber CoP, especially among international lawyers, by distinguishing the "sources of international law" from the (ostensibly) political sources of cybersecurity norms. However, as the preceding paragraphs have shown, the GGE had by this time become so attuned to the political dynamic between the US and Russia, that it was difficult for the Group to offer authoritative guidance on this issue or reassert itself as the pre-eminent forum that applied or identified rules for cyberspace. The "politicization of international cyber law",[46] as two prominent international lawyers noted at the time, was the only probable outcome of the GGE.

4 New Practices Emerge, and Old Beliefs Are Questioned in the UN

Indeed, tracing the practices of the fifth UN GGE shows how the Group's belief in consensus allowed Russia and other states to block the inclusion of the section on international law. Karsten Geier, the chair of the Group and Expert from Germany, reportedly made the decision to negotiate the text of the inter-

46 Michael Schmitt and Liis Vihul, "International Cyber Law Politicized: The UN GGE's Failure to Advance Cyber Norms," *Just Security* (blog), June 30, 2017, https://www.justsecurity.org/42768/international-cyber-law-politicized-gges-failure-advance-cyber-norms/.

national law section for the final sessions. In an interview, Geier argued that the consensus requirement of the GGE "was not a disadvantage".[47] "There are ways of playing if you want to come to a solution but cannot support the consensus", he said. "[An expert] can issue a declaration that I am not joining the consensus on certain points or the Report could say "consensus-1" or something like that. Consensus is not an obstacle to progress, the report could be an appendix with elements that are not agreed or take cognizance of a dissenting vote." In Geier's opinion, however, the "absolute refusal of a player to compromise", could result in "complete blockage". Geier implied, therefore, that the GGE's failure was owed primarily to the intransigence of Russia.

On the other hand, it is also likely that the Chair's practice of negotiating the international law section towards the end of GGE discussions could not be reconciled with beliefs closely held by members of the Group. As has been noted previously, GGE discussions that usually begin with grandstanding or the articulation of maximalist positions by Experts were followed by sessions where political compromises between powerful states produced eleventh-hour outcomes. "The fundamental mistake Karsten did", said a Western diplomat who was involved in the fifth GGE, "was thinking that if we covered all the easier stuff, that we get so close, then we would truly get over the finish line. That didn't happen. [International law] was a tough issue – but we simply ran out of time, people literally had flights that night, and once people started leaving the room, then you know you cannot agree. *It's a consensus body*. In retrospect, I think many people felt we should have worked on the tough issue [earlier]...maybe if he could have mediated a sort of a bilateral [between US and Russia] or a trilateral between Russia, China and the US..." [emphasis added].[48] Another GGE Expert from a European country corroborated this account: "geopolitics was a factor in the failed GGE, but equally the lack of time was also a factor. There were ambitious proposals on both sides, and of course, a lack of appetite to compromise."[49] Diplomats who had internalized the value of consensus-based decision-making in the group the GGE rejected a new negotiating practice. If states like Russia and China already perceived the compromise of the previous GGE as a major concession, they opposed any clarification on the precise legal rules or sources of international cybersecurity law since such clarification would undermine their strategy of influencing those rules through norms. As a result, consensus around the international law section in the fifth GGE proved elusive.

---

47 *Interview with Karsten Geier*, February 8, 2021.

48 *Interview with a diplomat*, 2021.

49 *Interview with Carmen Gonsalves*, October 14, 2021.

Finally, the claim that GGE Experts perceived consensus not simply as the outcome of their deliberations but as adherence to its established practices is strengthened by the Group's failure to change its working procedures even in the face of a crisis. When it became apparent that the last session of the GGE would not produce a result, the Chair proposed to extend the meeting. "After the 2017 GGE meeting did not end in consensus, we thought of organizing another meeting, because consensus was not very far – to forge at least some sort of compromise – [but] this procedure did not meet with consensus. The secretariat said it was fine, but there was at least one delegation that strenuously said we do not want to continue with this process."[50]

5 The 2019–2021 UN GGE and OEWG: A Reflexive Separation of Norms and Rules

The failure of the fifth GGE to produce a report and clarify the application of international cybersecurity law resulted in an isolation of the Group from the larger CoP. As the previous section notes, this isolation had already begun with the conclusion of the 2014–2015 GGE, which elicited an exacting political compromise for the sake of a consensus report. States that took part in the GGE, as well as stakeholders belonging to the cyber CoP, were aware of the limits of the Group, and began investing in other initiatives to promote their respective strategies. China, which was blindsided by the US–Russia compromise in the 2014–2015 GGE, moved the Asian-African Legal Consultative Organization (AALCO) in 2014 to consider how international law applied to cyberspace.[51] AALCO, an intergovernmental organization that owes its origins to the Non-Aligned Movement, includes many developing countries that are part of the G77 negotiating bloc in the UN. Just as the fourth GGE was concluding its work, the Fifty-Fourth Annual Session of AALCO held in Beijing decided to establish an Open-Ended Working Group (OEWG) within AALCO to discuss the matter on a continual basis. The AALCO OEWG was tasked with following the "deliberation and progress made in the UN framework and other forums", and paying "special attention to international law pertaining to State Sovereignty in cyberspace, peaceful use of cyberspace,[…] identification of the relevant provisions of the UN Charter and other international instruments related

50 *Interview with Karsten Geier*, February 8, 2021.

51 "International Law in Cyberspace" (New Delhi: Asian-African Legal Consultative Organization, May 20, 2016), https://www.aalco.int/userfiles/file/55thSession/Cyberspace%202016.pdf.

to cyberspace".[52] Through its championship of the AALCO OEWG, China attempted to ensure that the development of international cybersecurity law was favorable to its interests, and there was sufficient support from other states for its own views on the subject, so that China did not face a situation similar to that in the GGE again. Interestingly, the Rapporteur to the AALCO working group was also a prominent Chinese international lawyer.[53]

Western states too appear to have been pessimistic in their assessment of the GGE's ability to guide the CoP on international cybersecurity law. The work of the GCSC and the Paris Call has already been highlighted in Chapter 3, and it bears mentioning that exercises like the Tallinn Manual too were informally and overtly supported by Western powers. The Organization for Security and Cooperation in Europe (OSCE) similarly began stepping up its efforts in cyber diplomacy in 2016 and 2017. The OSCE, a group that includes the US and Russia, was able in December 2017 to produce a Ministerial Decision on "enhancing OSCE Efforts to reduce the risk of conflict stemming from the use of Information and Communication technologies".[54] The precarity of GGE negotiations played an important role in shaping the OSCE's high-level declaration. Germany also chaired the OSCE in 2016, and Geier acknowledged that the drafts of OSCE declarations during this period were "certainly inspired by the developments at the UN". The thinking, Geier said, was, "oh God, we must have progress in Vienna (Austria chaired the OSCE in 2017) even if you do not consensus in New York".[55]

The GGE's isolation within the CoP was hastened by efforts even within the UN to provide clarity on issues pertaining to international cybersecurity law. In the summer of 2017, Estonia and Singapore, both regionally influential states with established interest and significant national investments in cybersecurity, created a Group of Friends on e-Governance and Cybersecurity at the UN headquarters in New York to further discussions on, *inter alia*, interna-

52 *International Law in Cyberspace*, N.51, 1–2.

53 "Professor Huang Zhixiong Was Elected as Special Rapporteur of International Organizations," Wuhan University Institute of International Law, October 10, 2018, http://translaw.whu.edu.cn/en/index.php/index-view-aid-505.html.

54 "DECISION No. 5/17 ENHANCING OSCE EFFORTS TO REDUCE THE RISKS OF CONFLICT STEMMING FROM THE USE OF INFORMATION AND COMMUNICATION TECHNOLOGIES," Ministerial Council Decision (Vienna: Organization for Security and Co-operation in Europe, December 8, 2017), https://www.osce.org/files/f/documents/9/f/361561.pdf.

55 *Interview with Karsten Geier*, February 8, 2021.

tional law applicable to cyberspace.[56] The GoF, which attracted over 30 countries as "members", interacted not only with the GGE chair but also private initiatives and stakeholders over "what came next after the GGE". In this regard, remarks by two veterans of the UN GGE secretariat made at a debriefing session on the 2016–2017 GGE for the UN GA First Committee are also instructive. Kerstin Vignard, then deputy director of UNIDIR, argued "that instead of serving as an incubator leading to a wider 'process' – as GGEs do on other topics – the cyber GGEs themselves became the process".[57] With GGEs having a limited membership, several states were "feeling excluded", she noted. Crucially, she also argued that changes in composition made it "increasingly difficult to hold the line on past GGE achievements". "Not all new members to the group believed that the reports were cumulative; rather they believed that issues from past reports could be reopened", she said. James Lewis, an external consultant who was involved secretarially in all GGEs, confirmed the view "that the consensus reports were the outcome of bargains, some of them not always logical to external observers".[58] The GGE veterans were, in essence, underlining the fact that the Group had lent itself to political rivalry, competition, and compromise, that its main goal of offering authoritative (albeit confusing) guidance on international cybersecurity law and cyber norms to the broader CoP had been sidelined. Indeed, this period marks a phase where influential states began outlining their positions on international cybersecurity law through standalone statements and declarations, presumably in the hope that they will trigger and shape discussion within the broader CoP on the matter.

Given Great Power rivalry in the GGE, it became challenging for the process to continue to stay relevant in the cyber CoP through new iterations or norms, and make meaningful contributions. In fact, US–Russia rivalry within the GGE resulted in the creation of parallel processes to articulate cyber norms and clarify international cybersecurity law. Owing to Russia's efforts, the UN General Assembly in December 2018 decided to convene an "open-ended working group" (OEWG) on ICT security. The OEWG was not only tasked with "further

56 "Address by the President of the Republic of Estonia Kersti Kaljulaid at the General Debate of the 72nd United Nations General Assembly," September 19, 2017, 4 https://gadebate.un.org/sites/default/files/gastatements/72/ee_en.pdf.

57 "ICTs in the Context of International Peace and Security: Current Conditions and Future Approaches," UNIDIR Cyber Stability Conference 2017 (United Nations Institute for Disarmament Research, October 11, 2017), 4 https://unidir.org/sites/default/files/publication/pdfs//icts-in-the-context-of-international-peace-and-security-current-conditions-and-future-approaches-en-696.pdf.

58 *ICTs in the Context of International Peace and Security*, n.57, 5.

developing rules, norms and principles of responsible behavior of States" identified by previous GGEs but also "if necessary, to introduce changes to them *or elaborate additional rules of behavior*" [emphasis added]. Whereas this formulation should ordinarily have deepened confusion about the precise status of norms and their relationship to international law, the GGE's overt politicization was evident to all, as the following sections highlight. The OEWG was evidently a Russian initiative to ensure it was not isolated by the United States and the like-minded group within an exclusive "club" like the GGE.[59] With the OEWG "open-ended" as regards its membership to any UN state, Russia calculated that it would have more support within a larger group. Further, as the UN GA mandate made it clear, Russia persisted in its efforts to articulate rules of state behavior through cybersecurity norms and even persuaded the UN GA to allow the OEWG to "introduce changes" to previous GGE norms and even "elaborate additional rules of behavior".[60]

Concurrently, the UN GA also set up a sixth GGE tasked, like its predecessor, to study how international law applied to the use of ICTs. The US and the like-minded group co-sponsored the GGE proposal with a view to re-establishing the GGE as the authoritative arbiter, within the UN framework, of international cybersecurity law. Indeed, as one commentator notes, the proposal to create a sixth GGE was supposed to be a mutually exclusive proposal from that of the OEWG, but many states voted in favor of both groups, creating parallel tracks that neither Russia nor the US appears to have sought.[61]

With the origins of both proposals apparent to participants and observers within the CoP, the possibility of either group influencing the community's pronouncements on international law was slim.

---

59 Samuele De Tomas Colatin, "A Surprising Turn of Events: UN Creates Two Working Groups on Cyberspace," *NATO CCDCOE* (blog), accessed November 25, 2022, https://ccdcoe.org/incyder-articles/a-surprising-turn-of-events-un-creates-two-working-groups-on-cyberspace/.

60 "73/27. Developments in the Field of Information and Telecommunications in the Context of International Security" (UN General Assembly, Seventy-third session, December 11, 2018), 5 https://doi.org/10.18356/9789210021753c001.

61 Alex Grigsby, "The United Nations Doubles Its Workload on Cyber Norms, and Not Everyone Is Pleased," Council on Foreign Relations, accessed November 25, 2022, https://www.cfr.org/blog/united-nations-doubles-its-workload-cyber-norms-and-not-everyone-pleased.

5.1 Practices of the 2019–2021 GGE and OEWG

At the outset, it is worth highlighting how both processes unfolded, and evaluating how their practices reinforced Great Power rivalry, and thus, the proximate *habitus* of the UN negotiations. The UN OEWG met for the first time in June 2019, while the GGE met initially in December of that year. The GGE, being a closed group, did not publish versions of its draft report or inputs received from states at any time during the Group's negotiations. In contrast, the OEWG was more transparent: the Group published a pre-draft, Zero Draft, and First Draft of its report, not only inviting written comments and oral statements from states on those drafts, but also making them available to the public.

Interviews with diplomats from both Groups shed light on the working practices instituted by their Chairs. "I was aware of the [previous] GGE's debacle… it was very much on my mind", said Patriota, the sixth GGE chair. "Negotiations started before day one", he said. "There was a lot of interest to join the Group. Seventy countries applied to be a member of the GGE, and the secretariat had to find a political way to balance the composition, even [account for] gender balance because the UN Secretary-General wanted it, as well as regional balance."[62] Patriota, who had the advantage of dealing with a smaller, closed group of states, followed a different approach to negotiations than Jürg Lauber, the Swiss diplomat who was appointed as the chair of the OEWG. Patriota made the GGE "go through the *acquis* first". This was aimed at getting "an agreement on what are [states'] reading of the [GGE's] mandate, reading of the current circumstances, [and reaffirm] common understandings".[63] Subsequently, he turned the GGE's attention to the section on threats and norms, and on international law, in that order. Jürg Lauber had a different approach: "Lauber basically kept putting out drafts, kept listening to the general statements [from OEWG members", recounted one OEWG diplomat. "Literally the Thursday before the last day [and session of OEWG negotiations], he's like, 'this is the last draft, take it or leave it'… we were like 'what, we never negotiated'." "It was a huge gamble", the diplomat said, "a lot of people were pissed off about it, but it worked, so you have to give it to him. He went outside the box and it worked".[64] Lauber, for his part, has acknowledged that the challenge of producing a successful OEWG report lay in getting all 193 states to agree to its contents. Nevertheless, he argued that he and his team "made great

62 *Interview with Guilherme Patriota,* July 29, 2021.

63 *Interview with Guilherme Patriota,* July 29, 2021.

64 *Interview with a diplomat, 2021.*

efforts to reach out to the various regional and other groups of member States as well as to the so-called (non-governmental) stakeholders".[65] By all accounts, the chairs of both Groups seem to have had a good working relationship, coordinating their work, and also jointly engaging in a consultative exercise with regional organizations prior to the negotiations themselves. Although the processes and the Chairs' practices were different, many diplomats acknowledged the fact the GGE and OEWG were intertwined. The discussions were not very different from each other, said Regine Grienberger of Germany, "we were working hard to hard to make these two products complementary and not conflicting with each other, to some establish some kind of coherence".[66] "Ultimately, this was a dual track that no one wanted to destroy", said Henri Verdier of France, "you could not really call it a real negotiation". "It was mostly an effort *to spread the acquis and not progress it*", he said [emphasis added].[67] As previously mentioned, the research and support staff for both groups were also the same.

The onset of the COVID-19 pandemic affected the working of both Groups, albeit differently. Although the OEWG and GGE both met in December 2019 and February 2020, their schedules diverged thereafter. The OEWG met for a third and final session in March 2021, which resulted in the group producing a consensus report. In the interim, the Group met four times for informal, virtual discussions, as well as a separate, informal interaction with non-governmental stakeholders. Each informal meeting of OEWG states had a clear programme of work. In contrast, the GGE met twice – interspersed by several informal intersessional meetings – after its second meeting, in April and May 2021 respectively. The final meeting of the OEWG was organized in "hybrid" format, with some delegations based in New York, whereas the GGE report was negotiated entirely through virtual discussions.

On paper, the virtual nature of negotiations made them more transparent, and reduced the scope for closed-door huddles that, as previously noted, had been the hallmark of GGE negotiations. However, that did little to alter the competitive dynamic between the Great Powers that continued to shape GGE discussions, even before the negotiations. "Some filter was applied [in the selection of GGE experts]", said Patriota, "[the UN secretariat] tried in some ways not to include some spoilers…some 'exceedingly difficult' members".

65 Jürg Lauber and Lukas Eberli, "From Confrontation to Consensus: Taking Stock of the OEWG Process," Cyberstability Paper Series (Global Commission on the Stability of Cyberspace, September 30, 2021), 3, https://cyberstability.org/paper-series/from-confrontation-to-consensus-taking-stock-of-the-oewg-process/.

66 *Interview with Regine Grienberger*, August 23, 2021.

67 *Interview with Henri Verdier*, October 8, 2021.

While Patriota did not name these states or Experts, another non-Western GGE Expert had noted that "the introduction of belligerent countries like Cuba [in the fifth GGE]" made deliberations more difficult.[68] The presence of spoilers was likely to make agreement between the "core nucleus of the group – US and Russia" difficult.[69] Secondly, whether virtual or not, there was no doubt that each process had its own custodian. Russia was more invested in the OEWG, as the US was in the GGE. "Poor Patriota had to listen a lot to the Russians giving long speeches of how [the GGE] was useless", a senior GGE Expert said.[70] "The Americans became the sole owner of the [GGE] process", another diplomat said.[71] Patriota himself acknowledged that the "Russians refused to participate substantively [in the GGE] until the very end". "I had no idea whether they would conform or not."[72]

The outcome of both processes was linked to the dynamic of Great Power relations. The OEWG, holding its final session in March 2021, finished first. As mentioned earlier, the hybrid format of the final OEWG session meant that many delegations were in New York, while some others negotiated virtually. Of the delegations in attendance, only two cyber diplomats – Krutskikh of Russia and Johanna Weaver of Australia – were sent by their capitals specifically for the OEWG, while others were represented by their UN missions. The Russian and Australian diplomats became proxies for the two negotiating blocs, with Australia negotiating the OEWG and GGE texts for the like-minded group that included the US, EU states, Australia, and Japan.[73] "Johanna Weaver worked magic in New York in the spring of 2021", wrote Heli-Tiirma Klaar, the Estonian Expert, in a stocktaking assessment of the OEWG and GGE.[74] "During the ongoing pandemic, with limited international travel, she was volunteering to establish a presence in New York for three months and proved especially efficient in arbitraging final GGE disputes between key players." Krutskikh and Weaver, who struck a rapport over the course of the negotiations, ensured that its virtual format did not impede a consensus report. It helped, of course, that the OEWG was a Russian initiative, and therefore, the Russians were keen to see it succeed. On the other hand, the two cyber diplomats with subject-matter expertise had an obvious advantage over their gen-

68 *Interview with a diplomat, 2021.*

69 *Interview with Guilherme Patriota,* July 29, 2021.

70 Interview with *a diplomat, 2021.*

71 *Interview with a diplomat, 2021.*

72 *Interview with Guilherme Patriota,* July 29, 2021.

73 See generally, *CyCon 2022 DAY 1 Keynote by Johanna Weaver*, 2022, https://www.youtube.com/watch?v=O8eFiJaNzRU.

74 Tiirma-Klaar (2021), 11.

eralist UN counterparts present at the venue, and essentially turned the OEWG discussions into a discussion between two geopolitical poles.

This dynamic carried over to the GGE as well. "Johanna struck deals with Russia, then posted to the like-minded group, then to the whole group", said a GGE Expert. "[I thought,] OK we don't have time, let's accept. Then she had to redo that with China, luckily Michele participated in it, and so did Patriota – and so, we were like if US and Chair are there, it's OK with us. So yeah, there were no rules [of negotiation] and this is how it happened – but wish I had been there! At the end of the day, I applaud [Weaver's] efforts."[75] Ultimately, several negotiators including Weaver herself, acknowledged that the GGE arrived at a consensus report because "Russia was in a good mood [after the OEWG] and played ball".[76] "The fact that Russia and China edited the draft [prior to the GGE's final session] indicated to us that failure was not a foregone conclusion". said Michele Markoff, underlining the significance of the GGE's practices among its Experts.[77] But most importantly, the GGE negotiations were foreshadowed by the decision, announced on the first day of its final session, by the United States to hold a presidential summit with Russia in Geneva the following month. Multiple GGE Experts confirmed the announcement's contribution to the GGE's success. "The Biden-Putin meeting was extremely relevant", an Expert put it bluntly, "[there would have been] no agreement without the large powers".[78]

6 Reflexive Negotiations on Norms and Law Limit "Creeping Expertise" at the UN

The background of negotiations in the 2019–2021 UN GGE and OEWG is important to evaluate the extent of "creeping expertise" in these forums. As noted previously, UN negotiators became more reflexive in their assessment of the groups' outcomes, filtering them through the lens of Great Power rivalry. If voluntary norms previously incorporated legal formulations or left their precise status ambiguous as part of a compromise, the appetite for such compromise formulations was limited in 2019. There was no scope within the UN processes to discuss further norms or discuss the application of specific international law principles, because the group wanted to keep norms and law

75 *Interview with a diplomat, 2021.*

76 *Interview with Johanna Weaver*, June 15, 2021.

77 *Discussing the UN OEWG with the Mother of Norms*, N.24.

78 Interview with *Heli-Tiirma Klaar*, October 6, 2021.

distinct. And this limited the possibility of technical considerations shaping international cybersecurity law through "law-like" norms whose status was ambiguous.

There is strong evidence to support the argument that international lawyers associated with the GGE and OEWG had become more reflexive in evaluating the UN processes and their pronouncements on norms and international law, thus weakening creeping expertise in these forums. I offer some illustrations below.

The use of the term "*acquis*" by GGE negotiators to describe previous consensus reports of the GGE is a case in point. In Chapter 2, I noted how repeated references to the UN GGE's reports as "*acquis"* by diplomats in public and during interviews – the term *acquis communitair*e is specifically used in EU law parlance to denote the corpus of community rights and obligations between states[79] – reflected the diplomatic corps' and cyber CoP's strong belief that both norms and rules were considered equivalent tools in advancing responsible state behavior. During the 2019–2021 negotiations, however, the term "acquis" was used reflexively by states.

The US and like-minded countries, especially EU states, pushed back against Russia's efforts to articulate new norms at the UN, arguing that the *acquis* could not be reopened. They were opposed to efforts by Russia to create new norms that would have the effect of weakening or replacing altogether the UN GGE's eleven norms and its affirmation of the applicability of international law. The GGE chair Patriota, meanwhile, described the *acquis* as "fragile", warning that it was the duty of the GGE to "protect it".[80] He used the term to strategically remind the GGE of its own collective responsibility, and the urgency therefore of coming up with another consensus report. An international lawyer involved in the 2019–2021 GGE negotiations took note of its use: "Patriota deliberately used the word '*acquis*' a lot: this got a lot of attention. Somehow, we were protecting the *acquis*, even the Russians were protecting the *acquis*…of course, they said [we want the] *acquis* 'plus' Shanghai Cooperation Organization (SCO) norms. Then China said '[we want] *acquis* 'plus' SCO 'plus' supply chain norms.'"[81] In other words, the like-minded group invoked the term to mean that the norms and rules agreed upon by the 2015 GGE could not be renegotiated, while Russia reflexively sought an expansion of the *acquis* by way of new, similarly sacred norms. Indeed, the Russian GGE Expert Krut-

79 Jan Klabbers, "Safeguarding the Organizational Acquis: The EU's External Practice," *International Organizations Law Review* 4, no. 1 (January 1, 2007): 57–89.

80 *Interview with Guilherme Patriota,* July 29, 2021.

81 *Interview with Takeshi Akahori,* August 6, 2021.

skikh even suggested, quite improbably, at one point that the OEWG deal with "major political tasks" such as "developing the rules of responsible behavior of states", while the GGE could address the "specialized issue of applicability of the existing norms of international law".[82]

The reflexive debates among individual states on the draft reports of both groups are also illustrative. Take for instance, the pre-draft and the Zero Draft of the OEWG published by the group's Chair in April 2020 and January 2021 respectively. Japan sought to replace the OEWG pre-draft's formulation that norms "provide *additional* specific guidance [apart from states' obligations under international law] to responsible state behavior in cyberspace" [emphasis added] with the phrase that norms simply "reflect the expectations of the international community".[83] Rather contentiously, the OEWG pre-draft suggested that states had "proposed suggestions for 'upgrading' as well as the elaboration of norms".[84] "If 'upgrading' means 'transforming' a norm from a non-binding status to a legally binding status, the OEWG has no power to make a change", the US argued.[85] The UK similarly sought clarity on the term as well as a "range of references [in the report] to the interplay" between norms and international law.[86] On the other hand, China argued that norms do not just provide "additional guidance" but are "standard-setting" in nature. "An overstatement of 'voluntary, non-binding' [to describe norms in the OEWG report] may send an unconstructive message to the world that we are unwill-

82 Igor Chugunov, "Article by Andrei Krutskikh, Special Presidential Representative for International Cooperation in Information Security, Published in the Kommersant Business Daily on March 27, 2019," accessed November 25, 2022, https://thailand.mid.ru/en/key-issues/5399-statya-spetspredstavitelya-prezidenta-rossijskoj-federatsii-po-voprosam-mezhdunarodnogo-sotrudnichestva-v-oblasti-informatsionnoj-bezopasnosti-posla-po-osobym-porucheniyam-mid-rossii-a-v-krutskikh-opublikovannaya-v-gazete-kommersant-27-marta-2019-goda-2.

83 "Japan's Comments on OEWG Pre-draft," April 2020, accessed November 25, 2022, https://front.un-arm.org/wp-content/uploads/2020/04/japan-comments-on-oewg-pre-draft.pdf.

84 "Initial 'Pre-draft' of the Report of the OEWG on Developments in the Field of Information and Telecommunications in the Context of International Security," April 27, 2020, https://front.un-arm.org/wp-content/uploads/2020/03/200311-Pre-Draft-OEWG-ICT.pdf. (hereafter, OEWG Pre-Draft).

85 "United States Comments on the Chair's Pre Draft of the Report of the UN Open Ended Working Group (OEWG)," accessed November 25, 2022, https://ceipfiles.s3.amazonaws.com/pdf/CyberNorms/UNGGE/United+States+Comments+on+the+Chair%E2%80%99s+Pre-Draft+of+the+Report+of+the+UN+Open+Ended+Working+Group+(OEWG).pdf.

86 "UK Response to Chair's Initial 'Pre-draft' of the Report of the OEWG on Developments in the Field of Information and Telecommunications in the Context of International Security," April 15, 2020, https://front.un-arm.org/wp-content/uploads/2020/04/20200415-oewg-predraft-uk.pdf.

ing to abide by the hard-won norms established through strenuous negotiations", China argued.[87] Australia, meanwhile, argued that the "normative framework" guiding state behavior in cyberspace had a binding component, i.e., international law, and a non-binding component of norms.[88]

These debates on the precise relationship between norms and international law continued into the next stage, i.e., negotiations over the OEWG's Zero Draft. The Zero Draft noted the "exchange of views" among states on how international law applied to cyberspace, drawing specific attention to "general principles of law, treaties, and customary international law".[89] This formulation was criticized by a number of states, with the UK noting it is "unusual to define international law by [its] sources", and if they are at all listed, they should "follow the order in which they appeared in the ICJ statute [...] to read treaties, customary international law, and general principles of law".[90] Russia too recommended removing any reference to the sources, presumably because it did not want for the OEWG report to emphasize existing international law in a major way.[91] The entire formulation was removed in the final OEWG report, and moved to the "Chair's Summary" which contained statements that were "half-agreed"[92] by states.[93] Similarly, the Zero Draft sought to

87 "China's Contribution to the Initial Pre-Draft of OEWG Report," accessed November 26, 2022, https://ceipfiles.s3.amazonaws.com/pdf/CyberNorms/UNGGE/China%E2%80%99s+Contribution+to+the+Initial+Pre-Draft+of+OEWG+Report.pdf.

88 "Australia's Comments on the Initial 'Pre-draft' of the Report of the UN Open Ended Working Group in the Field of Information and Telecommunications in the Context of International Security (OEWG)," Aril 2020, https://www.internationalcybertech.gov.au/sites/default/files/2020-11/australias-response-to-the-oewg-pre-draft-report-april-2020.pdf.

89 "Draft Substantive Report (Zero Draft)" (Open-ended Working Group on Developments in the Field of Information and Telecommunications in the Context of International Security, January 19, 2021), 5, https://digitallibrary.un.org/record/3899168/files/A_AC.290_2021_L.2-EN.pdf.

90 "UK COMMENTS ON ZERO DRAFT REPORT OF THE OEWG ON DEVELOPMENT IN THE FIELD OF ICTs IN THE CONTEXT OF INTERNATIONAL SECURITY," accessed April 5, 2022, https://front.un-arm.org/wp-content/uploads/2021/02/UK-submission-to-OEWG-ICTs-zero-draft-002.pdf.

91 "Draft Substantive Report (Zero Draft): Open-Ended Working Group on Developments in the Field of Information and Telecommunications in the Context of International Security (As of January 19, 2021: With Russian Amendments)," accessed April 5, 2022, https://front.un-arm.org/wp-content/uploads/2021/02/RF-OEWG-zero-draft-report-with-the-Russian-amendments-ENG.pdf.

92 *Interview with Regine Grienberger*, August 23, 2021.

93 "Chair's Summary" (Open-ended Working Group on Developments in the Field of Information and Telecommunications in the Context of International Security, Third substantive session, March 10, 2021), https://front.un-arm.org/wp-content/uploads/2021/03/

"highlight specific principles of the UN Charter", including among others, "state sovereignty".[94] This formulation was criticized by a group of states comprising Australia, Egypt, Indonesia, Russia, and the United Kingdom, who argued the term "state sovereignty" is not found in Article 2 (or for that matter, anywhere else) of the UN Charter. Their joint recommendation was to replace "UN Charter" with the broader formulation of "international law",[95] which was opposed by Cuba in the final negotiating session.[96] Owing to the lack of consensus, this formulation too was moved to the Chair's Summary.[97] Israel similarly argued in its response to the Zero Draft that norms do not offer guidance on what *constitutes* state behavior in cyberspace, but only *indicate* what such behavior should be.[98] Finally, Russia sought to insert text in the section on international law suggesting that the OEWG considered the possibility of developing "complementary binding norms" along with the development of international law through *opinio juris* and state practice.[99] This attempt to conflate norms and international law made it to the next stage of negotiations, i.e., on the OEWG's First Draft, but was moved finally and expectedly to the Chair's Summary because it was rejected by other states.

Then there was the debate on the ordering of the OEWG report's sections on norms and international law, providing evidence of reflexive evaluation of its once taken-for-granted practices. The zero draft of the OEWG had also placed the "International Law" section above that on "Rules, Norms, and Principles of Responsible State Behavior". A number of states opposed the placement of the sections so, particularly China, which sought for norms to be moved ahead of the section on international law. Indeed, China sought the deletion of a paragraph in the OEWG First Draft that distinguished between international law and "voluntary non-binding norms", and also argued that

---

Chairs-Summary-A-AC.290–2021-CRP.3-technical-reissue.pdf. (hereafter Chair's Summary).

94 *OEWG Zero Draft*, 5.

95 "Joint Proposal on the Text of the 1st Draft," accessed April 5, 2022, https://front.un-arm.org/wp-content/uploads/2021/03/PDF-Joint-Contribution-OEWG-First-Draft-Suggested-amendments.pdf.

96 Oral statement by Cuba, Third substantive session of the OEWG, 8–12 March 2021 [*recorded via participant observation*].

97 *Chair's Summary*, 3.

98 "Israel's Response to Zero-Draft Report from the OEWG Chair," March 2021, https://front.un-arm.org/wp-content/uploads/2021/03/Israel-amendments-UN-OEWG-ZERO-DRAFT-Israel-amendments-sent.pdf.

99 *Russian Amendments to the Draft Substantive Report* (*Zero Draft*), N.91.

the correct placing of the sections was not simply a "procedural issue".[100] While several European states and others belonging to a like-minded group that included Japan and Australia wanted to retain the original order, they agreed to China's suggestion, which was also backed by Russia.[101] The ordering of the OEWG report's sections may seem like a procedural concern to outsiders, but to the members of the Group it had acquired new meaning.

Just as old practices had come to be reflexively evaluated, new practices emerged in the UN negotiations that sharpened the distinction between international law and cyber norms. The UNGA resolution setting up the sixth GGE had also invited states to submit views on how international law applied to cyberspace, and specifically requested the UNSG to annex those national contributions to the report.[102] "The Annex was an escape clause, a protection valve", said Patriota.[103] "If we can't get an agreement on international law, [we] attach it to a report, and annex it, and that's it. This was fine with many of the like-minded countries, but not others. The Annex became in and of itself a big issue [...] and a deal-breaker." "I had to remind some GGE members that 'there's no rule here to help you'", he continued. "They would question China's questioning of the [UNGA] mandate with respect to the Annex, saying it's clear. That is true, [but] if any one of these 25 members decide that they are not in agreement with the Annex, they will simply raise their hand and they will make the [overall] agreement fail." Finally, on China's insistence, the Annex did not include those contributions, although the national statements were separately reproduced in another report. The GGE's abandoning its Annex typifies how its proximate *habitus* had powerfully influenced the group's practices – in this case, even contradicting its parent UN GA mandate – and accentuating the distinction between norms and international law. If such an annexure document had been included with the GGE norms report, it would have once again served to conflate the sources of cyber norms and international cybersecurity law, but no such outcome was possible in light of the changed circumstances.

Similarly, as referenced above, the Chair of the OEWG came up with the innovative practice of including a Chair's Summary, published separately from

100 Oral statement by China, Third substantive session of the OEWG, 8–12 March 2021 [*recorded via participant observation*].

101 Oral statement by Russian Federation, Third substantive session of the OEWG, 8–12 March 2021 [*recorded via participant observation*].

102 "73/266. Advancing Responsible State Behaviour in Cyberspace in the Context of International Security" (UN General Assembly, Seventy-third session, January 2, 2019), https://doi.org/10.18356/9789210021753c001.

103 *Interview with Guilherme Patriota*, July 29, 2021.

the Group's Final Report. The Chair's Summary included those portions of previous OEWG drafts that could not secure consensus from states. The text of the summary includes several pronouncements that blurred the distinction between norms and international law, and it is telling that these were not included in the final report. These instances are highlighted below:

1. According to the Chair's Summary, OEWG States recalled that "voluntary, non-binding norms of responsible State behavior [...] *should be viewed as being consistent with international law*, including to maintain international peace and security[...] [emphasis added]".[104] This statement, retroactively aligning norms alongside interpretations of international law to cyberspace, was placed in the pre-draft's section on norms, but could not secure consensus in the final report.
2. The Summary noted that "states must not use proxies to commit internationally wrongful acts using ICTs, and should seek to ensure that their territory is not used by non-State actors *acting on the instruction or under the control of a State* to commit such acts"[105] [emphasis added]. This statement had found mention in the pre-draft of the OEWG, leading some states to question why the formulation on due diligence – which, as a general principle of international law, makes no distinction between harmful, transboundary activities caused by states or non-state actors – was seemingly confined only to cyber operations attributable to states.
3. OEWG states could not even agree to highlighting General Assembly resolution 73/27 – which established the 2019–2021 OEWG – as "presenting [...] a set of 13 rules, norms and principles for responsible State behavior" and "affirm[ing] the 11 voluntary, non-binding norms" contained in the 2015 GGE report.[106] There is no doubt that previous GGE norms, having been adopted by the UNGA, constitute *opinio juris*, but some states appear to have been against any attempt to constrain the OEWG's remit to re-open or re-interpret the scope of those norms. In other words, some states were reluctant to elevate some norms above others, and acknowledge potentially their progressive development into binding rules.
4. Finally, both the GGE and OEWG also witnessed debate on a Programme of Action on cybersecurity concerns that would fall under the remit of the UN GA's First Committee. The PoA, a joint proposal by

104 *Chair's Summary*, 5.
105 *Chair's Summary*, 3.
106 *Chair's Summary*, 5.

France and Egypt that found a significant number of supporters, sought to create a permanent home on discussions around lawful state behavior in cyberspace. Both the GGE and OEWG reports took cognizance of the PoA, but also called for greater clarity on the proposal. The PoA specifically mooted "review conferences [...] organized every five years, following the same model as the Small Arms and Light Weapons PoA, and be consensus driven". The proposal also suggested that the review conferences could consider if additional norms could be developed over time. However, reference to the PoA's proposal on review conferences could not meet with consensus and was moved to the Chair's summary.[107] Review conferences are traditionally associated with treaty bodies: a review conference to develop new cyber norms would be unusual, and further blur the role of norms vis-à-vis international cybersecurity law, which may have led to states' reluctance to support the proposal.

Finally, the concluding paragraph of the OEWG final report noted that "new ideas and important proposals [were put forward by States], including the possibility of *additional* legally binding obligations" [emphasis added].[108] This formulation appeared to suggest that existing cyber norms could potentially be a source of binding obligations. The eleventh-hour phrasing was extensively debated both within the OEWG as well as the broader CoP. At the OEWG, Japan argued against any reference to "additional legal obligations" in the report, declaring a new legal instrument would have "no meaning without affirmation that international customary law on state responsibility applies to the acts of ICTs".[109] Japan was responding primarily to China's claim, made during the GGE negotiations, that the principles of state responsibility did not amount to customary law. Cuba, on the other hand, not only favored the inclusion of this phrase but sought to move it into the section on international law.[110] Israel and Switzerland opposed its

107 *Chair's Summary*, 8.

108 "Final Substantive Report" (Open-ended Working Group on Developments in the Field of Information and Telecommunications in the Context of International Security, March 10, 2021), 11, https://front.un-arm.org/wp-content/uploads/2021/03/Final-report-A-AC.290-2021-CRP.2.pdf.

109 Oral statement by Japan, Third OEWG Session [*recorded via participant observation*].

110 Oral statement by Cuba, Third OEWG Session [*recorded via participant observation*].

inclusion,[111] while South Korea argued "legally binding norms [were] not a realistic option".[112]

The OEWG and GGE's reports were therefore influenced by reflexive deliberation among delegations on the precise distinction between cyber norms and applications of international law to cyberspace. The preceding paragraphs show how the negotiating practices of both groups brought those distinctions to the fore. With the sources of international law seemingly distinguished from the political or technical sources of cyber norms, did such reflexive deliberation in the GGE and OEWG limit creeping expertise?

The answer is largely in the affirmative. Delegations appear to have been cautious in letting technical considerations influence the framework of responsible state behavior in cyberspace, either through norms or international law interpretations of the GGE and OEWG. At least two separate instances can be highlighted in support of this claim.

The discussion on the attribution of cyber operations to states reflects the limits of "creeping expertise" in the GGE and OEWG. The 2019–2021 OEWG rejected the compromise language (preferred by Russia) of the 2014–2015 GGE on attribution, namely, the fact that "an ICT activity was launched or otherwise originated from the territory or the ICT infrastructure of a State [would be] insufficient in itself to attribute the activity to that State and that accusations of organizing and implementing wrongful acts brought against States should be substantiated".[113] As noted previously in this book, the compromise language on technical attribution was introduced in the 2015 GGE's section on international law. Its removal from the OEWG report – the statement was ultimately moved to the Chair's Summary – resulted in the unusual situation, where GGE language, adopted by UN member states in the General Assembly, was subsequently rejected by the same 193 states in the OEWG. The OEWG's removal of the statement is arguably linked to a larger effort to separate the technical aspects from the legal and political dimensions of attributing a cyber operation to a state. "The political and technical assessment of an attribution does not and should not take into account whether or not, you have the criteria to meet a legal attribution [under the customary law of state responsibility]", said one UN negotiator in an interview.[114] "I tried very hard in the GGE

111 Oral statement by Switzerland, Third OEWG Session [*recorded via participant observation*]; Oral statement by Israel, Third OEWG Session [*recorded via participant observation*].

112 Oral statement by South Korea, Third OEWG Session [*recorded via participant observation*].

113 Chair's Summary, 3.

114 *Interview with Johanna Weaver*, June 15, 2021.

process to have that clarified [but] we weren't able to get that level of detail into the report." This Expert's views were publicly mirrored in the statements of many states in the OEWG as well. The pre-draft of the OEWG noted that "developing a common approach to attribution at the technical level could [...] support legal recourse for those harmed by malicious acts".[115] Several states rejected this formulation, which could not even make it to the Chair's Summary. Estonia argued attribution remained the "sovereign decision of each individual state".[116] Germany stated that the "act of formally attributing a malicious cyber operation to a State under international law is first and foremost a national prerogative."[117] Mexico, which had proposed for the ILC to take up the identification of international rules to cyberspace, argued "issues of attribution should be set in a separate paragraph" – the pre-draft referred to attribution in the context of threats to international peace and security – because the topic went "beyond Charter principles", presumably referring to the state responsibility regime.[118] France too questioned the viability of a "universal" approach to technical attribution.[119] On the other hand, Russia argued it would be "unacceptable to include in the text the concept of political 'attribution' of cyber attacks" since the compromise language of the fourth GGE "clearly [indicated] the need to support any accusations against States with appropriate technical evidence".[120] China supported the view that

115 OEWG Pre-draft, 6.

116 "Estonia's Comments to the 'Initial "Pre-draft" of the Report of the OEWG on Developments in the Field of Information and Telecommunications in the Context of International Security,'" April 16, 2020, https://front.un-arm.org/wp-content/uploads/2020/04/comments-to-the-oewg-pre-draft-report-estonia.pdf.

117 "Initial 'Pre-draft' of the Report of the OEWG on Developments in the Field of Information and Telecommunications in the Context of International Security And Non-Paper Listing Specific Language Proposals under Agenda Item 'Rules, Norms and Principles' from Written Submissions Received before 2 March 2020 | COMMENTS FROM GERMANY," April 6, 2020, https://front.un-arm.org/wp-content/uploads/2020/04/20200401-oewg-german-written-contribution-to-pre-draft-report-1.pdf.

118 "Preliminary Comments of Mexico to the Initial 'Pre-draft' of the Report of the OEWG on Developments in the Field of Information and Telecommunications in the Context of International Security," April 2020, https://front.un-arm.org/wp-content/uploads/2020/04/mexico-inputs-pre-draft-oewg.pdf.

119 "France's Response to Zero-Draft Report from the OEWG Chair," February 2021, https://front.un-arm.org/wp-content/uploads/2021/02/France_OEWG_ENG_Vfclean.pdf.

120 "Commentary of the Russian Federation on the Initial 'Pre-draft' of the Final Report of the United Nations Openended Working Group on Developments In the Field of Information and Telecommunications in the Context of International Security," accessed November 26, 2022, https://front.un-arm.org/wp-content/uploads/2020/04/russian-commentary-on-oweg-zero-draft-report-eng.pdf.

an attribution mechanism under the UN would be "universally accepted".[121] Additionally, developing countries like Argentina and Brazil endorsed a common attribution mechanism at the technical level that would provide legal grounds for victims of malicious cyber operations.[122] However, in the face of strident opposition to this formulation, it was rejected even in the revised version of the OEWG pre-draft.

Another example of the limits of "creeping expertise" can be found in the discussion of the OEWG and GGE on supply chain integrity. In particular, both groups deliberated the obligations of states with respect to "harmful hidden functions" – a phrase introduced by the third UN GGE,[123] which has since been recognized across international forums. Harmful hidden functions could be software that exploits zero-day vulnerabilities or otherwise leverages aspects of supply chain hardware or software for purposes of surveillance, espionage, and potentially even destructive cyber operations ("backdoors"). The fourth UN GGE called on states prevent the proliferation of malicious ICT tools [...] and the *use* of harmful hidden functions" [emphasis added].[124] Initial drafts of the OEWG underlined states' concerns over the *creation* of such exploits, and "highlighted the responsibility [of states to notify users when significant vulnerabilities are identified".[125] This formulation could not secure agreement and was moved to the Chair's Summary[126] – although the reasons are unclear, the formulation arguably constrained the ability of states to develop zero-day exploits and backdoors, which was likely resisted by many in the OEWG. In contrast, references cautioning against the "use" or "introduction" – the latter and original terms were preferred by the sixth GGE[127] – of harmful hidden functions allowed states to exercise political discretion in

121 *China's Contribution to the Initial Pre-draft of OEWG Report*, N.87.

122 "Initial 'Pre-draft' of the Report of the OEWG on Developments in the Field of Information and Telecommunications in the Context of International Security | Comments by ARGENTINA," April 2020, https://front.un-arm.org/wp-content/uploads/2020/04/oewg-ict-comments-argentina-3.pdf; "Comments Submitted by Brazil to the Initial 'Pre-draft' of the Report of the OEWG on Developments in the Field of Information and Telecommunications in the Context of International Security," April 8, 2020, https://front.un-arm.org/wp-content/uploads/2020/04/comments-by-brazil-on-the-pre-draft-report-of-cyber-oewg-8-apr-2020.pdf.

123 Third UN GGE Report, 7.

124 Fourth UN GGE report, 8.

125 OEWG Pre-draft, 7; OEWG First Draft, 9.

126 Chair's Summary, 5.

127 "Report of the Group of Governmental Experts on Advancing Responsible State Behaviour in Cyberspace in the Context of International Security" (UN General Assembly, Seventy-sixth session, July 14, 2021), 14–15 https://documents-dds-ny.un.org/doc/UNDOC/GEN/N21/075/86/PDF/N2107586.pdf?OpenElement.

determining when to deploy such weapons, while retaining the prerogative to technically develop them. This is yet another instance where states appear to be conscious of technical considerations limiting or influencing the scope of their obligations in cyberspace.

7 "Confusion" Galore: What Next for the UN GGE?

As Chapter 2 notes, the UN GGE played a historic and critical role in shaping the thinking of practitioners within the cyber CoP on regulating state behavior in cyberspace. On account of GGE reports published since 2009, the "framework of responsible state behavior" in cyberspace came to be understood by the wider community of states and non-state actors as including "norms, rules *and* [legal] principles". The GGE's practices accommodated a compromise made between two important political camps within the group. While the United States and its European partners and allies wanted norms to reflect existing international law, Russia and other states wanted to negotiate new rules for the domain, and saw new norms as proxies for binding rules till such a time there was a cybersecurity treaty. To meet both interests, UN GGEs began devoting a section to "norms, rules and principles" where some norms sometimes borrowed the language of international law, or sounded like they reflected existing obligations, while leaving the door open for "additional norms", presumably whether they reflected existing international law or not. Even as the 2015 GGE notably laid down eleven norms that repeatedly referred to international law, the report itself called those norms "voluntary and non-binding". The ambiguity of the precise status of norms may have satisfied the political dynamic of the GGE, but to other practitioners in the CoP, it was a signal that norms could potentially advance international cybersecurity law.

Indeed, appreciating the role of norms as a vehicle to develop international cybersecurity law, many initiatives and entities, including technical and industry actors began to mimic the GGE's approach to articulating cyber norms. Chapters 3 and 4 highlighted the impact of the UN GGE on multistakeholder norms initiatives and law-ascertainment initiatives like the Tallinn Manual.

Even as the GGE's compromises shaped how the cyber CoP approached international cybersecurity governance, they sharpened the geopolitical fault-lines in the group. Great Power rivalry, long a feature of the UN group, became to define the GGE. Practices such as the selection of GGE Experts (who were nominated by their states) and closely held beliefs around who those Experts should be (professional cyber diplomats) and how they should function (negotiated consensus) accentuated the US–Russia centricism of the group. With this rivalry taking center stage, negotiators within the group began to analyze its pronouncements, norms, and international law from the prism of US–Russia competition. As a result, they reflexively evaluated and distinguished norms from international law in the GGE and OEWG's pronouncements. As this chapter has demonstrated, this reflexive separation meant naturally that technical concerns reflected in norms would remain political statements of aspirational value.

Notably, there is some evidence to suggest the GGE and OEWG's pronouncements on norms and international law from 2016 were reflexively evaluated not only by UN negotiators but also by some international lawyers and practitioners outside the UN groups as well. Writing in 2020, Francois Delerue, Frédérick Douzet, and Aude Géry noted "the ambiguous (sometimes **confusing**) role played by norms and international law in the regulation of cyberspace".[128] Noting the then ongoing discussions at the UN, they argued perceptively that "states will discuss norms and international law at two different moments because the working sessions [of both GGE and OEWG] are organized by themes, with one dedicated to norms and another to international law. Yet, *because they are both linked*, the risk is that states treat this issue twice and adopt two different, or even contradictory, positions." Writing in 2022, Lotrionte noted that the "UN Reports' lack of clarity on the terminology used has led to much **confusion**".[129] "Including a reference to the UN Charter treaty within a section on voluntary norms", Lotrionte argued, "[indicated that] the Experts [in 2013 and 2015 reports] did not fully recognize the nature of treaty or customary law".[130] At a June 2022 symposium of international lawyers on rules for cyberspace, Schmitt noted that he was "nervous that all the voluntary norms and other international cyber projects, the Tallinn Manuals included, are creating more **confusion** than clarity for States".[131] Writing in 2018 in an article titled "2018: The year that cyber peace became non-binding", Tikk described the "course of action" taken by states to declare norms as voluntary and non-binding as "**confusing**". "Many of these norms

128 François Delerue, Frédérick Douzet and Aude Géry, "The Geopolitical Representations of International Law In The International Negotiations On The Security And Stability Of Cyberspace", Report No. 75, IRSEM/EU Cyber Direct, November 2020, 16.

129 Catherine Lotrionte, "Bringing the Law In: Unlearned Lessons for Diplomats and Others." *The Cyber Defense Review* 7, no. 1 (2022): 23–32.

130 Lotrionte (2022), 28.

131 Asaf Lubin [@AsafLubin], "Tom Wingfield (@RANDCorporation): On Grey Zone Ops: 'The Dimmer Switch Option of Cyber Is Very Attractive to Policymakers.' @Schmitt_ILaw 'I'm Nervous That All the Voluntary Norms & Other Int'l Cyber Projects, TM Included, Are Creating More Confusion than Clarity for States.' https://T.Co/WvxW4JxqrZ," Tweet, *Twitter*, June 15, 2022, https://twitter.com/AsafLubin/status/1537146862796476418.

come with some very disturbing small print about international law", she wrote. "[…] UN experts have declared state responsibility and due diligence non-binding."[132] Writing in 2017, Tikk and Kerttunen argued that the 2015 GGE Report's emphasis on "voluntary" nature of cyber norms while retaining them in a section titled "norms, rules and principles" is "**confusing**".[133] Osula and Rõigas in a 2016 edited volume on cyber norms similarly described the UN GGE reports as a "good example" of the "somewhat **confusing** terminology" used in discussions on cyber norms.[134] Evaluating the national positions of Estonia and Latvia on the applicability of international law to cyberspace, Done pointed to an interesting development. The English version of Latvia's cyber strategy refers to the promotion of shared understanding of how "international treaties" should apply to cyberspace. The Latvian version, however, uses the term "international norms". This, she pointed out in a 2022 journal article, "is **confusing**" and criticizes the use of "vague terminology"[135] [all emphases added].

The use of the term "confusing" to describe the relationship between cyber norms and international law by noted practitioners[136] in the cyber CoP is not coincidental and telling in the context laid out by this chapter. Of course, they do not all agree on how norms and international law should be separated – Schmitt and Lotrionte, for instance, call for a distinction between political norms and legal norms, with the latter reflecting precisely the vocabulary of existing rules, while Delerue et al. call such a formal separation "artificial" and

132 "UN GGE – 2018: The Year That Cyber Peace Became Non-Binding," *ICT4Peace Foundation* (blog), December 31, 2018, https://ict4peace.org/activities/2018-the-year-that-cyber-peace-became-non-binding/.

133 Eneken Tikk and Mika Kerttunen, "The Alleged Demise of the UN GGE: An Autopsy and Eulogy" (Cyber Policy Institute, 2017), 14 https://cyber-peace.org/wp-content/uploads/2018/11/Tikk-Kerttunen-2017-The-Alleged-Demise-of-the-UN-GGE-An-Autopsy-and-Eulogy.pdf.

134 Anna-Maria Osula and Henry Rõigas, "International Cyber Norms," in *International Cyber Norms: Legal, Policy & Industry Perspectives*, ed. Anna-Maria Osula and Henry Rõigas, 14 (Tallinn: NATO CCD COE Publications, 2016).

135 Laura Done, "Applicability of International Law in Cyberspace: Positions by Estonia and Latvia," *Electronic Scientific Journal of Law* (*Socrates*) 3, no. 24 (2022), 37.

136 For example, Michael Schmitt, as noted here, has been the director of the Tallinn Manual exercises. Delerue's book, "Cyber Operations and International Law" won the European Society of International Law's 2021 Book Prize. Douzet was a Commissioner in the Global Commission on the Stability of Cyberspace. Lotrionte, a former intelligence lawyer for the US government, played an important role as a rapporteur in early discussions on international cybersecurity law of the MIT Cyber Norms conference. Tikk was not only part of the early GGEs as part of an Expert delegation but also the "project coordinator" of the first Tallinn Manual.

acknowledge a "normative gradation" between both – but all acknowledge that their relationship should be clarified. This is also not to say lawyers never evaluated the relationship between norms and international law prior to the failure of the UN GGE. But the evidence certainly points to a heightened degree of reflexive evaluation after the culmination of the fourth GGE. Such evaluation is conspicuous even as other institutions in the CoP such as multi-stakeholder bodies and even law-finding initiatives (detailed in Chapters 3 and 4) continued to conflate norm-articulation and rule-interpretation.

At the time of writing, the GGE process appears to have concluded, while a second OEWG (2021–2025) has been constituted to further develop the "framework of responsible state behavior" in cyberspace. The approval by UN member states of a Programme of Action (PoA) that can house permanent negotiations and discussions on cybersecurity is an interesting development, but it is too early to speculate how the PoA will relate to the OEWG. Retaining its character still as the preeminent intergovernmental forum for cybersecurity negotiations, the UN processes will remain influential in the CoP. For example, the PoA could incubate a conference of parties to establish a cybersecurity treaty in the future. However, the UN negotiations are unlikely to influence what is, at the time of writing, the main vector of "creeping expertise" – the influence by technical experts of international cybersecurity law through the articulation of norms. Evidence from the 2019–2021 UN GGE and OEWG provide ample evidence in support of such a claim.

CHAPTER 6

Protecting the "Public Core" of the Internet: An Evolving Cyber Norm and Its Legal Implications

1 A Cross-sectional View of "Creeping Expertise" in the Cyber CoP

This chapter examines the evolution of the norm to protect "the public core of the internet" (hereafter "the public core"), tracing its progress from a concept developed by a Dutch scientific council in 2015 to becoming the subject of norm-articulation at the 2019–2021 UN GGE and OEWG. The transformation of the public core norm as it traveled through various institutions within the cyber CoP offers a cross-sectional illustration of "creeping expertise". This chapter demonstrates that the public core norm was understood and interpreted simultaneously by the cyber CoP as a voluntary norm to strengthen cybersecurity around the internet's core protocols and as an affirmation of existing international law protections for such critical, "transnational" digital infrastructure. Various institutions within the CoP called on states to proactively ring-fence the internet's backbone from major cyber operations, while at the same time arguing that such protections were based on existing international law. In this manner, the public core norm, initially conceived as an aspirational guideline for states, gradually came to be seen as being based in existing international law.

Technical experts crucially influenced the CoP's understanding of what constituted the "public core" and practitioners' assessment of those functionalities or attributes of the public core that deserved protection from cyber operations by states. This chapter highlights their close involvement in norm articulation on public core protections across institutions of the cyber CoP. With some states and non-state actors in the CoP seeking "an additional layer of normative protection" for the public core through existing international law, these technical experts not only became important interlocutors in articulating the technical scope of the norm, but also determining how international law applied to it.

In particular, this chapter illustrates how a closed-door interaction (co-organized by the Dutch foreign ministry in 2016) between technical experts and international lawyers decisively shaped the final form of the norm that was presented by the Dutch government for consideration before the 2016–

2017 UN GGE and 2019–2021 UN GGE and OEWG. The practices of this meeting – specifically, the Dutch MFA's circulation of a non-paper that linked the norm to international law, and a briefing organized for meeting participants by a distinguished international lawyer on public core protections – were crucial to conflating the normative and legal status of public core protections. Equally notable was the group's explanation of what activities would not be proscribed by this norm – e.g., cyber-enabled espionage – based on the lack of corresponding proscriptions in international law.

The norm that was prepared in consultation with this beachhead group was not only tabled before the UN GGE by the Netherlands, but also before the GCSC for its consideration, given the Dutch were among the Commission's leading sponsors and promoters. The practices of the GCSC conflating norm-articulation and rule-interpretation have already been described in Chapter 3, and are not repeated here. Instead, the chapter focuses on (a) how technical experts' involvement in GCSC norm-articulation resulted in a fleshing out of the scope of public core protections and (b) how GCSC negotiations resulted in the notion, tied to international law, that the protection of the public core, and "therefore, the stability of the internet", might be a collective responsibility of states.

From the GCSC, the norm traveled to the sixth UN GGE and 2019–2021 OEWG, where the aspirational and legal aspects of public core protections were separated by negotiating states. This finding is not surprising. The preceding chapter noted that, following the failure of the fifth UN GGE, negotiators reflexively evaluated the relationship between voluntary norms and existing international law, with the like-minded group of countries in particular concerned that Russia would use "additional norms" to upset the delicate compromise agreed upon by previous UN GGEs in the 2019–2021 OEWG. Consequently, the public core norm was discussed at length through multiple drafts of the OEWG in particular, with the eventual formulation removing any references to international law.

Following the UN processes' rejection of any reference to international law in relation to public core protections, the Paris Call Working Group 4 had an opportunity to offer its own interpretation of the norm. In its final report – WG4 meetings were mostly organized after the conclusion of the UN processes – WG4 too rejected linkages between the public core norm and existing international rules. This is an interesting finding: as Chapter 3 notes, there are a number of instances that highlight "creeping expertise" in the commentaries of the Paris Call Working Groups. Out of the nine Paris Call norms, the protection of the public core was the only new topic to be addressed by the 2019–2021 UN GGE and OEWG. The remaining principles were either out of the UN First Committee's purview (e.g., intellectual property theft) or did not relate directly to the behavior of states (e.g., private hack backs). The UN processes' separation of the public core norm from any basis in international law appears to have influenced the view of Paris Call WG4 as well, which specifically notes that it does not generate new obligations on states.

The chapter is divided into four sections. The first section highlights the period from the articulation of the public core concept leading up to the creation of a norm around its protection, from 2015 to 2017. The second section outlines developments from 2017 to 2019 in the cyber CoP that saw norm articulation around public core protections by the GCSC and the Paris Call, and examines how the failure of the 2016–2017 GGE may have influenced the norm's evolution. The third section highlights the adoption of the public core concept by the 2019–2021 UN GGE and OEWG and explains how both forums reflexively separated and dismissed any legal basis for its protection. The final section examines how the UN negotiations and subsequent statements by Russia on public core protections shaped pronouncements by the Paris Call WG4 and the GCSC, which issued a note on the interpretation of its norm four years after its publication.

2 2015–2017: Conceptualizing the "Public Core" Norm

The concept of the "public core" was first advanced by the Netherlands Scientific Council for Government Policy (WRR) in 2015 through a brief published by Dennis Broeders, then one of its staff researchers.[1] That the idea emerged from a body like WRR is itself notable in the context of this book. The WRR is an "independent advisory" body which describes its objective as providing "science-based policy advice" to the Dutch government. Originally conceived as a "technocratic" planning body, but later recast as an advisory organization providing scientific assessments of societal problems, the WRR aims to ensure "expert representation of public interests".[2] WRR Council members include social scientists, most of whom are senior members of the Dutch academy,

1 Dennis Broeders, "The Public Core of the internet: An International Agenda for internet Governance" (The Hague: The Netherlands Scientific Council for Government Policy (WRR), 2015), https://english.wrr.nl/binaries/wrr-eng/documenten/reports/2015/10/01/the-public-core-of-the-internet/R094e-Public-core-internet.pdf (*hereafter* "Broeders Report").

2 "History – About Us – The Netherlands Scientific Council for Government Policy," (Ministerie van Algemene Zaken, May 20, 2022), https://english.wrr.nl/about-us/history-of-wrr.

while the Council's substantive work is primarily carried out by full-time research staff.[3]

Its framing of the public core concept in 2015 reflected the WRR's objective of isolating and amplifying a broad social concern: the stability of the internet as a whole. The internet had become "so important" that states had begun to abandon their "benign neglect" of the domain, the report argued – many had attempted to "'fence off' their own national area" of cyberspace.[4] Specifically, an "ever growing number of states have tampered with the internet's core infrastructure […] to further their own national interests", the report declared. The report formulated the public core as encompassing "infrastructure, protocols and standards that routes data so that it reaches all four corners of the globe".[5] They included the Domain Name System, TCP/IP protocols, and other routing, forwarding, and security protocols of the internet, as well as institutions and infrastructure such as internet registries, exchange points, and undersea cables. The overall theme of the report was that the public core – whose governance and upkeep was considered the remit of the technical community – was increasingly under stress from geopolitical and sovereign forces that the internet's "overall integrity and functionality" could no longer be guaranteed.

The report identified four major threats to the internet's public core:

a. Censorship and surveillance activities of governments, including through coercive actions on internet service providers, that often relied on DNS-based blocking and filtering, which affected the "free and open communication" that made the internet a success, and also limited its availability to users.
b. Military and intelligence-gathering operations that exploited vulnerabilities in public core protocols or attendant infrastructure that relied on them, which degraded the security of the core and reduced public trust in such infrastructure.
c. The "splintering of the internet" into national segments on account of policies such as data localization and attempts to reroute internet traffic within national borders; and

---

3 "Organization – About Us – The Netherlands Scientific Council for Government Policy," (Ministerie van Algemene Zaken, May 19, 2022), https://english.wrr.nl/about-us/organiza tion.

4 *Broeders Report*, 9.

5 *Broeders Report*, 9.

d. Interference with "deeper technical infrastructure" of the internet to enforce stringent intellectual property regimes, for example, through DNS filtering and blocking.

As this listing indicates, the WRR report accounted for cyber operations as one among the major threats facing the public core. In other words, the public core concept was linked to a series of national and international trends seen as undermining the functionality and stability of the internet – including legislative measures aimed at bolstering IP rights or control over territorial digital infrastructure and networks – of which cyber operations by state and non-state actors was a serious concern, but not necessarily the most prominent one. "Our main conclusion is that governments need to exercise enormous restraint when considering policies, legislation, and operational activities that intervene in the internet's core protocols", declared the report.

How could states be persuaded to exercise such restraint? Eliciting a commitment to keep the public core a "neutral zone" protected from national interference would be a "tall order for most countries", acknowledged the report. Nevertheless, a concerted diplomatic effort could raise awareness about nations' shared interests in its stability and trigger international discussions around concrete commitments. The report was clear-eyed in its assessment against prescribing an international legal route for global collective action. Articulating public core protections in the "form of a treaty or convention" would make them "subject to a multilateral negotiation game in which the outcome is often the lowest common denominator", it said.[6] Instead, "an international norm that designates the internet's core protocols as a neutral zone would have a broader and more potent impact if it were negotiated and disseminated *in parallel to the route of the* [*UN*] *GGE*", the report suggested[7] [emphases added].

It is notable that the WRR report called for the public core norm to be negotiated outside the GGE. The GGE focused on "national security and on preventing escalation of cyber conflicts", the report noted, implying that the scope of public core protections was wider than the remit of the UN First Committee on disarmament and international security. The original Dutch version of the WRR report expressly acknowledges that the public core norm should be pursued in a "wider and complementary" platform to the GGE. Indeed, the report noted that it was important to disentangle actors responsible for "internet security" from "national security". Additionally, it focused on the role of non-state actors, especially businesses and technical organizations,

6 *Broeders Report*, 95.

7 *Broeders Report*, 95.

and sought to broaden the "diplomatic arena" to include private parties as well.[8]

All this is to emphasize that the articulation of public core protections in the form of an international cybersecurity norm, and the eventual discussion of those protections in the 2019–2021 GGE and OEWG, were not a direct or even organic outcome of the WRR report. To be sure, the report called on the Netherlands government to champion public core protections through diplomatic outreach. But such cyber diplomacy would be more aimed at ensuring that public core protection was internalized by states, with its compliance subject not to international regimes, but to "national democratic and legal oversight". As far as companies were concerned, the report suggested the adoption of public core protection principles akin to the UN Guiding Principles on Business and Human Rights (or the "Ruggie principles", after John Ruggie, the UN SG's Special Representative on the topic) that could serve as a model for ISPs and other internet companies faced with coercive national measures.[9]

The report generated considerable interest from the Dutch government. WRR presented the report to the Dutch foreign ministry on the eve of the Netherlands hosting the 2015 Global Conference on Cyber Space (GCCS) in The Hague. In his opening remarks at The Hague conference, Foreign Minister Bert Koenders declared that states should "acknowledge the special status of the core infrastructure of the internet". It should be treated as a "public commons" like states "[treated] the high seas, in line with the writings of the Dutch jurist and philosopher Hugo Grotius in the early 17th century", he said.[10] Just as there are "treaties and practices" governing behavior in the high seas, the "tenets of international law" too apply to cyberspace. Consequently, states should be "able to count on other states not interfering with or harming their root servers and their critical infrastructure and services", he concluded. Koenders' speech marked the first instance where the notion of protecting the public core was tied to international law. It is, as previous paragraphs have argued, a departure from the WRR report, which argued that "international law [played] only a very limited role" in restraining states from operations targeting the public core for national security purposes.

Koenders' formulation is also interesting because it reframes public core protections from being an aspirational norm (as the WRR report sought) to

8 *Broeders Report*, 99–101.

9 *Broeders Report*, 75.

10 "Opening Speech GCCS Bert Koenders," *The Hague Online* (blog), April 16, 2015, https://www.thehagueonline.com/news/2015/04/16/opening-speech-gccs-bert-koenders.

an obligation grounded in existing international rules. In other words, this was the first indication that the Dutch government would champion a public core norm that borrowed the vocabulary of international law.

The Dutch decision to formulate public core protections in this manner can arguably be attributed to the closely held beliefs of the cyber CoP about interpreting international law through cyber norms. Importantly, the transformation of the public core norm in the hands of the Dutch government highlights how the CoP's beliefs structure the behavior of a new entrant into the community. 2015 was a watershed year for Dutch cyber diplomacy, because the Netherlands' hosting of the GCCS conference also set the stage for its participation in the 2016–2017 UN GGE for the first time. Its participation in the GGE marked the formal entry of the Netherlands government into the cyber CoP, and the foreign ministry sought to use the occasion to burnish the country's credentials in cyber diplomacy. "[Following the GCCS,] a lot of funding and leeway [was] given to us to build an agenda that did not stop with the Conference – we were constantly looking for the 'new thing', and what is the strategic direction to take this discussion in", said a Dutch diplomat who was closely involved in cyber negotiations during this period.[11] "That's when Dennis [Broeders]' report came out." The report offered an opportunity for the Netherlands to engage in what the diplomat termed "norm entrepreneurship". As he noted, there were also strategic reasons to articulate such a norm. "We had a particular interest in [the stability of the core] being one of the most important connection hubs in Europe, one of the largest IXPs in the world [AMS-IX], and generally, one of the more digitized countries in the world."

However, in articulating the public core norm to fit the GGE's agenda, the Dutch government framed it not only as an international cybersecurity concern, but also as a norm that reflected existing international law. Even as it transformed the scope of the norm in this manner, the government continued to engage the technical community and actively sought the help of technical experts to fine-tune the text of the norm prior to its presentation at the fifth UN GGE. This marked the beginning of "creeping expertise" in conversations around international law protections for the public core.

Soon after the GCCS conference, the Dutch MFA began laying the groundwork to promote the public core norm at the GGE. The first step involved drafting the norm and soliciting feedback from different stakeholders and equally, gathering regional perspectives about the norm's acceptability. On July 11, 2016, the MFA in collaboration with the Clingendael Institute, a prominent think-tank based in The Hague, organized an "expert meeting" to "brain-

---

11 *Interview with a Dutch diplomat*, June 14, 2021.

storm [and] draft a norm [on the public core] that could possibly be submitted to the 2016 UN GGE report".[12] Fifteen participants were invited to this brainstorming session, including diplomats, technical experts, international lawyers, and political scientists (including this author) from the Netherlands, the United States, Russia, India, and Malaysia. A "non-paper" for a "norm of non-intervention in the public core of the global internet" was circulated in advance to all participants. This non-paper contained a draft formulation of the norm, an explanation of its elements, possible "corollary norms" that could be taken up in other venues, and a list of considerations material to its acceptability and dissemination.[13] The day-long meeting was organized into two halves: the first half would involve presentations by Dutch policy experts involved in public core discussions, following which the participants would discuss the wording and effects of the proposed draft norm. The second half of the meeting was "public", in the sense that a wider range of stakeholders from the Netherlands were invited to express their views on the proposed norm.

The practices of this meeting reinforced the notion that the public core norm was grounded in existing international law. The circulation of the non-paper among participants, which not only offered a draft text of the norm, but also its connection to existing obligations was notable. The draft text of the norm read:[14]

> A state should not conduct or knowingly support ICT activity **contrary to its obligations under international law** that intentionally **damages the functionality and integrity of the public core of the global internet** or otherwise impairs the ability of the public core of the global internet to **provide services to other states.** [emphases added]

As the above text indicates, this draft norm was very closely worded to norm 13(f) of the 2014–2015 GGE report that addressed critical infrastructure protection. The draft norm adopted verbatim the formulation on international law used in norm 13(f), as well as the key operational phrases "intentionally damages [...] or otherwise impairs". This was deliberate. The non-paper acknowledged that the "normative protection" afforded to critical infrastructure under

12 Dennis Broeders, "Aligning the International Protection of 'the Public Core of the internet' with State Sovereignty and National Security," *Journal of Cyber Policy* 2, no. 3 (September 2, 2017): 366–376, https://doi.org/10.1080/23738871.2017.1403640.

13 "Non-paper: Proposal for a Norm of Non-intervention in the Public Core of the Global internet" (Clingendael Institute, July 4, 2016) [hereafter "*Public Core Non-Paper Version 1*"].

14 *Public Core Non-Paper Version 1*, 1.

paragraph 13(f) could be "extended to cover" the public core.[15] In adopting thus the language of the GGE, the non-paper reinforced the conflation of norms and international law among the invited participants. Like the GGE report, the non-paper also did not elaborate on those international law obligations pertaining to the public core, but noted that in certain circumstances, such as the use of force in self-defense or the adoption of countermeasures in response to internationally wrongful acts, states could take "legitimate" action that implicated the public core. Crucially, the non-paper also indicted that the use of the phrase "intentionally damages [...] or otherwise impairs" meant the norm "did not cover espionage activities".[16] This formulation too was a departure from the WRR report, which specifically pointed to the concerns raised by intelligence activities on the integrity of the public core. However, the Dutch government was arguably conscious of the reality that no agreement would be possible within the GGE on espionage-related measures.

The circulation of the non-paper was not the only relevant practice which reinforced the notion that the public core norm was based on international law. Following presentations by Broeders and the aforementioned Dutch diplomat in the first half of the meeting, the participants were briefed by a technical expert who identified elements of the public core, and subsequently, by an international lawyer who identified "obligations under existing international law" vis-à-vis state behavior and the public core.

This backdrop and outline of practices is necessary to evaluate the impact of the July 2016 meeting on the norm that the Dutch government finally presented to the GGE when the 2016–2017 group began deliberations two months later. The following paragraphs outline how international lawyers and technical experts respectively shaped the meeting and its outcomes. The meeting was private, and statements were not attributable to any participant, but notes from the meeting, and a second version of the non-paper circulated by the MFA soon after it shines light on how the group influenced the original draft norm and its explanatory text.[17]

15 *Public Core Non-Paper Version 1*, 1.

16 *Public Core Non-Paper Version 1*, 4.

17 "Non-Paper: Proposal for a Norm of Non-Interference in Core internet Functions [Revised]" (Clingendael Institute, July 19, 2016) [hereafter "*Public Core Non-Paper version 2*"].

2.1 International Law and the Public Core Norm

1. The meeting discussed the overall purpose of the norm: was it to clarify the scope of existing legal obligations or to lay the groundwork for a new, standalone obligation to protect the public core? The group concluded that "various components" of the public core already enjoy "normative protections under international law", but that the purpose of the norm was to provide an "additional layer of normative protection" to the public core. In this regard, some in the group felt that the original phrasing "contrary to [a state's] obligations under international law" was too narrow and could be construed as allowing actions targeting the public core that did not cause non-material damage to data or digital infrastructure.[18] Rather than allow for such permissive interpretation, it would be best to keep the overall focus on the integrity of the public core itself, they argued.
2. Given that the objective of the norm was equally to emphasize the applicability of international law to core cyberspace functions, the group sought to reinforce the point that the norm did not alter existing obligations in any way. Consequently, the norm should underline that its application was "without prejudice to the rights and obligations of states" under international law.
3. The group also felt that the scope of the norm – which was intended to only cover instances where cyber operations on the public core resulted in transboundary harm or disruption – was not properly clarified in the draft text.[19] For instance, a government's decision to block or filter the internet or internet-enabled services within its own jurisdiction would not be covered under the norm, although it was conceivable that some such actions could contravene international human rights obligations. The original formulation "otherwise impairs [...] the ability of the public core [...] to provide services to other states" was also not sufficiently clear. Technical experts in the meeting pointed out that the public core itself did not provide services to states, but the functioning of its core internet protocols was essential to all manner of digital services in a territory, whether public or private.

---

18 "Verslag Clingendael-Bijeenkomst Non-Interventie in de Publieke Kern van Het internet, 11 Juli 2016" (Clingendael Institute, July 2016).

19 *Verslag Clingendael-Bijeenkomst Non-Interventie in de Publieke Kern van Het internet, 11 Juli 2016.*

4. If espionage was outside the purview of the norm – a point on which there was no disagreement within the group – how could it be precisely articulated or reflected in the text? This was a question that the group addressed in some detail during its deliberations.[20]

2.2 Technical Formulations in the Public Core Norm

1. The term "public core", while connoting certain protocols, standards, and infrastructure that were critical to the functioning of the internet, may be too broad and ambiguous a term for a forum such as the GGE, felt some participants. Even the original non-paper had noted that the "notion of a 'public core' could be contentious in international negotiations". Technical experts also felt that such a broad formulation, with the link to "services", may be vague. One proposal was to divide the public core into three parts: a "technical level" (comprising protocols and standards), "functional level" (including carriers, internet Exchanges and ISPs), and "organization level" (stewards or custodians of such standards and protocols such as ISOC, IETF, ICANN, IANA, etc.). Eventually, the technical experts in the group persuaded the rest that the emphasis of the norm should be on what the public core does: ensuring critical forwarding and naming functions of the internet.[21] Participants agreed that the norm would cover protocols and standards relating to the routing and forwarding of data packets on the internet, as well as institutions and infrastructure responsible for those functions – ISPs, IXPs, undersea cables, routers, switches, etc. Similarly, the Domain Name System as well as ICANN, the entity responsible for its governance would be covered by the protections for "naming functions" as envisaged by the norm.
2. Once the object of protection – naming and forwarding functions of the internet – had been established, it was also important to identify the kind of activity that the norm proscribed. The group agreed that the norm should cover cyber operations targeting forwarding and naming functions that result in serious, large-scale impact or disruption.
3. Finally, it was also important to define precisely the threshold of damage caused by such large-scale disruptions. The group concluded that the "availability and integrity" of the internet's forwarding and naming functions were most critical, and any damage to them, whether intentional or unintentional, should be considered unacceptable. Technical experts within the group played a key role in illuminating the impor-

20 Meeting on the Public Core norm, The Hague, July 2016. [*via participant observation*].
21 Meeting on the Public Core norm, The Hague, July 2016. [*via participant observation*].

tance of packet availability and integrity to other participants, although it should be noted that the 2015 WRR report also highlighted these features as critical.[22] Availability, integrity, and confidentiality are the three critical tenets of data security, which also animate the transmission of data packets on the internet. "Availability" refers to the smooth and reliable use of a service or functionality at its "expected level". "Integrity" refers to the expectation that the data/packet has not been altered or tampered with in any manner. And "confidentiality" refers to the private nature of packet transmission or data exchange between users and machines. The group dropped confidentiality from the scope of the public core norm, because it did not cover espionage and other intelligence-centric, cyber-enabled operations.

Following these inputs from the expert meeting, the Dutch MFA revised the draft norm and non-paper, and circulated them among participants for further feedback.[23] The revised norm read:

> Without prejudice to its rights and obligations under international law, a State should not conduct or knowingly [support | condone | allow] [ICT] activity that **intentionally damages the general extraterritorial availability or integrity of the core forwarding and naming functions of the [internet | global public network].**

The revised norm notably omitted references to operations or activities that unintentionally caused damage to forwarding and naming functions, likely because many states would oppose such a formulation at the UN. In particular, the Dutch government was concerned that countries without the capacity to monitor their networks effectively would oppose the norm owing to their lack of control over non-state actors mounting operations from their territory. To highlight the scope of the norm as well as the damage it proscribed, the terms "general" and "extraterritorial" were added to its text. The revised language, it was hoped, would indicate that only cyber activities which caused general, i.e., widespread disruption of critical internet functions outside a state's own territory would be prohibited by the norm.

Finally, to illustrate the norm in action, the non-paper also offered a typology of cyber operations that would be considered impermissible. They included:[24]

---

22 *Broeders Report*, 11.

23 *Public Core Non-Paper version 2*, 2.

24 *Public Core Non-Paper version 2*, 5–6.

a. DNS root zone tampering;
b. DDoS attacks on the root zone servers as well as major internet exchange points;
c. (Physical) attacks on undersea internet cables;
d. Attacks on routing infrastructure and protocols, such as BGP hijacks, which resulted in misdirection of DNS queries to infrastructure or territory of the perpetrator;
e. Attacks on certificate authorities and protocols supporting public key infrastructure such as SSL/TLS; and
f. Cyber operations executed for domestic purposes, which result in "unintended extraterritorial consequences".

"The 2016 brainstorming session resulted in a markedly better definition that we put forward [to the GGE] after that meeting than with what we went in", said a Dutch diplomat. "We could not have come up with the phrasing on routing and forwarding just by ourselves as diplomats."[25]

The formulation of the norm and its dissemination by the Dutch government marked an important milestone in discussions on public core protections within the cyber CoP. Although the participants and the Dutch MFA emphasized that the norm did not alter existing legal obligations, the extent to which it added "a layer of normative protection" to those obligations was unclear. At the time of the July 2016 meeting, states were just beginning to discuss and articulate precisely how international rules applied to cyberspace. The Hague Process consultations on the Tallinn Manual 2.0, which were once again a joint initiative of the Dutch government, helped catalyze those discussions. However, owing to a lack of pronouncements from states on applicable law, it was not exactly clear at the time what obligations were triggered by this norm, let alone the precise scope of those obligations. While the Dutch proposal reflected a norm of "non-interference in core internet functions", it was not easy to draw comparisons with the customary international rule of non-intervention. Firstly, only states had the right against non-intervention: it would be difficult to extend this obligation to the public core functions or their steward organizations which were not subjects of public international law. Secondly, the rule of non-intervention would only be triggered when the cyber operation impinged on an activity within the *domaine reserve* of a state. An acknowledgment that routing or forwarding functions were somehow governmental in nature would come with its own set of problems, not least of which was the possibility of states' taking over these functions.

25 *Interview with a diplomat*, July 7, 2021.

The non-paper also hinted that the due diligence principle in cyber operations could be extended to stopping cyber operations that harmed the public core, but that further discussions would be required to define "the type of 'adverse [transboundary] effects'" that were covered by the proposed norm.[26] However, even the application of the due diligence principle would not be without potential concerns: for one, the requirement to monitor networks for cyber operations targeting the public core may compel some states to engage in DNS filtering or deep-packet inspection, and even use such measures as excuses to surveil their citizens. So while it was clear that the public core norm, as formulated by the Dutch government, would almost certainly advance international cybersecurity law through its application to core internet functions, the precise scope of applicable rules was less clear. As far as the typology and specific illustrations of public core attacks were concerned, they were a useful tool to understand the kind of activities proscribed by the norm. However, except for cyber operations that were implemented domestically but had extraterritorial consequences – which the non-paper hinted could violate the due diligence principle – the wrongfulness of these operations was not tied to any existing international legal obligation, which left their status uncertain.

3 2017–2019: Multistakeholder Bodies Address Public Core Protections

Given the closed nature of GGE negotiations as well as inter-departmental consultations within government that usually precede those negotiations, it is unclear whether the Dutch MFA made further changes to the revised norm and non-paper before presenting it to the fifth UN GGE. Notwithstanding its exact formulation, the norm on non-interference in the public core was indeed presented before the Group. Owing to the failure of this GGE, however, the norm on public core protections too never saw the light of day at the UN. "We had some language in the final draft of the GGE [on public core protections]", said a negotiator who participated in the fifth GGE. "No one objected to that part of the draft. If the whole stuff hadn't collapsed [because of international law], this could have also made it", he said.[27] Another negotiator however said that the public core formulation "was taken out from the last

26 *Public Core Non-Paper version 2*, 5.
27 *Interview with a diplomat*, June 14, 2021.

draft [of the GGE report] which ultimately was rejected [*in toto*]".[28] A Western diplomat said that the "thing that worked against [the public core norm] in 2017 [was the perception that] you essentially forbade states from doing the things they needed to do for law enforcement and even purposes of intelligence". Crucially, he also said that some among the "like-minded countries" felt that if the GGE started "*opening the door to door to new norms*", it would play to the advantage of Russia and China[29] [emphasis added].

The failure of the UN GGE marked an important moment for Dutch diplomacy with respect to its championship of the public core norm. The survival of the norm in this specific instance may have been tied to the fate of the fifth GGE, but it was clear that much work needed to be done to develop common understandings around its precise scope. A question had been cast over the GGE's ability to develop such common understandings, especially in light of US-Russia rivalry coming to dominate its discussions. Countries, including Western countries, had opposed the norm for its plausible circumspection of intelligence-gathering activities, and also for the fact that additional norms opened a Pandora's box for the group.

The Western diplomat's evaluation of the public core norm through the prism of Russian and Chinese interests is telling, and further evidence of the fact that the "proximate *habitus*" of the GGE had come to be characterized by Great Power competition, as noted in Chapter 5. The United States and the like-minded countries did not support the creation of new norms, which they felt would be used by Russia to undermine the delicate political compromise struck by the fourth GGE in 2014–2015. The Dutch MFA had expected for states to be wary of its implications for espionage – the non-paper even anticipated this possibility – but it was arguably less prepared for its rejection as a separate, standalone norm. If the Netherlands wanted to develop a new norm that underlined existing international legal obligations of states towards the public core, it had to find alternative avenues or institutions for this task.

The concept of the public core, meanwhile, had begun to gain traction among other actors and institutions in the cyber CoP. Both the technical community as well as institutions concerned with the political aspects of internet governance embraced the topic. The technical community "shares a sense of collective stewardship towards the public core of the internet", declared ISOC, while the Bildt Commission called on states "to agree not to use cyber weap-

28 *Interview with a diplomat*, October 19, 2021.

29 "A Policy Framework for an Open and Trusted internet" (internet Society), accessed January 31, 2023, https://www.internetsociety.org/resources/doc/2016/policy-framework-for-an-open-and-trusted-internet/.

ons" against the internet's "core infrastructure".[30] In an effort to bring together both these communities and articulate a standalone norm on the public core, the Dutch MFA decided to help establish a multistakeholder entity for this purpose. The Global Commission on the Stability of Cyberspace (GCSC) was thus launched in 2017 by the Netherlands government at the Munich Security Conference.

The GCSC's background and practices have been elaborated on in Chapter 3, but it is also important to highlight specifically the relevance of the public core norm to the Commission. The GCSC was launched mainly as a vehicle for disseminating the public core norm. "It is true that the Commission talked about a much broader set of topics, but this norm was always top of mind [for the Dutch government]", said Christopher Painter, a former US diplomat who joined as a GCSC Commissioner mid-way during its term.[31] "[The Netherlands] wanted to make sure [the public core norm] got through [to relevant constituencies] or got the right hearing", said Painter. Marina Kaljurand, the first chair of the GCSC, said that "the public core of the internet was among the first topics [the Commission] drew up for discussion".[32] Indeed, the first of its eight norms that the GCSC published was on the public core, indicating its pride of place.[33] The norm read:

> Without prejudice to their rights and obligations, **state and non-state actors** should not conduct or knowingly allow activity that intentionally **and substantially** damages the general availability or integrity of the public core of the internet, **and therefore the stability of cyberspace** [emphases added].

The formulation of the public core norm by the GCSC, as the emphasized segments highlight, differed in small but important ways from the Dutch government's articulation.

At the outset, it is important to assess what parts of the norm were retained by the GCSC. By retaining the phrase "without prejudice to their rights and obligations", the Commission too sought to project the public core norm as aligned with international law, and that the norm did not alter states' existing obligations in any way. Yet, the GCSC background paper to the norm noted that a "commitment to norms, *together with the application of international*

30 *Bildt Commission report*, 49–58.
31 *Interview with Christopher Painter*, October 19, 2021.
32 *Interview with Marina Kaljurand*, October 7, 2021.
33 Global Commission on the Stability of Cyberspace, "Call to Protect the Public Core of the internet – GCSC," November 21, 2017, https://web.archive.org/web/20220404013743/https://cyberstability.org/research/call-to-protect/.

law, [could] significantly enhance cyber stability" [emphasis added]. It was clear, therefore, that the GCSC was attempting to move the needle either by advancing a new obligation around the protection of the public core, or, as the Dutch government intended, extend the scope of existing obligations to include such protection. This view is consistent with the finding in Chapter 3 that the practices of the GCSC reinforced the beliefs of the cyber CoP that blurred the lines between norm articulation and law-interpretation.

The GCSC also retained the key formulation "general availability and integrity" while referring to critical functions of the internet that were sought to be protected by the norm. However, it dispensed with the reference to "forwarding and naming functions" in the Dutch government's norm, preferring instead the general phrase "public core of the internet". The GCSC may have felt that the original term was too technical in nature, or perhaps that the Commission needed to specifically highlight and embed the "public core of the internet" as a phrase with intersubjective meaning within the CoP. The consequence of this broad formulation, however, was that the onus of elaborating the concept of the public core fell on the Commission's shoulders. As later paragraphs in this section note, the GCSC sought to define the public core in the following years, and offer its own interpretations of the norm, even after the Commission's term had concluded.

The GCSC's modifications to the Dutch government's version of the norm were significant. Firstly, the GCSC norm addressed both state and non-state actors, calling on them to refrain from interference with the public core. As Chapter 3 highlighted, several norms articulated by the GCSC were targeted at non-state actors, although they are not subjects of public international law. Unlike its norm against 'hack backs' by private actors, the GCSC did not make any attempt to tie state responsibility to cyber operations by non-state actors targeting the public core.

The GCSC's raising of the threshold of unacceptable damage caused due to interference with public core functions arguably counts as its most significant modification to the Dutch government's norm. The GCSC's formulation indicated that only cyber operations which caused "substantial" damage to public core functions would be covered by the norm. Furthermore, such "intentional and substantial damage" also had to affect "the stability of cyberspace". This is arguably a high standard to meet. In an interview, a Dutch negotiator who was involved with the GCSC as well as subsequent negotiations at the UN confirmed this qualification as significant. "You could read it like this: *only* attacks on the general availability or integrity of the public core that impact [the stability of cyberspace] are covered by the norm", the negotiator said [emphasis added]. "[…] for example, intervening in one specific state [via a cyber operation] that doesn't have global reach is not prohibited by the norm. That's interesting, because this was signed off by all Commissioners including [those] from a country that opposed the public core norm later in the GGE [namely, the United States]."[34]

Although the GCSC's work in general, including on the public core norm, has been highlighted in academic and policy debates,[35] not much attention has been paid to this important qualification that it introduced to the norm. At the time of writing, other actors and institutions in the cyber CoP have also not offered their interpretation of the GCSC norm, so it is difficult to assess its acceptance by the community. The high threshold of cyber "instability" envisaged by the norm raises an important question: if, as the Dutch diplomat noted, the GCSC's norm excludes those cyber operations against the public core that are targeted towards a specific state and whose effects are limited to it, who can invoke state responsibility when such cyber operations do impair the general availability or integrity of core functions? If the cyber operation in question impairs the smooth functioning of the internet in a third state, can such manifestation really be equated with damaging the "stability of cyberspace" as a whole? Conversely, if the cyber operation has resulted in internet disruptions across a number of states and will likely cause more damage in the future, can a non-injured state invoke the responsibility of the wrongdoer state?

In other words, an interesting prospect raised by this formulation is whether the norm reflects a *collective obligation* on states to maintain the stability of public core functions. As noted previously, both the Dutch government and GCSC's versions of the public core norm attempt to align it with existing international obligations. However, the Dutch government sought primarily to frame those obligations vis-à-vis injured states. Its reference, for example, to the due diligence obligation in the non-paper indicated that the Dutch government sought for states that suffered harm owing to cyber operations targeting the public core to be able to take remedial measures. On the

34 *Interview with a diplomat,* July 7, 2021.

35 See generally, Jacqueline Eggenschwiler, "Expert Commissions and Norms of Responsible Behaviour in Cyberspace: A Review of the Activities of the GCSC," *Digital Policy, Regulation and Governance* 22, no. 2 (January 1, 2020): 93–107, https://doi.org/10.1108/DPRG-03-2019-0019; Christian Ruhl et al., "Cyberspace and Geopolitics: Assessing Global Cybersecurity Norm Processes at a Crossroads" (Carnegie Endowment for International Peace, February 2020), https://carnegieendowment.org/files/Cyberspace_and_Geopolitics_Carnegie_v1_web.pdf; Marja Lehto, "The Rise of Cyber Norms," in *Research Handbook on International Law and Cyberspace,* ed. Nicholas Tsagourias and Russell Buchan, 1st ed. (London: Edward Elgar Publishing, 2021).

other hand, the GCSC's introduction of the "stability" requirement – intended mainly as a compromise to convey to reluctant countries like the United States that the threshold of violation for this norm would be very high – arguably reframes the norm as a collective obligation. Would the protection of the public core, and therefore the stability of cyberspace, count as an obligation *erga omnes*, owed to the "international community as a whole"?[36] Although there is no doubt that the smooth functioning of core internet protocols is "the concern of all states", no state has offered a view in support of or against such an interpretation. There is virtually no state practice to this effect. For instance, despite many instances of states and criminal entities engaging in Border Gateway Protocol (BGP) hijacking over the years – rerouting through impersonation, internet traffic meant for another state's territory or organization's networks through its own – no governments have publicly criticized or responded to such measures as wrongful acts in international law.[37] BGP hijacking arguably counts as a violation of the public core norm.

Therefore, in the absence of *lex specialis* in the form of customary law or agreements to this effect, the GCSC norm can be interpreted as an effort to move towards solidifying or generating such a collective obligation. The GCSC's discussions lend credence to such an observation. "'Stability' has to be aspirational: we all agreed [in the Commission] that *status quo* is not a good thing", said Painter, referring to the increasing frequency of cyber attacks on public core functions.[38] Aspirational as the norm may be, its claim to advancing a collective *legal* obligation is arguably furthered by the GCSC's effort to ground it in existing international law. The phrases that bookend the GCSC norm on the public core – "without prejudice to their rights and obligations" and "therefore, the stability of cyberspace" – reflect how law-interpretation and norm-articulation in the cyber CoP went hand in hand.

The speed with which the GCSC published the norm after its creation – the Commission was launched in February 2017, and the public core norm published in November that year, whereas most of its eight norms were only pub-

36 For a brief discussion of this topic, *see*, Przemysław Roguski, "Collective Countermeasures in Cyberspace – Lex Lata, Progressive Development or a Bad Idea?," in *2020 12th International Conference on Cyber Conflict (CyCon)*, vol. 1300, 2020, 25–42, https://doi.org/10.23919/CyCon49761.2020.9131715.

37 "China Has Been 'Hijacking the Vital internet Backbone of Western Countries,'" ZDNET, accessed January 31, 2023, https://www.zdnet.com/article/china-has-been-hijacking-the-vital-internet-backbone-of-western-countries/; Derek B. Johnson, "Role of US Agencies Limited in Protecting against BGP Hijacks, Attacks on internet Architecture," SC Media, March 4, 2022, https://www.scmagazine.com/analysis/network-security/role-of-us-agencies-limited-in-protecting-against-bgp-hijacks-attacks-on-internet-architecture.

38 *Interview with Christopher Painter*, October 19, 2021.

lished in December 2018 – arguably reflected the desire of the Dutch government to keep this topic in timely circulation following the failure of the UN GGE in the summer of 2017. The rushed timeline did not offer a lot of opportunities for consultative engagement with the technical community, although the Commission managed to elicit the views of some technical experts through a survey administered prior to the norm's publication. Two GCSC commissioners, Bill Woodcock and Olaf Kolkman, were instrumental in outreach efforts towards the technical community before and after the publication of the public core norm. At the time, Woodcock was affiliated to Packet Clearing House, an NGO that offered crucial networking and security functions to IXPs and other DNS entities, while Kolkman was based at ISOC. With extensive experience and a professional interest in developing a norm around public core protections, both of them played an important role in shaping the formulation of the norm at the July 2016 meeting organized by the Dutch MFA in The Hague. As GCSC commissioners, they organized surveys and outreach sessions among the technical community to assess what it thought of the norm and to define the precise scope of the term "public core".

Woodcock chaired the GCSC's working group on "critical infrastructure assessment", which was tasked with identifying types of infrastructure that deserved protection, not only through the public core norm, but also other GCSC norms.[39] To gather inputs from the technical community, the working group circulated a survey that sorted infrastructure into different categories (e.g., transportation, communication, energy, etc.) and asked them to review their importance and worthiness for protection. "[We got the technical community's inputs] by issuing a general call on the network operators' group – [it's a] catch-all community, usually has everyone in it", said Woodcock.[40] An email-based discussion among technical experts in response to the circulation of the survey in the North American Network Operators' Group (NANOG) reveals how technical experts too mixed up the processes of articulating non-binding norms and application of existing laws. "Hi Bill", wrote one technical expert in response to Woodcock's circulation of the GCSC survey, "Aren't there already laws of war that forbid targeting civilians and civilian infrastructure as well as laying out the combatants' duties to mitigate collateral damage from strikes on government personnel and facilities? Is there some reason these laws should not continue to apply when the attacks are carried out

39 "Report of the GCSC Critical Infrastructure Assessment Working Group" (New Delhi: Global Commission on the Stability of Cyberspace, November 20, 2017), https://web.archive.org/web/20210626155229/https://www.pch.net/resources/Papers/GCSC/GCSC-CI-WG-Delhi-Nov-2017.pdf.

40 *Interview with Bill Woodcock*, September 24, 2021.

with bits instead of bombs?"[41] In response, Woodcock wrote that some states don't think "the old rules don't also apply in a new venue [i.e., cyberspace]". "Also, the rules by which *war* is conducted don't apply when it's not a *war*. And it's essentially never a *war* anymore", he wrote[42] [emphasis original]. The exchange indicates the extent to which technical experts had become essential interlocutors in the cyber CoP, actively participating in discussions around rulemaking for the domain. Woodcock's distinction between *jus ad bellum* and *jus in bello* rules highlights how technical experts too had internalized – through the CoP's discussions – important distinctions pertaining to the application of specific legal regimes. More to the context at hand, it is another example of how the articulation of norms and the identification of specific rules was conflated in the broader CoP.

Insofar as public core functions were concerned, the working group reported back to the Commission that its survey respondents were strongly in support of protection for "internet infrastructures", which included systems responsible for "naming and numbering" as well as "routing and forwarding" functions, as well as "supporting infrastructure", that included datacenters, certification and trust mechanisms, as well as the software used in maintaining public core functions.[43] Importantly, the working group also came up with non-exhaustive definitions of each of these categories, which are provided in Table 6.1.

This listing by the GCSC working group of public core infrastructure was the first systematic attempt by an actor in the cyber CoP to define the ambit of the term. The working group's findings and survey results were presented to the full Commission at its November 2017 meeting in New Delhi. While the GCSC published a pared-down summary of what constitutes public core infrastructure in November 2017 – "elements of the public core include, *inter alia,* internet routing, the domain name system, certificates and trust, and communications cables" – it published a more extensive listing of public core infrastructure in May 2018.[44] The 2018 document was called "Definition of The

41 "Re: GCSC Critical Infrastructure Protection Questions: Your Input Needed," November 15, 2017, The Mail Archive, accessed January 31, 2023, https://www.mail-archive.com/nanog@nanog.org/msg92412.html.

42 "Re: GCSC Critical Infrastructure Protection Questions: Your Input Needed," The Mail Archive, November 15, 2017, https://www.mail-archive.com/nanog@nanog.org/msg92414.html.

43 *Report of the GCSC Critical Infrastructure Assessment Working Group.*

44 "DEFINITION OF THE PUBLIC CORE, TO WHICH THE NORM APPLIES" (Bratislava: Global Commission on the Stability of Cyberspace, May 2018), https://hcss.nl/wp-content/uploads/2022/08/Definition-of-the-Public-Core-of-the-internet.pdf.

TABLE 6.1 Public core infrastructure and systems: GCSC Working Group Survey and Assessment

DNS systems and data	a. Root zone servers; b. DNS infrastructure and processes used to sign DNS records for authentication (DNSSEC); c. Generic (.com, .gov), country-code (.uk, .us, etc.), geographic, and internationalized top-level domains; d. Public recursive DNS resolvers
Routing infrastructure and protocols	a. Core and peering routers of major networks b. internet forwarding systems c. internet Exchange Points d. Systems that assure routing authenticity e. Regional internet registries, f. Systems for defensive routing of attack traffic g. Routing protocols and the integrity of protocol development processes
Cables	Physical cable systems and installations for wired communications, including high-capacity trunk lines and landing stations for undersea cables.
Wireless communication	Infrastructure and systems for wireless communications, including back-end 4G/5G infrastructure.
Datacenters and cloud infrastructure	
Certificates and trust	Cryptographic keys used to authenticate users and make internet transactions like web browsing and email secure and private a. Keyservers b. Certificate Authorities and their Public Key Infrastructure c. Password managers (e.g., iCloud Keychain) d. Wi-Fi roaming authenticators (e.g., Boingo) e. Social-media authentication services f. Spam and malware blacklists and whitelists
Software	Source code and patch-distribution infrastructure of software used in the core of the internet, and by large portions of the internet-using public a. Widely-used operating systems and compilers b. Common DNS servers c. Mail transport, delivery, and user agents d. Web servers and browsers.
World Wide Web	Network infrastructure enabling web browsing, including search engines and content distribution networks (CDNs).

Public Core, To Which The Norm Applies". Not only did this document incorporate most infrastructure identified by the working group, it even suggested that the definition "may be broadened in the future" to include "far more categories of internet and ICT-enabled infrastructure".[45]

45 *DEFINITION OF THE PUBLIC CORE, TO WHICH THE NORM APPLIES*, 2.

The crystallization of the norm by the GCSC arguably generated the impetus for its acceptance by the wider cyber CoP. Following the publication of the norm and the definition of the public core by the GCSC, the Paris Call adopted it as one of nine important principles of international cybersecurity. Principle 2 of the Call sought to "prevent activity that intentionally and substantially damages the general availability or integrity of the public core of the internet".[46] As the text of this principle indicates, the Paris Call adopted the language of the GCSC except for its qualification that the public core norm only covered cyber operations that endangered the stability of cyberspace. As with other Paris Call principles, it was also not clear whether the "principle" was directed only at states, or if it included actions by states and non-state actors. The Call noted the work of the GCSC, and announced the creation of a "community of interest" to "further refine the concept [and] discuss propagation" of the norm. The "community of interest" would be led by The Hague Centre for Strategic Studies, one of the institutional directors of the GCSC process.[47] As noted previously, the GCSC was itself a signatory to the Paris Call.

4 2019–2021: The Public Core Norm at the United Nations

The announcement of the Paris Call by the French government in November 2018 also coincided with the UN General Assembly's passing of two separate resolutions to establish the sixth UN GGE and the first OEWG. Given that debates around the public core had gained momentum in the cyber CoP, with a number of high-profile states and non-state actors signing up to the Paris Call in particular, it was perhaps inevitable that the topic would eventually be tabled for consideration at these intergovernmental forums. However, the form and substance of the public core norm as it was presented before the UN bodies was notable. A Dutch diplomat closely involved in tabling the public core norm before both the UN GGE and OEWG said there were "three elements to the [Dutch] strategy" the second time around.[48] The diplomat's detailing of the strategy also throws into relief how the practices of the GGE had acquired meaning to practitioners. "The GGE report has a certain system [of ordering]. You start with the threats, and the threats need to be addressed by a norm or law or CBM or some capacity building measure", the negotiator

46 "The Call and the 9 Principles – Paris Call," Paris Call, November 11, 2018, https://pariscall.international/en/principles.

47 *The Call and the 9 Principles – Paris Call.*

48 *Interview with a diplomat,* July 7, 2021.

said. "The moment you agree [attacks on the public core are] a threat, you need to at least deal with it in the [report's] norm section, and we have worked internationally to get support around this idea."

However, the negotiator continued, this "was not the most controversial part. We had originally proposed to have a new norm [in 2016–17], which was clearly not happening [this time]." The next best solution was to include it in the wording of an existing norm, so it was "read into the context of the critical infrastructure norm" (13(f) of the 2014–2015 UN GGE report), the negotiator said. The third element of this strategy was to ensure that the international character of the public core – "it's not confined to national boundaries" – was retained even if it were embedded in a norm on (national) critical infrastructure.

Did this strategy succeed? Given that the GGE was a closed negotiation, it is difficult to track the evolution of the norm through the course of its term. However, discussions at the OEWG highlight how the norm was received and negotiated by specific states, and how their response shaped its eventual formulation in both reports.

Prior to the publication of the OEWG's pre-draft in March 2020, the Netherlands suggested the inclusion of the public core norm in the report as "guidance for implementation of UN GGE 2015 recommendation 13(f), and [for also bringing it] under the scope of UN

GGE 2015 re commendation 13(g)".[49] Notably, the text supplied by the Dutch government included the GCSC's qualification that only cyber operations "affecting the stability of cyberspace" would be prohibited by the norm. However, the UN version dropped the norm's original proviso that it was "without prejudice to the rights and obligations" of states.[50] This is not surprising. As Chapter 5 has highlighted, discussions at the UN after the failure of the fifth GGE were characterized by a high degree of reflexive evaluation on the precise relationship between norms and international law. Arguably, the Dutch did not want to make any overt reference to international law in its proposal, given the perception among the like-minded group that new norms were an avenue for Russia and China to create new obligations around state behavior, and a new norm that used the language of international law would be even more problematic.

49 "The Kingdom of the Netherlands' Response to the Pre-Draft Report of the OEWG," accessed February 1, 2023, https://front.un-arm.org/wp-content/uploads/2020/02/letter-to-chair-of-oewg-kingdom-of-the-netherlands.pdf.

50 *OEWG Pre-Draft*, 7.

The OEWG pre-draft included a reference to the Dutch proposal as one among those "suggestions [received from states] for the 'upgrading' as well as further elaboration of norms". In addition to the proposal on public core protections, the pre-draft also noted that some states wanted for "supranational critical information infrastructure [to] be considered a special category of critical infrastructure, and that its protection [to be considered] the shared responsibility of all States". Although the language of this proposal did not correspond to the Dutch formulation, interviews with multiple diplomats involved in UN negotiations suggest that at least one state – namely, Singapore – viewed the notion of "supranational critical infrastructure" to be aligned with the concept of the public core.[51] The Dutch delegation too acknowledged the similarities between both proposals.[52]

As Trepykhalin and Markovski note, a number of states and influential non-state actors supported the inclusion of public core protections in the OEWG report at the pre-draft stage.[53] Such support was not, however, unqualified. Countries such as the UK, France, and Canada, which were "generally supportive" of the proposal, noted that it should aim to clarify existing norms, as new norms were not necessary.[54] Part of the like-minded grouping, these states were not only concerned about new norms in general, as noted earlier, but specifically that the articulation of new norms in the Russian-sponsored OEWG would result in their supplanting or modifying those norms published by the UN GGE in 2015. Developing countries like Brazil supported the concept but suggested that infrastructure for electoral processes should also have the same level of protection as the public core.[55] Some countries were con-

51 *Interview with Henri Verdier*, October 8, 2021; *Interview with Elizabeth Tan*, August 3, 2021.

52 *Interview with Joost Bunk*, July 7, 2021.

53 Trepykhalin and Markovski (2021), 5–8.

54 "Letter to OEWG Chair: Canadian Comments on Draft OEWG Report," April 6, 2020, https://front.un-arm.org/wp-content/uploads/2020/04/letter-to-oewg-chair-canadian-comments-on-draft-oewg-report-april-6-final.pdf; "France's response to the pre-draft report from the OEWG Chair," April 2020, https://front.un-arm.org/wp-content/uploads/2020/04/contribution-fr-oewg-eng-vf.pdf; "UK response to Chair's initial 'Pre-draft' of the report of the OEWG on developments in the field of information and telecommunications in the context of international security," April 15, 2020, https://front.un-arm.org/wp-content/uploads/2020/04/20200415-oewg-predraft-uk.pdf.

55 "Comments submitted by Brazil to the Initial 'Pre-draft' of the report of the OEWG on developments in the field of information and telecommunications in the context of international security," April 8, 2020, https://front.un-arm.org/wp-content/uploads/2020/04/comments-by-brazil-on-the-pre-draft-report-of-cyber-oewg-8-apr-2020.pdf.

cerned that the use of the phrase "upgrading of norms" to describe new proposals and suggestions from states signified their elevation into something more legalistic. As a result, countries like Switzerland opposed this specific phrasing.[56]

But it was the response of Great Powers to the public core norm that was most decisive. China sought for the OEWG to "avoid introducing concepts that have not gained global consensus yet", specifically pointing to the term "public core".[57] The United States refrained from publicly criticizing the Netherlands, an important ally in the like-minded group, but commented on the language of the sister proposal (floated by Singapore) on "supranational infrastructure".[58] "'Supranational,' 'trans-border,' and 'transnational' critical infrastructure were terms used by OEWG delegates, but it is unclear to us if delegates were using those terms interchangeably or not", the US said in written comments on the pre-draft. "If delegates view those terms as synonymous, we should choose one term to describe such critical infrastructure with international implications. [...] We are also unsure what it means to declare 'supranational critical information infrastructure' a 'special category' of such infrastructure, with protection that is a 'shared responsibility' of all States." Additionally, the US also commented seemingly in a veiled reference to the Dutch proposal that the creation of "entirely new normative concepts" will take away from the OEWG's goal to be "productive" in "international cyber stability" discussions. Russia, meanwhile, did not make any observations at the pre-draft stage, but as this chapter later highlights, was closely following discussions on the public core concept.

The opposition of China and the United States in the UN negotiations put paid to any possibility of the term "public core" appearing in either the GGE or OEWG reports. In fact, the Zero Draft of the OEWG report simply took note of proposals that, *inter alia*, "drew attention [to] the importance of ensuring the general availability and integrity of the internet".[59] Faced with a significantly watered-down formulation from the pre-draft, the Dutch delegation negoti-

56 "UN Open-ended working group on developments in the field of information and telecommunications in the context of international security, 2019/2020: Written feedback by Switzerland to the first pre-draft report of the OEWG," April 9, 2020, https://front.un-arm.org/wp-content/uploads/2020/04/20200409-switzerland-remarks-oewg-pre-draft.pdf.

57 *China's Contribution to the Initial Pre-Draft of OEWG Report*, 4.

58 "United States Comments on the Chair's Pre-draft of the Report of the UN Open Ended Working Group (OEWG)," April 6, 2020, https://front.un-arm.org/wp-content/uploads/2020/04/oewg-pre-draft-usg-comments-4-6-2020.pdf.

59 *OEWG Zero Draft*, 8.

ated with partners in the final stages of OEWG deliberations to ensure the report contained stronger references to the concept. As a "compromise text", the First Draft of the OEWG noted that states had agreed that "ensuring the general availability and integrity of the internet" was "vital".[60] The final OEWG report included an additional reference to the concept, noting that "malicious ICT activities against CI and CII [...] that impact the general availability or integrity of the internet are [a] real and growing concern". The UN GGE report, meanwhile, noted that "critical infrastructure *may* also refer to those infrastructures that provide services across several States such as the technical infrastructure essential to the general availability or integrity of the internet"[61] [emphasis added]. In offering this definition, the GGE fully subsumed the concept under Norm 13(f) pertaining to critical infrastructure. But the use of the term "may" left the door open for states to subjectively interpret what constitutes such "essential" infrastructure. Indeed, the OEWG expressly notes that it is State's prerogative to determine which infrastructures it designates as critical, leaving therefore the status of public core protocols and infrastructure ambiguous.

Thus, just as the public core norm picked up specialized legal meaning as it traveled through institutions like the GCSC and Paris Call within the cyber CoP, it was reflexively shorn of those connotations in the UN GGE and OEWG. The UN GGE and OEWG references to the public core make no references to existing international obligations, and offer no guidance as to the threshold of damage to such infrastructure, protocols, or institutions that would be considered unacceptable. To be sure, the subsuming of public core protections within Norm 13(f) means that the references to international law in the "parent" norm apply to the concept as well. In other words, the UN GGE and OEWG reports could be interpreted to mean that "states should not conduct or knowingly support ICT activity contrary to its obligations under international law that intentionally damages or otherwise impairs the use and operation" of infrastructure "essential to the general availability or integrity of the internet". However, as the previous paragraph notes, the reports leave it to states to subjectively consider what would be essential infrastructure. Furthermore, by dropping the term "public core" and replacing it simply with "internet", both UN reports raise the question how and whether any single infrastructure can be considered "essential to the general availability or integrity" of the internet as a whole. The resilience and redundancy features built into internet networking infrastructure and protocols make it possible for it to

60 *OEWG First Draft*, 6.

61 *Sixth GGE Report*, 13.

be functional even in the face of serious cyber operations, or specific regional disruptions. No infrastructure or institution can be identified and isolated as a single point of critical failure for the internet, precisely because its "network of networks" design can withstand such failures.[62] Therefore, even if the 2021 UN reports can be interpreted to extend the reach of its critical infrastructure obligations in international law to the public core, the specific object of protection is still unclear.

The transformation of the public core norm as is traveled across the cyber CoP provides evidence of the arguments laid out in Chapters 2 and 5 of this book. Following the failure of its fifth iteration, the GGE (and its sister UN initiative, the OEWG) had become isolated from the CoP, resulting in UN negotiators reflexively assessing the relationship between norms and international law through the prism of Great Power politics. The public core norm, which had successfully "picked up" legal formulations as it traveled through institutions in the cyber CoP, was accordingly scrutinized for its implications by Great Powers and its allies in both UN processes. Whereas the practices of the GCSC and the Paris Call reinforced the closely held beliefs of the CoP – facilitating the conflation between articulating an aspirational norm on the public core and the application of existing obligations to protect it – this was not the case at the UN. The US and like-minded countries did not want for the Dutch to float a new norm, for concern that Russia may similarly propose additional norms that threatened the GGE's *acquis*. China was wary of attaching any international obligation to a norm or term that had no prior existence at the GGE. The initial Dutch proposal to the UN processes itself removed any references to the norm being aligned with international law. The final outcome was that the public core formulation at the UN not only "lost parts of the norm here and there",[63] as a Dutch diplomat said, but also lost its precise technical scope and legal "cover".

The influence of the post-2016 UN processes and its misalignment with the broader CoP is illustrated in the French response to the public core norm in the Paris Call and the UN negotiations. Whereas the Paris Call – a document in which the French government was the penholder and final arbiter – embraced the public core formulation of the Dutch government and GCSC, French negotiators were more reflexive in their approach towards the norm at the UN. "A lot of technical researchers have an issue with the [formulation] 'public' core

62 *See generally*, "Akamai Blog | internet Resilience, Part 2: What It Takes to 'Just Work,'" accessed February 1, 2023, https://www.akamai.com/blog/performance/internet-resilience-part2-what-it-takes-to-just-work.

63 *Interview with a diplomat*, July 7, 2021.

of the internet: in the early days, everything was public, but now that is not the case. What you are really trying to protect is more and more private", said Henri Verdier, the lead French negotiator at the UN, explaining his reluctance to using the term "public core" in the UN reports.[64] "Most of my friends... like Singapore... when they started talking about the public core [at the OEWG], they spoke about 'supranational' infrastructures...things without sovereignty. I had to explain to them there is no such thing as infrastructure without sovereignty. We spent some time [discussing] to avoid the idea that the internet is a new space without any sovereignty, and also that there are no sacred infrastructures and other infrastructures that you *can* attack", he said [emphasis added]. Verdier's comments – other UN negotiators considered him to be favorable to the public core proposal – indicate that the UN's avoiding of the term "public core" and its replacement with a general reference to the internet was to avoid a technical formulation that somehow made it acceptable to attack either private infrastructure or those infrastructure that could be excluded from "core" forwarding and naming functions. France's attempts, which were supported by the like-minded group, were to ensure that attaching technical and legal meaning to the public core norm rendered some actions permissible. "Creeping expertise" had met its limits at the UN.

5 2021 Onwards: Whither the Public Core Norm?

The treatment of the public core norm and concept at the 2019–2021 UN GGE and OEWG also generated discussion from unexpected quarters. Following the publication of the UN reports in the first half of 2021, Russia submitted a proposal before the International Telecommunication Union's (ITU) Council Working Group on International internet-related Public Policy Issues (CWG – internet) titled "RISK ANALYSIS OF THE EXISTING internet GOVERNANCE AND OPERATIONAL MODEL".[65] "Currently, there is not a single international legal act that would guarantee the integrity and security of the internet's public core", read the Russian proposal, "and without such fundamental instruments, it is impossible to ensure the long-term and productive development of the internet [...]" Calling on states to "act as guarantors of the stability and integrity of the internet's public core", Russia sought for CWG-internet to convene con-

64 *Interview with Henri Verdier*, October 8, 2021.

65 "Contribution by the Russian Federation | RISK ANALYSIS OF THE EXISTING internet GOVERNANCE AND OPERATIONAL MODEL" (ITU Council Working Group on International internet-related Public Policy Issues, September 9, 2021), https://www.itu.int/md/S21-RCLINTPOL16-C-0004/en.

sultations among ITU stakeholders on the "role of states" and "the need for international legal acts" to "guarantee the integrity, resilience, and stability" of the public core.[66] Russia capped the proposal with a reference to the GCSC's public core norm – the GCSC norm and background paper were appended to the proposal – and called on states to look at the Commission's definition of the term.

The ITU CWG-internet is an important policy institution in the organization's apparatus, whose inputs are evaluated by the ITU Council as policy proposals for the ITU Plenipotentiary Conference. Given that the next ITU Plenipot was scheduled for the following year, this proposal by Russia in 2021 drew a lot of attention in the cyber CoP.[67] To critics of the public core formulation and the norm, the Russian proposal vindicated their stance. The technical community, certain sections of which were always cautious about the proposal, saw it as yet another attempt by Russia and the ITU to usurp internet governance from the remit of multistakeholder bodies onto closed, intergovernmental institutions. For them, the proposal was the natural outcome of articulating or promoting such a norm in an intergovernmental venue such as the UN GGE, where Great Power politics was the defining theme. Notably, ICANN CEO Göran Marby in 2020 had coined the phrase "technical internet governance" *per contra* "internet governance" to pointedly highlight and distinguish the work of technical entities and experts in maintaining "core internet infrastructure" and "avoid the development of new legislations, regulations, and policy missteps that could negatively impact the technical function of the internet".[68] The Russian ITU proposal sought for exactly such a new law on a global scale, leveraging the heightened attention paid to the public core concept in the cyber CoP. To the US and like-minded partners, the Russian proposal illustrated the problems of articulating new norms in the UN GGE or OEWG, which they were concerned would be used as elements of a separate cybersecurity treaty.

66 *RISK ANALYSIS OF THE EXISTING internet GOVERNANCE AND OPERATIONAL MODEL*, 2.

67 "Country Focus Report Update: Russian Federation internet-Related Laws and UN Deliberations" (ICANN, June 6, 2022), https://itp.cdn.icann.org/en/files/government-engagement-ge/ge-011-06-06-2022-en.pdf.

68 Göran Marby, "ICANN President & CEO Goals for Fiscal Year 2021," ICANN, July 2020, https://www.icann.org/en/blogs/details/icann-president–ceo-goals-for-fiscal-year-2021-20-7-2020-en; Mark Datysgeld, "Is There Such a Thing as Technical internet Governance?," CircleID, September 2, 2020, https://circleid.com/posts/20200902-is-there-such-a-thing-as-technical-internet-governance.

In sum, the Russian proposal changed the nature of the discussion around public core protections in the CoP by transforming it from an aspirational norm based on existing international obligations to a security concern that required an altogether new legal regime for its management. The consequence of this reframing and proposal was that it halted efforts by other actors, including its own promoters, to advance international cybersecurity law around public core protections through the norm. In less than two weeks after Russia floated its proposal at the ITU, the GCSC issued a "statement on the interpretation of the norm on non-interference with the public core".[69] In this statement, the GCSC addressed two important aspects related to its original formulation:

a. First, the Commission said that the norm of restraint "largely orientated towards states" In the "vast majority of historic cases", the "interference [against public core functions] in question (whether intentional or not) was attributed to state-backed or state-affiliated organizations", wrote the Commission. On the other hand, the original norm of the Commission had called on both "states and non-state actors" not to interfere and damage public core functions.
b. Second, the GCSC argued that the public core norm pertained to "governance 'on' the internet" and not "of" the internet. In other words, the norm was simply aimed at moderating state activity, and not related to internet governance. internet governance was the privy of the constellation of multistakeholder institutions designated to address various core functions, which the norm did not affect in any way. This was somewhat of a strategic retreat for a body that had explicitly based its agenda on being relevant for the "regime complex" of global cyber activities, which included internet governance entities. Framed differently, it was a candid admission by the GCSC that its work on the technical formulations around the public core may have resulted in an overreach that was now being exploited by political actors. "There is nothing in the GCSC norm to suggest that these key elements of the public core are not being well cared for by these [technical/ internet governance] actors", said the Commission.

Similarly, the Paris Call community had an opportunity in late 2021 to evaluate the public core norm through Working Group 4. WG4, as Chapter 3 notes, was tasked with elaborating and advancing common interpretations of Paris Call

69 "Statement on the Interpretation Of the Norm On Non-Interference with the Public Core" (Global Commission on the Stability of Cyberspace, September 22, 2021), https://hcss.nl/wp-content/uploads/2022/06/GCSC-statement-public-core_final.pdf.

principles. WG4 report on the Paris Call principle of public core protection made three relevant points:

a. Stakeholders should use the term "public core" instead of "infrastructure", as the OEWG did, noted WG4, because critical infrastructure could be nationalized during a crisis. The word "'infrastructure' can undermine the **multistakeholder model of internet governance**", said the report [emphasis original].
b. The public core norm should not "invoke the broader issue of the global commons" which was a "broader than necessary" concept for this formulation, noted the report.
c. "Efforts to advance the norm should make clear that it does not create new obligations as it relates to the due diligence principle", noted the report. Such a recommendation went against the 2016 suggestion of the Dutch government's non-paper to consider whether public core protections would require an advancement of the due diligence rule as applicable to cyberspace.

The GCSC's subsequent clarification of its own norm, and the Paris Call WG4's commentary both separate the aspirational character of public core protections from any existing obligation in international law. The GCSC's clarification walks a fine line between acknowledging that states will have to exercise some restraint against interfering with public core functions and noting that "protection" of the public core simply refers to the already-robust system of technical protections afforded by internet governance entities to its various aspects. The GCSC note explicitly rejects the proposition, advanced by Russia, that "states must act as guarantors of the stability and integrity" of the public core. It is difficult to see, then, how international law plays in any potential system of protection of these core functions. WG4's commentary on the other hand stresses that it is important to retain the formulation "public core" precisely because classifying it as critical infrastructure may "legalize" its protection – whether under domestic or international law. Furthermore, it makes a pointed note to avoid analogizing the public core with the global commons: the notion of cyberspace as a "global commons" has often been invoked by states, especially developing countries, calling for a binding legal regime for cyberspace.

The Russian proposal at the ITU certainly heightened concerns within multistakeholder groups like the GCSC and Paris Call WGs that states could use the pretext of public core protection to assume and centralize control over key aspects of internet governance. More broadly, however, the treatment of public core protections by the UN GGE and OEWG made practitioners in the cyber CoP realize the challenges of linking the norm with existing legal obligations. The US and like-minded group's opposition to "additional norms" in the UN reports for fear that Russia would use them as proxies to establish new legal obligations, as the previous chapter highlighted, meant that public core protections would not be articulated as a separate norm. But the UN's subsuming of public core functions under the framework of critical infrastructure also meant that states would have a greater say in determining not only what aspects of the "core" were CI, but also how to protect them under national and international law. The fact that the US provided Russia with a list of CI considered as "off-limits" for cyber attacks during the Biden-Putin summit of June 2021 raised the possibility that some kind of political framework may emerge around the topic.[70] Should public core concerns be addressed through Great Power negotiations on CI protection, multistakeholder entities would have a limited role in shaping the scope of such rules. Further, any reference to the obligations of states vis-à-vis the public within this framework would likely be used by those countries to seek greater control over internet governance functions. The rejection by the multistakeholder WG4 of the Dutch proposition that public core protections could be linked to a due diligence obligation should be seen in this vein.

At the time of writing, therefore, it would appear that discussions at the UN GGE and OEWG on the public core not only resulted in a de-linking of legal and normative aspects of its protection at the UN but also other forums in the cyber CoP. This development limits the possibility of "creeping expertise": technical experts may continue to play an important role in how voluntary norms around public core protection are articulated, but are unlikely to shape how new or existing rules are identified or applied to this issue.

70 Morgan Phillips, "Biden Gave Putin List of 16 Critical Infrastructure Entities 'off Limits' to Cyberattacks," FOXBusiness, June 16, 2021, https://www.foxbusiness.com/politics/biden-putin-critical-infrastructure-entities-off-limits-cyberattacks.

CHAPTER 7

Conclusion

The problems of global governance have grown increasingly complex even as states' appetite for collective action has diminished. Climate change, cybersecurity, the advent of Lethal Autonomous Weapons Systems, the growing use of spyware, and the governance of Artificial Intelligence (AI) are but a few issues that take top billing in the global governance agenda of the 21st century. More complex issues are on the horizon: guidelines around the use of quantum technology in civil and military domains, the regulation of nanomaterials, and managing the potential ubiquity of human-robot interactions. Some global governance challenges, such as climate change and cybersecurity, have been tabled at the UN and elsewhere for more than a decade. At the time of writing, momentum towards new binding instruments on these problems at multilateral forums appears to be slow. Yet, the business of global governance has endured. The action has shifted, at least in part, towards informal and ad hoc settings where states and non-state actors rub shoulders to tackle specific, pre-defined issues for short periods of time. These "task-specific"[1] entities have articulated non-binding guidelines but have also advanced intersubjective understandings of how existing international law applies to those issues. Framing the contours of legal discourse is critical to shaping state practice and advancing policy, both at the domestic and international level. It is also possible that legal discourse shaped by these informal entities will influence negotiations over a formal instrument, should one materialize. As Meyer notes, "informal lawmaking allows States to update [formal] law when circumstances have changed".[2]

Several aspects of these global governance challenges require technical inputs and assessments. Therefore, it is not out of the ordinary to see technical experts serving as advisers or consultants to states on policy matters, includ-

1 Yf Reykers et al., "Ad Hoc Coalitions in Global Governance: Short-Notice, Task – and Time-Specific Cooperation," *International Affairs* 99, no. 2 (2023): 727–745, https://doi.org/10.1093/ia/iiac319.

2 Timothy Meyer, "Alternatives to Treaty-Making – Informal Agreements," in *The Oxford Guide to Treaties*, ed. Duncan B Hollis (Oxford University Press, 2020), https://doi.org/10.1093/law/9780198848349.003.0004.

ing security concerns. But the "pervasive informality"[3] of governance mechanisms in domains such as cybersecurity heightens experts' involvement and places them in a position where they can also shape the application of international law to state behavior in those domains. As Iván Fuentes and Santiago Villalpando note, "a significant part of the treaty-making process takes place behind closed doors".[4] Informal governance bodies on the other hand tend to be more inclusive or expressly multi-stakeholder in composition, sometimes offering a chance for non-legal actors to shape legal reasoning and interpretation. This book highlights how technical experts in this vein have shaped states' and non-state actors' perceptions of lawful state behavior in cyberspace. This concluding chapter summarizes some of its key findings and empirical methods, and picking up the thread from Chapter 1, highlights some of its modest contributions to international legal theory.

1 Summary of Findings

It has been 25 years since Russia first brought the UN General Assembly's attention to the topic of cybersecurity. The institutional landscape of international cybersecurity governance has since become highly fragmented, with intergovernmental, multistakeholder, and private initiatives all vying to frame "responsible state behavior" from the perspectives and interests of their respective stakeholders. In 2025, as in 1998, there remains a big void in this landscape, namely, the absence of a formal, authoritative mechanism to set or interpret rules for cyberspace. The *ad hoc* nature of international cybersecurity governance has however not prevented states and non-state actors from coalescing around key themes and issues, or from articulating norms and rules around those topics. Shared understandings among actors in these institutions on what rules are applicable to state behavior in cyberspace and how they apply contribute to the development of international cybersecurity law. Even if these institutions are informal and fluid, their interpretations of international cybersecurity law have already gained traction among influential states, and could arguably shape a future cybersecurity treaty.

3 Arun Sukumar et al., "The Pervasive Informality of the International Cybersecurity Regime: Geopolitics, Non-State Actors and Diplomacy," *Contemporary Security Policy* 45, no. 1 (2024): 7–44, https://doi.org/10.1080/13523260.2023.2296739.

4 Carlos Iván Fuentes and Santiago Villalpando, "Making the Treaty," in *The Oxford Guide to Treaties*, ed. Duncan B Hollis (Oxford University Press, 2020), https://doi.org/10.1093/law/9780198848349.003.0010.

This book has demonstrated how technical expertise shapes the determination of what rules should apply to state activities in cyberspace, and the scope of those rules. In the absence of authoritative institutions to set rules for the domain, international cybersecurity law has primarily developed through the articulation of cyber norms. Ordinarily, norms described as "voluntary" and "non-binding" by states themselves could simply be classified as aspirational statements or "soft law", as international lawyers usually refer to it, which may crystallize into binding rules in the future. However, actors and institutions involved in international cybersecurity governance – collectively referred to in this book as the "cyber Community of Practice" (CoP) – have habitually conflated voluntary norms and existing international law. This conflation has resulted in two broad outcomes. First, norms articulated by these institutions have often echoed the language of binding law, implying that they are not in fact voluntary guidelines, but interpretations of existing international rules. Technical experts, who play an important role in the articulation of voluntary norms, have therefore had an influential say in ascertaining what aspects of state behavior should be regulated, what rules should apply to those activities, and how the application of certain rules should be conditioned by technical considerations. Second, even private exercises like the Tallinn Manuals and the Oxford Process, set up to interpret and apply existing rules to specific scenarios, have been orchestrated like non-binding norms-articulation processes. These initiatives sought to ensure that their interpretations accommodated the views of interested actors as to what should count as existing law, and ultimately secure their acceptance, even if such interpretations could not be ascertained through formal sources of international law. Their attempts thus at "managing" key stakeholders, including the technical community, meant that the Tallinn Manuals and Oxford Process drafters were influenced as much by technical considerations as they were by legal-doctrinal sources in identifying and applying existing rules.

In sum, the conflation of norms and rules in the cyber CoP created a permissive environment for technical expertise to shape the development of international cybersecurity law through statements and interpretations by these *ad hoc* groups. I termed the tacit internalization of technical knowledge and considerations by actors involved in the identification and application of international law in international cybersecurity as "creeping expertise".

This book offered an explanation as to why actors and institutions within the cyber CoP became disposed to conflating voluntary norms and rules. A compromise made in the early UN GGEs between two political camps – led by the US and Russia, respectively – resulted in GGE reports suggesting that norms drawn from existing international law and "additional norms" could both guide state behavior in cyberspace. The GGE did not specify whether these "additional norms" were equivalent to legal norms, i.e., interpretations of international law, or whether they were simply aspirational guidelines. Ambiguity regarding the precise character of norms led future UN GGEs to club norms and rules together. In other words, voluntary norms and international law were treated as functionally equivalent tools in regulating state activities in cyberspace. From 2013, UN GGE reports contained a separate section on "norms, rules and principles of responsible state behavior" that likened legal norms as well as "additional norms". In 2015, the UN GGE formally described all norms as "non-binding" but continued to refer to or incorporate international law principles in those norms, further conflating norm-articulation and rule-interpretation. I pointed to two instances of "creeping expertise" owed to this conflation of rules and norms: the 2015 GGE report appeared to identify, through its norm on the subject, a legal obligation not to undertake or knowingly allow cyber operations that caused "damage" or "unintentional impairment" to others' critical infrastructure. Second, the UN GGE norm on the responsibility of states for "internationally wrongful acts" suggested that the attribution of cyber operations to states should be "substantiated". However, the GGE did not specify what such substantiation entailed or whether the substantiation referred to legal attribution of wrongful acts or technical attribution of cyber operations.

Following the UN GGE, other institutions which are a part of the cyber CoP similarly conflated rules and norms. Multistakeholder initiatives such as the GCSC and Paris Call based some of the voluntary norms they articulated on existing international rules, not only identifying specific rules as applicable, but also describing how they would apply. The GCSC's norms on foreign election interference and cyber "hack backs", both of which were crafted with the help of technical experts, were justified on the basis of their alignment with existing rules on non-intervention and state responsibility. The GCSC's norm on election interference suggested that only technical infrastructure involved in the conduct and evaluation of elections and plebiscites was protected under international law, but that any form of interference in their functioning should be interpreted as coercive, thereby breaching the obligation of non-intervention. With respect to hack backs, the GCSC's definition of active cyber defense was broadly framed in a manner so as to place the territorial state responsible for the most intrusive measures taken by private entities outside their networks.

The Paris Call Working Groups, through their commentaries on the nine "principles" articulated by the Call, similarly scoped the definitions of election interference, ICT supply chain integrity, and private hack backs in technical terms, and noted that the protection or regulations of these activities were based on existing legal obligations. Chapter 3 also highlighted a separate, interesting dimension of "creeping expertise" in relation to the work of Paris Call Working Group 3: the conflation of norms and rules allowed technical experts to not only influence the development of rules for this domain, but also *how* shared understandings of international cybersecurity law could be developed. This chapter highlighted how technical experts within WG3 advocated for multistakeholder cybersecurity governance mechanisms similar to the Programme of Action (PoA) on Small Arms and Light Weapons or the process that led to the Montreux Document/International Code of Conduct Association on private military and security companies. The Montreux Document and PoA SALW reflect and generate, respectively, interpretations of existing rules considered authoritative by states and non-state actors. WG3's report drew from briefings made by international lawyers to the group, who brought these processes to the attention of technical experts.

Finally, this book has demonstrated how technical expertise shaped the findings and statements of the Tallinn Manuals and the Oxford Process, because both initiatives were managed like a norms-articulation process that accommodated technical and political concerns as much as they accounted for the legal-doctrinal ascertainment of applicable international law. Although both Tallinn Manual and Oxford Process lawyers suggested they were identifying *lex lata,* their discussions resembled those of the UN GGE or multistakeholder norms initiatives than a strictly doctrinal law-finding or interpretation exercise. This was not surprising: unlike the International Law Commission that engages in identifying or progressively developing rules for a domain when there is sufficient state practice to do so, international cybersecurity law initiatives like the Tallinn Manuals and the Oxford Process had no such luxury. To secure policy purchase from states, businesses, and the technical community alike, therefore, they sought to ensure their findings reflected the concerns of all those practitioners. The credibility and legitimacy that both initiatives enjoy, even if stakeholders might disagree with their interpretations, is owed to this management, I argued. I pointed to three instances of creeping expertise in the Tallinn Manuals. Apprised of the interconnected and ubiquitous nature of cloud computing by technical experts, the Tallinn Manual drafters acknowledged that cyber attacks could quite easily have extraterritorial effects. Sovereignty violations of third states could occur through cyber operations, TM2 found, even if it was not the intention of the perpetrator state. TM2 balanced its doing away of intent with a sufficiently high threshold for damage for a cyber operation to constitute a violation of sovereignty. The "law" of cyber countermeasures articulated by TM2 was a significant departure from the customary law on the subject, primarily because the drafters factored in some of the technical-operational realities of implementing such measures in cyberspace. Finally, in what is arguably the most prominent illustration of the "norms-like" approach of the Tallinn Manuals, I highlighted how TM2 adopted the UN GGE's compromise language – which in turn was shaped by technical considerations – in its voluntary norm on the application of the due diligence principle to cyberspace. The UN GGE and TM2 attached the due diligence principle to the state responsibility regime, despite no state practice to suggest a primary due diligence obligation existed for cyberspace. It is also probable that TM2 linked both to ensure victim states had recourse to cyber countermeasures in the event territorial states failed to stop malicious cyber activity originating from or transiting through their networks.

Technical experts also played a crucial role in helping shape the statements of the Oxford Process. Expert briefings on the importance of data integrity to clinical trials and vaccine research prompted Oxford Process lawyers to declare as prohibited cyber operations targeting such data, even if for the purposes of espionage. A presentation by a Meta employee provoked discussions on how the group viewed "coercive" behavior (and therefore, prohibited interventions) in cyberspace in relation to influence operations. The group sought more clarity on whether the degree of "inauthenticity" of a cyber operation could help infer its goals and thus determine its coercive character, as opposed to its actual effects. Lastly, Chapter 4 also pointed out that the Oxford Process group's exposure to the wide range of technical harms that could be caused by ransomware attacks led them to suggest that states would only be in breach of their due diligence obligations for territorial ransomware operations that violated existing rights of states, and not for causing "significant adverse consequences" alone.

When actors within the cyber CoP reflexively evaluated the relationship between voluntary norms and existing rules, the effect of "creeping expertise" was muted. Chapter 5 noted how tensions between the United States and Russia – particularly in the aftermath of Russian electoral interference in the 2016 US presidential elections – prompted a shift in how UN negotiators evaluated rules and norms. Whereas voluntary norms and existing rules were previously seen as functionally similar tools to advance responsible state behavior, UN negotiators began to assess how the interplay between norms and rules would shape the dynamic between Great Powers in cyberspace. The US and like-minded countries were not keen to re-open or re-interpret previously agreed-upon norms and to articulate new norms that might dilute interpretations of existing rules. Russia and to a lesser extent, China, sought "additional binding obligations" in the form of new norms, and to avoid any references to existing rules.

The heightened awareness of US and Russian positions and the reflexive assessment of how norms and rules shaped the bilateral dynamic made actors in the UN insist on a separation of voluntary norms and existing rules in their reports. A noticeable outcome of such separation was the removal of some references to international law language in voluntary norms. As a result, there were limited avenues for technical considerations to shape interpretation of rules through those norms.

Chapter 5 highlighted two instances that illustrate the limits of "creeping expertise" in the 2019–2021 UN negotiations. The UN OEWG rejected the 2015 GGE report's finding that cyber attribution should be "substantiated", making it clear that the legal standard of attribution for internationally wrongful acts in cyberspace did not have to meet an additional, technical requirement of substantiation. The OEWG pre-draft's language on supporting legal attribution through a commonly developed technical standard was also rejected by states. Secondly, early drafts of the OEWG report sought to "upgrade" the 2015 UN GGE norm on ICT supply chain integrity, to suggest states had an obligation not to "create" zero-day exploits and other "harmful hidden functions" that weaponized vulnerabilities in the ICT supply chain. The 2015 UN GGE norm had only sought to prevent their "use", not "creation". The framing of this norm as a legal obligation ("upgrading") would have had the effect of suggesting that states should not develop harmful exploits at all. This language was ultimately rejected in the OEWG, which preferred to retain the 2015 UN GGE formulation.

Chapter 6 illustrated "creeping expertise" across institutions in the CoP with the case study of the norm to protect the public core of the internet. Initially floated by the Dutch government as a non-binding proposal to protect technical infrastructure (located across territories) essential to maintaining the "general availability and integrity" of the internet, this norm picked up legal meaning as it was discussed by various institutions within the CoP. Technical experts contributed in a significant way to understanding exactly what infrastructure was sought to be protected, and consequently, what existing obligations should apply to its protection. However, when the public core norm was taken up by the 2019–2021 UN GGE and UN OEWG, negotiators chose to separate and strip the norm of any existing legal obligation. This finding is consistent with the broader conclusion that the UN groups had begun to reflexively evaluate the relationship between norms and law, which limited "creeping expertise".

To illustrate "creeping expertise" in international cybersecurity law, this book relied on an empirical research method called "practice tracing". Practice tracing involves, *inter alia*, immersive observation in a CoP to identify everyday practices of actors within its various institutions. It is an inductive method that involves three steps: researchers first gather data on practices within the CoP; then infer the social meaning of those practices; and finally, trace the role of practices in contributing to the observed social phenomena. Practice tracing is based on the underlying theory – drawn conceptually from the work of theorists such as Pierre Bourdieu – that everyday, taken-for-granted practices in a community or society reflect and reinforce its deeply held background dispositions. As manifestations of how the community should think and act about any specific issue, these practices influence how actors learn new ideas or apply such learning to their work.

There is a compelling reason to specifically study practices of the cyber CoP to analyze the emergence of international cybersecurity law. In fluid global governance environments where there is no formal institution to set or apply rules, actors learn by doing. International cybersecurity governance, as this book noted, typifies such an environment and most institutions involved in norm-articulation or rule-interpretation are informal. States and non-state actors participate in multiple and overlapping institutions, often have serendipitous interactions with technical experts or other specialists at these venues, and address ongoing or unexpected cyber incidents and developments on the fly. However serendipitous, deliberations between technical experts, diplomats, international lawyers and NGOs are ultimately shaped by the practices of said institutions. While institutional practices can be specific and not shared among all groups within the CoP, they do reflect common beliefs and dispositions towards cybersecurity governance. The same actors are engaged across these institutions, and they acknowledge, despite differences, the joint nature of their enterprise. Practice tracing helps develop a working explanation of how background beliefs arise, their role in shaping different practices across institutions, and finally to develop a theory of how social phenomena are owed to such practices and beliefs.

This book used practice tracing to highlight how actors within the cyber CoP have become habitually disposed to conflate norms and rules. Through practices that reflected this conflation, technical expertise that contributed to the articulation of cyber norms also tacitly shaped the development of rules for the domain. The following table presents an overview of practices within the cyber CoP that were surveyed in Chapters 2 to 5. This book identified and analyzed these practices, as well as their role in facilitating "creeping expertise", with the help of 67 interviews with diplomats, international lawyers,

TABLE 7.1 Overview of practices within the cyber CoP

Institutions	Practices
UN GGE (2004–2015)	– Clubbing of "norms, rules and principles" in GGE reports – Use of international law language in formulations of voluntary norms – Technical expert serving as a facilitator for a section on international law – Repeated invocations of consensus GGE reports as the "*acquis*"
GCSC	– Recruitment of international lawyers into the Commission and RAG to draft non-binding norms – RfPs issued by the Commission soliciting legal expertise and inputs into norms on the offensive use of cyber capabilities – Publication of background papers and additional notes, defending norms in existing international rules
Paris Call	– Briefings and presentations by international lawyers to WG3 and WG4 – "Memo-like" notes on existing rules interspersed among WG4's commentary on norms
Tallinn Manuals	– Hague Process consultations with states on TM2 – Consensus-based decision-making among international law scholars who helped draft the manuals – Interactions with states and technical experts on the margins of conferences such as CyCon

TABLE 7.1 Overview of practices within the cyber CoP (*cont.*)

Institutions	Practices
Oxford Process	– Consensus-based decision-making among drafters of Oxford Process statements – Briefings by technical experts – Framing of "objects and methods" of international law protection in response to contemporary cyber incidents or developments

UN GGE and UN OEWG (2019–2021) (Reflexive evaluation and rejection of old UN GGE practices)	– Extended debate on the precise positioning of sections on voluntary norms and international law
	– Calls by some states to re-open the *acquis*, to include an "*acquis+*" formulation
	  – GGE's rejection of the UN GA mandate to include Annex of international law positions of states along with GGE report
	  – Debate on, and in some cases, rejection of international law language in text of voluntary norms

technical experts, and other actors in the CoP, alongside immersive observation of their various discussions over a period of nine months.

2 Contribution to International Legal Theory

The introduction to this book foregrounded the contribution of this book in three aspects.

Firstly, the book offers insights into the close involvement and contribution of technical experts in the development of international cybersecurity law. It is no revelation to say that scientific and technical expertise has played an important role in assisting states, multilateral organizations, and international courts in interpreting and applying rules.[5] Experts also help states implement their international obligations at the sub-national or provincial level.[6] The case of international cybersecurity, however, is different from these instances of expert involvement.

The difference is primarily that in multilateral organizations or international courts, technical expertise contributes to the application or adjudication of international law by formal entities. The "scientific fact-finding" of experts is different from law-ascertainment,[7] which is very much the remit of judicial or legal officers. As Simma notes with reference to the ICJ, technical experts are often called on to clarify facts that influence the court's legal pronouncements, but that determination is made by judges (and in other contexts, legal professionals) alone. Experts are necessary to "understand fully the meaning of these facts [and] their relevance for the proper application of the law to the facts. I would never have left the exercise of the Court's judicial function to experts", notes the former ICJ judge.[8] The extent to which subject-matter expertise – or, as it is widely characterized, "extra-legal expertise"[9] – is relied upon for adjudication or interpretation depends on the forum. The WTO, as Pauwelyn (2002) and others have noted, has a system that relies

5 *See generally*, Bruno Simma, "The International Court of Justice and Scientific Expertise," *Proceedings of the ASIL Annual Meeting* 106 (January 2012): 230–33, https://doi.org/10.5305/procannmeetasil.106.0230; Joost Pauwelyn, "The Use of Experts in WTO Dispute Settlement," *The International and Comparative Law Quarterly* 51, no. 2 (2002): 325–364; Gian Luca Burci, "Global Health," in *The Cambridge Companion to International Organizations Law*, ed. Jan Klabbers, Cambridge Companions to Law (Cambridge University Press, 2022), https://doi.org/10.1017/9781108574242.013; Makane Moïse Mbengue and Rukmini Das, "Temporal Aspects of the Use of Experts in the Proceedings before the ICJ and ITLOS," in *Time and International Adjudication*, ed. Andrea Gattini (Brill, 2024), https://doi.org/10.1163/9789004716377_019; "Techniques for Judicial Engagement with Science in the Practice of International Courts and Tribunals," in *Science and Judicial Reasoning: The Legitimacy of International Environmental Adjudication*, ed. Katalin Sulyok (Cambridge University Press, 2020); Jean D'Aspremont and Makane Moïse Mbengue, "Strategies of Engagement with Scientific Fact-Finding in International Adjudication," *Journal of International Dispute Settlement* 5, no. 2 (2014): 240–272, https://doi.org/10.1093/jnlids/idu004.

6 Daniel Bodansky and Harro van Asselt, "Who's Who in the Legal Process: Actors beyond the State," in *The Art and Craft of International Environmental Law*, ed. Daniel Bodansky and Harro van Asselt (Oxford University Press, 2024), https://doi.org/10.1093/oso/9780197672365.003.0007; David Fidler, "Global Health Jurisprudence: A Time of Reckoning," *96 Georgetown Law Journal*, 393 (2008), January 1, 2008, https://www.repository.law.indiana.edu/facpub/141.

7 *See generally*, d'Aspremont and Mbengue (2014), n.5.

8 Simma (2012), n.4, 232.

9 Makane Moïse Mbengue and Rukmini Das, "Experts," Oxford Public International Law, https://doi.org/10.1093/law-mpeipro/e1553.013.1553.

extensively on technical and scientific expertise in the dispute settlement process, as well as the preparation of reports by the WTO secretariat. The secretariat arguably even has the capacity to augment the expert resources available to developing countries during treaty negotiations, although states usually rely on in-house experts. The same applies to forums like the International Tribunal for the Law of the Sea or the World Health Organization.

To be sure, there is a "broader interpretive community"[10] of NGOs, experts, and IO secretariats that often coalesce around institutions and governance regimes. This community is a check on "radical indeterminacy" in rule-interpretation and shapes the justificatory discourse of states around compliance.[11] But even such communities accord pride of place to legal advisers and officials trained in international law. Johnstone describes an interpretive community as having three concentric circles: an inner circle of government and intergovernmental officials directly responsible for articulating and implementing a rule; a second circle of legal advisers and legal experts who pass judgment on the inner circle's interpretations – both from a disciplinary perspective and as custodians of the "community judgment"; and a third outer circle of NGOs and technical experts, among others.[12] Certainly, "community judgment" should account for expert opinions, especially in domains which have an element of scientific assessment, such as non-proliferation or climate change.[13] But expert inputs are woven into legal argumentation and discourse, which in turn is centered around a treaty and/or a formal institution, whose rules of engagement between legal and non-legal experts are structured.

In the domain of international cybersecurity governance, neither do such instruments or institutions exist nor can engagement between lawyers and non-legal actors – as chapters in this book have shown – be considered structured in any meaningful way. *Ad hoc* bodies created to advance cybersecurity governance began their work by framing international cybersecurity law as *one* pillar of responsible state behavior. International lawyers were only one (albeit important) piece of the governance puzzle, and they could not be considered sole, authoritative sources of legal interpretation because the latter was always conjoint with norm-articulation. Non-binding norms and binding rules were conflated in an iterative process of discovering: (a) what state or

10 Ian Johnstone, *The Power of Deliberation: International Law, Politics and Organizations* (Oxford University Press, 2011), https://doi.org/10.1093/acprof:oso/9780195394931.001.0001.

11 Johnstone (2011), 36.

12 Johnstone (2011), 41.

13 Ian Johnstone, *Treaty Interpretation: The Authority of Interpretive Communities*, 12 MICH. J. INT'L L. 371 (1991), 289.

state-backed operations in cyberspace should be addressed, (b) what objects should be considered worthy of legal or normative protection, and (c) what technical and strategic considerations encouraged or constrained the implementation of "responsible state behavior". In this discovery process, technical experts were as influential in shaping governance (including legal) outcomes as international lawyers.

Secondly, the emergence of "international cybersecurity law" illustrates how legal discourse around domains of global governance can advance even in the absence of treaties. The evolution of such discourse this book shows, is often driven by practice, and not doctrine alone. International legal scholarship has turned its gaze towards practices in a significant way. Yet, as Chapter 1 highlighted, most works tend to focus on legal practices, especially practices of formal institutions such as international courts and tribunals. In many specialized domains of law, there are no authoritative institutions to apply or interpret rules for the domain as a whole. Yet, the lack of formal mechanisms does not imply the absence of rulemaking or interpretation. Communities of Practice in these domains still coalesce in informal and *ad hoc* settings, which discuss and eventually generate shared understandings about rules for the domain. Some of them may concern themselves expressly with international law (e.g., Tallinn Manuals, Oxford Process), but in many cases, international law will only be one among many agenda-items on the table (e.g., UN GGE, GCSC, Paris Call). Studying the "non-legal" or "extra-legal" practices of these institutions is therefore important. Furthermore, in technology-centric domains such as international cybersecurity, Lethal Autonomous Weapons Systems (LAWS), and artificial intelligence, even the applicability of existing international law or its precise scope is unclear and even questioned by many influential actors. In such cases, it is reasonable to assume that technical experts, diplomats, NGOs, and businesses all play some role in influencing what rules apply and how they apply. This book demonstrated how non-law professionals such as technical experts and non-legal practices, such as those relating to recruitment, deliberation, and decision-making in informal institutions, can contribute to the development of specialized rules for these domains.

Thirdly, the book offers a working account of the fragmentation of international law, albeit one limited to the domain of cybersecurity. Two decades ago, the ILC's Study Group on the topic noted that international lawyers are equipped with a "professional toolbox" to respond to "most substantive fragmentation problems".[14] Chapters in this book show interpretative techniques and doctrine certainly play an important role in lawyers reconciling specialized rules of cybersecurity with principles of public international law. But these professional tools are not deployed in a vacuum. Closely held beliefs of states and non-state actors on how to advance cybersecurity governance – which are in turn reflected in the practices of various governance institutions – have shaped what lawyers determine to be applicable international law and how such rules are applied to cyber operations. In other words, how lawyers use their toolbox to address rule-interpretation for specialized domains is guided by the beliefs and practices of the community responsible for the governance of that domain.

At an early stage in the evolution of the cyber CoP, the UN GGE's compromise formulation on cyber norms structured legal argumentation and interpretation within the broader community. The articulation of norms (notwithstanding their characterization as "voluntary" or "non-binding") by the GGE would not only embrace legal principles but also lay down markers as to what states considered deserving of legal protection. The UN GGE's 2015 norm on critical infrastructure is a good example. By articulating Norm 13(f), the GGE not only determined that critical infrastructure is considered protected under international law from cyber operations, but also set a benchmark ("intentional damage" or "impairment of use") to assess the legality of such operations. The policy priorities of major cyber powers, identified in this manner via norms, set the tone for legal discourse. International lawyers in the cyber CoP then addressed the potential legal implications of the norm (or any legal formulation contained therein), and scope of state obligations around it.

The work of multistakeholder bodies like the GCSC and Paris Call also speaks to this approach. The protection of the public core, cyber operations tampering with election infrastructure, and hack backs by private actors were evidently concerns that promoters and participants in these bodies wanted to bring to the attention of the cyber CoP. The GCSC and Paris Call mimicked the UN GGE's approach of articulating cyber norms and principles that were important to its founders and ascribing legal connotations to some of them. Technical experts played an important role in framing normative concerns – e.g., were all election-related processes protected from cyber operations, or was it only technical infrastructure essential to the holding of an election? –

14 International Law Commission, "Fragmentation of International Law: Difficulties Arising from the Diversification and Expansion of International Law – Report of the Study Group of the International Law Commission," *UN Doc. A/CN.4/L.682/Corr.1* (Aug. 11, 2006), 100.

but lawyers worked with these framings to shape applicable law. At the time of writing, states widely associate cyber-enabled election interference with the rule against non-interference. Although the precise contours of the rule as it pertains to cyberspace, and the extent to which cyber operations constitute "coercion" are still debated, it is the early work of the GCSC and Paris Call lawyers that laid the groundwork for intersubjective legal discourse on the topic. Practices of these institutions – RFPs, "law-like" memos, background notes, etc. – that allowed for international lawyers to interact with, and influence the deliberations diplomats, technical experts, and other stakeholders were therefore critical to the overall discourse.

It is the work of the Tallinn Manuals and the Oxford Process that merits special mention here, not least because they were explicitly designed as law-ascertainment initiatives. Lawyers in both entities have been engaged in an essentially balancing act that, on the one hand, resolves doctrinal tensions between general and specialized international rules, and, on the other, applies general PIL rules in a way that is likely to elicit acceptance from states and influential non-state actors. Whether it was in relation to the "rule" of sovereignty or applying the law of countermeasures to cyber operations, Tallinn Manual lawyers were sensitized to the technical and operational realities of cyberspace by experts, and sought to interpret the law in a way that induced compliance from states. Unlike the "justificatory discourse" of states around their performance/non-performance of known and internalized obligations,[15] TM1 and TM2 lawyers were holding forth on legal principles that had seldom been addressed within the cyber CoP. The articulation of norms by the UN GGE and other multistakeholder initiatives flagged policy priorities for the Tallinn Manual lawyers. The entanglement of international law interpretation with norm-articulation gave the Tallinn team latitude to absorb policy and operational concerns from various corners of the cyber CoP, including from technical experts. As Chapter 4 demonstrates, the "managerial practices" of the Tallinn Manuals offer insight into how their law-ascertainment was closely linked with consultations with other actors in the CoP who were engaged in articulating norms. Notwithstanding the disagreements that several states have expressed with the Manuals' pronouncements, it is no exaggeration to say that both TM1 and TM2 have become critical references for legal discourse on international cybersecurity. Many states have offered their views on international law applicable to cyberspace that closely mirrors the framing of the

15 *See* Abram Chayes and Antonia Handler Chayes, *The New Sovereignty: Compliance with International Regulatory Agreements. The New Sovereignty* (Harvard University Press, 1998), https://doi.org/10.4159/9780674262638.

Tallinn Manuals. Their influence has arguably as much to do with their management of the cyber CoP – aided by the opening that the CoP's norms-law conflation provided – as with their legal pronouncements themselves.

The Oxford Process, being a more exploratory exercise to identify international law protections for cyberspace, arguably has had more latitude. The Process' explicit focus on specific themes and infrastructures – what it calls "objects of protection in international law" – is aligned with the approach of norms bodies, and is intrinsically geared towards policy purchase by actors in the cyber CoP. Yet, even in the Oxford Process meetings, there is ample evidence of tension among lawyers as to interpreting PIL for cybersecurity. There was no consensus on proscribing cyber-enabled espionage in certain cases within the group; lawyers could not agree whether "coordinated authentic behavior" would constitute coercion when supported by a state; and they could also not agree on a threshold of harm for the due diligence obligation vis-à-vis ransomware. Practices of the Oxford Process, such as systematic briefings by technical experts, certainly spurred robust debate within the group on these matters. Yet, international lawyers, even while engaged in an exercise whose objective is as much to identify international cybersecurity law as to advance it, can be conservative while addressing fragmentation issues.

In the final analysis, this book aims to contribute towards a new wave of scholarship that explores how legal argumentation is shaped by "socially shared cognitive processes".[16] For over two decades, legal scholars have honed in on Bourdieusian concepts, especially the notion of "fields" – characterized by structured relations, hierarchies, and the twin dynamics of competition and cooperation between legal professionals – to explain the emergence of specialized rules of international law or of specific judicial cultures and outcomes. These seminal works drew on the study of legal practices, to explain the "logic of the field" in different institutional/judicial settings or domains of global governance.[17] In contrast, concepts like the *habitus*, denoting the underlying core disposition(s) that generated and reified such practices, were "underused"[18] in legal scholarship (compared especially to works of IR). There is an intuitive and close connection between core dispositions and beliefs

16 Moshe Hirsch, "Sociological Analysis of International Law and the Cognitive Turn," in *International Legal Theory and the Cognitive Turn*, ed. Anne van Aaken and Moshe Hirsch (Oxford University Press, 2025), https://doi.org/10.1093/9780198909293.003.0010.

17 Yves Dezalay and Mikael Rask Madsen, "The Force of Law and Lawyers: Pierre Bourdieu and the Reflexive Sociology of Law," *Annual Review of Law and Social Science* 8, no. Volume 8, 2012 (2012): 433, https://doi.org/10.1146/annurev-lawsocsci-102811-173817.

18 Mikael Rask Madsen and Salvatore Caserta, "International Judicial Habitus: Pierre Bourdieu and the Cognitive Turn," in *International Legal Theory and the Cognitive Turn*, ed.

held by those within a community of practice and the socio-cognitive mechanisms that trigger it.[19] As communities of practice in global governance draw in a wider range of disciplines and stakeholders, the causal micro-processes that allow "extra-legal" practices to shape legal argumentation invite closer scrutiny. Indeed, the question that arises is whether practices can truly be classified as "extra-legal" in ad hoc or informal settings of global governance, where lawyers share space with technical experts and governance specialists to discuss frontier domains around which legal argumentation is itself new. Much will depend on experimental work that tests behavioral and cognitive science precepts – work that is already underway in some sections of international legal scholarship.[20]

But the preliminary evidence of the impact that a CoP's internalized beliefs can have on legal reasoning, as presented by this book, is sufficiently compelling to pursue such investigative avenues. Take specifically the impact that the cyber norms-international law articulation has had on legal professionals alone. Why did lawyers who were part of the GCSC's research advisory groups clarify the scope of non-binding norms using legal reasoning? Why did lawyers, including very distinguished legal experts in foreign ministries, refer to UN GGE reports as the UN's "*acquis*", when it is clear they don't bind states? Why do international lawyers agree to write law-like memos to commentaries of Paris Call reports? Evidence presented in these chapters suggests a level of tacit internalization of the cyber CoP's core view on how to advance cybersecurity governance. It is difficult to imagine today a corpus of rules called "international cybersecurity law" that makes no reference to negotiated norms, either in scope or substance, however obliquely. As the CoP's discussions shift from quasi-legal to strictly legal settings like the Tallinn Manual drafting or Oxford Process meetings, norms are not explicitly conflated with law. But the impact that norms have had in signaling states' priorities and desired levels of protection has meant even legal-interpretative exercises have borrowed their language or managed the process of law ascertainment like norms-articulation.

Anne van Aaken and Moshe Hirsch (Oxford University Press, 2025), 220 https://doi.org/10.1093/9780198909293.003.0011.

19 *See generally*, Quentin Bruneau, "Converging Paths: Bounded Rationality, Practice Theory and the Study of Change in Historical International Relations," *International Theory*, September 2020, 1–27, https://doi.org/10.1017/S1752971920000494.

20 *See generally*, Anne van Aaken and Tomer Broude, "From Economic to Behavioral Analysis of International Law: What Have We Learned So Far?," in *International Legal Theory and the Cognitive Turn*, ed. Anne van Aaken and Moshe Hirsch (Oxford University Press, 2025), https://doi.org/10.1093/9780198909293.003.0009.

It is also hoped that the pathways of "creeping expertise" studied in this book lend themselves to an accounting of the legitimacy concerns associated with expert involvement. Nine out of 19 technical experts interviewed for this book were based in the Global South, but that cannot be considered an indication of the overall state of North-South representation within the technical community involved in international cybersecurity governance. International lawyers, notably critical theorists, have powerfully framed the accountability and "deliberative" deficit in global governance settings that are exclusive, and rely increasingly on epistemic authority in decision making.[21] The challenge is compounded as IOs trend towards informality and ad hoc forums.[22] The question as to whether technical expertise itself is a proxy for strategic framing[23] of a cybersecurity problem by powerful states is entirely valid: we saw this in debates on technical attribution of cyber operations at the UN GGE. As Shires notes drawing on the rich IR scholarship on the politicization of expertise, cybersecurity expertise too tends to have a performative dimension, appealing via ritualized conferences and symposia to marketplaces for ideas, commerce, policy, and ultimately, power.[24] Whether such ritualization and competitive dynamic facilitates the co-opting of expertise for strategic and commercial gain is certainly a valid question. That begs the question, as Koskenniemi framed it several years ago: "does international cyber law exist at all?"[25] But even as we debate whether "technical idioms" have been co-opted by the grammar of commerce or strategy, we can be surer that technical vocabulary has "crept" into legal argumentation.

21 *See generally*, David Kennedy, *A World of Struggle: How Power, Law, and Expertise Shape Global Political Economy* (Princeton University Press, 2016); Michael Zürn, *A Theory of Global Governance: Authority, Legitimacy, and Contestation* (Oxford University Press, 2018); Fleur Johns, *Non-Legality in International Law: Unruly Law*, Cambridge Studies in International and Comparative Law (Cambridge University Press, 2013); Ian Johnstone, "Legislation and Adjudication in the UN Security Council: Bringing down the Deliberative Deficit," *The American Journal of International Law* (Washington, United Kingdom) 102, no. 2 (2008): 275–308; Galit Sarfaty, *Values in Translation: Human Rights and the Culture of the World Bank* (Stanford University Press, 2012).

22 Jan Klabbers, *The Normative Gap in International Organizations Law*, Brill, December 16, 2019, https://doi.org/10.1163/15723747-01602004.

23 Martti Koskenniemi, "The Politics of International Law – 20 Years Later," *European Journal of International Law* 20, no. 1 (2009): 7–19, https://doi.org/10.1093/ejil/chp006.

24 James Shires, "Enacting Expertise: Ritual and Risk in Cybersecurity," *Politics and Governance* 6, no. 2 (2018): 31–40.

25 *Prof. Martti Koskenniemi | International Cyber Law: Does It Exist and Do We Need It? (Full Lecture)*, directed by EU Cyber Direct, 2019, 43:39, https://www.youtube.com/watch?v=nh5FGswBImo.

APPENDIX 1

Interview Questionnaire 1 – Technical Experts

1. From the perspective of the GGE/OEWG or any other norm-setting institution, what is perhaps an issue that concerns you the most – given your area of technical expertise, interest or frequent professional engagement?
2. Have you interacted with an international lawyer, or a diplomat to discuss this concern or any technical concern related to cybersecurity? Could you briefly describe this interaction? (If you have done so several times, please describe your most recent, substantive interaction.) [Are you formally/informally involved in any norms making process?]
3. Is there an international lawyer whom you follow professionally, or whose work you know of? Would you recommend that I speak to one?
4. How would you evaluate public and private efforts in your country/region to bring together technical experts and international lawyers? What can be done to improve such interactions?

HTTPS://DOI.ORG/10.1163/9789004737617-009

APPENDIX 2

Interview Questionnaire 2 – International Lawyers

It may often be the case that a negotiator or lawyer learns about the technical dimensions of a hard problem they are trying to solve (e.g., attribution, countermeasures, or due diligence in cyberspace), which expands or constrains their view of how a specific cyber rule should be applied or interpreted. My book, driven by empirical assessment, examines whether lawyer-technical expert interactions contribute to such learning.

I was wondering if I could interview you in relation to this topic. The purpose of the interview would be two-fold:

- To have a broad and free-ranging conversation on your views regarding the application or interpretation of rules to cyberspace, and if/how they have evolved over the years; and
- To understand whether/how such views have been shaped by technical expertise. So far, my interviews suggest that technical experts, too, have begun to think in terms of legal thresholds in relation to cyber attacks, so the process of learning is a two-way street. I would, therefore, be interested in hearing about your engagements with the technical community generally.
- To what extent have various norms initiatives influenced your work as an international lawyer? How would you reflect on your role as a legal scholar vis-à-vis the articulation or implementation of these norms?
- Norms are often the product of political negotiations or, in multistakeholder formats, the preferred outcomes of vested interests. In your opinion, is there an ideal way to address the relationship between IL and norms? Or do you feel these processes in fact are *the* ideal way to help develop "international cyber law" as a body of rules?
- In relation to the [name of the process], could you please talk briefly about the processes of recruitment, deliberation, and external engagement with international lawyers as well as the larger "cyber" community? I am aware [the process] extensively consulted technical experts, so if you are at liberty to touch on that, I would be grateful.
- Thresholds: Many critical issues around the precise application of state responsibility and due diligence regimes to cyberspace revolve around thresholds. What is the threshold to satisfy attribution, of "serious, adverse consequences", significant transboundary harm, etc.? I would like to speak with you, if possible, about whether and how your interactions with technical experts may have influenced your views on some of these topics.

 | HTTPS://DOI.ORG/10.1163/9789004737617-010

APPENDIX 3

Interview Questionnaire 3 – Diplomats/Negotiators

My book examines whether technical experts influence how lawyers and negotiators identify and apply rules for cyberspace. It may often be the case that a diplomat or lawyer learns about the technical dimensions of a hard problem they are trying to solve (e.g., attribution, "proportionate" countermeasures, or "due diligence" in cyberspace), which expands or constrains their view of how a specific cyber rule should be applied or interpreted.

Since several institutional and *ad hoc* forums exist to discuss cyber norms, lawyers, diplomats, and technical experts have many opportunities to interact and exchange views – this could be on the margins of a conference, during a panel discussion, in formal negotiations, or even through Twitter exchanges! Part of my research therefore entails gathering data on the "everyday" aspects of cyber diplomacy, including such meetings.

I would be very grateful for an opportunity to interview you, as part of my research, on such common practices. To be sure, I am not really looking for "smoking gun" instances where technical experts have influenced your views on issues as a diplomat (if there are any, I would be grateful if you could share them!). I am hoping to speak with you about the practices of the UN GGE, and numerous other forums where you have been actively involved, to get your perspective on those discussions generally, and the role (if any) of technical experts. These would include not only norms processes but also regional consultations and capacity-building dialogues, which you have long been a part of.

Interviewees

Abdul-Hakeem Ajijola African Union Cyber Security Expert Group Abuja, Nigeria	Alexander Isavnin Russian Pirate Party Moscow, Russia
Alexandra Kulikova London, UK	Alissa Cooper IETF Chair (2017–2021), USA
Amandeep Gill UN Special Envoy on Technology Geneva, Switzerland	Amir Sagie Ministry of Foreign Affairs Israel
Anastasiya Kazakova Kaspersky Moscow, Russia	Annalaura Gallo APCO Worldwide
Anne-Marie Buzatu ICT4Peace Geneva, Switzerland	Bastiaan Goslings The Netherlands
Bill Woodcock Packet Clearing House Paris, France	Brett van Niekerk Durban University of Technology South Africa
Carmen Gonsalves Ministry of Foreign Affairs The Netherlands	Chris Doten National Democratic Institute USA
Chris Painter USA	Claudio Lucena Paraíba State University UEPB, Brazil
Cormac Callanan Aconite internet Solutions Dublin, Ireland	Dai Mochinaga Shibaura Institute of Technology Japan
Dan Efrony Hebrew University of Jerusalem Israel	Dan McBryde Ministry of Foreign Affairs Canada
Dennis Broeders Leiden University The Netherlands	Duncan Hollis Temple University USA

Elizabeth Tan
Cybersecurity Agency of Singapore
Singapore
Everton Rodrigues
NIC.Br
Brazil
Fredrik Hansen
London, UK

Guillherme Patriota
Ministry of Foreign Affairs
Brazil
Henri Verdier
Ministry of Foreign Affairs
France
Jeff Bedser
CleanDNS
USA
Joanna Kulesza
Lodz University
Poland
Joost Bunk
Ministry of Foreign Affairs
The Netherlands
Karsten Geier
Ministry of Foreign Affairs
Germany
Kerstin Vignard
Johns Hopkins University
USA
Kubo Macak
ICRC
Geneva, Switzerland
Leonid Todorov
APTLD.ru
Russia

Eneken Tikk
Meta
Helsinki
Francois Delerue
IE University
Spain
Gary Corn
American University
USA
Heli Tiirma-Klaar
Ministry of Foreign Affairs
Estonia
Horst Kremers
Berlin, Germany

Jim Lewis
CSIS
USA
Johanna Weaver
Ministry of Foreign Affairs
Australia
Kaja Ciglic
Microsoft
Slovenia
Kate Getao
Ministry of ICT
Kenya
Koichiro Komiyama
JPCERT
Japan
Lars Steffen
ECO International
Germany
Margaret Nyambura
GFA Consulting Group GmbH
Kenya

Mariana Salazar
OAS
Mexico

Marina Kaljurand
Tallinn, Estonia

Michael Schmitt
Reading University
UK

Michiel Steltman
DINL
The Netherlands

Motohiro Tsuchiya
Keio University
Japan

Nemanja Malisevic
Microsoft
Austria

Nnenna Ajufo
Swansea University
UK

Olaf Kolkman
ISOC
The Netherlands

Olga Cavalli
ISOC
Argentina

Przemyslaw Roguski
Jagiellonian University
Poland

Regine Grienberger
Ministry of Foreign Affairs
Germany

Rutger van Marissing
Ministry of Foreign Affairs
The Netherlands

Savvyo Vinicius
Instituto Federal do Rio
Grande do Norte

Serge Droz
FIRST
Geneva, Switzerland

Sherif Hashem
SUNY
New York

Sico van der Meer
Clingendael Institute
The Netherlands

Takeshi Akahori
Ministry of Foreign Affairs
Japan

Thomas Wingfield
RAND Corporation
USA

Toshiya Jitzusumi
Chuo University
Japan

Vittorio Bertola
Open X-change
Italy

Vrikson Acosta
Venezuela

Bibliography

"A Call to Cyber Norms: Discussions at the Harvard-MIT–University of Toronto Cyber Norms Workshops, 2011 and 2012," March 2015. https://www.americanbar.org/content/dam/aba/administrative/law_national_security/A_Call_to_Cyber_Norms.authcheckdam.pdf.

"A Policy Framework for an Open and Trusted internet." *internet Society*, June 2016, https://www.internetsociety.org/resources/doc/2016/policy-framework-for-an-open-and-trusted-internet/.

Aaken, Anne van, and Tomer Broude. "From Economic to Behavioral Analysis of International Law: What Have We Learned So Far?" In *International Legal Theory and the Cognitive Turn*, edited by Anne van Aaken and Moshe Hirsch. Oxford University Press, 2025. https://doi.org/10.1093/9780198909293.003.0009.

Aaken, Anne van, and Moshe Hirsch, eds. *International Legal Theory and the Cognitive Turn*. Oxford University Press, 2025. https://doi.org/10.1093/9780198909293.001.0001.

Aaken, Anne van, and Moshe Hirsch. "Introduction: International Legal Theory and the Cognitive Turn." In *International Legal Theory and the Cognitive Turn*, edited by Anne van Aaken and Moshe Hirsch. Oxford University Press, 2025. https://doi.org/10.1093/9780198909293.003.0001.

Aalberts, Tanja, and Ingo Venzke. "Moving beyond Interdisciplinary Turf Wars: Towards an Understanding of International Law as Practice." In *International Law as a Profession*, edited by Jean d'Aspremont, Tarcisio Gazzini, Andre Nollkaemper, and Wouter Werner, 287–310. Cambridge: Cambridge University Press, 2017. https://doi.org/10.1017/9781316492802.013.

Abbott, Kenneth W. "Hybrid Institutional Complexes in Global Governance." *The Review of International Organizations* 17, no. 2 (April 1): 263–291. https://doi.org/10.1007/s11558-021-09431-3.

Abbott, Kenneth W., and Benjamin Faude. "Choosing Low-Cost Institutions in Global Governance." *International Theory* 13, no. 3 (November 2021): 397–426. https://doi.org/10.1017/S1752971920000202.

Abbott, Kenneth W., Jessica F. Green, and Robert O. Keohane. "Organizational Ecology and Institutional Change in Global Governance." *International Organization* 70, no. 2 (2016): 247–277.

Abbott, Kenneth W., Robert O. Keohane, Andrew Moravcsik, Anne-Marie Slaughter, and Duncan Snidal. "The Concept of Legalization." *International Organization* 54, no. 3, (2000): 401–419. https://doi.org/10.1162/002081800551271.

Abbott, Kenneth W., and Duncan Snidal. "Law, Legalization, and Politics." In *Interdisciplinary Perspectives on International Law and International Relations: The State of the Art*, edited by Jeffrey L. Dunoff and Mark A. Pollack, 33–56. Cambridge: Cambridge University Press, 2012. https://doi.org/10.1017/CBO9781139107310.003.

Abdurashitov, Oleg. "The Collateral Damage of the World War Web." In Www.Kaspersky.Com, 2019. https://www.kaspersky.com/about/policy-blog/general-cybersecurity/the-collateral-damage-of-the-world-war-web.

"Accreditation: ICT OEWG Session 2. 'Forum of Incident Response and Security Teams (FIRST).pdf,' January 20, 2020. https://drive.google.com/file/d/1Rr7yjnDhl3-AbuQjPQtIweXiEGZGjCaQ/view?usp=drive_open&usp=embed_facebook.

"Accreditation: ICT OEWG Session 2. 'Rapid7.pdf,' January 23, 2020. https://drive.google.com/file/d/1fNoBtX_FtsVgzKI1txTkAomgR-Nsv5pD/view?usp=drive_open&usp=embed_facebook.

Acheson, Ray. "Presentation on Consensus, Political Will, Nuclear Disarmament, and the Conference on Disarmament." *Reaching Critical Will*, October 11, 2012. https://www.reachingcriticalwill.org/resources/statements/7062-presentation-on-consensus-political-will-nuclear-disarmament-and-the-conference-on-disarmament.

Acheson, Ray. "The CCW Is Still Standing, but to What End?" In *Reaching Critical Will*, 2019. https://reachingcriticalwill.org/disarmament-fora/ccw/2019/laws/ccwreport/14445-ccw-report-vol-7-no-8.

Adams, Michael J. "A Warning about Tallinn 2.0 … Whatever It Says," January 4, 2017. https://www.lawfareblog.com/warning-about-tallinn-20-%E2%80%A6-whatever-it-says.

"Additional Note to the Norm against Offensive Cyber Operations by Non-state Actors (Archived." In *Singapore: Global Commission on the Stability of Cyberspace*, 2022. https://web.archive.org/web/20220807221137/http://cyberstability.org/wp-content/uploads/2018/11/Additional-Note-to-the-Norm-Against-Offensive-Cyber-Operations-by-Non-state-Actors-Norm-Package-Singapore.pdf.

"Address by the President of the Republic of Estonia Kersti Kaljulaid at the General Debate of the 72nd United Nations General Assembly," September 19, 2017. https://gadebate.un.org/sites/default/files/gastatements/72/ee_en.pdf.

Adler, Emanuel. "Seeds of Peaceful Change: The OSCE's Security Community-Building Model." In *Security Communities*, edited by Emanuel Adler and Michael Barnett, 119–160. Cambridge: Cambridge University Press, 1998. https://doi.org/10.1017/CBO9780511598661.004.

Adler, Emanuel. *World Ordering: A Social Theory of Cognitive Evolution. Cambridge Studies in International Relations*. Cambridge: Cambridge University Press, 2019. https://doi.org/10.1017/9781108325615.005.

Adler, Emanuel, and Michael Barnett. "A Framework for the Study of Security Communities." In *Security Communities*, edited by Emanuel Adler and Michael Barnett, 29–66. Cambridge: Cambridge University Press, 1998. https://doi.org/10.1017/CBO9780511598661.002.

Adler, Emanuel, and Vincent Pouliot. "International Practices." In *International Practices*, edited by Emanuel Adler and Vincent Pouliot, 3–35. Cambridge Studies in International Relations. Cambridge: Cambridge University Press, 2011. https://doi.org/10.1017/CBO9780511862373.003.

Adler, Emanuel, Niklas Bremberg, and Maïka Sondarjee. "Communities of Practice in World Politics: Advancing a Research Agenda." *Global Studies Quarterly* 4, no. 1 (2024): ksad070. https://doi.org/10.1093/isagsq/ksad070.

Adler-Nissen, Rebecca. *Opting Out of the European Union: Diplomacy, Sovereignty and European Integration.* Cambridge: Cambridge University Press, 2014. https://doi.org/10.1017/CBO9781107337916.001.

Adler-Nissen, Rebecca, and Alena Drieschova. "Track-Change Diplomacy: Technology, Affordances, and the Practice of International Negotiations." *International Studies Quarterly* 63, no. 3 (September 1): 531–545. https://doi.org/10.1093/isq/sqz030.

"Advancing Cyberstability – Final Report | Global Commission on the Stability of Cyberspace." *The Hague Centre for Strategic Studies and East-West Institute*, November 2019. https://hcss.nl/wp-content/uploads/2019/11/GCSC-Final-Report-November-2019.pdf.

"Advancing Cyberstability Final Report Fact Sheet." In *Global Commission on the Stability of Cyberspace*, 2019. https://hcss.nl/wp-content/uploads/2022/08/GCSC-Fact-Sheet.pdf.

"Advancing International Cyber Norms: Multistakeholder Recommendations," Accessed March 10, 2023 https://pariscall.international/assets/files/WG4-Final-Report-101121.pdf.

"Advancing Responsible State Behavior in Cyberspace in the Context of International Security." In *UN General Assembly, Seventy-Third Session*, 2019. https://doi.org/10.18356/9789210021753c001.

"Agreement between the Governments of the Member States of the Shanghai Cooperation Organization on Cooperation in the Field of International Information Security." In *Shanghai Cooperation Organization, 61st Plenary Meeting*, 2009. https://ccdcoe.org/uploads/2018/10/SCO-090616-IISAgreement.pdf.

"Akamai Blog | internet Resilience, Part 2: What It Takes to 'Just Work,'" Accessed March 10, 2023 https://www.akamai.com/blog/performance/internet-resilience-part2-what-it-takes-to-just-work.

Akami, Tomoko. "A Quest to Be Global: The League of Nations Health Organization and Inter-colonial Regional Governing Agendas of the Far Eastern Association of Tropical Medicine 1910–1925." *The International History Review* 38, no. 1 (January 1, 2016): 1–23. https://doi.org/10.1080/07075332.2015.1018302.

Akami, Tomoko. "Imperial Polities, Intercolonialism, and the Shaping of Global Governing Norms: Public Health Expert Networks in Asia and the League of Nations Health Organization, 1908–1937." *Journal of Global History* 12, no. 1 (March 2017): 4–25. https://doi.org/10.1017/S1740022816000310.

Akande, Dapo, Antonio Coco, and Talita Souza Dias. "Drawing the Cyber Baseline: The Applicability of Existing International Law to the Governance of Information and Communication Technologies." *International Law Studies* 99, no. 1 (February 3, 2022). https://digital-commons.usnwc.edu/ils/vol99/iss1/2.

Akande, Dapo, Antonio Coco, and Talita Souza Dias. "The Second Oxford Statement on International Law Protections of the Healthcare Sector during COVID-19: Safeguarding Vaccine Research." *EJIL: Talk!*, August 11, 2020. https://www.ejiltalk.org/the-second-oxford-statement-on-international-law-protections-of-the-healthcare-sector-during-covid-19-safeguarding-vaccine-research/.

Alter, Karen J. "The International Court of Justice in Comparison: Understanding the Court's Limited Influence." *Melbourne Journal of International Law* 21, no. 3 (January 2021): 676–697. https://doi.org/10.3316/informit.243545899752250.

Alter, Karen J. "The Promise and Perils of Theorizing International Regime Complexity in an Evolving World." *The Review of International Organizations* 17, no. 2 (2022): 375–396. https://doi.org/10.1007/s11558-021-09448-8.

Alter, Karen J., and Kal Raustiala. "The Rise of International Regime Complexity." *Annual Review of Law and Social Science* 14, (2018): 329–349. https://doi.org/10.1146/annurev-lawsocsci-101317-030830.

Alter, Karen J., Laurence R. Helfer, and Mikael Rask Madsen. "How Context Shapes the Authority of International Courts." *Law and Contemporary Problems* 79, no. 1 (2016): 1–36.

Amazon Web Services, Inc. "What Is Cloud Computing," https://aws.amazon.com/what-is-cloud-computing/.

Amstel, Nelleke, and Tilman Rodenhäuser. "The Montreux Document and the International Code of Conduct: Understanding the Relationship between International Initiatives to Regulate the Global Private Security Industry." In *Public Private Partnerships Series*. Geneva: DCAF, 2016. https://www.dcaf.ch/sites/default/files/publications/documents/DCAF_PPPs_Series_Paper_The_MD_and_ICoC_Understanding_the_Relationship.pdf.

Anghie, Antony. *Imperialism, Sovereignty and the Making of International Law*. 1st ed. Cambridge University Press, 2005. https://doi.org/10.1017/CBO9780511614262.

Anghie, Antony. "Western Discourses of Sovereignty." In *Sovereignty*, edited by Julie Evans, Ann Genovese, Alexander Reilly, and Patrick Wolfe, 19–36. Frontiers of Possibility. University of Hawai'i Press, 2013. http://www.jstor.org/stable/j.ctt6wqd3c.5.

Arangio-Ruiz, Gaetano. "Fifth Report on State Responsibility (Extract from the Yearbook of the International Law Commission." *International Law Commission*, 1993. https://legal.un.org/ilc/documentation/english/a_cn4_453.pdf.

Arimatsu, Louise. "A Treaty for Governing Cyber-Weapons: Potential Benefits and Practical Limitations." In *2012 4th International Conference on Cyber Conflict*, edited by C. Czosseck, K. Ziolkowski, and R. Ottis, 2012.

"ASEAN Cyber Capacity Development Project," Accessed March 10, 2023 https://www.interpol.int/en/Crimes/Cybercrime/Cyber-capabilities-development/ASEAN-Cyber-Capacity-Development-Project.

Atkinson, Will. "Bourdieu and Schutz." In *The Oxford Handbook of Pierre Bourdieu*, 2018. https://doi.org/10.1093/oxfordhb/9780199357192.013.17.

"Australia's Comments on the Initial 'Pre-draft' of the Report of the UN Open Ended Working Group in the Field of Information and Telecommunications in the Context of International Security (OEWG." *Aril*, 2020. https://www.internationalcybertech.gov.au/sites/default/files/2020-11/australias-response-to-the-oewg-pre-draft-report-april-2020.pdf.

"Australia's International Cyber Engagement Strategy." *Australian Government*, October 2017. https://www.internationalcybertech.gov.au/sites/default/files/2020-11/The%20Strategy.pdf.

Australian Government "Annex B: Australia's Position on How International Law Applies to State Conduct in Cyberspace | Australia's International Cyber and Critical Tech Engagement," Accessed March 10, 2023 https://www.internationalcybertech.gov.au/our-work/annexes/annex-b.

Autesserre, Séverine. *Peaceland: Conflict Resolution and the Everyday Politics of International Intervention. Problems of International Politics*. Cambridge: Cambridge University Press, 2014. https://doi.org/10.1017/CBO9781107280366.

Baldwin, John, and Gwynn Davis. "Empirical Research in Law." In *The Oxford Handbook of Legal Studies*, 2005. https://doi.org/10.1093/oxfordhb/9780199248179.013.0039.

Ballard, A.J. "The League of Nations and Public Health." Ph.D., University of Southern California, 1941. http://search.proquest.com/docview/1646485621/abstract/A343688F34C24F45PQ/1.

Barnett, Michael. *Eyewitness to a Genocide: The United Nations and Rwanda*. Cornell University Press, 2003.

Barton, John H., Judith L. Goldstein, Timothy E. Josling, and Richard H. Steinberg. "The Politics of the GATT/WTO Legal System: Legislative and Judicial Processes." In *The Evolution of the Trade Regime, 61–90. Politics, Law, and Economics of the GATT and the WTO.* Princeton University Press, 2006. https://doi.org/10.2307/j.ctt7t1bb.7.

Baumgärtel, Moritz. "'Part of the Game': Government Strategies against European Litigation Concerning Migrant Rights." In *The Changing Practices of International Law*, edited by Tanja Aalberts and Thomas Gammeltoft-Hansen, 103–128. Cambridge: Cambridge University Press, 2018. https://doi.org/10.1017/9781108349420.006.

Bendiek, Annegret, and Matthias Schulze. "Attribution: A Major Challenge for EU Cyber Sanctions." In *SWP Research Paper 2021.* Berlin: Stiftung Wissenschaft und Politik (SWP, 2021). https://www.swp-berlin.org/en/publication/attribution-a-major-challenge-for-eu-cyber-sanctions.

Bennett, Andrew, and Jeffrey T. Checkel. "Process Tracing." In *Process Tracing*, edited by Andrew Bennett and Jeffrey T. Checkel, 3–38. Cambridge: Cambridge University Press, 2014. https://doi.org/10.1017/CBO9781139858472.003.

Benzecry, Claudio E. "Habitus and Beyond: Standing on the Shoulders of a Giant Looking at the Seams." In *The Oxford Handbook of Pierre Bourdieu*, edited by Thomas Medvetz and Jeffrey J. Sallaz. Oxford: Oxford University Press, 2018. https://academic.oup.com/edited-volume/28103/chapter/212231522.

Besson, Samantha. "Sovereignty." Oxford Public International Law, April 2011. http://opil.ouplaw.com/view/10.1093/law:epil/9780199231690/law-9780199231690-e1472.

Besson, Samantha, and Jean D'Aspremont. "The Sources of International Law: An Introduction." In *The Oxford Handbook of the Sources of International Law*, edited by Jean d'Aspremont and Samantha Besson. Oxford: Oxford University Press, 2018. https://academic.oup.com/edited-volume/41302/chapter/352052586.

Bevir, Mark. "Adhocracy." In *Encyclopedia of Governance*, 9–10. Thousand Oaks: SAGE Publications, Inc, 2007. https://doi.org/10.4135/9781412952613.

Beyer, Christian. "Edmund Husserl." In *The Stanford Encyclopedia of Philosophy*, edited by Edward N. Zalta. Metaphysics Research Lab, Stanford University, 2020. https://plato.stanford.edu/archives/win2020/entries/husserl/.

Bianchi, Andrea. "Epistemic Communities." In *Concepts for International Law*, edited by Jean d'Aspremont and Sahib Singh, 251–66. Edward Elgar Publishing, 2019. https://www.elgaronline.com/view/edcoll/9781783474677/9781783474677.00022.xml.

Bodansky, Daniel, and Harro van Asselt. "Who's Who in the Legal Process: Actors beyond the State." In *The Art and Craft of International Environmental Law*, edited by Daniel Bodansky and Harro van Asselt. Oxford University Press, 2024. https://doi.org/10.1093/oso/9780197672365.003.0007.

Bode, Ingvild. "Reflective Practices at the Security Council: Children and Armed Conflict and the Three United Nations." *European Journal of International Relations* 24, no. 2 (June 1): 293–318. https://doi.org/10.1177/1354066117714529.

Boer, Lianne J.M. *International Law As We Know It: Cyberwar Discourse and the Construction of Knowledge in International Legal Scholarship*. 1st ed. Cambridge University Press, 2021. https://doi.org/10.1017/9781108676564.

Boer, Lianne J.M. "Restating the Law as It Is: On the Tallinn Manual and the Use of Force in Cyberspace." *Amsterdam Law Forum* 5, no. 3 (2013): 4–18.

Bohman, James, and William Rehg. "Jürgen Habermas." In *The Stanford Encyclopedia of Philosophy*, edited by Edward N. Zalta. Metaphysics Research Lab, Stanford University, 2017. https://plato.stanford.edu/archives/fall2017/entries/habermas/.

Bonneuil, Christophe and Levidow. "How Does the World Trade Organization Know? The Mobilization and Staging of Scientific Expertise in the GMO Trade Dispute." *Social Studies of Science* 42, no. 1 (2012): 75–100.

"Book Reviews and Notes." *American Journal of International Law* 20, no. 1 (1926): 207–229.

Borowy, Iris. *Coming to Terms with World Health: The League of Nations Health Organisation 1921–1946*. Peter Lang, 2009.

Bourdieu, Pierre. *In Other Words: Essays Towards a Reflexive Sociology*. Stanford University Press, 1990.

Bourdieu, Pierre. *Outline of a Theory of Practice*. Translated by Richard Nice. Cambridge: Cambridge University Press, 1977. https://doi.org/10.1017/CBO9780511812507.004.

Bourdieu, Pierre. "Some Properties of Fields." In *Media Studies*, edited by Sue Thornham, Caroline Bassett, and Paul Marris, 94–99. A Reader. Edinburgh University Press, 2009. http://www.jstor.org/stable/10.3366/j.ctvxcrv1h.14.

Bourdieu, Pierre. "The Force of Law: Toward a Sociology of the Juridical Field Essay." Translated by Richard Terdiman. *Hastings Law Journal* 38, no. 5 (1987): 805–813.

Bourdieu, Pierre. *The Logic of Practice*. Stanford University Press, 1990.

Brewer, John. *Ethnography*. McGraw-Hill Education (UK, 2000).

Broeders, Dennis. "Aligning the International Protection of 'the Public Core of the internet' with State Sovereignty and National Security." *Journal of Cyber Policy* 2, no. 3 (September 2, 2017): 366–376. https://doi.org/10.1080/23738871.2017.1403640.

Broeders, Dennis. "Private Active Cyber Defense and (International) Cyber Security – Pushing the Line?" *Journal of Cybersecurity* 7, no. 1 (January 1, 2021): 010. https://doi.org/10.1093/cybsec/tyab010.

Broeders, Dennis. "The Public Core of the internet: An International Agenda for internet Governance." In *The Hague: The Netherlands Scientific Council for Government*

Policy (*WRR*), 2015. https://english.wrr.nl/binaries/wrr-eng/documenten/reports/2015/10/01/the-public-core-of-the-internet/R094e-Public-core-internet.pdf.

Broeders, Dennis, and Fabio Cristiano. “Cyber Norms and the United Nations: Between Strategic Ambiguity and Rules of the Road.” *SSRN Electronic Journal*, 2020. https://doi.org/10.2139/ssrn.3819171.

Broude, Tomer. “Keep Calm and Carry on: Martti Koskenniemi and the Fragmentation of International Law” *Temple International & Comparative Law Journal* 27, no. 2 (2013): 279–292.

Broude, Tomer, and Yahli Shereshevsky. “Explaining the Practical Purchase of Soft Law: Competing and Complementary Behavior Hypotheses.” In *International Law as Behavior*, edited by Harlan Grant Cohen and Timothy Meyer. Cambridge: Cambridge University Press, 2021. https://doi.org/10.1017/9781316979792.005.

Brownlie, Ian. “To What Extent Are the Traditional Categories of Lex Lata and Lex Ferenda Still Viable.” In *Change and Stability in International Law-Making*, edited by Antonio Cassese and Joseph H.H. Weiler, 1st ed., 66–72. Berlin: Walter de Gruyter, 1988.

Bruneau, Quentin. “Converging Paths: Bounded Rationality, Practice Theory and the Study of Change in Historical International Relations.” *International Theory*, September 2020, 1–27. https://doi.org/10.1017/S1752971920000494.

Brunnée, Jutta, and Stephen J. Toope, eds. “Shared Understandings.” In *Legitimacy and Legality in International Law: An Interactional Account, 56–87. Cambridge Studies in International and Comparative Law*. Cambridge: Cambridge University Press, 2010. https://doi.org/10.1017/CBO9780511781261.004.

Brutger, Ryan, and Julia C. Morse. “Balancing Law and Politics: Judicial Incentives in WTO Dispute Settlement.” *The Review of International Organizations* 10, no. 2 (June 2015): 179–205. https://doi.org/10.1007/s11558-015-9216-x.

Buchan, Russell. “Cyberspace, Non-state Actors and the Obligation to Prevent Transboundary Harm.” *Journal of Conflict and Security Law* 21, no. 3 (December 2016): 429–53. https://doi.org/10.1093/jcsl/krw011.

Bueger, Christian. “Experimenting with Global Governance: Learning Lessons in the Contact Group on Piracy.” In *Knowing Governance*, edited by Jan-Peter Voß and Richard Freeman, 87–105. London: Palgrave Macmillan UK, 2016. https://doi.org/10.1057/9781137514509.

Bueger, Christian. “Territory, Authority, Expertise: Global Governance and the Counter-Piracy Assemblage.” *European Journal of International Relations* 24, no. 3 (September 1): 614–37. https://doi.org/10.1177/1354066117725155.

Burci, Gian Luca. “Global Health.” In *The Cambridge Companion to International Organizations Law*, edited by Jan Klabbers. Cambridge Companions to Law. Cambridge University Press, 2022. https://doi.org/10.1017/9781108574242.013.

Cannizzaro, E. "The Role of Proportionality in the Law of International Countermeasures." *European Journal of International Law* 12, no. 5 (December 1, 2001): 889–916. https://doi.org/10.1093/ejil/12.5.889.

Cardenas, Fabian, and Jean d'Aspremont. "Epistemic Communities in International Adjudication." Oxford Public International Law, April 2020. https://doi.org/10.1093/law-mpeipro/e2425.013.2425.

Caserta, Salvatore, and Mikael Rask Madsen. "The Situated and Bounded Rationality of International Courts: A Structuralist Approach to International Adjudicative Practices." *Leiden Journal of International Law* 35, no. 4 (December 2022): 931–43. https://doi.org/10.1017/S0922156522000486.

Caserta, Salvatore, and Mikael Rask Madsen. "Between Community Law and Common Law: The Rise of the Caribbean Court of Justice at the Intersection of Regional Integration and Post-colonial Legacies." *Law and Contemporary Problems* 79, no. 1 (2016): 89–115.

"Chair's Summary," Accessed March 10, 2023 https://front.un-arm.org/wp-content/uploads/2021/03/Chairs-Summary-A-AC.290-2021-CRP.3-technical-reissue.pdf.

"Chair's Summary." Open-Ended Working Group on Developments in the Field of Information and Telecommunications in the Context of International Security." *Third Substantive Session*, March 10, 2021. https://front.un-arm.org/wp-content/uploads/2021/03/Chairs-Summary-A-AC.290-2021-CRP.3-technical-reissue.pdf.

Charmaz, Kathy. *Constructing Grounded Theory*. 1st ed. SAGE, 2006.

Charmaz, Kathy. "Constructionism and the Grounded Theory Method." In *Handbook of Constructionist Research*, edited by James A. Holstein and Jaber F. Gubrium, 397–410. Guilford Press, 2008.

Charmaz, Kathy. "Constructivist Grounded Theory." *The Journal of Positive Psychology* 12, no. 3 (May 4, 2017): 299–300. https://doi.org/10.1080/17439760.2016.1262612.

Chayes, Abram, and Antonia Handler Chayes. *The New Sovereignty: Compliance with International Regulatory Agreements*. Harvard University Press, 1998.

Checkel, Jeffrey T. "Methods in Constructivist Approaches." In *The Oxford Handbook of International Security*. Oxford University Press, 2018. https://doi.org/10.1093/oxfordhb/9780198777854.013.11.

Checkel, Jeffrey T. "Process Tracing and International Political Economy." In *The Oxford Handbook of International Political Economy*, edited by Jon C.W. Pevehouse and Leonard Seabrooke, 0. Oxford University Press, 2021. https://doi.org/10.1093/oxfordhb/9780198793519.013.47.

"China's Contribution to the Initial Pre-draft of OEWG Report," Accessed March 10, 2023 https://ceipfiles.s3.amazonaws.com/pdf/CyberNorms/UNGGE/China%E2%80%99s±Contribution±to±the±Initial±Pre-Draft±of±OEWG±Report.pdf.

"China's Contribution to the Initial Pre-draft of OEWG Report," April, 2020. https://front.un-arm.org/wp-content/uploads/2020/04/china-contribution-to-oewg-pre-draft-report-final.pdf.

Chircop, Luke. "A Due Diligence Standard of Attribution in Cyberspace." *International & Comparative Law Quarterly* 67, no. 3 (July 2018): 643–68. https://doi.org/10.1017/S0020589318000015.

Chircop, Luke. "Territorial Sovereignty in Cyberspace after Tallinn Manual 2.0." *Melbourne Journal of International Law* 20, no. 2 (2019): 349.

Christoforou, Theofanis. "Settlement of Science-Based Trade Disputes in the WTO: A Critical Review of the Developing Case Law in the Face of Scientific Uncertainty." *New York University Environmental Law Journal* 8 (2000): 622.

"Chronological Index of Treaties Index." League of Nations Treaty Series Index, 1926.

Chugunov, Igor. "Article by Andrei Krutskikh, Special Presidential Representative for International Cooperation in Information Security, Published in the Kommersant Business Daily on March 27, 2019," Accessed March 10, 2023 https://thailand.mid.ru/en/key-issues/5399-statya-spetspredstavitelya-prezidenta-rossijskoj-federatsii-po-voprosam-mezhdunarodnogo-sotrudnichestva-v-oblasti-informatsionnoj-bezopasnosti-posla-po-osobym-porucheniyam-mid-rossii-a-v-krutskikh-opublikovannaya-v-gazete-kommersant-27-marta-2019-goda-2.

Coco, Antonio, and Talita Souza Dias. "'Cyber Due Diligence': A Patchwork of Protective Obligations in International Law." *European Journal of International Law* 32, no. 3 (August 1): 771–806. https://doi.org/10.1093/ejil/chab056.

Coco, Antonio, Talita Souza Dias, and Tsvetelina Benthem. "Dust in the (Solar)Winds: Was It 'Just." In *Espionage or Does International Law Have More to Say on the Protection of IT Supply Chains?" The Oxford Process on International Law Protections in Cyberspace*, 2021. https://www.elac.ox.ac.uk/wp-content/uploads/2022/10/Oxford-Process-Compendium-Digital.pdf.

"Coding | Key Concepts in Ethnography – Credo Reference," Accessed March 10, 2023 https://access.infobase.com/article/1181701-coding?aid=99224.

Cohen, Harlan G. "Finding International Law, Part II: Our Fragmenting Legal Community," 2011.

Cohn, Carol. "Motives and Methods: Using Multi-Sited Ethnography to Study US National Security Discourses." In *Feminist Methodologies for International Relations*, edited by Brooke A. Ackerly, Maria Stern, and Jacqui True. Cambridge University Press, 2006.

Colatin, Tomas and Samuele. "A Surprising Turn of Events: UN Creates Two Working Groups on Cyberspace." In *NATO CCDCOE* (*Blog*, Accessed March 10, 2023 https://ccdcoe.org/incyder-articles/a-surprising-turn-of-events-un-creates-two-working-groups-on-cyberspace/.

Collins, Richard. "The League of Nations and the Emergence of International Administration: Finding the Origins of International Institutional Law." *Revista Española de Derecho Internacional* 71, no. 2 (2019): 285–294.

Collins, Richard, and Alexandra Bohm. "International Law as Professional Practice: Crafting the Autonomy of International Law." In *International Law as a Profession*, edited by Jean d'Aspremont, Tarcisio Gazzini, Andre Nollkaemper, and Wouter Werner, 67–92. Cambridge: Cambridge University Press, 2017. https://doi.org/10.1017/9781316492802.005.

"Comments Submitted by Brazil to the Initial 'Pre-draft' of the Report of the OEWG on Developments in the Field of Information and Telecommunications in the Context of International Security," April 8, 2020. https://front.un-arm.org/wp-content/uploads/2020/04/comments-by-brazil-on-the-pre-draft-report-of-cyber-oewg-8-apr-2020.pdf.

"Contribution by the Russian Federation RISK ANALYSIS OF THE EXISTING INTERNET GOVERNANCE AND OPERATIONAL MODEL." In *ITU Council Working Group on International internet-Related Public Policy Issues*, 2021. https://www.itu.int/md/S21-RCLINTPOL16-C-0004/en.

Cook, Graham. *A Digest of WTO Jurisprudence on Public International Law Concepts and Principles*. Cambridge: Cambridge University Press, 2015. https://doi.org/10.1017/CBO9781316212691.

Corbin, Juliet. "Grounded Theory." *The Journal of Positive Psychology* 12, no. 3 (May 4, 2017): 301–302. https://doi.org/10.1080/17439760.2016.1262614.

Cornut, Jérémie. "The Practice Turn in International Relations Theory." In *The International Studies Encyclopedia*. Wiley-Blackwell, 2017. https://www.oxfordreference.com/display/10.1093/acref/9780191842665.001.0001/acref-9780191842665-e-0456.

Cornut, Jérémie, and Nicolas Zamaróczy. "How Can Documents Speak about Practices? Practice Tracing, the Wikileaks Cables, and Diplomatic Culture." *Cooperation and Conflict* 56, no. 3 (September 1): 328–345. https://doi.org/10.1177/0010836720972426.

"Country Focus Report Update: Russian Federation internet-Related Laws and UN Deliberations." *ICANN*, June 6, 2022. https://itp.cdn.icann.org/en/files/government-engagement-ge/ge-011-06-06-2022-en.pdf.

Cowan, Jane K. "'The Feeling of Pursuing an Ideal': A League of Nations Civil Servant Reflects on His Work." *Social Anthropology* 28, no. 1 (2020): 17–34. https://doi.org/10.1111/1469-8676.12744.

Cowan, Jane K. "Who's Afraid of Violent Language?: Honor, Sovereignty and Claims-Making in the League of Nations." *Anthropological Theory* 3, no. 3 (September 1): 271–291. https://doi.org/10.1177/14634996030033002.

Craven, Matthew. “Theorizing the Turn to History in International Law.” In *The Oxford Handbook of the Theory of International Law*, 2016. https://doi.org/10.1093/law/9780198701958.003.0002.

Crawford, James R. “Responsibility to the International Community as a Whole.” *Indiana Journal of Global Legal Studies* 8 (2001).

Creemers, Rogier. *China's Approach to Cyber Sovereignty*. Berlin: Konrad-Adenauer-Stiftung, 2020. https://www.kas.de/documents/252038/7995358/China%E2%80%99s±Approach±to±Cyber±Sovereignty.pdf/2c6916a6-164c-fb0c-4e29-f933f472ac3f?version=1.0&t=1606143361537.

Crootof, Rebecca. “International Cybertorts: Expanding State Accountability in Cyberspace.” *Cornell Law Review* 103, no. 3 (2018): 565–644.

Cussó, Roser. “Building a Global Representation of Trade through International Quantification: The League of Nations' Unification of Methods in Economic Statistics.” *The International History Review* 42, no. 4 (July 3): 714–36. https://doi.org/10.1080/07075332.2019.1619611.

Cussó, Roser. “La défaite de la sdn face aux nationalismes des majorités : la Section des minorités et l'irrecevabilité des pétitions « hors traité ».” *Études internationales* 44, no. 1 (2013): 65–88. https://doi.org/10.7202/1015123ar.

“Cyber Operations Tracker | Council on Foreign Relations. “Denial of Service Attacks against U.S. Banks in 2012–2013,” Accessed March 10, 2023 https://www.cfr.org/cyber-operations/denial-service-attacks-against-us-banks-2012-2013.

“Cyber Peace & Security Monitor,” Accessed March 10, 2023 https://reachingcritical will.org/disarmament-fora/ict/oewg/cyber-monitor/15214-cyber-peace-security-monitor-vol-1-no-10.

“Cyber-Attacks: Council Extends Sanctions Regime until 18 May 2025,” Accessed March 10, 2023 https://www.consilium.europa.eu/en/press/press-releases/2022/05/16/cyber-attacks-council-extends-sanctions-regime-until-18-may-2025/.

CyberScoop. “U.S. Can Respond to Cyberattacks without Showing Proof First, Legal Expert Says.” *January* 11 (2017). https://cyberscoop.com/us-evidence-proof-on-hacking/.

Cybersecurity, and Infrastructure Security Agency. “Iranian State Actors Conduct Cyber Operations against the Government of Albania | CISA.” *September* 21 (2022). https://www.cisa.gov/uscert/ncas/alerts/aa22-264a.

Cybersecurity Tech Accord. “A Statement on the Programme of Action: A Standing UN Body to Uphold International Expectations Is the Best Hope for Stability in Cyberspace.” *October* 18 (2021). https://cybertechaccord.org/a-statement-on-the-programme-of-action-a-standing-un-body-to-uphold-international-expectations-is-the-best-hope-for-stability-in-cyberspace/.

Cybersecurity Tech Accord. “Cybersecurity Tech Accord,” https://cybertechaccord.org/accord/.

Cybersecurity Tech Accord. "Paris Call for Trust and Security in Cyberspace: Six Working Groups Launched to Advance Global Cybersecurity," March 1, 2021. https://cybertechaccord.org/paris-call-for-trust-and-security-in-cyberspace-six-working-groups-launched-to-advance-global-cybersecurity/.

Cyberspace, Global Commission. "Call to Protect the Public Core of the internet – GCSC," November 21, 2017. https://web.archive.org/web/20220404013743/https://cyberstability.org/research/call-to-protect/.

"Cyberwarfare and International Humanitarian Law: The ICRC's Position." In *International Committee of the Red Cross (ICRC)*, 2013. https://www.icrc.org/en/doc/assets/files/2013/130621-cyberwarfare-q-and-a-eng.pdf.

"Cybil Portal," September 27, 2022 https://cybilportal.org/projects/?_sft_themes=international-law-in-cyberspace.

CyCon 2012 | Michael Schmitt: Tallinn Manual Part I," 2012. https://www.youtube.com/watch?v=wY3uEo-Itso.

CyCon. "DAY 1 Keynote by Johanna Weaver," 2022. https://www.youtube.com/watch?v=O8eFiJaNzRU.

d'Aspremont, Jean. "The Professionalization of International Law." In *International Law as a Profession*, edited by André Nollkaemper, Jean d'Aspremont, Tarcisio Gazzini, and Wouter Werner, 19–37. Cambridge: Cambridge University Press, 2017. https://doi.org/10.1017/9781316492802.003.

d'Aspremont, Jean, and Makane Moïse Mbengue. "Strategies of Engagement with Scientific Fact-Finding in International Adjudication." *Journal of International Dispute Settlement* 5, no. 2 (2014): 240–272. https://doi.org/10.1093/jnlids/idu004.

D.A.R.T.-Information. "Journal Editors Statement (JETS," 2014. https://www.dartstatement.org/2014-journal-editors-statement-jets.

"Data Integrity – Glossary | CSRC." In *NIST Computer Security Resource Center*, Accessed April 8, 2023 https://csrc.nist.gov/glossary/term/data_integrity.

Datysgeld, Mark. "Is There Such a Thing as Technical internet Governance?" *CircleID*, September 2, 2020. https://circleid.com/posts/20200902-is-there-such-a-thing-as-technical-internet-governance.

de Traz, Robert. "L'Esprit de Genève." *Journal of the Royal Institute of International Affairs* 8, no. 6 (1929): 637. https://doi.org/10.2307/3015688.

"DECISION No. 5/17 Enhancing OSCE Efforts to Reduce the Risks of Conflict Stemming from the Use of Information and Communication Technologies." In *Ministerial Council Decision. Vienna: Organization for Security and Co-Operation in Europe*, 2017. https://www.osce.org/files/f/documents/9/f/361561.pdf.

"Declaration on Principles of International Law Concerning Friendly Relations and Cooperation among States in Accordance with the Charter of the United Nations." *UN General Assembly, Twenty-Fifth Session*, 1970. https://digitallibrary.un.org/record/202170.

Deeks, Ashley. "Tallinn 2.0 and a Chinese View on the Tallinn Process." *Lawfare (Blog), May* 31 (2015). https://www.lawfareblog.com/tallinn-20-and-chinese-view-tallinn-process.

Deer, Cécile. "Doxa." In *Pierre Bourdieu: Key Concepts*, edited by Michael Grenfell, 119–130. Acumen Publishing, 2008. https://doi.org/10.1017/UPO9781844654031.011.

"Definition of the Public Core, to Which the Norm Applies." In *Bratislava: Global Commission on the Stability of Cyberspace*, 2018. https://hcss.nl/wp-content/uploads/2022/08/Definition-of-the-Public-Core-of-the-internet.pdf.

"Delegates Propose New Programme of Action for Struggle against Threats to Cybersecurity, in First Committee Thematic Debate | UN Press," Accessed April 8, 2023 https://press.un.org/en/2021/gadis3673.doc.htm.

Delerue, François. *Cyber Operations and International Law*. 1st ed. Cambridge University Press, 2020. https://doi.org/10.1017/9781108780605.

Delerue, François, Frédérick Douzet, and Aude Géry. "The Geopolitical Representations of International Law in the International Negotiations on the Security and Stability of Cyberspace," 2017.

DENIC internet Governance Radar. "Q3/2021 – International Telecommunication Union (ITU," 2021. https://internet-governance-radar.de/aktuelles/blogpost/q3-2021-international-telecommunication-union-itu.

Dev, Priyanka R. "Use of Force and Armed Attack Thresholds in Cyber Conflict: The Looming Definitional Gaps and the Growing Need for Formal U.N. Response Notes." *Texas International Law Journal* 50, no. 2–3 (2016): 381–402.

"Developments in the Field of Information and Telecommunications in the Context of International Security." *UN General Assembly, Sixty-Eighth Session*, January 9, 2014. https://doi.org/10.18356/9789210021753c001.

"Developments in the Field of Information and Telecommunications in the Context of International Security." In *UN General Assembly, Seventy-Third Session*, 2018. https://doi.org/10.18356/9789210021753c001.

"Developments in the Field of Information and Telecommunications in the Context of International Security – UNODA," https://www.un.org/disarmament/ict-security/.

"Developments in the Field of Information and Telecommunications in the Context of International Security – UNODA," https://www.un.org/disarmament/ict-security/.

Dezalay, Yves, and Bryant G. Garth. *Dealing in Virtue: International Commercial Arbitration and the Construction of a Transnational Legal Order*. University of Chicago Press, 1996.

Dezalay, Yves, and Mikael Rask Madsen. "The Force of Law and Lawyers: Pierre Bourdieu and the Reflexive Sociology of Law." *Annual Review of Law and Social Science* 8, no. 1 (2012): 433–52. https://doi.org/10.1146/annurev-lawsocsci-102811-173817.

Dias, Talita, and Tsvetelina Benthem. "Online Electoral Disinformation: A Human Rights Law Perspective." In *The Oxford Process on International Law Protections in Cyberspace*, 2022. https://www.elac.ox.ac.uk/wp-content/uploads/2022/10/Oxford-Process-Compendium-Digital.pdf.

Dinniss, Heather A. Harrison. "A Room Full of Experts: Expert Manuals and Their Influence on the Development of International Law." In *Yearbook of International Humanitarian Law*, edited by Terry D. Gill, Robin Geiß, Heike Krieger, and Rebecca Mignot-Mahdavi, 23:21–34. Springer Nature, 2020.

Dinstein, Yoram. "Computer Network Attacks and Self-Defense." *International Law Studies* 76, no. 1 (June 1, 2002). https://digital-commons.usnwc.edu/ils/vol76/iss1/20.

Disarmament Affairs, United Nations Office. "Convention on Certain Conventional Weapons – Informal Meeting of Experts (2016) | United Nations," Accessed April 8, 2023 https://meetings.unoda.org/ccw-ime/convention-certain-conventional-weapons-informal-meeting-experts-2016.

Disarmament Affairs, United Nations Office. "Accreditation: ICT OEWG, Session 2 – Google Drive," January 23, 2020. https://drive.google.com/drive/folders/1fdv-FQtqpUMsGKwk4QMi8CyeXrXbXRwm.

Disarmament Affairs, United Nations Office. "Note Verbale by the Secretariat Regarding the Accreditation of NGOs at the Second Substantive Session of the Open-Ended Working Group (10–14 February 2020," January 24, 2020. https://unoda-web.s3.amazonaws.com/wp-content/uploads/2020/01/NV-OEWG-session-2-NGO-accreditation.pdf.

Disarmament Affairs, United Nations Office. "Small Arms and Light Weapons – UNODA," Accessed April 8, 2023 https://www.un.org/disarmament/convarms/salw/.

Done, Laura. "Applicability of International Law in Cyberspace: Positions by Estonia and Latvia." *Electronic Scientific Journal of Law* (*Socrates* 3, no. 24 (2022).

Doswald-Beck, Louise, ed. *San Remo Manual on International Law Applicable to Armed Conflicts at Sea*. Cambridge: Cambridge University Press, 1995. https://doi.org/10.1017/CBO9780511622052.

Douek, Evelyn. "What Does 'Coordinated Inauthentic Behavior' Actually Mean?" *Slate*, July 2, 2020. https://slate.com/technology/2020/07/coordinated-inauthentic-behavior-facebook-twitter.html.

Draft Articles on Prevention of Transboundary Harm from Hazardous Activities, with Commentaries (*as Submitted to the UN General Assembly*. Dordrecht: International Law Commission, 2008. https://doi.org/10.1007/978-1-4020-8367-9_23.

Draft Rules of Procedure of the Fifth Review Conference of the High Contracting Parties to the Convention on Prohibitions or Restrictions on the Use of Certain Conventional Weapons Which May Be Deemed to Be Excessively Injurious or to Have Indiscrimi-

nate Effects. Geneva: UN Office of Disarmament Affairs, 2016. https://documents-dds-ny.un.org/doc/UNDOC/GEN/G16/215/36/PDF/G1621536.pdf?OpenElement.

"Draft Substantive Report (Zero Draft)." In *Open-Ended Working Group on Developments in the Field of Information and Telecommunications in the Context of International Security*, 2021. https://documents-dds-ny.un.org/doc/UNDOC/LTD/N20/378/94/PDF/N2037894.pdf?OpenElement.

"Draft Substantive Report (Zero Draft) : Open-Ended Working Group on Developments in the Field of Information and Telecommunications in the Context of International Security (As of January 19, 2021: With Russian Amendments," Accessed April 8, 2023 https://front.un-arm.org/wp-content/uploads/2021/02/RF-OEWG-zero-draft-report-with-the-Russian-amendments-ENG.pdf.

Drezner, Daniel W. "The Power and Peril of International Regime Complexity." *Perspectives on Politics* 7, no. 1 (2009): 65–70.

Droz, Serge, and Daniel Stauffacher. "Trust and Attribution in Cyberspace: A Proposal for an Independent Network of Organizations Engaging in Attribution Peer-Review." In *ICT4Peace Cybersecurity Policy Process Brief*, 2018.

Ducheine, Paul @ducheine@mastodon.social [@paulducheine]. "@Schmitt_ILaw to Paul Walker on His Proposal on the Law of Countermeasures: How Would That Have to Be Change, given the Customary Status?" *Tweet. Twitter*, May 27, 2015. https://twitter.com/paulducheine/status/603517003354214400.

Dunkelberg, Alonso Gurmendi. "Obligation to Negotiate Access to the Pacific Ocean (Bolivia v. Chile." *American Journal of International Law* 113, no. 2 (April 2019): 347–53. https://doi.org/10.1017/ajil.2019.9.

Dunlap, Charlie and J.D. "International Law and Cyber Ops: Q & A with Mike Schmitt about the Status of Tallinn 3.0." *Lawfire (Blog), October* 3 (2021). https://sites.duke.edu/lawfire/2021/10/03/international-law-and-cyber-ops-q-a-with-mike-schmitt-about-the-status-of-tallinn-3-0/.

Dunoff, Jeffrey L. "Perspectives on the Perils, Promise, Politics – and Practice – of Interdisciplinarity." In *The Power of Legality: Practices of International Law and Their Politics*, edited by Nikolas M. Rajkovic, Tanja E. Aalberts, and Thomas Gammeltoft-Hansen, 345–70. Cambridge: Cambridge University Press, 2016. https://doi.org/10.1017/CBO9781316535134.014.

Dunoff, Jeffrey L., and Mark A. Pollack. "Practice Theory and International Law." In *Research Handbook on the Sociology of International Law*, edited by Mosche Hirsch and Andrew Lang, 252–72. Edward Elgar Publishing, 2018. https://www.elgaronline.com/display/edcoll/9781783474486/9781783474486.00019.xml

Dunoff, Jeffrey, and Mark Pollack. "International Judicial Practices: Opening the 'Black Box' of International Courts." *Michigan Journal of International Law*, no. 40.1 (2018): 47. https://doi.org/10.36642/mjil.40.1.international.

Dunoff, Jeffrey, and Joel Trachtman. "Economic Analysis of International Law." *Yale Journal of International Law*, January 1, 1999. https://openyls.law.yale.edu/handle/20.500.13051/6390.

Duvall, Raymond D., and Arjun Chowdhury. "Practices of Theory." In *International Practices*, edited by Emanuel Adler and Vincent Pouliot, 335–354. Cambridge: Cambridge University Press, 2011. https://doi.org/10.1017/CBO9780511862373.019.

dwcom. "Reports: Berlin Plans Cyberattack 'Hackback' – DW – 04/20/2017," Accessed April 8, 2023 https://www.dw.com/en/reports-german-government-plans-cyberattack-hackback-ahead-of-election/a-38506101.

Dworkin, Ronald. *Law's Empire*. 1st ed. Cambridge, MA: Harvard University Press, 1986.

"Procès-Verbaux of the Proceedings of the Committee, June 16th-July 24th 1920, with Annexes =: Procès-Verbaux Des Séances Du Comité." In *League of Nations*. Clark, NJ: Lawbook Exchange, 1920.

Efrony, Dan, and Yuval Shany. "A Rule Book on the Shelf? Tallinn Manual 2.0 on Cyberoperations and Subsequent State Practice." *American Journal of International Law* 112, no. 4 (October 2018): 583–657. https://doi.org/10.1017/ajil.2018.86.

Egan, Brian. "Remarks on International Law and Stability in Cyberspace." *U.S. Department of State*, November 10, 2016, 2009–2017 264303.

Eggenschwiler, Jacqueline. "Expert Commissions and Norms of Responsible Behavior in Cyberspace: A Review of the Activities of the GCSC." *Digital Policy, Regulation and Governance* 22, no. 2 (January 1, 2020): 93–107. https://doi.org/10.1108/DPRG-03-2019-0019.

Eichensehr, Kristen E. "Review of Tallinn Manual on the International Law Applicable to Cyber Warfare." Edited by Michael N. Schmitt. *The American Journal of International Law* 108, no. 3 (2013): 585–89. https://doi.org/10.5305/amerjintelaw.108.3.0585.

Emery, Bond Huberman and David. "Snopestionary: What Is 'Coordinated Inauthentic Behavior'?" *Snopes*, September 4, 2021. https://www.snopes.com/articles/366947/coordinated-inauthentic-behavior/.

Encyclopedia Britannica. "Sociology – The Historical Divide: Qualitative and Establishment Sociology," April 3, 2023. https://www.britannica.com/topic/sociology.

English, John, and Andrew F. Cooper. "International Commissions and the Mind of Global Governance." In *International Commissions and the Power of Ideas*, edited by Ramesh Thakur, Andrew F. Cooper, and John English, 1st ed. United Nations University Press, 2005.

ENISA. "Coordinated Vulnerability Disclosure Policies in the EU." *News Item*, Accessed April 8, 2023 https://www.enisa.europa.eu/news/enisa-news/coordinated-vulnerability-disclosure-policies-in-the-eu.

"Estonia's Comments to the 'Initial "Pre-draft" of the Report of the OEWG on Developments in the Field of Information and Telecommunications in the Context of International Security.'" *April* 16 (2020). https://front.un-arm.org/wp-content/uploads/2020/04/comments-to-the-oewg-pre-draft-report-estonia.pdf.

EU Cyber Direct, dir. *Prof. Martti Koskenniemi | International Cyber Law: Does It Exist and Do We Need It? (Full Lecture)*. 2019. 43:39. https://www.youtube.com/watch?v=nh5FGswBImo.

"EU Statement – On Consideration of the Implementation of the International Tracing Instrument." In *8th Biennial Meeting of States on the UN POA to Prevent, Combat & Eradicate the Illicit Trade in Small Arms & Light Weapons | EEAS Website."*, Accessed April 8, 2023 https://www.eeas.europa.eu/delegations/un-new-york/eu-statement-consideration-implementation-international-tracing-instrument_en?s=63.

European Commission. "Speech by the President at the Paris Peace Forum." *Text*, November 11, 2021 https://ec.europa.eu/commission/presscorner/detail/en/speech_21_5977.

"European Cyber Agora, June 2–3 2021 – Microsoft." https://www.microsoft.com/en-eu/cyber-agora/.

"European Cyber Agora, June 14–16 2022 – Microsoft." https://www.microsoft.com/en-eu/cyber-agora/.

Farnsworth, Valerie, Irene Kleanthous, and Etienne Wenger-Trayner. "Communities of Practice as a Social Theory of Learning: A Conversation with Etienne Wenger." *British Journal of Educational Studies* 64, no. 2 (April 2, 2016): 139–60. https://doi.org/10.1080/00071005.2015.1133799.

Federal Office of Culture, Confederation of Switzerland. "L'Esprit de Genève (Spirit of Geneva," n.d. https://www.lebendige-traditionen.ch/tradition/en/home/traditionen/l_esprit-de-geneve--der-geist-von-genf-.html.

Fidler, David. "Global Health Jurisprudence: A Time of Reckoning." *96 Georgetown Law Journal 393 (2008)*, January 1, 2008. https://www.repository.law.indiana.edu/facpub/141.

Fidler, David P. "The Globalization of Public Health: The First 100 Years of International Health Diplomacy." *World Health Organization. Bulletin of the World Health Organization; Geneva* 79, no. 9 (2001): 842–49.

"Final Substantive Report." In *Open-Ended Working Group on Developments in the Field of Information and Telecommunications in the Context of International Secu-*

rity, 2021. https://front.un-arm.org/wp-content/uploads/2021/03/Final-report-A-AC.290-2021-CRP.2.pdf.

Finnemore, Martha, and Duncan B. Hollis. "Constructing Norms for Global Cybersecurity." *The American Journal of International Law* 110, no. 3 (2016): 425–79.

Fioretos, Orfeo. "Historical Institutionalism in International Relations." *International Organization* 65, no. 2 (April 2011): 367–99. https://doi.org/10.1017/S0020818311000002.

"First Committee 13th Meeting| Monday, 17 October 2005, 10 a.m." *UN General Assembly, Sixtieth Session*, October 17, 2005. https://documents-dds-ny.un.org/doc/UNDOC/GEN/N05/555/42/PDF/N0555542.pdf?OpenElement.

Fitzmaurice, Malgosia. "The History of Article 38 of the Statute of the International Court of Justice." In *The Oxford Handbook of the Sources of International Law*, 2017. https://doi.org/10.1093/law/9780198745365.003.0009.

Five Principles for Shaping Cybersecurity Norms. Microsoft, 2013. https://query.prod.cms.rt.microsoft.com/cms/api/am/binary/REVmc9.

Fleck, Dieter. "Searching for International Rules Applicable to Cyber Warfare – A Critical First Assessment of the New Tallinn Manual." *Journal of Conflict and Security Law* 18, no. 2 (July 1): 331–51. https://doi.org/10.1093/jcsl/krt011.

Flowers, Zachary. "The Role of Precedent and Stare Decisis in the World Trade Organization's Dispute Settlement Body." *International Journal of Legal Information* 2, no. ed (2019): 90–104. https://doi.org/10.1017/jli.2019.21.

Foreign Affairs FDFA, Confederation of Switzerland. "The Montreux Document," n.d. https://www.eda.admin.ch/eda/en/home/foreign-policy/international-law/international-humanitarian-law/private-military-security-companies/montreux-document.html.

"Form and Substance in International Agreements." *American Journal of International Law* 99, no. 3 (2005): 581–614.

"Fragmentation of International Law: Difficulties Arising from the Diversification and Expansion of International Law – Report of the Study Group of the International Law Commission," 2006.

"France 24. "'Paris Call': 51 States Vow Support for Global Rules on Cyberweapons." *November* 12 (2018). https://www.france24.com/en/20181112-france-internet-paris-call-51-states-support-cybersecurity-rules-cyberweapons-peace-forum.

France, O.N.U. "Cybersecurity: Paris Call for Trust and Security in Cyberspace," Accessed March 2, 2023 https://onu.delegfrance.org/Cybersecurity-Paris-Call-for-Trust-and-Security-in-Cyberspace.

France24. "'Paris Call': 51 States Vow Support for Global Rules on Cyberweapons." *November* 11 (2018). https://www.france24.com/en/20181112-france-internet-paris-call-51-states-support-cybersecurity-rules-cyberweapons-peace-forum.

France-Désarmement. “The Resolution on PoA Cyber, Co-Sponsored by 74 States and Adopted with 157 Votes in Favor, Supports a Future Programme of Action to Strengthen Capacity-Building to Address #cyber Attacks and Advance Responsible Behavior in the #cyberspace #77unga @francediplo_ASD https://T.Co/FAYLqwUo-nw.” *Tweet. Twitter*, November 3, 2022. https://twitter.com/FR_Desarmement/status/1588195825968156673.

“France’s Response to Zero-Draft Report from the OEWG Chair,” February 2021. https://front.un-arm.org/wp-content/uploads/2021/02/France_OEWG_ENG_Vfclean.pdf.

Friedmann, Wolfgang. *The Changing Structure of International Law*. New York: Columbia University Press, 1964. http://archive.org/details/changingstructur0000wolf.

Frost, Mervyn, and Silviya Lechner, eds. “Introduction: Mapping Out the Problem of Practices.” In *Practice Theory and International Relations, 1–30. Cambridge Studies in International Relations*. Cambridge: Cambridge University Press, 2018. https://doi.org/10.1017/9781108645775.001.

“Further Practical Measures for the Prevention of an Arms Race in Outer Space.” In *UN General Assembly, Seventy-Second Session*, 2018. https://doi.org/10.18356/9789210021753c001.

“G7 Declaration on Responsible States Behavior in Cyberspace,” September 12, 2021. http://www.g7.utoronto.ca/foreign/170411-cyberspace.html.

Galindo, George Rodrigo Bandeira. “Martti Koskenniemi and the Historiographical Turn in International Law.” *European Journal of International Law* 16, no. 3 (June 1): 539–559. https://doi.org/10.1093/ejil/chi130.

Gammeltoft-Hansen, Thomas, and Tanja Aalberts. “Introduction: The Changing Practices of International Law.” In *The Changing Practices of International Law*, edited by Tanja Aalberts and Thomas Gammeltoft-Hansen, 1st ed., 1–25. Cambridge University Press, 2018. https://doi.org/10.1017/9781108349420.002.

Garfinkel, Harold. “Studies of the Routine Grounds of Everyday Activities.” *Social Problems* 11, no. 3 (1964): 225–50.

Garrett, Geoffrey, and Barry R. Weingast. “Ideas, Interests, and Institutions: Constructing the European Community’s Internal Market.” In *Ideas and Foreign Policy: Beliefs, Institutions, and Political Change*, edited by Judith Goldstein and Robert O. Keohane, 173–206. Cornell University Press, 1993. http://www.jstor.org/stable/10.7591/j.ctvv4147z.11.

Garwood-Gowers, Andrew. “Case Concerning Oil Platforms (Islamic Republic of Iran v United States of America) – Did the ICJ Miss the Boat on the Law on the Use of Force?” *Melbourne Journal of International Law* 5, no. 1 (2004). http://classic.austlii.edu.au/au/journals/MelbJIL/2004/10.html.

GCSC. "GCSC Request for Proposals: Call for Research [Closed]," Accessed February 8, 2023 https://web.archive.org/web/20210423120218/https://cyberstability.org/wp-content/uploads/2017/12/GCSC_Request_For_Proposals_2018.pdf.

GCSC. "Request for Consultation: Definition of Stability of Cyberspace," n.d. https://cyberstability.org/news/request-for-consultation-definition-of-stability-of-cyberspace/.

GCSC. "Request for Proposals Archives," n.d. https://cyberstability.org/?research_category=request-for-proposals/.

"GCSC Meeting Singapore: Attendance List." In *Global Commission on the Stability of Cyberspace*, 2018.

Gehring, Thomas, and Thomas Dörfler. "Constitutive Mechanisms of UN Security Council Practices: Precedent Pressure, Ratchet Effect, and Council Action Regarding Intrastate Conflicts." *Review of International Studies* 45, no. 1 (January 2019): 120–140. https://doi.org/10.1017/S0260210518000268.

"General and Complete Disarmament." In *UN General Assembly, Fifty-Fifth Session*, 2001. https://documents-dds-ny.un.org/doc/UNDOC/GEN/N00/561/37/PDF/N0056137.pdf?OpenElement.

"General Assembly First Committee Sixty-Fifth Session," 2010. https://meetings.unoda.org/meeting/29603/documents?f%5B0%5D=author_documents_%3AGeneral%20Assembly%20First%20Committee&f%5B1%5D=document_type_meeting%3AVerbatim%20records.

"General Assembly First Committee Sixty-Fourth Session (2009) | United Nations," Accessed March 2, 2023 https://meetings.unoda.org/meeting/29602/documents?f%5B0%5D=author_documents_%3AGeneral%20Assembly%20First%20Committee.

"General Assembly First Committee Sixty-Seventh Session (2012) | United Nations," Accessed March 2, 2023 https://meetings.unoda.org/meeting/29605/documents?f%5B0%5D=author_documents_%3AGeneral%20Assembly%20First%20Committee.

"General Assembly First Committee Sixty-Sixth Session," 2011. https://meetings.unoda.org/meeting/29604/documents?f%5B0%5D=author_documents_%3AGeneral%20Assembly%20First%20Committee&f%5B1%5D=document_type_meeting%3AVerbatim%20records.

"General Assembly Resolution 73/27, Developments in the Field of Information and Telecommunications in the Context of International Security, A/RES/73/27," 2018. https://documents-dds-ny.un.org/doc/UNDOC/GEN/N18/418/04/PDF/N1841804.pdf.

"General Assembly Resolution 73/266, Advancing Responsible State Behavior in Cyberspace in the Context of International Security, A/RES/73/266," 2018. https://

documents-dds-ny.un.org/doc/UNDOC/GEN/N18/465/01/PDF/N1846501.pdf.

Gjelten, Tom. "Shadow Wars: Debating Cyber 'Disarmament.'" *World Affairs* 173, no. 4 (November 1, 2010): 33–43.

Glas, Aarie, Clifton Linden, Matthew J. Hoffmann, and Robert A. Denemark. "Understanding Multilateral Treaty-Making as Constitutive Practice." *Journal of Global Security Studies* 3, no. 3 (July 1): 339–57. https://doi.org/10.1093/jogss/ogy014.

"Global Commission on internet Governance | One internet." *Centre for International Governance Innovation and The Royal Institute for International Affairs*, 2016. https://www.cigionline.org/static/documents/gcig_final_report_-_with_cover.pdf.

Goldsmith, Jack, and Alex Loomis. *Defend Forward and Sovereignty*. Aegis Series Paper. Hoover Institution, 2021. https://doi.org/10.1093/oso/9780197601792.003.0008.

GOV UK. "Security and Freedom in the Cyber Age – Seeking the Rules of the Road," February 4, 2011. https://www.gov.uk/government/speeches/security-and-freedom-in-the-cyber-age-seeking-the-rules-of-the-road.

Gram-Skjoldager, Karen, and Haakon A. Ikonomou. "Making Sense of the League of Nations Secretariat – Historiographical and Conceptual Reflections on Early International Public Administration." *European History Quarterly* 49, no. 3 (July 1): 420–444. https://doi.org/10.1177/0265691419854634.

Graves, Tom. "Active Cyber Defense Certainty Act." *Pub* L, no. H. R. 4036 (2017). https://www.congress.gov/bill/115th-congress/house-bill/4036/text?q=%7B%22search%22%3A%5B%22Active±Cyber±Defense±Certainty±Act%22%5D%7D&r=1.

Graves, Tom. "Text – H.R.4036 – 115th Congress (2017–2018): Active Cyber Defense Certainty Act." *Legislation*, November 1, 2017. http://www.congress.gov/.

Grenfell, Michael James. *Pierre Bourdieu : Key Concepts*. 2nd ed. London: Routledge, 2014. https://web.p.ebscohost.com/ehost/ebookviewer/ebook/ZTAwMHh3d19fODUwMTY3X19BTg2?sid=28e6d1fd-2ce4-4655-940c-3d0c2b5e6206@redis&vid=0&format=EB&lpid=lp_114&rid=0.

Grewe, Wilhelm Georg. *The Epochs of International Law*. Walter de Gruyter, 2000.

Grigsby, Alex. "The United Nations Doubles Its Workload on Cyber Norms, and Not Everyone Is Pleased." *Council on Foreign Relations*, November 15, 2018 https://www.cfr.org/blog/united-nations-doubles-its-workload-cyber-norms-and-not-everyone-pleased.

"Group of Governmental Experts – UNODA," Accessed April 28, 2023 https://www.un.org/disarmament/group-of-governmental-experts/.

"Group of Governmental Experts on Developments in the Field of Information and Telecommunications in the Context of International Security." In *UN General Assembly, Sixty-Fifth Session*, 2010. https://documents-dds-ny.un.org/doc/UNDOC/GEN/N10/469/57/PDF/N1046957.pdf?OpenElement.

"Group of Governmental Experts on Developments in the Field of Information and Telecommunications in the Context of International Security." *UN General Assembly, Sixty-Eighth Session*, June 24, 2013. https://documents-dds-ny.un.org/doc/UNDOC/GEN/N13/371/66/PDF/N1337166.pdf?OpenElement.

"Group of Governmental Experts on Developments in the Field of Information and Telecommunications in the Context of International Security." *UN General Assembly, Seventieth Session*, July 22, 2015. https://documents-dds-ny.un.org/doc/UNDOC/GEN/N15/228/35/PDF/N1522835.pdf?OpenElement.

Guest, Stephen. *Ronald Dworkin*. 2nd ed. Stanford University Press, 1997.

Guieu, Jean-Michel. "La SDN et Ses Organisations de Soutien Dans Les Ann□es 1920: Entre Promotion de Années; l'esprit; Genéve: volonté; d'Influence." *Relations Internationales*, no. 151 (2012): 11–24.

Gusterson, Hugh. "Ethnographic Research." In *Qualitative Methods in International Relations: A Pluralist Guide*, edited by Audie Klotz and Deepa Prakash, 93–113. Research Methods Series. London: Palgrave Macmillan UK, 2008. https://doi.org/10.1057/9780230584129_7.

Gusterson, Hugh. *Nuclear Rites: A Weapons Laboratory at the End of the Cold War*. University of California Press, 1996.

Guzman, Andrew T. "A Compliance-Based Theory of International Law." *California Law Review* 90, no. 6 (2002): 1823–1887. https://doi.org/10.2307/3481436.

Guzman, Andrew T., and Timothy L. Meyer. "International Soft Law." *Journal of Legal Analysis* 2, no. 1 (March 1, 2010): 171–225. https://doi.org/10.1093/jla/2.1.171.

Guzzini, Stefano. "Power." In *Bourdieu in International Relations Rethinking Key Concepts in IR*, edited by Rebecca Adler-Nissen, 1st ed. New York: Routledge, 2013.

Haas, Peter M. "Banning Chlorofluorocarbons: Epistemic Community Efforts to Protect Stratospheric Ozone." *International Organization* 46, no. 1 (1992): 187–224. https://doi.org/10.1017/S002081830000148X.

Haas, Peter M. "Introduction: Epistemic Communities and International Policy Coordination." *International Organization* 46, no. 1 (1992): 1–35.

"Habitus | Social Theory Rewired," Accessed April 13, 2023 https://routledgesoc.com/category/profile-tags/habitus.

Hagan, John, and Ron Levi. "Crimes of War and the Force of Law." *Social Forces* 83, no. 4 (2005): 1499–1534.

Hansen-Magnusson, Hannes. "Arctic Geopoetics: Russian Politics at the North Pole." *Cooperation and Conflict* 54, no. 4 (December 1): 466–87. https://doi.org/10.1177/0010836718815526.

Hart, H.L.A., Herbert Lionel Adolphus Hart, and Leslie Green. *The Concept of Law*. OUP Oxford, 2012.

Heinl, Caitriona. "Can ASEAN Continue to Improve Cybersecurity in the Region and Beyond?" In *Council on Foreign Relations*, March 22, 2018. https://www.cfr.org/blog/can-asean-continue-improve-cybersecurity-region-and-beyond.

Helal, Mohamed. "On Coercion in International Law." *NYU Journal of International Law and Politics* 52 (2019). https://doi.org/10.2139/ssrn.3357513.

Hirsch, Moshe. "Sociological Analysis of International Law and the Cognitive Turn." In *International Legal Theory and the Cognitive Turn*, edited by Anne van Aaken and Moshe Hirsch. Oxford University Press, 2025. https://doi.org/10.1093/9780198909293.003.0010.

Hofmann, Stephanie C., and Andrew Yeo. "Historical Institutionalism and Institutional Design: Divergent Pathways to Regime Complexes in Asia and Europe." *European Journal of International Relations* 30, no. 2 (2024): 306–32. https://doi.org/10.1177/13540661231170717.

Hoffman, Wyatt and Steven Nyikos. "Governing Private Sector Self-Help in Cyberspace: Analogies from the Physical World." Carnegie Endowment for International Peace, December 6, 2018. https://carnegieendowment.org/2018/12/06/governing-private-sector-self-help-in-cyberspace-analogies-from-physical-world-pub-77832.

Hofius, Maren. "Towards a 'Theory of the Gap': Addressing the Relationship between Practice and Theory." *Global Constitutionalism* 9, no. 1 (March 2020): 169–82. https://doi.org/10.1017/S2045381719000431.

Holmes, Marcus, Richard Jordan, and Eric Parajon. "Assessing the Renaissance of Individuals in International Relations Theory." *PS: Political Science & Politics* 54, no. 2 (April 2021): 214–219. https://doi.org/10.1017/S1049096520001699.

Hopf, Ted. "Critiques of the Practice Turn in IR Theory: Some Responses." In *Conceptualizing International Practices*, edited by Alena Drieschova, Christian Bueger, and Ted Hopf, 1st ed., 28–44. Cambridge University Press, 2022. https://doi.org/10.1017/9781009052504.002.

Hopf, Ted. "The Logic of Habit in International Relations." *European Journal of International Relations* 16, no. 4 (December 1, 2010): 539–61. https://doi.org/10.1177/1354066110363502.

Horenbeeck, Maarten, Joanna Kulesza, and Andrii Paziuk. "IGF2018 Best Practice Forum on Cybersecurity: Cybersecurity Culture, Norms and Values," December 2018. http://www.intgovforum.org/multilingual/filedepot_download/6764/1437.

HPCR Manual on International Law Applicable to Air and Missile Warfare. Cambridge: Cambridge University Press, 2013. https://doi.org/10.1017/CBO9781139525275.

Huang, Zhixiong, and Kubo Mačák. "Towards the International Rule of Law in Cyberspace: Contrasting Chinese and Western Approaches." *Chinese Journal of International Law* 16, no. 2 (June 1): 271–310. https://doi.org/10.1093/chinesejil/jmx011.

Hudec, Robert E. "GATT Legal System: A Diplomat's Jurisprudence." *Journal of World Trade Law* 4 (1970): 615.

Hudec, Robert E. "The New WTO Dispute Settlement Procedure: An Overview of the First Three Years." *Minnesota Journal of Global Trade* 8 (1999): 1.

Hurd, Ian. "The International Rule of Law and the Domestic Analogy." *Global Constitutionalism* 4, no. 3 (November 2015): 365–395. https://doi.org/10.1017/S2045381715000131.

ICoCA. "International Code of Conduct Association. "The Code," Accessed April 28, 2023 https://icoca.ch/the-code/.

ICT4Peace Foundation. "First Session of Paris Call Working Group 3 Moderated by Anne-Marie Buzatu, ICT4Peace," May 25, 2021. https://ict4peace.org/activities/first-session-of-paris-call-working-group-3-moderated-by-anne-marie-buzatu/.

ICT4Peace Foundation. "UN GGE – 2018: The Year That Cyber Peace Became Non-binding." *December* 31 (2018). https://ict4peace.org/activities/2018-the-year-that-cyber-peace-became-non-binding/.

"Icts in the Context of International Peace and Security: Current Conditions and Future Approaches." In *UNIDIR Cyber Stability Conference 2017*. United Nations Institute for Disarmament Research, 2017. https://unidir.org/sites/default/files/publication/pdfs//icts-in-the-context-of-international-peace-and-security-current-conditions-and-future-approaches-en-696.pdf.

"IGF 2018 Speech by French President Emmanuel Macron." *Text. internet Governance Forum*, November 14, 2018. https://www.intgovforum.org/multilingual/content/igf-2018-speech-by-french-president-emmanuel-macron.

"IGF 2021 – Day 3 – OF #50 Protecting the Public Core: Next Steps after the OEWG & GGE | internet Governance Forum," Accessed April 13, 2023 https://www.intgovforum.org/en/content/igf-2021-%E2%80%93-day-3-%E2%80%93-of-50-protecting-the-public-core-next-steps-after-the-oewg-gge.

"Informal Australian Research Paper What next for Advancing Responsible State Behavior at the United Nations?," April 2021. https://www.internationalcybertech.gov.au/sites/default/files/2021-04/australian-research-paper-what-next-advancing-responsible-state-behavior-united-nations_1.pdf.

"Informal Multi-Stakeholder Cyber Dialogue," Accessed March 2, 2023 https://letstalkcyber.org/.

"Initial 'Pre-draft' of the Report of the OEWG on Developments in the Field of Information and Telecommunications in the Context of International Security," April 27, 2020. https://front.un-arm.org/wp-content/uploads/2020/03/200311-Pre-Draft-OEWG-ICT.pdf.

"Initial 'Pre-draft' of the Report of the OEWG on Developments in the Field of Information and Telecommunications in the Context of International Security | Comments by ARGENTINA," April 2020. https://front.un-arm.org/wp-content/uploads/2020/04/oewg-ict-comments-argentina-3.pdf.

"Initial 'Pre-draft' of the Report of the OEWG on Developments in the Field of Information and Telecommunications in the Context of International Security and Non-paper Listing Specific Language Proposals under Agenda Item 'Rules, Norms and Principles," Accessed March 2, 2023 https://front.un-arm.org/wp-content/uploads/2020/04/20200401-oewg-german-written-contribution-to-pre-draft-report-1.pdf.

"International Convention Relating to Economic Statistics." Lake Success, N.Y, 1950. http://hdl.handle.net/2027/mdp.39015038406180.

"International Cyber Law: Interactive Toolkit," Accessed March 2, 2023 https://cyberlaw.ccdcoe.org/wiki/Main_Page.

International Cyber Law: Interactive Toolkit. "Due Diligence." *September* 12 (2022). https://cyberlaw.ccdcoe.org/wiki/Due_diligence.

International Cyber Law: Interactive Toolkit. "Prohibition of Intervention." *September* 12 (2022). https://cyberlaw.ccdcoe.org/wiki/Prohibition_of_intervention.

International Cyber Law: Interactive Toolkit. "Sony Pictures Entertainment Attack (2014," June 9, 2021. https://cyberlaw.ccdcoe.org/wiki/Sony_Pictures_Entertainment_attack_(2014).

International Cyber Law: Interactive Toolkit. "Sovereignty," September 19, 2022. https://cyberlaw.ccdcoe.org/wiki/Sovereignty.

"International Information Security Legal Acts and Fundamental Documents," Accessed April 13, 2023 https://namib.online/wp-content/uploads/2019/03/МИБ_английская-версия.pdf.

"International Law and Cyber Operations – Launch of the Tallinn Manual 2.0," 2017. https://www.youtube.com/watch?v=riP4kStBBJs.

"International Law and Cyberspace | Finland's National Positions." In *Ministry of Foreign Affairs*. Finland, Accessed April 13, 2023 https://um.fi/documents/35732/0/Cyber±and±international±law%3B±Finland%27s±views.pdf/41404cbb-d300-a3b9-92e4-a7d675d5d585?t=1602758856859.

"International Law and the Trump Administration: Strengthening Cybersecurity [7–19-2017," 2017. https://www.youtube.com/watch?v=gBxt7sUPeMA.

"International Law Commission," https://legal.un.org/ilc/elections/2021election_outcome.shtml.

"International Law Commission," https://legal.un.org/ilc/league.shtml.

International Law Commission. "Draft Articles on Responsibility of States for Internationally Wrongful Acts, with Commentaries – 2001." *State Responsibility*, 2001, 114.

International Law Commission. "Summaries of the Work of the International Law Commission | International Liability for Injurious Consequences Arising out of

Acts Not Prohibited by International Law," Accessed April 13, 2023 https://legal.un.org/ilc/summaries/9.shtml.

International Law Commission. "Responsibility of States for Internationally Wrongful Acts." In *UN General Assembly, Fifty-Third Session*, 2001. https://doi.org/10.1007/978-1-4020-8367-9_22.

International Law in Cyberspace. New Delhi: Asian-African Legal Consultative Organization, 2016. https://www.aalco.int/userfiles/file/55thSession/Cyberspace%2020 16.pdf.

"International Law in Future Frontiers." *GOV.UK*, May 19, 2022. https://www.gov.uk/government/speeches/international-law-in-future-frontiers.

"International Liability for Injurious Consequences Arising out of Acts Not Prohibited by International Law." In *International Law Commission, Fifty-Second Session*, 2000. https://legal.un.org/ilc/reports/2000/english/chp8.pdf.

International Liability for Injurious Consequences Arising out of Acts Not Prohibited by International Law | Comments and Observations Received from Governments: Report of the Secretary-General. Fifty-second session: International Law Commission, 2000. https://legal.un.org/ilc/documentation/english/a_cn4_509.pdf.

"International Tracing Instrument | Weapons Law Encyclopedia," Accessed April 13, 2023 https://www.weaponslaw.org/instruments/2005-international-tracing-instrument.

internet Society. "Reflections from the Global Commission on the Stability of Cyberspace." *December* 13 (2017). https://www.internetsociety.org/blog/2017/12/reflec tions-global-commission-stability-cyberspace/.

"Israel's Response to Zero-Draft Report from the OEWG Chair," March 2021. https://front.un-arm.org/wp-content/uploads/2021/03/Israel-amendments-UN-OEWG-ZE RO-DRAFT-Israel-amendments-sent.pdf.

"Japan's Comments on OEWG Pre-draft," April 2020. https://front.un-arm.org/wp-content/uploads/2020/04/japan-comments-on-oewg-pre-draft.pdf.

Jensen, Eric Talbot, and Sean Watts. "A Cyber Duty of Due Diligence: Gentle Civilizer or Crude Destabilizer? Symposium: Tallinn Manual 2.0 on the International Law Applicable to Cyber Operations." *Texas Law Review* 95, no. 7 (2017): 1555–1578.

"Jessup World Championship," 2022. https://www.youtube.com/watch?v=JuPWCU qBsxA.

Johns, Fleur. *Non-legality in International Law: Unruly Law*. Cambridge Studies in International and Comparative Law. Cambridge University Press, 2013. https://doi.org/10.1017/CBO9781139012959.

Johnson, Derek B. "Role of US Agencies Limited in Protecting against BGP Hijacks, Attacks on internet Architecture." *SC Media*, March 4, 2022. https://www.scmaga zine.com/analysis/network-security/role-of-us-agencies-limited-in-protecting-aga inst-bgp-hijacks-attacks-on-internet-architecture.

Johnstone, Ian. "Between Bureaucracy and Adhocracy: Crafting a Spectrum of UN Peace Operations." *Global Peace Operations Review*, March 2016. https://peaceoperationsreview.org/thematic-essays/from-bureaucracy-to-adhocracy-crafting-a-spectrum-of-un-peace-operations/.

Johnstone, Ian. "Interpretive Communities." In *The Power of Deliberation: International Law, Politics and Organizations*. Oxford University Press, 2011. https://doi.org/10.1093/acprof:oso/9780195394931.003.0003.

Johnstone, Ian. "Law-Making by International Organizations: Perspectives from IL/IR Theory." In *Interdisciplinary Perspectives on International Law and International Relations: The State of the Art*, edited by Jeffrey L. Dunoff and Mark A. Pollack, 266–92. Cambridge: Cambridge University Press, 2012. https://doi.org/10.1017/CBO9781139107310.014.

Johnstone, Ian. "Security Council Deliberations: The Power of the Better Argument." *European Journal of International Law* 14, no. 3 (June 1): 437–480. https://doi.org/10.1093/ejil/14.3.437.

Johnstone, Ian. "Legislation and Adjudication in the UN Security Council: Bringing down the Deliberative Deficit." *The American Journal of International Law* (Washington, United Kingdom) 102, no. 2 (2008): 275–308.

Johnstone, Ian, and Arun Mohan Sukumar. "Constructivism, Interpretation, and Cognitive Studies." In *International Legal Theory and the Cognitive Turn*, edited by Anne van Aaken and Moshe Hirsch. Oxford University Press, 2025. https://doi.org/10.1093/9780198909293.003.0004.

"Joint Proposal on the Text of the 1st Draft," March 2021. https://front.un-arm.org/wp-content/uploads/2021/03/PDF-Joint-Contribution-OEWG-First-Draft-Suggested-amendments.pdf.

Jolley, Jason. "Recommendation 13(F)." In *Voluntary, Non-binding Norms for Responsible State Behavior in the Use of Information and Communications Technology: A Commentary*, edited by Eneken Tikk, 171. New York: United Nations Publication, 2017. https://www.un.org/disarmament/wp-content/uploads/2018/04/Civil-Society-2017.pdf.

Joseph, Jonathan, and Milja Kurki. "The Limits of Practice: Why Realism Can Complement IR's Practice Turn." *International Theory* 10, no. 1 (March 2018): 71–97. https://doi.org/10.1017/S175297191700015X.

Kahlert, Torsten. "Pioneers in International Administration: A Prosopography of the Directors of the League of Nations Secretariat." *New Global Studies; Berlin* 13, no. 2 (2019): 191–228.

Kapiszewski, Diana, Lauren M. MacLean, and Benjamin L. Read. *Field Research in Political Science: Practices and Principles*. Cambridge: Cambridge University Press, 2015. https://doi.org/10.1017/CBO9780511794551.

Kavanagh, Camino. *The United Nations, Cyberspace and International Peace and Security: Responding to Complexity in the 21st Century*. Geneva: United Nations Institute for Disarmament Research, 2017. https://unidir.org/sites/default/files/publication/pdfs//the-united-nations-cyberspace-and-international-peace-and-security-en-691.pdf.

Kelle, Udo. "'Emergence' vs. 'Forcing' of Empirical Data? A Crucial Problem of 'Grounded Theory' Reconsidered." *Forum Qualitative Sozialforschung / Forum: Qualitative Social Research* 6, no. 2 (May 31, 2005). https://doi.org/10.17169/fqs-6.2.467.

Kennedy, David. *A World of Struggle: How Power, Law, and Expertise Shape Global Political Economy*. Princeton University Press, 2016.

Keohane, Robert O., and Lisa L. Martin. "The Promise of Institutionalist Theory." *International Security* 20, no. 1 (June 22, 1995): 39–52.

Kessler, Oliver, and Wouter Werner. "Expertise, Uncertainty, and International Law: A Study of the Tallinn Manual on Cyberwarfare." *Leiden Journal of International Law* 26, no. 4 (December 2013): 793–810. https://doi.org/10.1017/S0922156513000411.

Kilovaty, Ido. "Cyber Warfare and the Jus Ad Bellum Challenges: Evaluation in the Light of the Tallinn Manual on the International Law Applicable to Cyber Warfare," National Security Law Brief 5, no. 5 (2014): 90–124. 103.

Kilovaty, Ido. "The Elephant in the Room: Coercion." *AJIL Unbound* 113 (2019): 87–91. https://doi.org/10.1017/aju.2019.10.

Kilovaty, Ido. "The International Law of Cyber Intervention." In *Research Handbook on International Law and Cyberspace*, edited by Nicholas Tsagourias and Russell Buchan, 97–112. Edward Elgar Publishing, 2021. https://www.elgaronline.com/view/edcoll/9781789904246/9781789904246.00014.xml.

Klabbers, Jan. "Safeguarding the Organizational Acquis: The EU's External Practice." *International Organizations Law Review* 4, no. 1 (January 1): 57–89. https://doi.org/10.1163/157237307X223620.

Klabbers, Jan. "The EJIL Foreword: The Transformation of International Organizations Law." *European Journal of International Law* 26, no. 1 (February 1, 2015): 9–82. https://doi.org/10.1093/ejil/chv009.

Klabbers, Jan. "The Relative Autonomy of International Law or the Forgotten Politics of Interdisciplinary Theory." *Journal of International Law and International Relations* 1, no. 1–2 (2005): 35–48.

Klabbers, Jan. *The Normative Gap in International Organizations Law*. Brill, December 16, 2019. https://doi.org/10.1163/15723747-01602004.

Klett, Taylor Wessing-Detlef. "Hackback Plans – Cyber Security through an Active Cyber Defence?" *Lexology*, November 3, 2019. https://www.lexology.com/library/detail.aspx?g=0e512994-ccb0-4ac2-8b1c-57a7efd88309.

Klimburg, Alexander. "New Conditions and Constellations in Cyber." *The Hague: The Hague Centre for Strategic Studies*, 2021. https://hcss.nl/report/cyberstability-paper-series-new-conditions-and-constellations-in-cyber/.

Klotz, Audie, and Cecelia Lynch. "Strategies for Research in Constructivist International Relations." *M.E. Sharpe*, 2007.

Kolkman, Olaf. "Rough Guide to IETF 102," July 29, 2018 https://www.ietfjournal.org/rough-guide-to-ietf-102/.

Koh, Harold Hongju. "International Law in Cyberspace." *Harvard International Law Journal Online* 54 (December 2012). https://harvardilj.org/2012/12/online_54_koh/.

Koivurova, Timo, and Krittika Singh. *Due Diligence*. Oxford Public International Law, 2022. http://opil.ouplaw.com/view/10.1093/law:epil/9780199231690/law-9780199231690-e1034?prd=OPIL.

Korzak, Elaine. "National Views on the Application of International Law to Cybersecurity." In *Perspectives on Responsible Behavior in State Uses of ICT. ICT4Peace Foundation & Cyber Policy Institute*, 2017. https://ict4peace.org/wp-content/uploads/2017/02/ICT4Peace-Book-Draft.pdf.

Korzak, Elaine. *Russia's Cyber Policy Efforts in the United Nations*. Tallinn Papers: NATO CCDCOE, 2021.

Korzak, Elaine. "The 2015 GGE Report: What Next for Norms in Cyberspace?," September 23, 2015. https://www.lawfareblog.com/2015-gge-report-what-next-norms-cyberspace.

Koskenniemi, Martti. "A History of International Law Histories." In *The Oxford Handbook of the History of International Law*, edited by Anne Peters and Bardo Fassbender, 2012. https://doi.org/10.1093/law/9780199599752.003.0040.

Koskenniemi, Martti. "Out of Europe: Carl Schmitt, Hans Morgenthau, and the Turn to 'International Relations.'" In *The Gentle Civilizer of Nations The Rise and Fall of International Law 1870–1960*. Cambridge University Press, 2001. https://www.cambridge.org/core/services/aop-cambridge-core/content/view/A1FCD2F7A0B4C1AB655C59B8DAD162E8/9780511494222c6_p413-509_CBO.pdf/out_of_europe_carl_schmitt_hans_morgenthau_and_the_turn_to_international_relations.pdf.

Koskenniemi, Martti. "The Fate of Public International Law: Between Technique and Politics." *The Modern Law Review* 70, no. 1 (2007): 1–30.

Koskenniemi, Martti. "The Politics of International Law – 20 Years Later." *European Journal of International Law* 20, no. 1 (2009): 7–19. https://doi.org/10.1093/ejil/chp006.

Kratochwil, Friedrich. "Making Sense of 'International Practices.'" In *International Practices*, edited by Emanuel Adler and Vincent Pouliot, 36–60, 2012. https://doi.org/10.1017/CBO9780511862373.004.

Крутских, Андрей, и Анатолий Стрельцов. «Международное право и проблема обеспечения международной информационной безопасности». Международ ная жизнь, №," 11 (2014). https://interaffairs.ru/jauthor/material/1167.

Kratochwil, Friedrich. "Practicing Law: Spoudaios, Professional, Expert or 'Macher'? Reflections on the Changing Nature of an Occupation." In *The Law of International Lawyers: Reading Martti Koskenniemi*, edited by Alexis Galán, Marieke Hoon, and Wouter Werner, 225–264. Cambridge: Cambridge University Press, 2017. https://doi.org/10.1017/9781108147620.010.

Kritsiotis, Dino. "Theorizing International Law on Force and Intervention." In *The Oxford Handbook of the Theory of International Law*, 2016. https://doi.org/10.1093/law/9780198701958.003.0034.

Kruse, Megan. "At IETF 102: The Global Commission on the Stability of Cyberspace – Cyber Diplomacy Meets InfoSec and Technology." *internet Society* (*Blog*, June 26, 2018. https://www.internetsociety.org/blog/2018/06/at-ietf-102-the-global-commission-on-the-stability-of-cyberspace-cyber-diplomacy-meets-infosec-and-technology/.

Lamp, Nicolas. "The 'Practice Turn' in International Law: Insights from the Theory of Structuration." In *Research Handbook on the Sociology of International Law*, edited by Mosche Hirsch and Andrew Lang, 273–295. Edward Elgar Publishing, 2018. https://www.elgaronline.com/edcollchap/edcoll/9781783474486/9781783474486.00020.xml.

Lang, Andrew. *Against Objectivism*. Edited by Andrew Lang. Oxford University Press, 2011. https://doi.org/10.1093/acprof:oso/9780199592647.003.0006.

Lang, Andrew. "The Double Movement of Law and Expertise." In *Expert Knowledge in Global Trade*, edited by Erin Hannah, James Scott, and Silke Trommer, 124–48. Abingdon, UK: Routledge, 2015. https://www.routledge.com/.

Lang, Andrew. *World Trade Law after Neoliberalism: Reimagining the Global Economic Order*. Oxford University Press, 2011.

Laqua, Daniel, ed. *Internationalism Reconfigured: Transnational Ideas and Movements between the World Wars*. 1st ed. London: Bloomsbury Academic, 2011.

Laski, Harold Joseph. "The Limitations of the Expert." *Harper's Magazine*, December 1, 1930. https://harpers.org/archive/1930/12/the-limitations-of-the-expert/.

Lau, Justin, Arindrajit Basu, and Irene Poetranto. "The UN Struggles to Make Progress on Securing Cyberspace." Carnegie Endowment for International Peace, May 19, 2021. https://carnegieendowment.org/2021/05/19/un-struggles-to-make-progress-on-securing-cyberspace-pub-84491.

Lauber, Jürg, and Lukas Eberli. "From Confrontation to Consensus: Taking Stock of the OEWG Process." In *Cyberstability Paper Series. Global Commission on the Stability of Cyberspace*, 2021. https://cyberstability.org/paper-series/from-confrontation-to-consensus-taking-stock-of-the-oewg-process/.

Laudrain, P.B. and Arthur. "Avoiding A World War Web: The Paris Call for Trust and Security in Cyberspace," December 4, 2018. https://www.lawfareblog.com/avoiding-world-war-web-paris-call-trust-and-security-cyberspace.

"Launch of Global Commission on the Stability of Cyberspace." *HSD SecurityDelta.Nl*, March 7, 2017. https://securitydelta.nl/news/interviews/launch-of-global-commission-on-the-stability-of-cyberspace.

Lave, Jean. "Situating Learning in Communities of Practice." In *Perspectives on Socially Shared Cognition*, 63–82. Washington, DC, US: American Psychological Association, 1991. https://doi.org/10.1037/10096-003.

Lave, Jean, and Etienne Wenger. *Situated Learning: Legitimate Peripheral Participation*. Cambridge University Press, 1991.

"Law of the Horse to Law of the Submarine: The Future of State Behavior in Cyberspace." *CyCon*, 2015. https://www.youtube.com/watch?v=rFeK4jAQvE0.

Lawfare. "Legislative Hackback: Notes on the Active Cyber Defense Certainty Act Discussion Draft," March 7, 2017. https://www.lawfareblog.com/legislative-hackback-notes-active-cyber-defense-certainty-act-discussion-draft.

Le Monde. "La France veut relancer les négociations sur la paix dans le cyberespace." *November* 8 (2018). https://www.lemonde.fr/pixels/article/2018/11/08/la-france-veut-relancer-les-negociations-sur-la-paix-dans-le-cyberespace_5380571_4408996.html.

Leander, Anna. "Habitus and Field." *Oxford Research Encyclopedia of International Studies*, March 1, 2010. https://doi.org/10.1093/acrefore/9780190846626.013.51.

Lehto, Marja. "The Rise of Cyber Norms." In *Research Handbook on International Law and Cyberspace*, edited by Nicholas Tsagourias and Russell Buchan, 1st ed. London: Edward Elgar Publishing, 2021.

Lehto, Marja. "The Rise of Cyber Norms." *Research Handbook on International Law and Cyberspace*, December 14, 2021, 32–45.

"Letter to OEWG Chair: Canadian Comments on Draft OEWG Report," April 6, 2020. https://front.un-arm.org/wp-content/uploads/2020/04/letter-to-oewg-chair-canadian-comments-on-draft-oewg-report-april-6-final.pdf.

Let's Talk Cyber. "Events :: Let's Talk Cyber," https://letstalkcyber.org/events?page=1&q=&tags%5B%5D=lets-talk-cyber2020-events&year=2020.

Let's Talk Cyber. "Let's Talk Cyber 2020 | International Law :: Let's Talk Cyber," https://letstalkcyber.org/events/let-s-talk-cyber-2020-international-law.

Let's Talk Cyber. "Let's Talk Cyber 2020 | Rules, Norms and Principles :: Let's Talk Cyber," https://letstalkcyber.org/events/let-s-talk-cyber-2020-rules-norms-and-principles.

Lewis, James A., and Christopher Painter. "Discussing the UN OEWG with the Mother of Norms." In *Inside Cyber Diplomacy*, 2021. https://www.csis.org/podcasts/inside-cyber-diplomacy/discussing-un-oewg-mother-norms.

Lin, Herbert, and Joel Trachtman. "Diagonal Export Controls to Counter Diagonal Transnational Attacks on Civil Society." *European Journal of International Law* 31, no. 3 (August 1, 2020): 917–939. https://doi.org/10.1093/ejil/chaa053.

"List of Questions for WRITTEN ANSWERS." Lok Sabha, February 11, 2022. https://loksabhadocs.nic.in/questionslist/MyFolder/11022022.pdf.

Loh, Dylan M.H. "Institutional Habitus, State Identity, and China's Ministry of Foreign Affairs." *International Studies Review* 22, no. 4 (November 26, 2020): 879–902. https://doi.org/10.1093/isr/viz051.

Lotrionte, Catherine. "Bringing the Law In: Unlearned Lessons for Diplomats and Others." *The Cyber Defense Review* 7, no. 1 (2022): 23–32.

Lotrionte, Catherine, and Enekken Tikk. *Panel 3: Applicability of International Law to Cyberspace & Characterization of Cyber Incidents*. Cambridge, MA: Cyber Norms Workshop, 2012. https://citizenlab.ca/cybernorms2012/panel3summary.pdf.

Lu, Catherine. "Introduction." In *Roundtable 2–5 on International Security in Practice: The Politics of NATO-Russia Diplomacy. H-Diplo | ISSF*, 2012. https://issforum.org/roundtables/2-5-international-security-in-practice.

Lu, Catherine, Peter Jackson, James Goldgeier, Robert Jervis, Ole Jacob Sending, Jennifer Sterling-Folker, Andrei Tsygankov, and Vincent Pouliot. "Roundtable 2–5 on International Security in Practice: The Politics of NATO-Russia Diplomacy." In *H-Diplo | ISSF*, 2011. https://issforum.org/roundtables/2-5-international-security-in-practice.

Lubin, Asaf. "Judge Simma during the Championship Round of @The_Jessup, Asking the Applicant on the Use of @TallinnManual as a Source of Law: 'Aren't You a Bit Quick to Elevate the Tallinn Manual into a 38(1)(d) Source. Is @Schmitt_ILaw Really like Grotius or Brownlie of Our Time?'" *Tweet. Twitter*, April 9, 2022. https://twitter.com/AsafLubin/status/1512790447374094338.

Lubin, Asaf. "Tom Wingfield (@RANDCorporation): On Grey Zone Ops: 'The Dimmer Switch Option of Cyber Is Very Attractive to Policymakers.' @Schmitt_ILaw 'I'm Nervous That All the Voluntary Norms & Other Int'l Cyber Projects, TM Included, Are Creating More Confusion than Clarity for States.' Https://T.Co/WvxW4JxqrZ." *Tweet. Twitter*, June 15, 2022. https://twitter.com/AsafLubin/status/1537146862796476418.

Lupia, Arthur, and Colin Elman. "Openness in Political Science: Data Access and Research Transparency." *PS: Political Science & Politics* 47, no. 01 (January 2014): 19–42. https://doi.org/10.1017/S1049096513001716.

Mačák, Kubo. "From Cyber Norms to Cyber Rules: Re-Engaging States as Law-Makers." *Leiden Journal of International Law* 30, no. 4 (December 2017): 877–899. https://doi.org/10.1017/S0922156517000358.

Mačák, Kubo. "Is the International Law of Cyber Security in Crisis?" In *2016 8th International Conference on Cyber Conflict* (*CyCon*, 127–139, 2016. https://doi.org/10.1109/CYCON.2016.7529431.

Mačák, Kubo. "Military Objectives 2.0: The Case for Interpreting Computer Data as Objects under International Humanitarian Law." *Israel Law Review* 48, no. 1 (March 2015): 55–80. https://doi.org/10.1017/S0021223714000260.

Mačák, Kubo Laurent Gisel, and Tilman Rodenhäuser. "International Law Protections against Malicious Cyber Operations Targeting the Healthcare Sector." In *The Oxford Process on International Law Protections in Cyberspace*, 2020. https://www.elac.ox.ac.uk/wp-content/uploads/2022/10/Oxford-Process-Compendium-Digital.pdf.

Madsen, Mikael Rask. "Reflexivity and the Construction of the International Object: The Case of Human Rights." *International Political Sociology* 5, no. 3 (September 1): 259–275. https://doi.org/10.1111/j.1749-5687.2011.00133.x.

Madsen, Mikael Rask, and Salvatore Caserta. "International Judicial Habitus: Pierre Bourdieu and the Cognitive Turn." In *International Legal Theory and the Cognitive Turn*, edited by Anne van Aaken and Moshe Hirsch. Oxford University Press, 2025. https://doi.org/10.1093/9780198909293.003.0011.

Mälksoo, Lauri. "The Tallinn Manual as an International Event." *ICDS*, August 8, 2013. https://icds.ee/en/the-tallinn-manual-as-an-international-event/.

Marby, Göran. "ICANN President & CEO Goals for Fiscal Year 2021." *ICANN*, July 2020. https://www.icann.org/en/blogs/details/icann-president–ceo-goals-for-fiscal-year-2021-20-7-2020-en.

Marceau, Gabrielle Z., and Jennifer K. Hawkins. "Experts in WTO Dispute Settlement." *Journal of International Dispute Settlement* 3, no. 3 (November 1): 493–507. https://doi.org/10.1093/jnlids/ids014.

March, James G., and Johan P. Olsen. "The Logic of Appropriateness." In *The Oxford Handbook of Public Policy*, edited by Robert Goodin, Michael Moran, and Martin Rein, 0. Oxford University Press, 2008. https://doi.org/10.1093/oxfordhb/9780199548453.003.0034.

Markoff, John. "A Silent Attack, but Not a Subtle One." *The New York Times*, September 27, 2010. https://www.nytimes.com/2010/09/27/technology/27virus.html.

Martin, Lisa L., and Beth A. Simmons. "Theories and Empirical Studies of International Institutions." *International Organization* 52, no. 4 (1998): 729–57. https://doi.org/10.1162/002081898550734.

Maurer, Tim. *Cyber Norm Emergence at the United Nations – - An Analysis of the Activities at the UN Regarding Cyber-Security*. Cambridge, MA: Belfer Center for Science and International Affairs, 2011. https://www.belfercenter.org/sites/default/files/legacy/files/maurer-cyber-norm-dp-2011-11-final.pdf.

Maurer, Tim, and Wyatt Hoffman. "The Privatization of Security and the Market for Cyber Tools and Services," 2019.

Maurer, Tim, Christian Ruhl, Duncan Hollis, and Wyatt Hoffman. *Cyberspace and Geopolitics: Assessing Global Cybersecurity Norm Processes at a Crossroads*. Carnegie Endowment for International Peace, 2020. https://carnegieendowment.org/2020/02/26/cyberspace-and-geopolitics-assessing-global-cybersecurity-norm-processes-at-crossroads-pub-81110.

Maurushat, Alana, and Kathy Nguyen. "The Legal Obligation to Provide Timely Security Patching and Automatic Updates." *International Cybersecurity Law Review* 3, no. 2 (December 1): 437–65. https://doi.org/10.1365/s43439-022-00059-6.

McKay, Angela, Jan Neutze, Paul Nicholas, and Kevin Sullivan. "International Cybersecurity Norms: Reducing Conflict in an internet-Dependent World," December 14, 2014. https://query.prod.cms.rt.microsoft.com/cms/api/am/binary/REVroA.

McNeil, Adam. "How Did the WannaCry Ransomworm Spread? | Malwarebytes Labs." *Malwarebytes*, May 19, 2017. https://www.malwarebytes.com/blog/news/2017/05/how-did-wannacry-ransomworm-spread.

"Means to Reinforce Research on Nuclear Disarmament Verification: Report on a Series of Regional Conversations." *Matters*, no. 13 (November 2017). http://www.vertic.org/media/assets/Publications/VM13.pdf.

"MEETING WITH ICANN GOVERNMENTAL ADVISORY COMMITTEE | ICANN 65, Marrakesh." In *Global Commission on the Stability of Cyberspace*, 2019. https://gac.icann.org/presentations/public/ICANN65-13.1-GCSC.pdf?language_id=1.

Mégret, Frédéric. "International Criminal Justice as a Juridical Field." *Champ Pénal/Penal Field*, no. Vol. XIII (February 29, 2016). https://doi.org/10.4000/champpenal.9284.

Mégret, Frédéric. "Thinking about What International Humanitarian Lawyers 'Do': An Examination of the Laws of War as a Field of Professional Practice." In *The Law of International Lawyers*, edited by Wouter Werner, Marieke Hoon, and Alexis Galán, 1st ed., 265–296. Cambridge University Press, 2017. https://doi.org/10.1017/9781108147620.011.

Meierhenrich, Jens. "The Practice of International Law: A Theoretical Analysis." *Law and Contemporary Problems* 76, no. 3/4 (2013): 1–83.

Meston. "The Spirit of Geneva." *International Affairs* 15, no. 4 (July 1, 1936): 576–576. https://doi.org/10.1093/ia/15.4.576.

Meta. "Coordinated Inauthentic Behavior," https://about.fb.com/news/tag/coordinated-inauthentic-behavior/.

Meyer, Paul. "Does the Conference of Disarmament Have a Future?" *Journal for Peace and Nuclear Disarmament* 4, no. 2 (July 3): 287–94. https://doi.org/10.1080/25751654.2021.1993632.

Michael, James Bret, Eneken Tikk, Peter Wahlgren, and Thomas C. Wingfield. "From Chaos to Collective Defense." *Computer* 43, no. 8 (August 2010): 91–94. https://doi.org/10.1109/MC.2010.228.

Michele G. Markoff, Statement. "Delegation of the United States of America." *October* 30 (2013). https://unoda-documents-library.s3.amazonaws.com/General_Assembly_First_Committee_Sixty-eighth_session_(2013)/united-states_4.pdf.

Mikanagi, Tomohiro. "Application of the Due Diligence Principle to Cyber Operations." *International Law Studies* 97 (2021): 21.

"Militair Rechtelijk Tijdschrift Jaargang 111 – 2018 – 3 Cyber Special." *Netherlands Military Law Review*, 2018. https://puc.overheid.nl/mrt/doc/PUC_248137_11/1/.

Miller, Seumas, and Michael J. Selgelid. "Ethical and Philosophical Consideration of the Dual-Use Dilemma in the Biological Sciences." *Science and Engineering Ethics* 13, no. 4 (2007): 523–580. https://doi.org/10.1007/s11948-007-9043-4.

Ministère de l'Europe et Des Affaires. "Cybersecurity: Paris Call of 12 November 2018 for Trust and Security in Cyberspace." In *France Diplomacy – Ministry for Europe and Foreign Affairs*, Accessed April 13, 2023 https://www.diplomatie.gouv.fr/en/french-foreign-policy/digital-diplomacy/france-and-cyber-security/article/cybersecurity-paris-call-of-12-november-2018-for-trust-and-security-in.

Ministère de l'Europe et Des Affaires. "Ministère de l'Europe et Des Affaires. 'Guaranteeing Cybersecurity.' France Diplomacy – Ministry for Europe and Foreign Affairs," Accessed April 13, 2023 https://www.diplomatie.gouv.fr/en/french-foreign-policy/digital-diplomacy/france-s-international-digital-strategy/article/guaranteeing-cybersecurity.

Ministère de l'Europe et Des Affaires. "Multilateralism: A Principle of Action for France." France Diplomacy – Ministry for Europe and Foreign Affairs," Accessed April 13, 2023 https://www.diplomatie.gouv.fr/en/french-foreign-policy/united-nations/multilateralism-a-principle-of-action-for-france/.

Ministerie van Algemene Zaken. "History – About Us – The Netherlands Scientific Council for Government Policy." *Webpagina. Ministerie van Algemene Zaken*, May 20, 2022. https://english.wrr.nl/about-us/history-of-wrr.

Ministerie van Algemene Zaken. "Organization – About Us – The Netherlands Scientific Council for Government Policy." In *Webpagina. Ministerie van Algemene Zaken*, 2022. https://english.wrr.nl/about-us/organization.

Ministerie van Algemene Zaken. "WRR Highlights Urgent Need to Protect the internet through International Policy – Persbericht – WRR." *Persbericht. Ministerie van Algemene Zaken*, April 10, 2015.

Ministry of Foreign Affairs, Republic of Korea. In "Foreign Ministry to Hold the Pre-workshop on International Security for Seoul Conference on Cyberspace 2013 View|Press Releases | Ministry of Foreign Affairs, Republic of Korea." June 27, 2013 https://www.mofa.go.kr/eng/brd/m_5676/view.do?seq=312480&srchFr=&%

3BsrchTo=&%3BsrchWord=&%3BsrchTp=&%3Bmulti_itm_seq=0&%3Bitm_seq_1=0&%3Bitm_seq_2=0&%3Bcompany_cd=&%3Bcompany_nm=.

Mitrany, David. "The Prospect of Integration: Federal or Functional." *JCMS: Journal of Common Market Studies* 4, no. 2 (1965): 119–49. https://doi.org/10.1111/j.1468-5965.1965.tb01124.x.

Monroe, Kristen Renwick. "The Rush to Transparency: DA-RT and the Potential Dangers for Qualitative Research." *Perspectives on Politics* 16, no. 1 (March 2018): 141–48. https://doi.org/10.1017/S153759271700336X.

"Montreux Five Years On: An Analysis of State Efforts to Implement Montreux Document Legal Obligations and Good Practices." American University Washington College of Law, 2013. https://www.wcl.american.edu/index.cfm?LinkServID=B1E626D9-095E-4A28-94A94551CEA3488E.

Moody, Glyn. "France Says 'No' to Company Hack-Backs Following Online Attacks – But Wants to Keep the Option Open for Itself," February 20, 2018. https://www.techdirt.com/2018/02/20/france-says-no-to-company-hack-backs-following-online-attacks-wants-to-keep-option-open-itself/.

Moomaw, William R. "Scientist Diplomats or Diplomat Scientists: Who Makes Science Diplomacy Effective?" *Global Policy* 9, no. S3 (2018): 78–80. https://doi.org/10.1111/1758-5899.12520.

Moraes, M. "Internationalism as an Organisational Practice: The League of Nations Secretary-General, 1918–1946." Http://purl.org/dc/dcmitype/Text, University of Oxford, 2020. https://ora.ox.ac.uk/objects/uuid:b5c37bd9-fc74-4a18-8e28-5655aa7345cd.

Moravcsik, Andrew. "Transparency: The Revolution in Qualitative Research." *PS: Political Science & Politics* 47, no. 1 (January 2014): 48–53. https://doi.org/10.1017/S1049096513001789.

Morgan, Patrick M. "The Practice of Deterrence." In *International Practices*, edited by Emanuel Adler and Vincent Pouliot, 139–73. Cambridge: Cambridge University Press, 2011. https://doi.org/10.1017/CBO9780511862373.010.

Morris, P.Sean. "The Advisory Committee of Jurists and the Historical Origins of Scholarly Writings as a Source of International Law." In *SSRN Scholarly Paper*. Rochester, NY: Social Science Research Network, 2019. https://papers.ssrn.com/abstract=3373294.

"Multistakeholder Diplomacy: Building a Cybersecurity Regime," 2021. https://sites.tufts.edu/cilg/multistakeholderdiplomacy/.

Multi-Stakeholder Insights| A Compendium on Countering Election Interference. Canada: Microsoft, 2021. https://www.canada.ca/content/dam/di-id/documents/compendium-eng.pdf.

"Multistakeholder Participation at the UN: The Need for Greater Inclusivity in the UN Dialogues on Cybersecurity," November 2021. https://pariscall.international/

assets/files/10-11-WG3-Multistakeholder-participation-at-the-UN-The-need-for-greater-inclusivity-in-the-UN-dialogues-on-cybersecurity.pdf.

Nair, Deepak. "Saving Face in Diplomacy: A Political Sociology of Face-to-Face Interactions in the Association of Southeast Asian Nations." *European Journal of International Relations* 25, no. 3 (September 1): 672–697. https://doi.org/10.1177/1354066118822117.

Nakashidze, Giorgi. "Cyberattack against Georgia and International Response: Emerging Normative Paradigm of 'Responsible State Behavior in Cyberspace'?," February 28, 2020. https://www.ejiltalk.org/cyberattack-against-georgia-and-international-response-emerging-normative-paradigm-of-responsible-state-behavior-in-cyberspace/.

NATO. "Brussels Summit Communiqué Issued by NATO Heads of State and Government (2021) https://www.nato.int/cps/en/natohq/news_185000.htm.

NATO CCDCOE "Over 50 States Consult Tallinn Manual 2.0," 2016. https://ccdcoe.org/news/2016/over-50-states-consult-tallinn-manual-2-0/.

NATO CCDCOE. "@paulducheine @alexsib17 We're Planning for Second Half of 2016 for Completion and Publication. @Schmitt_ILaw @lvihul." *Tweet. Twitter*, October 9, 2015. https://twitter.com/ccdcoe/status/652392532404514816.

NATO CCDCOE. "Tallinn Manual 2.0 to Be Completed in 2016," 2015. https://ccdcoe.org/news/2015/tallinn-manual-2-0-to-be-completed-in-2016/.

Neumann, Iver B. "Returning Practice to the Linguistic Turn: The Case of Diplomacy." *Millennium* 31, no. 3 (July 1): 627–651. https://doi.org/10.1177/03058298020310031201.

Newman, Abraham, and Elliot Posner. "Transnational Feedback, Soft Law, and Preferences in Global Financial Regulation." *Review of International Political Economy* 23, no. 1 (January 2, 2016): 123–152. https://doi.org/10.1080/09692290.2015.1104375.

"Non-paper: Proposal for a Norm of Non-interference in Core internet Functions [Revised." *Clingendael Institute*, July 19, 2016.

"Non-paper: Proposal for a Norm of Non-intervention in the Public Core of the Global internet." *Clingendael Institute*, July 4, 2016.

"Norm Package | Singapore." In *Global Commission on the Stability of Cyberspace*, 2018. https://cyberstability.org/wp-content/uploads/2018/11/GCSC-Singapore-Norm-Package-3MB.pdf.

"NTI Nuclear Security Index." *The Nuclear Threat Initiative*, April 16, 2024. https://www.nti.org/about/programs-projects/project/nti-index/.

Nye, Joseph S., Jr, "Opinion | Cyberspace Wars." *The New York Times*, February 27, 2011. https://www.nytimes.com/2011/02/28/opinion/28iht-ednye28.html.

"Official Compendium of Voluntary National Contributions on the Subject of How International Law Applies to the Use of Information and Communications Technologies by States Submitted by Participating Governmental Experts." In *Group of Governmental Experts on Advancing Responsible State Behavior in Cyberspace in the*

Context of International Security Established Pursuant to General Assembly Resolution 73/266." UN General Assembly, Seventy-Sixth Session, 2021. https://front.unarm.org/wp-content/uploads/2021/08/A-76-136-EN.pdf.

"Official Records of the 15th Meeting of the First Committee." New York: UN, 2001. https://documents-dds-ny.un.org/doc/UNDOC/GEN/N10/594/32/PDF/N1059432.pdf?OpenElement.

Official Records of the 17th Meeting of the First Committee. New York: UN General Assembly, Sixty-fourth Session, 2009. https://documents-dds-ny.un.org/doc/UNDOC/GEN/N09/571/73/PDF/N0957173.pdf?OpenElement.

"OHCHR | Call for Inputs: Report on the Provision of Military and Security Cyber Products and Services by 'Cyber Mercenaries' and Its Human Rights Impact," 2021. https://www.ohchr.org/en/calls-for-input/2021/call-inputs-report-provision-military-and-security-cyber-products-and-services.

Olejnik, Lukasz. "French Application of International Rules to Cyberwarfare." *Security, Privacy & Tech Inquiries*, September 10, 2019. http://blog.lukaszolejnik.com/french-application-of-international-rules-to-cyberwarfare/.

"Open-Ended Working Group – UNODA," https://www.un.org/disarmament/open-ended-working-group/.

"Open-Ended Working Group on Information and Communication Technologies (2021) | United Nations," https://meetings.unoda.org/open-ended-working-group-information-and-communication-technologies-2021.

"Opening Speech GCCS Bert Koenders." *The Hague Online* (*blog*), *April* 16 (2015). https://www.thehagueonline.com/news/2015/04/16/opening-speech-gccs-bert-koenders.

O'Reilly, Karen. "Coding." In *Key Concepts in Ethnography*, 34–38. London: SAGE Publications Ltd, 2009. https://doi.org/10.4135/9781446268308.

Orford, Anne. "International Law and the Limits of History." In *The Law of International Lawyers*, edited by Wouter Werner, Marieke Hoon, and Alexis Galan, 297–320. Cambridge: Cambridge University Press, 2017. https://doi.org/10.1017/9781108147620.012.

Orford, Anne. "Scientific Reason and the Discipline of International Law." In *International Law as a Profession*, edited by Jean d'Aspremont, Tarcisio Gazzini, Andre Nollkaemper, and Wouter Werner, 93–114. Cambridge: Cambridge University Press, 2017. https://doi.org/10.1017/9781316492802.006.

"Organization of Work of the First Substantive Session (Open-Ended Working Group on Developments in the Field of Information and Telecommunications in the Context of International Security," July 23, 2019. https://unoda-web.s3.amazonaws.com/wp-content/uploads/2019/08/A-AC.290-2019-2.pdf.

Osula, Anna-Maria, and Henry Rõigas. "International Cyber Norms." In *International Cyber Norms: Legal, Policy & Industry Perspectives*, edited by Anna-Maria Osula and Henry Rõigas. Tallinn: NATO CCD COE Publications, 2016.

Oxford Institute for Ethics, Law and Armed Conflict. "Behind the Scenes." https://www.elac.ox.ac.uk/the-oxford-process/behind-the-scenes/.

Oxford Public International Law. "Conference (Meeting) of States Parties," Accessed April 13, 2023 https://opil.ouplaw.com/view/10.1093/law:epil/9780199231690/law-9780199231690-e909.

Oxford Reference. "Intersubjectivity," 2011 https://doi.org/10.1093/oi/authority.20110803100008603.

Paganini, Pierluigi. "German Government Prepares Law for Backdoors and Hacking Back." *Security Affairs*, December 5, 2017. https://securityaffairs.co/wordpress/66370/digital-id/german-government-backdoors-law.html.

Paltiel, Daniel. "Russian Newspaper Kommersant Interviews Special Representative Krutskikh on UN GGE Cyber Arrangements." *Center for Strategic and International Studies*, August 17, 2015. https://www.csis.org/blogs/strategic-technologies-blog/russian-newspaper-kommersant-interviews-special-representative.

Paris Call. "The Call and the 9 Principles – Paris Call." *November* 11 (2018). https://pariscall.international/en/principles.

Paris Call. "The Paris Call." *November* 12 (2018). https://pariscall.international/en/call.

Patel, Bimal N., ed. "Case Concerning Military and Paramilitary Activities in and against Nicaragua: (Nicaragua v. USA." In *The World Court Reference Guide*, 487–511. Brill | Nijhoff, 2000. https://doi.org/10.1163/9789004481237_119.

Pauwelyn, Joost. "Foreword." In *A Digest of WTO Jurisprudence on Public International Law Concepts and Principles*, edited by Graham Cook and xiii–xix. Cambridge: Cambridge University Press, 2015. https://doi.org/10.1017/CBO9781316212691.001.

Pauwelyn, Joost. "The Use of Experts in WTO Dispute Settlement." *The International and Comparative Law Quarterly* 51, no. 2 (2002): 325–364.

Pauwelyn, Joost, Ramses Wessel, and Jan Wouters. *Informal International Lawmaking*. Oxford: Oxford University Press, 2012.

Peat, Daniel, and Matthew Windsor. "An Interpretive Turn to Practice Part II: Interpretation in International Law Symposium." *Cambridge Journal of International and Comparative Law* 3, no. 2 (2014): 444–449.

Pellet, Alain, and Daniel Müller. "Part Three Statute of the International Court of Justice, Ch.Ii Competence of the Court, Article 38." In *The Statute of the International Court of Justice*, edited by Andreas Zimmermann, Christian J. Tams, Karin Oellers-Frahm, and Christian Tomuschat, 3rd ed. Oxford, UK: Oxford University Press, 2019. https://opil.ouplaw.com/view/10.1093/law/9780198814894.001.0001/law-9780198814894-chapter-50.

Petersmann, Ernst-Ulrich. "The Establishment of a GATT Office of Legal Affairs and the Limits of 'Public Reason' in the GATT/WTO Dispute Settlement System." In *A History of Law and Lawyers in the GATT/WTO: The Development of the Rule of Law in the Multilateral Trading System*, edited by Gabrielle Marceau, 182–207. Cambridge: WTO Internal Only, 2015. https://doi.org/10.1017/CBO9781316048160.016.

Phillips, Morgan. "Biden Gave Putin List of 16 Critical Infrastructure Entities 'off Limits' to Cyberattacks." *Text.Article. FOXBusiness. Fox Business*, June 16, 2021. https://www.foxbusiness.com/politics/biden-putin-critical-infrastructure-entities-off-limits-cyberattacks.

Pomson, Ori. "The Prohibition on Intervention Under International Law and Cyber Operations." *International Law Studies* 99 (2022): 41.

Porges, Amelia. "The New Dispute Settlement: From the GATT to the WTO." *Leiden Journal of International Law* 8, no. 1 (1995): 115–33. https://doi.org/10.1017/S0922156500003137.

Pouliot, Vincent. "Evolution in International Practices." In *Conceptualizing International Practices*, edited by Alena Drieschova, Christian Bueger, and Ted Hopf, 1st ed., 170–190. Cambridge University Press, 2022. https://doi.org/10.1017/9781009052504.008.

Pouliot, Vincent. "Global Governance in the Age of Epistemic Authority." *International Theory* 13, no. 1 (March 2021): 144–156. https://doi.org/10.1017/S1752971920000433.

Pouliot, Vincent. *International Security in Practice: The Politics of NATO–Russia Diplomacy*. Cambridge: Cambridge University Press, 2010. https://doi.org/10.1017/CBO9780511676185.

Pouliot, Vincent. "Practice Tracing." In *Process Tracing: From Metaphor to Analytic Tool*, edited by Andrew Bennett and Jeffrey T. Cambridge: Cambridge University Press, 2014. https://doi.org/10.1017/CBO9781139858472.013.

Pouliot, Vincent. "The Gray Area of Institutional Change: How the Security Council Transforms Its Practices on the Fly." *Journal of Global Security Studies* 6, no. 3 (September 1, 2021): 043. https://doi.org/10.1093/jogss/ogaa043.

Pouliot, Vincent. "The Logic of Practicality: A Theory of Practice of Security Communities." *International Organization* 62, no. 2 (2008): 257–288.

Pouliot, Vincent. "The Logic of Practicality: A Theory of Practice of Security Communities." In *International Security in Practice: The Politics of NATO-Russia Diplomacy, 11–51. Cambridge Studies in International Relations*. Cambridge: Cambridge University Press, 2010. https://doi.org/10.1017/CBO9780511676185.003.

Pouliot, Vincent, and Frédéric Mérand. "Bourdieu's Concepts: Political Sociology in International Relations." In *Bourdieu in International Relations: Rethinking Key Concepts in IR*, edited by Rebecca Adler-Nissen. Routledge, 2012.

Pouliot, Vincent, and Jean-Philippe Thérien. "Global Governance in Practice." *Global Policy* 9, no. 2 (2018): 163–172. https://doi.org/10.1111/1758-5899.12529.

"Preliminary Comments of Mexico to the Initial 'Pre-draft' of the Report of the OEWG on Developments in the Field of Information and Telecommunications in the Context of International Security," April 2020. https://front.un-arm.org/wp-content/uploads/2020/04/mexico-inputs-pre-draft-oewg.pdf.

"Professor Huang Zhixiong Was Elected as Special Rapporteur of International Organizations." *October* 10 (2018). http://translaw.whu.edu.cn/en/index.php/index-view-aid-505.html.

"Programme of Action on Small Arms and Its International Tracing Instrument – UNODA," https://www.un.org/disarmament/convarms/salw/programme-of-action/.

"Proposal for a DIRECTIVE OF THE EUROPEAN PARLIAMENT AND OF THE COUNCIL on Measures for a High Common Level of Cybersecurity across the Union, Repealing Directive (EU) 2016/1148," 2020. https://eur-lex.europa.eu/legal-content/EN/TXT/?uri=celex:52020PC0823.

"Provisional Rules of Procedure of the Conference." In *United Nations Conference on the Illicit Trade in Small Arms and Light Weapons in All Its Aspects*, 2001. https://documents-dds-ny.un.org/doc/UNDOC/GEN/N01/410/92/PDF/N0141092.pdf?OpenElement.

Pytlak, Allison. "Cyber Peace & Security Monitor." *Reaching Critical Will*, July 31, 2022. https://www.reachingcriticalwill.org/disarmament-fora/ict/oewg-ii/cyber-monitor/16310-cyber-peace-security-monitor-vol-2-no-7.

"Qualitative Transparency Deliberations on Behalf of the APSA Section for Qualitative and Multi-Method Research," 2021. https://doi.org/10.7910/DVN/SWVFV8.

Rajkovic, Nikolas M., Tanja E. Aalberts, and Thomas Gammeltoft-Hansen. "Introduction: Legality, Interdisciplinarity and the Study of Practices." In *The Power of Legality: Practices of International Law and Their Politics*, edited by Nikolas M. Rajkovic, Tanja E. Aalberts, and Thomas Gammeltoft-Hansen, 1–26. Cambridge: Cambridge University Press, 2016. https://doi.org/10.1017/CBO9781316535134.002.

Rao, Pemmaraju Sreenivasa. "Third Report on International Liability for Injurious Consequences Arising out of Acts Not Prohibited by International Law (Prevention of Transboundary Damage from Hazardous Activities." *International Law Commission, Fifty-Second Session*, June 9, 2000. https://legal.un.org/ilc/documentation/english/a_cn4_510.pdf.

Ratner, Steven. "Persuasion About/Without International Law: the Case of Cybersecurity Norms." In *Talking International Law: Legal Argumentation Outside the Courtroom*, edited by Ian Johnstone and Steven Ratner, 2021st ed. New York: Oxford University Press, 2021.

Ratner, Steven R. "Persuading to Comply: On the Deployment and Avoidance of Legal Argumentation." In *Interdisciplinary Perspectives on International Law and International Relations: The State of the Art*, edited by Jeffrey L. Dunoff and Mark A. Pollack, 568–590. Cambridge: Cambridge University Press, 2012. https://doi.org/10.1017/CBO9781139107310.028.

Raustiala, Kal. "Form and Substance in International Agreements." *American Journal of International Law* 99, no. 3 (2005): 581–614.

Rawls, John. "The Idea of an Overlapping Consensus." *Oxford Journal of Legal Studies* 7, no. 1 (1987): 1–25.

Reaching Critical Will. "Arms Trade Treaty," Accessed April 2, 2023 https://www.reachingcriticalwill.org/disarmament-fora/att.

Reay, Diane. "'It's All Becoming a Habitus': Beyond the Habitual Use of Habitus in Educational Research." *British Journal of Socioltogy of Education* 25, no. 4 (2004): 431–444.

redazione@ispionlineit. "Cyber Norms and the United Nations: Between Strategic Ambiguity and Rules of the Road." *Text. ISPI*, March 18, 2020. https://www.ispionline.it/en/pubblicazione/cyber-norms-and-united-nations-between-strategic-ambiguity-and-rules-road-25417.

Redman, Renee Colette. "The League of Nations and the Right to Be Free from Enslavement: The First Human Right to Be Recognized as Customary International Law – Freedom." *Beyond the United States"* 70 (1994): 43.

Redwood, Henry, and Hannah Goozee. "Shifting Accounts of Justice: The Legalization and Politicization of International Criminal Justice." *Social & Legal Studies* 31, no. 4 (August 1): 623–43. https://doi.org/10.1177/09646639211058832.

Reinsberg, Bernhard, and Oliver Westerwinter. "The Global Governance of International Development: Documenting the Rise of Multi-Stakeholder Partnerships and Identifying Underlying Theoretical Explanations." *The Review of International Organizations* 16, no. 1 (January 2021): 59–94. https://doi.org/10.1007/s11558-019-09362-0.

"Report – Global Commission on the Stability of Cyberspace," https://cyberstability.org/report/.

Report of the 2016 Informal Meeting of Experts on Lethal Autonomous Weapons Systems (*LAWS*. UN Office of Disarmament Affairs, 2016. https://documents-dds-ny.un.org/doc/UNDOC/GEN/G16/117/16/PDF/G1611716.pdf?OpenElement.

"Report of the Group of Governmental Experts on Advancing Responsible State Behavior in Cyberspace in the Context of International Security." In *UN General Assembly, Seventy-Sixth Session*, 2021. https://documents-dds-ny.un.org/doc/UNDOC/GEN/N21/075/86/PDF/N2107586.pdf?OpenElement.

"Report of the Group of Governmental Experts on Developments in the Field of Information and Telecommunications in the Context of International Security

(A/65/201," July 30, 2010. https://documents-dds-ny.un.org/doc/UNDOC/GEN/N10/469/57/PDF/N1046957.pdf?OpenElement.

"Report of the International Law Commission on the Work of Its Fifty-First Session," May 3, 1999. https://legal.un.org/ilc/documentation/english/reports/a_54_10.pdf.

Report of the International Security Cyber Issues Workshop Series. UNIDIR/ Center for Strategic and International Studies, 2016. https://www.unidir.org/files/publications/pdfs/report-of-the-international-security-cyber-issues-workshop-series-en-656.pdf.

Report of the International Security Cyber Issues Workshop Series. Geneva: UNIDIR/ Center for Strategic and International Studies, 2016. https://unidir.org/sites/default/files/publication/pdfs/report-of-the-international-security-cyber-issues-workshop-series-en-656.pdf.

Reykers, Yf, John Karlsrud, Malte Brosig, Stephanie Claudia Hofmann, Cristiana Maglia, and Pernille Rieker. "Ad Hoc Coalitions in Global Governance: Short-Notice, Task- and Time-Specific Cooperation." *International Affairs*, 2023. https://doi.org/10.1093/ia/iiac319.

Richmond, Oliver P. "UN Peace Operations and the Dilemmas of the Peacebuilding Consensus." *International Peacekeeping* 11, no. 1 (March 2004): 83–101. https://doi.org/10.1080/1353331042000228403.

Riecke, Lena. "Unmasking the Term 'Dual Use' in EU Spyware Export Control." *European Journal of International Law* 34, no. 3 (2023): 697–720. https://doi.org/10.1093/ejil/chad039.

Riles, Annelise. "Infinity within the Brackets." *American Ethnologist* 25, no. 3 (August 1998): 378–398. https://doi.org/10.1525/ae.1998.25.3.378.

Ringmar, Erik. "The Search for Dialogue as a Hindrance to Understanding: Practices as Inter-Paradigmatic Research Program." *International Theory* 6, no. 1 (March 2014): 1–27. https://doi.org/10.1017/S1752971913000316.

Risse, Thomas. "'Let's Argue!': Communicative Action in World Politics." *International Organization* 54, no. 1 (2000): 1–39.

Roguski, Przemysław. "Layered Sovereignty: Adjusting Traditional Notions of Sovereignty to a Digital Environment." In *2019 11th International Conference on Cyber Conflict* (*CyCon*, 900:1–13, 2019. https://doi.org/10.23919/CYCON.2019.8756900.

"Roundtable 2–5 on International Security in Practice: The Politics of NATO-Russia Diplomacy," March 14, 2011. https://issforum.org/roundtables/2-5-international-security-in-practice.

"Rules of Procedure of the Conference on Disarmament." Conference on Disarmament, 2022. https://documents-dds-ny.un.org/doc/UNDOC/GEN/G22/439/18/PDF/G2243918.pdf?OpenElement.

Russian Federation." "Commentary of the Russian Federation on The Final Report of The United Nations Open-Ended Working Group on Developments in The Field of

Information and Telecommunications in The Context of International Security.", Accessed April 2, 2023 https://front.un-arm.org/wp-content/uploads/2020/04/russian-commentary-on-oweg-zero-draft-report-eng.pdf.

Sacriste, Guillaume, and Antoine Vauchez. "The Force of International Law: Lawyers' Diplomacy on the International Scene in the 1920s." *Law & Social Inquiry* 32, no. 1 (2007): 83–107.

Samuel, Cherian. *UN Cyber OEWG Ends after Five-Year Run*. Manohar Parrikar Institute for Defence Studies and Analyses, 2025. https://www.idsa.in/publisher/issuebrief/un-cyber-oewg-ends-after-five-year-run.

Samuel, Herbert. "The World Economic Conference." *International Affairs (Royal Institute of International Affairs 1931–1939* 12, no. 4 (1933): 439–459. https://doi.org/10.2307/2603601.

Sarfaty, Galit. *Values in Translation: Human Rights and the Culture of the World Bank*. Stanford University Press, 2012.

Sarson, Leah, Val Muzik, Brandon Ray, Glenn Gambrell, Leehi Yona, and Robert Comeau. "The Model Arctic Council: Simulated Negotiations as Pedagogy and Embodied Diplomacy." *American Review of Canadian Studies* 49, no. 1 (January 2, 2019): 105–122. https://doi.org/10.1080/02722011.2019.1570955.

Schachter, Oscar. "Invisible College of International Lawyers." *Northwestern University Law Review* 72 (1978): 217.

Schatz, Edward. "Disciplines That Forget: Political Science and Ethnography." *PS: Political Science & Politics* 50, no. 1 (January 2017): 135–138. https://doi.org/10.1017/S1049096516002304.

Schatz, Edward. "Methods Are Not Tools: Ethnography and the Limits of Multiple-Methods Research." C&M Political Methodology Working Paper Series." *The Committee on Concepts and Methods*, January 12, 2007. https://concepts-methods.org/Files/WorkingPaper/PM%2012%20Schatz.pdf.

Schia, Niels Nagelhus. "Being Part of the Parade – 'Going Native' in the United Nations Security Council." *PoLAR: Political and Legal Anthropology Review* 36, no. 1 (2013): 138–56. https://doi.org/10.1111/plar.12007.

Schindler, Sebastian, and Tobias Wille. "Change in and through Practice: Pierre Bourdieu, Vincent Pouliot, and the End of the Cold War." *International Theory* 7, no. 2 (July 2015): 330–59. https://doi.org/10.1017/S1752971915000068.

Schmitt, Michael. "In Defense of Sovereignty in Cyberspace," May 8, 2018. https://www.justsecurity.org/55876/defense-sovereignty-cyberspace/.

Schmitt, Michael. "Tallinn Manual 2.0 on the International Law of Cyber Operations: What It Is and Isn't," February 9, 2017. https://www.justsecurity.org/37559/tallinn-manual-2-0-international-law-cyber-operations/.

Schmitt, Michael. "The United Kingdom on International Law in Cyberspace." *EJIL: Talk!*, May 24, 2022. https://www.ejiltalk.org/the-united-kingdom-on-international-law-in-cyberspace/.

Schmitt, Michael. "Foreign Cyber Interference in Elections." *International Law Studies* 97 (2021): 27.

Schmitt, Michael. "Grey Zones in the International Law of Cyberspace." *Yale Journal of International Law Online* 42, no. 2 (2017). https://cpb-us-w2.wpmucdn.com/campuspress.yale.edu/dist/8/1581/files/2017/08/Schmitt_Grey-Areas-in-the-International-Law-of-Cyberspace-1cab8kj.pdf.

Schmitt, Michael. "In Defense of Due Diligence in Cyberspace." *The Yale Law Journal Forum* 125 (2015). https://www.yalelawjournal.org/forum/in-defense-of-due-diligence-in-cyberspace.

Schmitt, Michael. "International Cyber Law Politicized: The UN GGE's Failure to Advance Cyber Norms," June 30, 2017. https://www.justsecurity.org/42768/international-cyber-law-politicized-gges-failure-advance-cyber-norms/.

Schmitt, Michael, ed. *Tallinn Manual on the International Law Applicable to Cyber Warfare*. 1st ed. Cambridge University Press, 2013. https://doi.org/10.1017/CBO9781139169288.001.

Schmitt, Michael, ed. *Tallinn Manual 2.0 on the International Law Applicable to Cyber Operations*. 2nd ed. Cambridge University Press, 2017. https://doi.org/10.1017/9781316822524.006.

Schmitt, Michael N., Louise Arimatsu, and Tim McCormack, eds. "Vol. 13." In *Yearbook of International Humanitarian Law*. TMC Asser Press, 2010.

Schmitt, Michael N., and Liis Vihul. *The Nature of International Law Cyber Norms*. Tallinn Papers: NATO CCDCOE, 2014.

Schmitz, Andreas, Daniel Witte, and Vincent Gengnagel. "Pluralizing Field Analysis: Toward a Relational Understanding of the Field of Power." *Social Science Information* 56, no. 1 (March 1): 49–73. https://doi.org/10.1177/0539018416675071.

Schneier, Bruce. *Cyberconflicts and National Security*. UN Chronicle. United Nations, 2013. https://www.un.org/en/chronicle/article/cyberconflicts-and-national-security.

Schöndorf, Roy. "Israel's Perspective on Key Legal and Practical Issues Concerning the Application of International Law to Cyber Operations." *International Law Studies* 97 (2021): 13.

Schroeder, Matt, and Rachel Stohl. "Small Arms, Large Problem: The International Threat of Small Arms Proliferation and Misuse | Arms Control Association." *Arms Control Today*, June 2006. https://www.armscontrol.org/act/2006-06/features/small-arms-large-problem-international-threat-small-arms-proliferation-misuse.

Schwartz-Shea, Peregrine, and Dvora Yanow. *Interpretive Research Design*. Routledge, 2013. https://learning.oreilly.com/library/view/interpretive-research-design/9780415878081/12_ch3.xhtml.

Scott-Jones, Julie, and Sal Watt. "Making Sense of It All: Analysing Ethnographic Data." In *Ethnography in Social Science Practice*, edited by Julie Scott-Jones and Sal Watt, 1st ed. London: Routledge, 2010. https://www.taylorfrancis.com/books/edit/10.4324/9780203876305/ethnography-social-science-practice-julie-scott-jones-sal-watt.

Sealey, Anne. "Globalizing the 1926 International Sanitary Convention." *Journal of Global History* 6, no. 3 (November 2011): 431–455. https://doi.org/10.1017/S1740022811000404.

Sealey, Patricia Anne. "The League of Nations Health Organisation and the Evolution of Transnational Public Health." PhD Thesis, The Ohio State University, 2011.

Security Council Report. "In Hindsight: The Security Council and Cyber Threats, an Update," February 2022. https://www.securitycouncilreport.org/monthly-forecast/2022-02/in-hindsight-the-security-council-and-cyber-threats-an-update.php.

Sending, Ole Jacob. "Diplomats, Lawyers, and the Emergence of International Rule." In *The Politics of Expertise, 33–54. Competing for Authority in Global Governance.* University of Michigan Press, 2015. http://www.jstor.org/stable/10.3998/mpub.4016693.7.

"Seventh Biennial Meeting of States on the United Nations Programme of Action on Small Arms (BMS7)." IANSA, 2021. https://iansa.org/seventh-biennial-meeting-of-states-on-the-united-nations-programme-of-action-on-small-arms/.

Shaffer, Gregory, Manfred Elsig, and Sergio Puig. "The Extensive (but Fragile) Authority of the WTO Appellate Body." *Law and Contemporary Problems* 79, no. 1 (2016): 237–273.

Shaffer, Gregory, and Tom Ginsburg. "The Empirical Turn in International Legal Scholarship." *American Journal of International Law* 106, no. 1 (January 1, 2012): 1–47.

Shaffer, Gregory, and Mark A. Pollack. "Hard and Soft Law." In *Interdisciplinary Perspectives on International Law and International Relations: The State of the Art*, edited by Jeffrey L. Dunoff and Mark A. Pollack, 197–222. Cambridge: Cambridge University Press, 2012. https://doi.org/10.1017/CBO9781139107310.011.

Shaffer, Gregory, and Joel Trachtman. "Interpretation and Institutional Choice at the WTO." *Virginia Journal of International Law* 52 (2012): 103.

Shahabuddeen, Mohamed. "Stare Decisis." In *Precedent in the World Court*, 1st ed. Cambridge University Press, 1996. https://doi.org/10.1017/CBO9780511720840.

Shelton, Dinah. *Soft Law*. GW Law Faculty Publications & Other Works, 2008. https://scholarship.law.gwu.edu/faculty_publications/1049.

Shinohara, Hatsue. "International Law and World War I." *Diplomatic History* 38, no. 4 (2014): 880–893. https://doi.org/10.2307/26376611.

Shires, James. "Enacting Expertise: Ritual and Risk in Cybersecurity." *Politics and Governance* 6, no. 2 (2018): 31–40.

Singer, P.W. "Stuxnet and Its Hidden Lessons on the Ethics of Cyberweapons." *Case Western Reserve Journal of International Law* 47 (2015): 9.

Sivakumaran, Sandesh. "The Influence of Teachings of Publicists on the Development of International Law." *International & Comparative Law Quarterly* 66, no. 1 (January 2017): 1–37. https://doi.org/10.1017/S0020589316000531.

Smith, Brad. "The Need for a Digital Geneva Convention." *Microsoft on the Issues*, February 14, 2017. https://blogs.microsoft.com/on-the-issues/2017/02/14/need-digital-geneva-convention/.

Smith, James McCall. "WTO Dispute Settlement: The Politics of Procedure in Appellate Body Rulings." *World Trade Review* 2, no. 1 (March 2003): 65–100. https://doi.org/10.1017/S1474745603001356.

Sondarjee, Maïka. "Change and Stability at the World Bank: Inclusive Practices and Neoliberal Technocratic Rationality." *Third World Quarterly* 42, no. 2 (February 1): 348–65. https://doi.org/10.1080/01436597.2020.1838893.

Sonne, Paul. "Data-Security Expert Kaspersky: There Is No More Privacy." *The Wall Street Journal*, September 3, 2013. https://www.wsj.com/articles/SB10001424127887324432404579053091175949708.

Sorcher, Sara. "Influencers: Companies Should Not Be Allowed to Hack Back." *Christian Science Monitor*, April 1, 2015. https://www.csmonitor.com/World/Passcode/Passcode-Influencers/2015/0401/Influencers-Companies-should-not-be-allowed-to-hack-back.

Spaargaren, Gert, Don Weenink, and Machiel Lamers. *Practice Theory and Research: Exploring the Dynamics of Social Life*. Routledge, 2016.

Spiermann, O. "'Who Attempts Too Much Does Nothing Well': The 1920 Advisory Committee of Jurists and the Statute of the Permanent Court of International Justice." *British Yearbook of International Law* 73, no. 1 (January 1, 2003): 187–260. https://doi.org/10.1093/bybil/73.1.187.

Stappert, Nora. "Practice Theory and Change in International Law: Theorizing the Development of Legal Meaning through the Interpretive Practices of International Criminal Courts." *International Theory* 12, no. 1 (March 2020): 33–58. https://doi.org/10.1017/S1752971919000150.

"Statement at Budapest Conference on Cyber Issues," October 2012, http://vienna.china-mission.gov.cn/eng/zgbd/201210/t20121009_8848606.htm.

"Statement by Vassily Nebenzia, Permanent Representative of the Russian Federation to the United Nations, at the 'Arria-Formula' VTC of the UNSC Members on Cyber-Attacks against Critical Infrastructure." In *Permanent Mission of the Russian Feder-*

ation to the United Nations, 2020. https://kemlu.go.id/download/L1NoYXJlZCUyMERvY3VtZW50cy9SdXNzaWFuJTIwRmVkZXJhdGlvbi5wZGY=.

"Statement by Vladimir Yermakov, Deputy Director of the Department for Security and Disarmament Affairs, MFA of Russia, Acting Head of the Delegation of the Russian Federation to the First Committee of the 68th Session of the UN General Assembly." *October* 30 (2013). https://unoda-documents-library.s3.amazonaws.com/General_Assembly_First_Committee_Sixty-eighth_session_(2013)/russian-federation.pdf.

"Statement on the Interpretation of the Norm on Non-interference with the Public Core." In *Global Commission on the Stability of Cyberspace*, 2021. https://hcss.nl/wp-content/uploads/2022/06/GCSC-statement-public-core_final.pdf.

Stein, Janice Gross. "Background Knowledge in the Foreground." In *International Practices*, edited by Emanuel Adler and Vincent Pouliot, 87–107, 2012, https://doi.org/10.1017/CBO9780511862373.007.

Streltsov, Anatoly A. "Application of International Humanitarian Law to Armed Conflicts in Cyberspace," 2012. https://digital.report/wp-content/uploads/2016/04/169747-Streltsov-ENG.pdf.

"Suits and Spooks DC 2017: Tallinn 2.0: How We Addressed Issues Of," Accessed April 2, 2023 https://suitsandspooksdc2017.sched.com/event/800R/tallinn-20-how-we-addressed-issues-of-sovereignty-attribution-espionage-countermeasures-and-other-key-points-of-cyber-warfare-under-international-law.

Sukumar, Arun Mohan. "'Responsibility to Detect?': Autonomous Threat Detection and Its Implications for Due Diligence in Cyberspace." In *2022 14th International Conference on Cyber Conflict: Keep Moving!*, 700:173–87, 2022. https://doi.org/10.23919/CyCon55549.2022.9811012.

Sullivan, Jonathan, and Weixiang Wang. "China's 'Wolf Warrior Diplomacy': The Interaction of Formal Diplomacy and Cyber-Nationalism." *Journal of Current Chinese Affairs*, March 14, 2022, 18681026221079840. https://doi.org/10.1177/18681026221079841.

Sulyok, Katalin, ed. "Techniques for Judicial Engagement with Science in the Practice of International Courts and Tribunals." In *Science and Judicial Reasoning: The Legitimacy of International Environmental Adjudication*. Cambridge Studies on Environment, Energy and Natural Resources Governance. Cambridge University Press, 2020. https://www.cambridge.org/core/books/science-and-judicial-reasoning/techniques-for-judicial-engagement-with-science-in-the-practice-of-international-courts-and-tribunals/1EC9EA2E42F73DF76D445838AFA8EE43.

"Supporters – Paris Call," https://pariscall.international/en/supporters.

"Tallinn Manual 2.0 Approach to State Responsibility." *CyCon*, 2015. https://www.youtube.com/watch?v=108uuZsPvms.

"Tallinn Manual Experts Meet for Intense Drafting Session," 2015. https://www.youtube.com/watch?v=pu1ZuCbqOeo.

Tanodomdej, Papawadee. "The Tallinn Manuals and the Making of the International Law on Cyber Operations." *Masaryk University Journal of Law and Technology* 13, no. 1 (2019): 67–86.

Tanodomdej, Papawadee. "The Tallinn Manuals and the Making of the International Law on Cyber Operations." *Masaryk University Journal of Law and Technology* 13, no. 1 (2019): 67–86.

Tanzi, Attila. *Liability for Lawful Acts*. Oxford Public International Law, 2021. http://opil.ouplaw.com/view/10.1093/law:epil/9780199231690/law-9780199231690-e1065.

"The Art of Technical Attribution in Cyberspace: Kaspersky Launches Simulation Game Training for Diplomats and Non-techie Cyber Experts." *October* 25 (2021). https://www.kaspersky.com/about/press-releases/2021_the-art-of-technical-attribution-in-cyberspace-kaspersky-launches-simulation-game-training-for-diplomats-and-non-techie-cyber-experts.

"The Attorney General's Office. "Cyber and International Law in the 21st Century." GOV.UK, May 23, 2018. https://www.gov.uk/government/speeches/cyber-and-international-law-in-the-21st-century.

"The Attorney General's Office. "International Law in Future Frontiers." GOV.UK, May 19, 2022. https://www.gov.uk/government/speeches/international-law-in-future-frontiers.

"The Call and the 9 Principles." Paris Call, November 12, 2018. https://pariscall.international/en/principles.

"The Future of Discussions on ICTs and Cyberspace at the UN." *August* 10 (2020). https://front.un-arm.org/wp-content/uploads/2020/10/joint-contribution-poa-future-of-cyber-discussions-at-un-10-08-2020.pdf.

"The Kingdom of the Netherlands' Response to the Pre-draft Report of the OEWG," February 2020, https://front.un-arm.org/wp-content/uploads/2020/02/letter-to-chair-of-oewg-kingdom-of-the-netherlands.pdf.

The Hague Centre for Strategic Studies, "Cyberstability Paper Series: New Conditions and Constellations in Cyber," Accessed April 2, 2023 https://hcss.nl/report/cyberstability-paper-series-new-conditions-and-constellations-in-cyber/.

The Hague Centre for Strategic Studies. "Global Commission on the Stability of Cyberspace – About," Accessed April 2, 2023 https://hcss.nl/global-commission-on-the-stability-of-cyberspace-about/.

The Hague Centre for Strategic Studies. "Global Commission on the Stability of Cyberspace – Norms," Accessed April 2, 2023 https://hcss.nl/gcsc-norms/.

The Hague Centre for Strategic Studies. "Norm Package Singapore | Global Commission Introduces Six Critical Norms Towards Cyber Stability," Accessed April 2, 2023

https://hcss.nl/report/norm-package-singapore-global-commission-introduces-six-critical-norms-towards-cyber-stability/.
The Hague Centre for Strategic Studies. "The GCSC Research Advisory Group Is Recruiting," June 26, 2017. https://hcss.nl/news/the-gcsc-research-advisory-group-is-recruiting/.
"The League and the Minorities Treaties." *Bulletin of International News* 5, no. 18 (1929): 3–10.
"The Montreux Document on Pertinent International Legal Obligations and Good Practices for States Related to Operations of Private Military and Security Companies during Armed Conflict." In *Montreux: Swiss Federal Department of Foreign Affairs; International Committee of the Red Cross*, 2008.
"The Oxford Process | People," https://www.elac.ox.ac.uk/the-oxford-process/people/.
"The Oxford Process on International Law Protections in Cyberspace," https://www.elac.ox.ac.uk/the-oxford-process-on-international-law-protections-in-cyberspace.
"The Oxford Process on International Law Protections in Cyberspace: A Compendium." Oxford, UK: Oxford Institute for Ethics, October 2022, https://www.elac.ox.ac.uk/wp-content/uploads/2022/10/Oxford-Process-Compendium-Digital.pdf.
"The Oxford Statement on International Law Protections against Foreign Electoral Interference through Digital Means," https://www.elac.ox.ac.uk/the-oxford-process/the-statements-overview/the-oxford-statement-on-international-law-protections-against-foreign-electoral-interference/.
"The Oxford Statement on The Regulation of Information Operations and Activities," https://www.elac.ox.ac.uk/the-oxford-process/the-statements-overview/the-oxford-statement-on-the-regulation-of-information-operations-and-activities/.
"The Second Oxford Statement on International Law Protections of the Healthcare Sector during Covid-19: Safeguarding Vaccine Research," https://www.elac.ox.ac.uk/the-oxford-process/the-statements-overview/the-second-oxford-statement/.
"The Tallinn Manual," https://ccdcoe.org/research/tallinn-manual/.
Theeuwen, Wieteke. "Attribution for the Purposes of State Responsibility." *Netherlands Military Law Review*, August 17, 2018. https://puc.overheid.nl/mrt/doc/PUC_248325_11/.
Thorne, Devin. "China's Vulnerability Disclosure Regulations Put State Security First." *The Strategist*, August 31, 2021. https://www.aspistrategist.org.au/chinas-vulnerability-disclosure-regulations-put-state-security-first/.
Tiirmaa-Klaar, Heli. "The Evolution of the UN Group of Governmental Experts on Cyber Issues." In *Cyberstability Paper Series New Conditions and Constellations in Cyber. The Hague Centre for Strategic Studies*, 2021. https://hcss.nl/wp-content/uploads/2021/12/Klaar.pdf.
Tikk, Eneken. *Parabasis: Cyber-Diplomacy in Stalemate*. Oslo: Norwegian Institute of International Affairs, 2018. https://nupi.brage.unit.no/nupi-xmlui/bitstream/

handle/11250/2569401/NUPI_Report_5_18_Tikk_Kerttunen.pdf?sequence=1&isAllowed=y.

Tikk, Eneken, and Mika Kerttunen. "The Alleged Demise of the UN GGE: An Autopsy and Eulogy." *Cyber Policy Institute*, 2017. https://cyber-peace.org/wp-content/uploads/2018/11/Tikk-Kerttunen-2017-The-Alleged-Demise-of-the-UN-GGE-An-Autopsy-and-Eulogy.pdf.

T.L.S. *Day 2 – Roundtable 5 – Get Your House in Order – What Diligence Is Due?* Washington D.C: American University Washington College of Law, 2022. https://media.wcl.american.edu/Mediasite/Play/999ce17eb3f04fe3ab28559de68fff0d1d.

"Top International Law Experts Discuss Tallinn Manual 2.0 (VIDEO," 2015. https://ccdcoe.org/news/2015/21-top-international-law-experts-discuss-tallinn-manual-2-0-video/.

Tournès, Ludovic. "American Membership of the League of Nations: US Philanthropy and the Transformation of an Intergovernmental Organisation into a Think Tank." *International Politics; Basingstoke* 55, no. 6 (November 2018): 852–869.

Trachtman, Joel P. "Regulatory Jurisdiction and the WTO." *Journal of International Economic Law* 10, no. 3 (September 1): 631–651. https://doi.org/10.1093/jiel/jgm025.

"Transparency and Confidence-Building Measures in Outer Space Activities." In *UN General Assembly, Sixty-Fifth Session*, 2011. https://doi.org/10.18356/9789210021753c001.

Treaties. "Other International Agreements of the United States of America 1776–1949 (Bevans). "International Sanitary Convention," 1926.

"Treaty Banning the Production of Fissile Material for Nuclear Weapons or Other Nuclear Explosive Devices." In *UN General Assembly, Sixty-Seventh Session*, 2013. https://doi.org/10.18356/9789210021753c001.

Tsagourias, Nicholas. "Cyber Attacks, Self-Defence and the Problem of Attribution." *Journal of Conflict and Security Law* 17, no. 2 (2012): 229–244.

Tsagourias, Nicholas. "Electoral Cyber Interference, Self-Determination, Non-intervention." In *Governing Cyberspace: Behavior, Power and Diplomacy*, edited by Dennis Broeders and Bibi Berg, 1st ed. London: Rowman & Littlefield, 2020.

Tsagourias, Nicholas. "The Tallinn Manual on the International Law Applicable to Cyber Warfare: A Commentary on Chapter II – The Use of Force." In *Yearbook of International Humanitarian Law*, edited by Terry D. Gill, Robin Geiß, Robert Heinsch, Tim McCormack, Christophe Paulussen, and Jessica Dorsey, 15:19–43. The Hague: T.M.C. Asser Press, 2012. https://doi.org/10.1007/978-90-6704-924-5_2.

U.D.T. "US 'Hacking Back' Law Could Create a Cyber Wild West of Vigilantism." Edited by U.D.T., July 3, 2018. https://udtonline.com/us-hacking-back-law-could-create-a-cyber-wild-west-of-vigilantism-jeff-engle/.

"UK Response to Chair's Initial 'Pre-draft' of the Report of the OEWG on Developments in the Field of Information and Telecommunications in the Context of

International Security," April 15, 2020. https://front.un-arm.org/wp-content/uploads/2020/04/20200415-oewg-predraft-uk.pdf.

United Nations. "58/32. Developments in the Field of Information and Telecommunications in the Context of International Security." In *UN General Assembly, Fifty-Eighth Session*, 2003. https://doi.org/10.18356/9789210021753c001.

"United Nations and Office for Disarmament Affairs. Voluntary Non-binding Norms for Responsible State Behavior in the Use of Information and Communications Technology: A Commentary," 2017.

"United Nations Office for Disarmament Affairs (UNODA). "Meetings of the High Contracting Parties," Accessed April 2, 2023 https://www.un.org/disarmament/the-convention-on-certain-conventional-weapons/meetings-and-documents/.

"United Nations Office for Disarmament Affairs (UNODA). "Programme of Action on Small Arms and Its International Tracing Instrument – UNODA," Accessed April 2, 2023 https://www.un.org/disarmament/convarms/salw/programme-of-action/.

"United Nations Study on Disarmament and Non-proliferation Education – UNODA," Accessed April 2, 2023 https://www.un.org/disarmament/topics/education/.

United States Department of State. "Joint Statement on Advancing Responsible State Behavior in Cyberspace," September 23, 2019 https://www.state.gov/joint-statement-on-advancing-responsible-state-behavior-in-cyberspace/.

United States Department of State. "The United States Supports the Paris Call for Trust and Security in Cyberspace," 2021 https://www.state.gov/the-united-states-supports-the-paris-call-for-trust-and-security-in-cyberspace/.

"United States Comments on the Chair's Pre Draft of the Report of the UN Open Ended Working Group (OEWG," Accessed April 2, 2023 https://ceipfiles.s3.amazonaws.com/pdf/CyberNorms/UNGGE/United±States±Comments±on±the±Chair%E2%80%99s±Pre-Draft±of±the±Report±of±the±UN±Open±Ended±Working±Group±(OEWG).pdf.

"Unpacking the GGE's Framework on Responsible State Behavior: Cyber Norms." *Global Partners Digital*, December 2019. https://www.gp-digital.org/wp-content/uploads/2019/12/unpacking_gge_cyber-norms.pdf.

"Updated List of Experts for the Presentations on the Six Areas Outlined in Paragraph 5 (a)-(f) of the Provisional Agenda of the OEWG (A/AC.290/2019.1) as of 28 August 2019." In *Open-Ended Working Group on Developments in the Field of Information and Telecommunications in the Context of International Security*, 2019. https://front.un-arm.org/wp-content/uploads/2019/09/280819-Updated-list-of-experts-first-substantive-session-OEWG-on-developments-in-the-field-of-information-and-telecommunications.pdf.

Vabulas, Felicity, and Duncan Snidal. "Cooperation under Autonomy: Building and Analyzing the Informal Intergovernmental Organizations 2.0 Dataset." *Journal of Peace Research* 58, no. 4 (July 1): 859–69. https://doi.org/10.1177/0022343320943920.

Varisco, Andrea Edoardo, Jonah Leff, and Himayu Shiotani. *The International Tracing Instrument: Examining Options to Support Operationalization*. Geneva: United Nations Institute for Disarmament Research, 2018. https://unidir.org/sites/default/files/publication/pdfs//the-international-tracing-instrument-examining-options-to-support-operationalization-en-712.pdf.

Vauchez, Antoine. *Brokering Europe: Euro-Lawyers and the Making of a Transnational Polity. Cambridge Studies in European Law and Policy*. Cambridge: Cambridge University Press, 2015. https://doi.org/10.1017/CBO9781107326323.

Venzke, Ingo. "Semantic Authority, Legal Change and the Dynamics of International Law." In *Legal Authority beyond the State*, edited by Henrik Palmer Olsen and Patrick Capps, 102–126. Cambridge: Cambridge University Press, 2018. https://doi.org/10.1017/9781108100045.005.

Verfassungsblog. "Hacking Back and International Law: An Irreconcilable Pair?," July 16, 2020, https://verfassungsblog.de/hacking-back-and-international-law-an-irreconcilable-pair/.

"Verslag Clingendael-Bijeenkomst Non-interventie in de Publieke Kern van Het internet." *Clingendael Institute*, July 11, 2016.

Visoka, Gëzim. "Metis Diplomacy: The Everyday Politics of Becoming a Sovereign State." *Cooperation and Conflict* 54, no. 2 (June 1, 2019): 167–190. https://doi.org/10.1177/0010836718807503.

Volo, Bayard, Lorraine, and Edward Schatz. "From the Inside Out: Ethnographic Methods in Political Research." *Political Science and Politics* 37, no. 02 (April 2004): 267–271. https://doi.org/10.1017/S1049096504004214.

Waag-Cowling, Noëlle, Brett Niekerk, and Trishana Ramluckan. "Submission to the Call for Inputs: Report on the Provision of Military and Security Cyber Products and Services by 'Cyber Mercenaries' and Its Human Rights Impact," 2021. https://www.ohchr.org/sites/default/files/Academia-van-der-Waag-Cowling.docx.

Wacquant, Loïc. "A Concise Genealogy and Anatomy of Habitus." *The Sociological Review* 64, no. 1 (February 1): 64–72. https://doi.org/10.1111/1467-954X.12356.

Wacquant, Loïc. "Homines in Extremis: What Fighting Scholars Teach Us about Habitus." *Body & Society* 20, no. 2 (June 1, 2014): 3–17. https://doi.org/10.1177/1357034X13501348.

Wedeen, Lisa. "Ethnography as Interpretive Enterprise." In *Political Ethnography: What Immersion Contributes to the Study of Power*, edited by Edward Schatz. University of Chicago Press, 2013.

Weiler, Joseph H.H. "The Rule of Lawyers and the Ethos of Diplomats: Reflections on the Internal and External Legitimacy of WTO Dispute Settlement." *Journal of World Trade* 35 (2001): 191.

Weindling, Paul. "Philanthropy and World Health: The Rockefeller Foundation and the League of Nations Health Organisation." *Minerva* 35, no. 3 (1997): 269–281.

Wenger, Etienne. *Communities of Practice: Learning, Meaning, and Identity*. Cambridge University Press, 1999.

Werner, Wouter. *Repetition and International Law*. 1st ed. Cambridge University Press, 2022. https://doi.org/10.1017/9781009039666.

Werner, Wouter, Marieke Hoon, and Alexis Galán, eds. *The Law of International Lawyers: Reading Martti Koskenniemi*. Cambridge: Cambridge University Press, 2017. https://doi.org/10.1017/9781108147620.

"What Is Multitenancy? | Multitenant Architecture | Cloudflare," Accessed April 2, 2023 https://www.cloudflare.com/learning/cloud/what-is-multitenancy/.

"Why We Urgently Need a Digital Geneva Convention," December 29, 2017 https://www.microsoft.com/en-us/cybersecurity/blog-hub/why-we-urgently-need-digital-geneva-convention.

Wiersema, Annecoos. "The New International Law-Makers? Conferences of the Parties to Multilateral Environmental Agreements." *Michigan Journal of International Law* 31, no. 1 (January 1, 2009): 231–287.

Wille, Tobias. "Practice Turn in International Relations." *Oxford Bibliographies*, May 24, 2018. https://www.oxfordbibliographies.com/view/document/obo-9780199743292/obo-9780199743292-0231.xml.

Williams, Peter. "Law and Lawyers in the Multilateral Trading System: Back to the Future." In *A History of Law and Lawyers in the GATT/WTO*, edited by Gabrielle Marceau, 85–108. Cambridge: Cambridge University Press, 2015. https://doi.org/10.1017/CBO9781316048160.007.

XXIII). "Question of General and Complete Disarmament." In *UN General Assembly, Twenty-Third Session*, 1968. https://www.unoosa.org/pdf/gares/ARES_23_2453E.pdf.

Yang, Yang. "Bourdieu, Practice and Change: Beyond the Criticism of Determinism." *Educational Philosophy and Theory* 46, no. 14 (December 6, 2014): 1522–1540. https://doi.org/10.1080/00131857.2013.839375.

"Yearbook of the International Law Commission 1982." *International Law Commission, Thirty-Fourth Session*, 1982. https://legal.un.org/ilc/publications/yearbooks/english/ilc_1982_v2_p1.pdf.

"Yearbook of the International Law Commission 1998 | Summary Records of the Meetings of the Fiftieth Session 20." *International Law Commission, Fiftieth Session*, April 12, 1998. https://legal.un.org/ilc/publications/yearbooks/english/ilc_1998_v1.pdf.

Young, Michael K. "Dispute Resolution in the Uruguay Round: Lawyers Triumph over Diplomats," 1995.

ZDNET. "China Has Been 'Hijacking the Vital internet Backbone of Western Countries.'" October 26, 2018, https://www.zdnet.com/article/china-has-been-hijacking-the-vital-internet-backbone-of-western-countries/.

Zhang, Binxin. "Cyberspace and International Humanitarian Law: the Chinese Approach." In *Asia-Pacific Perspectives on International Humanitarian Law*, edited by Sandesh Sivakumaran, Suzannah Linton, and Tim McCormack, 323–337. Cambridge: Cambridge University Press, 2019. https://doi.org/10.1017/9781108667203.020.

Zhang, Li. "A Chinese Perspective on Cyber War." *International Review of the Red Cross* 94, no. 886 (June 2012): 801–807. https://doi.org/10.1017/S1816383112000823.

Zürn, Michael. "On the Role of Contestations, the Power of Reflexive Authority, and Legitimation Problems in the Global Political System." *International Theory* 13, no. 1 (March 2021): 192–204. https://doi.org/10.1017/S1752971920000391.

Zürn, Michael. *A Theory of Global Governance: Authority, Legitimacy, and Contestation*. Oxford University Press, 2018. https://doi.org/10.1093/oso/9780198819974.001.0001.

Index

www.ingramcontent.com/pod-product-compliance
Lightning Source LLC
LaVergne TN
LVHW011216150926
848065LV00003B/28
* 9 7 8 9 0 0 4 7 3 7 6 0 0 *